Strategies for Technical Professionals

NOV 20 ~~10:00~~ 10:00 p.m

System NO

NO Longer ~~except~~ allow

work

PEARSON

Custom
Publishing

Printed in the United States of America

10 9 8 7 6 5 4 3

ISBN 0-536-90396-4

2004160653

JC

Please visit our web site at *www.pearsoncustom.com*

PEARSON CUSTOM PUBLISHING
75 Arlington Street, Suite 300, Boston, MA 02116
A Pearson Education Company

CONTENTS

Introduction

Chapter 1—Strategies for Independent Learning

Chapter 2—Overview of Technology Tools

Chapter 3—Styles of Learning

Chapter 4—Information from Electronic Sources

Chapter 5—Word Processing Tools

Chapter 6—Presentation Tools

Chapter 7—Spreadsheet and Database Tools

Chapter 8—Soft Skills of Technical Professionals

Chapter 9—Project Planning and Execution

Chapter 10—The Impact of Technology

About the Book

This book is to be used as an introductory text for the course Strategies for Technical Professionals, which itself is an introductory course in the associate degree programs in Information Technology run by ITT Technical Institute. The book is suitable for delivery of the course in both onsite and online environments. It blends a unique learning pedagogy with a well-designed mix of onsite and online learning strategies to equip students with the tools they will need to become technical professionals in this information age. The course introduces students to the techniques of basic information processing and Internet research, as well as to techniques used by independent technical learners. A review of the characteristics and trends of the global society provides a backdrop of what being technical professional means in today's information age.

The first section of the book provides students an overview of the entire course. It presents tips and techniques that will help students be successful, both in this course as well as in their career. As technical professionals in this information age, students will realize the importance of becoming lifelong learners. The objective is to motivate students and provide them information on attributes and techniques of becoming a successful independent learner. This section encourages and motivates students to identify their individual learning styles and to develop a strategy of personal management and success. It also equips students with basic technical skills required to pursue an online course. The online course management system at ITT Technical Institute is also covered in this section.

The second section focuses on the knowledge of technology tools required to become technical professionals. Technology tools are an integral part of a technical professional's work life. This section describes the characteristics and mechanisms used to share information over the Internet and the Microsoft Office applications that will be used in their daily work life. Students are guided on using these applications to showcase their ideas and enhance their work efficiency. They are also encouraged to explore more features of these applications by using the inbuilt and online Help features of the applications.

The third section explores the essential soft skills required of technical professionals, such as time and people management, critical thinking, creative thinking, problem solving, effective communication, and stress, career, and project management skills that will enhance their professionalism. The skills discussed in this part are important both for success in this program of study as well as for overall career success.

The last section of the book helps students recognize the effects of technology on organizations, society, and individuals. The dawn of the twenty-first century has changed the way people live, work, think, and learn. Understanding the scope and impact of these changes on political, social, and business environments will help students plan their lifelong learning process as well as help them contribute positively to society and the organizations in which they will work.

Conventions Used in the Book

This book contains features, identified by various icons, each presenting a different type of information. These features are:

 Notes provide information about a topic in context. This is additional information related to the topic.

 Tips provide an alternative method for performing a task. It can also contain a simplified, although unconventional, method of doing a task.

 Just-a-Minute presents nice-to-know information or a quick question that checks learners' understanding of the current topic.

 Warnings inform you about the dire effects of an action. Focusing on these warnings reduces the likelihood that learners will make the same errors.

 References provide links to Web sites, relevant books, and white papers for further study on a particular topic.

 Objectives begin each topic and inform learners about the learning outcome of a topic.

In addition, *italicized text* represents newly-introduced items.

Strategies for Independent Learning

1

This chapter presents some strategies for independent learning essential to e-learning. You will be required to use these strategies when you are taking an online course, such as this Strategies for the Technical Professional course. The information and strategies presented in this chapter will help you achieve optimal results and also introduce you to how to access online resources when you are taking an online course at ITT Tech.

This chapter prepares you to:

- Describe several strategies and skills that will help you to be a successful independent learner.

- Describe how to access resources in the ITT Tech Virtual Library.

- Describe how to access the ITT Tech Course Management System.

1.1 Independent Learning

1.2 E-Learning at ITT Tech

1.1 Independent Learning

Independent learning requires a lot of discipline. Whether you are in a classroom or on your own in an online learning environment, planning your activities, discussing ideas, obtaining feedback, and assessing your progress are critical to learning. In a classroom situation, you have an instructor and a room full of classmates who provide structure and motivation. However, when you are an independent online learner or are completing projects and assignments by yourself, you need to generate your own structure and motivation. You need to make an effort to discuss and obtain feedback on your ideas. This is true whether you are learning in a structured course program, such as this, or whether you are learning in unstructured situations, such as business, career, or life. *You* must take the initiative to be successful.

This section presents the course rationale for the Strategies for the Technical Professional course and the skills and techniques that will help you to be successful in independent learning.

1.1.1 Course Rationale

Explain the relevance of the course to the current program of study.

This course is an introductory course in the associate and bachelor degree programs in Information Technology. Students in the Strategies for the Technical Professional course may be enrolled in any degree program.

Despite the different subjects and areas of expertise addressed in the differing programs, some skills and requirements are common to all students. To be successful in your chosen career field, certain skills are essential. These include:

■ Identifying your learning style and formulating a strategy for continuous lifelong independent learning.

■ Exploring and validating information found on the Internet and using the information in a responsible manner.

■ Learning to use popular applications, such as word processing, spreadsheet, database, and presentation software to enhance productivity in both business and personal situations.

- Practicing personal and professional management skills that are critical for success.
- Analyzing how technology can have a positive impact on business, society, and personal achievement.

This course presents skills and concepts in all of these areas. In essence, the course is designed to give you the skills that will allow you to take advantage of technology and will enhance your likelihood of success in your chosen career. You will learn how to analyze and evaluate information and apply technology in general situations. With these foundational skills in place, you will be well positioned to learn the more detailed and specific topics presented later in your program of study and throughout your career.

1.1.2 Strategies for Independent Learning

 Describe several personal characteristics that enhance independent learning.

Independent learning is becoming a very popular alternative for professionals in the information age. With widespread access to the Internet and innovative software design, distance learning and self-paced Internet courses are quickly gaining acceptance and popularity. Learning in a classroom using traditional methods is no longer an absolute necessity.

Discussion forums, interactive Internet software, improved Internet security, and robust course management systems make it possible to generate an interactive and stimulating learning experience wherever a computer with Internet access is available. As depicted in Figure 1.1, independent online learning is a popular alternative for professionals.

Figure 1.1: Independent Online Learning is a Popular Alternative for Professionals

But does all of this modern technology enhance learning? In many situations it can. The freedom to take courses anywhere and anytime has made learning more accessible. The wealth of information available online can make research and learning more efficient and comprehensive. The availability of online simulations gives students opportunities for hands-on experience and interaction that were not previously possible. However, students need to be ready to take advantage of all the enhancements that technology can bring to learning.

Online independent learning requires students to be disciplined, motivated, and emotionally mature. In the absence of a strict classroom schedule, an instructor to present the information, or peers to interact with, an independent online learner can feel isolated and lost. Independent learners need to stay motivated and keep to a strict schedule without the benefit of constant interaction with classmates and the instructor. They also need to recognize when they need help or advice and then to seek it proactively.

Remember that the habits of independent learning will not only help you do well in an online course, they will also help you in the fast changing technical world. Since today's technology may quickly become obsolete, it is important that you keep your skills current. Improving your independent learning skills will be critical to your future success in this area.

Table 1.1 outlines some characteristics of successful independent learners and provides some tips on developing these yourself.

Characteristic	Description	Development Suggestions
Locus of control	Refers to your beliefs on how external events control the outcomes in your life. If you believe that you are responsible for the outcomes in your life, then you have an internal locus of control. If you believe that external events, rather than personal initiative, determine outcomes in your life, then you have an external locus of control.	Successful independent learners tend to have more of an internal locus of control. They take responsibility for actions and drive their actions toward success. They do not make excuses. If you tend towards an external locus of control, you believe that circumstances beyond your control will affect your outcomes. As an independent learner, you will have to make a determined effort to stick to your schedule and seek guidance and feedback on your progress. You will also need to recognize external circumstances that could inhibit your progress, and make conscious efforts to overcome them.
Emotional maturity	Refers to your ability to take action, control your responses to situations, and develop a broad perspective in terms of ideas. In short, it refers to how you view situations and react to them.	People are constantly maturing. Each experience and encounter can change a person's maturity level. Keep an open mind and take time for personal reflection to help develop your emotional maturity.
Achievement motivation	Refers to a person's need to achieve results. If you are focused on achieving results and seeking out challenging opportunities, you have a higher degree of achievement motivation. If you are more focused on relationships than achievements, you tend to	Successful independent learners tend to have a higher degree of achievement motivation. They are driven to success and stretch their abilities to introduce more challenges and realize their goals. This usually produces positive learning results. However, people with a high degree of achievement motivation may need to remember to take time to reflect upon learning, rather than be satisfied simply with achieving the goal. If you find that you are more focused on

Characteristic	Description	Development Suggestions
	have a lower degree of achievement motivation.	maintaining relationships and seeking feedback on how you are doing, you probably have a lower degree of achievement motivation. You may need to focus on developing a schedule and sticking to it to complete tasks on time. You may also need encouragement from your instructor or an advisor to ensure that you are staying focused on getting the most benefit out of your activities. You should make an effort to develop and maintain relationships with others in the class to get the feedback you need in the course of your studies.
Questioning techniques	Asking questions is an important aspect of learning. Questions can help you to clarify and assimilate information to ensure that you have a full understanding of the material that is presented.	Open-ended questions require long or in-depth explanations. They can be useful in helping you understand reasons or concepts. Closed-ended questions require short answers, such as yes or no. They can be helpful in confirming that you have the correct understanding of a topic. With all questions, take care to ensure that they are well-prepared, sincere, positive, and focused on further learning.
Preferred learning style	There are three general learning styles: Visual learners prefer to see or read information. Auditory learners prefer to hear information or have it explained to them. Kinesthetic learners prefer to learn through hands-on experience.	If you are a visual learner, you will be successful in reading the text and online material presented with the course as this is your preferred learning style. If you are an auditory learner, you may want to form a study group and have telephone conversations about course material to reinforce your learning of the material. Simply reading the material may not be enough for you to learn it thoroughly. If you are a kinesthetic learner, you will look for ways to practice and apply the skills that are taught, either by working on projects or by using software tools to practice skills. Completing the assignments and class projects will be helpful to reinforce your learning.

Table 1.1: Personal Characteristics for Success in Independent Learning

Additional techniques for identifying and maximizing your learning style are presented in Chapter 3, "Learning Styles."

1.1.3 Communication and Participation

 Describe the strategies and techniques for communicating and participating in courses designed for independent learning.

In many ways, online independent learning requires more discipline and effort than classroom-based learning. To be successful in an online program, you need to make an extra effort to communicate and participate in online team activities.

Effective communication usually involves more than just spoken or written words. Facial expressions, body language, and tone of voice can convey important meanings in conversations. When you are taking part in an online session, these visual communication aspects are missing. You typically do not have the benefit of seeing the person with whom you are communicating. Communicating through e-mail can be even more challenging, because you do not have the benefit of hearing the tone or manner in which the words are spoken. You also do not have the benefit of clarifying points or asking questions, so misinterpretations can be frequent occurrences. Communicating with others in an online training session can feel like participating in a meeting wearing a blindfold.

In addition to the challenges in online communication, as depicted in Figure 1.2, independent learning also requires you to take initiative to communicate as this will help you to enhance your learning.

Figure 1.2: Challenge of Online Communication in the Absence of Visual Cues

You may have few reminders from others to encourage you to interact with your classmates and instructor. While online independent learning gives you the flexibility to schedule your studies when it is convenient, you may also find it tempting to overlook difficulties or questions you may have in order to finish the lesson quickly. While cutting corners in this area may help you in the short run, you will only be compromising your learning in the long run. Table 1.2 lists some tips and techniques for effective communication in online courses.

Communication area	Suggested tips and techniques
E-mail	Avoid using all capital letters because it gives the impression of shouting.
	Be cautious when replying to messages. Use discretion when using the 'Reply to All' feature as you want to ensure that your replies go only to intended e-mail addresses.
	Avoid potentially emotional or unflattering

Communication area	Suggested tips and techniques
	discussions in e-mail.
	Use e-mail to clarify points. Resort to telephone conversations if you are having trouble reaching an understanding.
	Be courteous when sending large e-mail messages. Be aware of size limits that may exist or file attachments that may be blocked by a firewall. Ensure that recipients can open the attachments you send.
Telephone conversations	Speak clearly and identify yourself. On conference calls, be sure to identify yourself whenever you speak as it can be difficult to recognize voices over the phone.
	Limit background noise and other distractions. Barking dogs, doorbells, and other phones ringing can be disruptive to a telephone meeting.
	Always ask for permission from other callers before placing them on a speaker phone.
	When using a speaker phone, keep the phone on mute unless you are talking. This will minimize disruptions caused by background noise.
	Remember to turn off mute before you speak.
	Listen attentively and give others a chance to speak. Do not monopolize the conversation.
	Ensure that you can hear the conversation and that your voice can be heard clearly by others. Do not allow a meeting to continue if you cannot clearly hear the conversation.
	Be prompt for telephone meetings. Treat these meetings as you would a face-to-face meeting.

Table 1.2: Communication Tips and Techniques for Online Courses

Active participation involves frequent interaction with your instructor and classmates. In the online portion of this course, these interactions will be over e-mail, discussion forums, chat, and phone. As shown in Figure 1.3, such interactions can help you to enhance your online work.

Figure 1.3: Active Participation is Important for Success in an Online Program

Table 1.3 lists some tips and techniques for participation in an online course.

Suggestion	Rationale	Tips/Techniques
Actively participate in discussions	You will learn more when you express your ideas and get feedback from your classmates. Being an active participant in online discussions will help you establish your routine for independent study, and increase your learning.	Contribute ideas to enrich your thinking and to help make yourself known to your classmates. Give feedback to your classmates on their ideas.

Suggestion	Rationale	Tips/Techniques
Build relationships with classmates	You will have two sessions to meet your classmates in a face-to-face session. You will need to build or maintain the relationships further during the online portion of the course. Good relationships will help you to enrich your learning and build a strong professional network.	Do not let problems grow. If you are having difficulty completing assignments, ask your instructor for help. Keep your instructor's contact information handy on your computer. You can use Microsoft Outlook to store contact information.
Ask for help	To maximize your learning, you need to ask questions to clarify and confirm your understanding of topics. You are not likely to receive help if you do not ask for it.	Do not let problems grow. If you are having difficulty completing assignments, ask your instructor for help. Keep your instructor's contact information handy on your computer. You can use Microsoft Outlook to store contact information.

Table 1.3: Suggestions for Effective Participation in Online Courses

1.1.4 Study Habits

 Describe strategies and techniques to develop effective study habits for independent learning.

Independent learning requires a strong discipline in study habits. The Strategies for the Technical Professional course also requires you develop sound study habits. Communication and active participation are key elements for success. However, you must also develop good study habits as well.

You may review the material on study habits in the ITT Tech Virtual Library. Use the link http://www.library.itt-tech.edu/ to log on to the virtual library. From the main menu, select **Reference Resources**. Scroll down and select **Study Skills**. Browse through the list of learning resources.

You will learn more about accessing the ITT Tech Virtual Library in section 1.2 of this chapter.

Planning is essential in establishing good study habits. The tips and techniques for creating an effective study plan are:

- Know the course schedule. You cannot create a plan if you are not aware of the schedule for sessions, discussions, and projects.

- For each day, create a list of tasks to accomplish. Ensure that you can realistically accomplish the list.

- Set aside dedicated time each day to complete the tasks. Limit your distractions. Take a short break every 1 to 1.5 hours.

- Build a buffer into your schedule to handle unforeseen circumstances.

- Do not forget required projects. Schedule time each week to work on the projects. Develop a list of milestones for the projects.

- Do not fall behind. If you are not keeping to your planned schedule, revise it. Catch problems early and do not let them linger from week to week. Talk with your instructor if you are having problems.

Remember that you are responsible for creating your own motivation and success. Keep to your schedule and seek help early if you start falling behind.

 If you establish and stick to a plan, you can avoid stress related to completing the course. This strategy also will help you reduce stress in your professional life as well.

Figure 1.4 shows a sample template you could use to plan your study activities for the course. Using this or a similar template can help you to complete the required course work on time and alert you to potential problems before it is too late to correct them.

Completed		Completed by	Notes
	Required projects		
	1.		
	2.		
	3.		
	4.		
	Quizzes		
	1.		
	2.		
	3.		
	4.		
	5.		
	Chapter assignments/labs		
	1.		
	2.		
	3.		
	4.		
	5.		
	6.		
	7.		
	8.		
	9.		
	10.		

Figure 1.4: Sample Template for Planning Course Activities

The process you can follow to study online chapters is:

1. Read the introduction and objectives for a chapter. Familiarize yourself with the topics covered in it.

2. Assess your proficiency level with each objective for the chapter using the worksheet in Figure 1.5. Note the areas in which you need to improve your proficiency level.

3. Read through the online content. Read the summary as an overview of the key skills and concepts that were presented. Review material as necessary.

4. Complete assignments, projects, quizzes, and practice questions to get feedback on your learning.

5. Take another look at the skill assessment you completed in step two. Did you make gains in the areas that you needed to improve? If not, develop a plan for raising your skill level in those areas. You can use the ITT Tech Virtual Library as a source for additional information.

Figure 1.5 shows a sample worksheet to assess your proficiency levels.

Chapter:			
	Pre-chapter proficiency level	Post-chapter proficiency level	Area for further study
Chapter objectives			
Topic objectives			

Instructions:
1. List the chapter and topic objectives for the chapter you are studying.
2. Using your own judgment, rate your proficiency level for each objective before studying the chapter. Record your rating in the pre-chapter proficiency level column of the chart.
3. After studying the chapter, use your judgment to rate your proficiency level for the objectives. Record your rating in the pre-chapter proficiency level column of the chart.
4. In the area for further study column, place a check to indicate the objectives where you need further improvement.
Proficiency rating scale: **Developing:** low level of knowledge or experience   **Competent:** capable of explaining or demonstrating the knowledge   **Expert:** able to apply the knowledge in new situations

Figure 1.5: Sample Worksheet to Assess Proficiency Levels[MSOffice1]

Practice Questions

1. The Strategies for the Technical Professional course is designed to give you the skills to use _____ to enhance your lifelong learning.

   a. technology

   b. the ITT Technical Institute

   c. the Internet

   d. past experience

2. People who exhibit an internal locus of control would:

   a. Cite a slow Internet connection as a reason for not completing a project on time.

   b. Take personal responsibility for their results.

   c. Rely on other team members to complete projects.

   d. Need help to create and stick to a schedule.

3. Achievement motivation refers to:

   a. A person's desire to be liked by others.

   b. Setting grading standards such that students will be motivated by the grade they receive.

   c. A person's need or desire to achieve results.

   d. Using slogans and case studies to motivate people.

4. Identify the type of learner who prefers to learn by a hands-on approach:

   a. Elementary

   b. Auditory

   c. Visual

   d. Kinesthetic

5. Which of the following statements is true?

   Statement A: It is important to create a daily list of tasks to accomplish, though it is not necessary to have a realistic list.

   Statement B: Building a buffer into a schedule helps to handle unforeseen circumstances.

   a. Statement A is true, but Statement B is false.

   b. Statement A is false, but Statement B is true.

   c. Both statements are true.

   d. Both statements are false.

6. Which of the following statements is true?

   Statement A: You should assess your proficiency level with each objective for the chapter to determine the areas in which you need to improve your proficiency level.

   Statement B: Completing assignments, projects, quizzes, and practice questions provide feedback on your learning.

   a. Statement A is true, but Statement B is false.

   b. Statement A is false, but Statement B is true.

   c. Both statements are true.

   d. Both statements are false.

1.2 E-Learning at ITT Tech

E-learning is an online training medium that allows for a flexible, 'anytime, anywhere' learning environment. In today's fast-paced culture, organizations that implement e-learning provide their work force with the ability to change to their advantage. In the e-learning environment, users can learn about a particular subject at their own pace from any location. However, self-paced learning requires discipline. Independent learners need to maintain a high level of self-motivation.

In tune with the times, ITT Tech provides you the opportunity to take online courses and to be familiar with e-learning modes of instruction. While taking an online course, you should be comfortable using online resources. ITT Tech provides many online resources to you in its Virtual Library. To use this storehouse of information, you must have access to a computer with an Internet connection. In addition, to access an online course at ITT Tech, you must be familiar with the interface used to administer the course.

1.2.1 Requirements for Online Access

 State the hardware and software requirements for accessing resources online.

You will need to have access to a computer and the Internet to complete an online course. The minimum requirements for hardware and software are:

- Minimum hardware requirements: Pentium II, 133Mhz, 64MB RAM, CD-ROM drive, 3.5" diskette drive, and 1.2GB free disk space (master drive).
- Minimum software requirements: Windows 95™, Microsoft Office™, Internet Explorer™ version 5.5, and e-mail with file attachment capabilities.
- Internet connection: 56K dialup modem.
- Display settings: 800 × 600 or 1024 × 768 pixels.

While these are the minimum requirements, it is recommended that you use the most robust hardware and Internet connection you have available. For instance, a DSL or cable modem connection to the Internet is recommended, while a faster processor and more recent version of the Windows operating system will improve your online experience.

1.2.2 ITT Tech Virtual Library Resources

 Describe the resources available in the ITT Tech Virtual Library.

As a student of the ITT Technical Institute, you have access to the ITT Tech Virtual Library, which is a wealth of online reference information. The resources provided by this virtual library are:

- Full text books and periodicals.
- Reference resources, such as encyclopedias, dictionaries, and Web site directories.
- Information relevant to ITT Tech programs.
- Learning guides and tutorials on a variety of software applications.
- E-mail access to a librarian for personalized help.

In addition to these resources, you also have the ability to catalog links to references you find interesting. This feature, called **My Links**, can provide a useful catalog of Web sites and other reference information that will be useful to you as you complete your program.

As you initially explore the library, you may be impressed and yet overwhelmed by the vast content it provides. Keep in mind that the virtual library is analogous to a traditional library in that within it are many resources available for many different types of needs. By becoming familiar with the general types of resources available in the library and identifying the type of information you need prior to visiting the library, you can ensure that the library will be a more productive and less overwhelming resource for you. The next topic explains how to set up your user account to access the library.

1.2.3 Accessing the ITT Tech Virtual Library

 Explain how to access the ITT Tech Virtual Library and use its features.

The ITT Tech Virtual Library is available over the Internet. The URL for the library is http://library.itt-tech.edu.

You may want to create a bookmark for the ITT Tech Virtual Library by adding it to your **Favorites** in Internet Explorer. Use **Help** in Internet Explorer to learn how to do this.

You need a user name and password to access the library. On your first visit to the library, click the **Registration** link for new students to create your user name and password. On subsequent visits to the library, type them in the appropriate fields and then click the **Login** button to gain access to the library.

Figure 1.6 shows the ITT Tech Virtual **Login** Page.

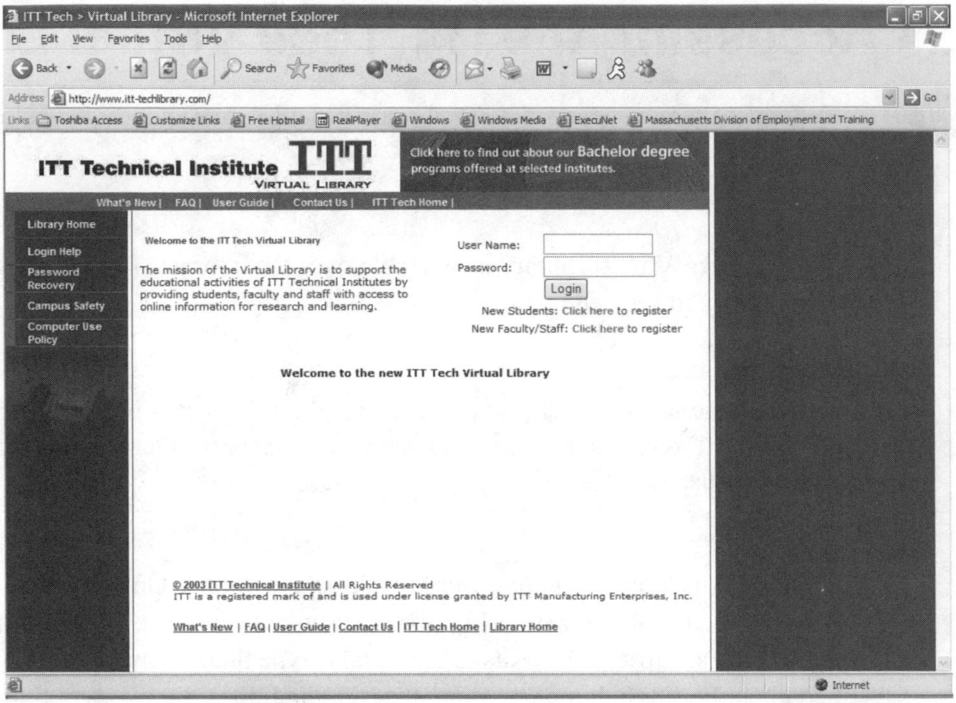

Figure 1.6: ITT Tech Virtual Library Login Page

To register and create your user name and password, you will need to know the following information:

- The user name that you wish to use, which:

    - Must have at least seven and not more than 15 letters or numbers.

    - Cannot contain spaces or special characters, such as, !, #, and &.

- The password, which:

    - Must have at least seven and not more than 15 letters or numbers.

    - Cannot contain spaces or any special characters, such as, !, #, and &.

- Your student ID number.

- Location of your school campus.

In addition, you will need to supply your name and at least one of the following pieces of information: home phone number, work phone number, or e-mail address.

It is a good idea to have this information on hand before you register for the library. Figure 1.7 shows a screen shot of the online registration form. Comprehensive information about the registration process is provided online. There is no waiting period after registration. Once you complete the registration process by clicking **Send Registration Information** at the bottom of the form you can begin using the library.

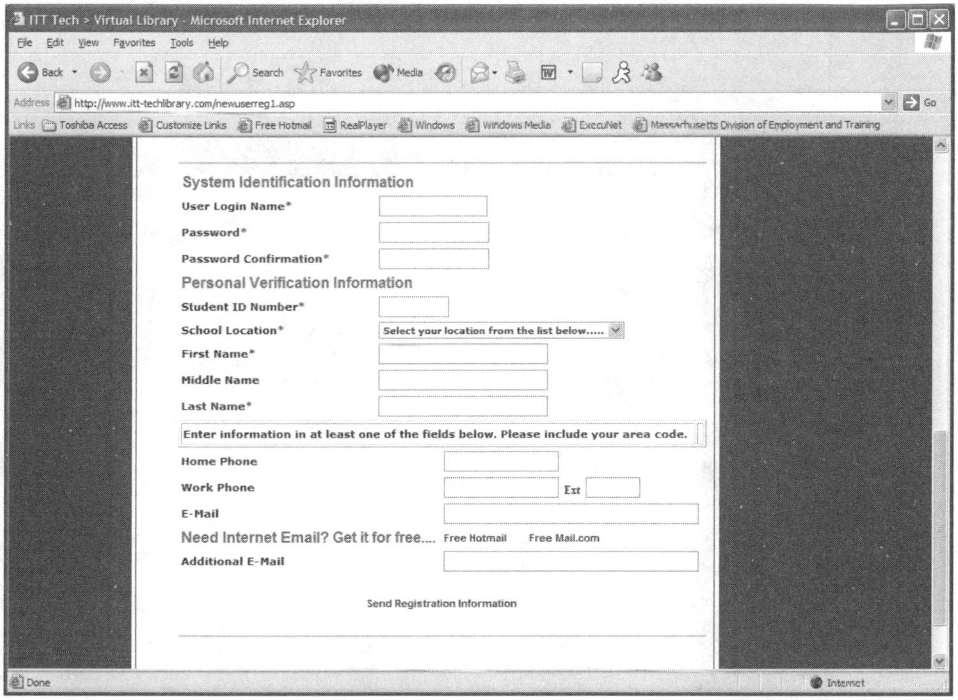

Figure 1.7: Student Registration Form for the ITT Tech Virtual Library

The library resources are also listed in the menu bar on the left side of the page. This menu is visible as you browse the general categories of resources available in the library. However, when you click on a link that takes you to a specific resource in the library, the menu of resources may not be available. You can use the **Back** button on your browser to return to the library menu, or return to the library home page and log on again to access the menu.

After you enter the library, you will see the main menu with the list of available resources, as shown in Figure 1.8. You can access these resources by clicking the link in the menu. Navigating the ITT Tech Virtual Library is similar to navigating the Internet, and while you may intuitively use many of the resources, there is also online help available for some resources.

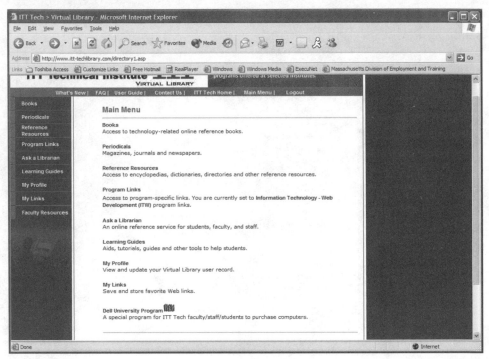

Figure 1.8: ITT Tech Virtual Library Menu of Resources

1.2.4 ITT Tech Course Management System for Online Learning

 Describe the purpose and benefits of the ITT Tech Course Management System.

Pursuing an online course requires you to access instructional material over the Internet. At ITT Technical Institute, the ITT Tech Course Management System provides a standard look and feel for accessing required course information. You will use this interface for all online courses in your program of study. The ITT Tech Course Management System can be described as a learning management system portal. It provides you:

- Access to information on your course of study.
- Online content, assignments, and quizzes that are required for your course.
- Links to additional information related to your studies.
- Forums for discussion and additional help.

In addition, the interface also helps you plan and track your progress through the course. Planned durations for each session of the course are provided. You can also view your results on quizzes. In short, the ITT Tech Course Management System acts as your resource and guide throughout the course by giving you the tools you need to complete the online version of the program.

1.2.5 Accessing the ITT Tech Course Management System

Explain how to access and use the ITT Tech Course Management System for online learning.

You access the ITT Tech Course Management System using the URL, http://www.distance-education.itt-tech.edu/ in Internet Explorer. After providing your assigned PIN (username) and password, you gain access to the information intended for you.

Figure 1.9 shows the interface of the ITT Tech Course Management System.

ITT Technical Institute ITT

Welcome **Admin,**   Wed Jan 21 21:27:02 EST 2004   VIRTUAL LIBRARY   LOGO

Home   My Desk Learning Tools Curriculum Delivery Course Preparation Collaborate Resources Setup Reports Search Virtual Library Help

QUICK LINKS

Ask the Instructor
Discussion Forum
My Instructor Links
Reset Password
Message Center
My Workspace
My Favorites
Course FAQs
Perf. Dashboard
Survey

MY COURSE KIT

Registered Courses	Start Date	End Date	Status	Performance
Instructor Orientation Program	08/17/2003	11/17/2003			
COMPOSITION I - DE2	09/08/2003	11/30/2003			
COMPOSITION I - DE3	09/08/2003	11/30/2003			
COMPOSITION I - DE4	09/08/2003	11/30/2003			
GE127: College Mathematics I	08/27/2003	12/27/2003			
IS314: Security Architecture of Common IT Platforms	09/03/2003	12/03/2003			
IS315: IS Risk Management and Intrusion Detection	09/03/2003	12/03/2003			
GE117: Composition I	09/03/2003	12/03/2003			
IS316: Fundamentals of Network Security, Firewalls, and VPNs	09/03/2003	12/03/2003			
COMPOSITION I - DE1	09/08/2003	11/30/2003			
GE192: College Mathematics II	09/02/2003	12/02/2003			
GE253: Physics	09/02/2003	12/02/2003			
GE332: Economics	09/02/2003	12/02/2003			

Figure 1.9: ITT Tech Course Management System Interface

Table 1.4 provides an overview of the components of the course management system that will be useful to you as you complete your online study.

Component	Description
My Desk	Provides access to courses for which you are currently registered and allows you to update your account profile information.
Learning Tools	Provides information about your course performance, messages, and other notes, links, and answers to questions.
Curriculum	Provides information about programs of study.
Collaborate	Gives access to discussion forums, chats, surveys, and your personal workspace.
Resources	Gives access to resources, such as a glossary and knowledge base.
Search	Allows you to search the knowledge base.

Component	Description
Virtual Library	Provides access to the ITT Tech Virtual Library (separate log-in required.)
Help Desk	Provides technical support information.

Table 1.4: Components of the ITT Tech Course Management System

1.2.6 Additional Help

State how to obtain help and ask questions during an online course at ITT Tech.

Asking questions is a natural part of learning. You need to interact with others and ask questions to clarify and confirm your understanding of the material. During an online course at ITT Tech, there are several ways for you to ask questions and get additional help. These include:

- Asking questions:
  - You can ask your instructor questions, either by sending e-mail or using the **Ask the Instructor** link in the ITT Tech Course Management System.
  - You can ask your classmates questions or discuss material by forming a study group. The ITT Tech Course Management System provides **Chat** and **Discussion** capabilities to facilitate discussions with other students.
- Seeking technical help: Administrative Support can help you with technical problems you may encounter during the online portion of the course. You can call the **Administrative Support** help desk at 1-877-456-7134.
- Seeking information about the programs of study offered by ITT Technical Institute: The **Administrative Support** desk can help you with questions about your registration or program of study. You can call the **Administrative Support** Help Desk at 1-877-456-7134
- Seeking help on research topics: The ITT Tech Virtual Library provides an **Ask a Librarian** service to provide assistance in researching topics.

All these resources are provided to support your online learning. Take advantage of them to help you work through any problems you may encounter during your studies.

Practice Questions

1. What version of Microsoft Internet Explorer is required for accessing an online portion of the course?
   a. 5.0 or higher
   b. 5.5 or higher
   c. 6.0 or higher
   d. No specific version requirements

2. Which of the following statements is true?
   Statement A: The ITT Tech Virtual Library contains tutorials on popular software products.
   Statement B: The ITT Tech Virtual Library contains full text books in an online format.
   a. Statement A is true, but Statement B is false.
   b. Statement A is false, but Statement B is true.
   c. Both statements are true.
   d. Both statements are false.

3. Which of the following is a valid user name for an ITT Tech Virtual Library user?
   I. rsmith
   II. rumplestiltskin2
   III. Paul&Jim
   IV. rlsmith
   a. I, II, III, and IV.
   b. I and IV.
   c. I, II, and IV.
   d. IV only.

4. Which of the following statements is true?

   Statement A: You must supply a PIN and password to log on to the ITT Tech Course Management System.

   Statement B: You must supply a PIN, password, and course name to log on to the ITT Tech Course Management system.

   a. Statement A is true, but Statement B is false.

   b. Statement A is false, but Statement B is true.

   c. Both statements are true.

   d. Both statements are false.

5. The Search function in the ITT Tech Course Management System allows

   you to search the:

   a. ITT Tech Virtual Library.

   b. Internet.

   c. Knowledge Base.

   d. ITT Technical Institute Web site.

6. If you are having trouble accessing online course resources in the ITT Tech

   Course Management system, how can you get help?

   a. Ask your instructor.

   b. Call the Administrative Support desk.

   c. Call the ITT Tech Technical Support desk.

   d. Post a discussion question.

Summary

In this chapter, you learned:

- The Strategies for the Technical Professional course presents skills and concepts in the following areas:

  - Analyzing the impact technology can have on business, society, and personal achievement.

  - Learning how to use popular applications for word processing, spreadsheet, database, and presentations to enhance productivity in both business and personal situations.

  - Exploring and validating information found on the Internet and in the ITT Tech Virtual Library and using that information in a responsible manner.

  - Identifying personal learning styles and formulating a strategy for continuous lifelong learning.

  - Practicing personal and professional management skills that are critical for success.

- Independent learning requires you to take the initiative to plan, ask questions, obtain feedback, and assess your results. Several personal characteristics play a factor in the success of independent learning: locus of control, emotional maturity, achievement motivation, and preferred learning style.

- Communication etiquette and good study habits are essential to your success as an independent online learner.

- During an online course at ITT Tech, additional help is available from a number of sources, including your instructor, discussions with classmates, the ITT Tech Administrative Support desk, and the Ask a Librarian service in the ITT Tech Virtual Library.

- The ITT Tech Virtual Library provides a variety of resources for learning and research. The ITT Tech Course Management System provides a mechanism to help you track your progress in the course and also serves as a portal to tools that can support online learning.

References

Book Reference

- Davis, James R. and Adelaide B. Davis. 2000. *Managing Your Own Learning*. San Francisco, CA: Berrett-Koehler Publishers, Inc.

Web Site References

- Discoveryhealth.com, Discovery Health Tools, *Locus of Control and Attribution Test Style*, <http://discoveryhealth.queendom.com/lc_short_access.html> (14 September 2003).

- McClelland, David C., *The Three Basic Approaches to Improving Productivity*, 2003, Accel-Team.com, <http://www.accel-team.com/human_relations/hrels_06_mcclelland.html> (14 September 2003).

Overview of
Technology Tools

2

The computer industry provides us with a vast number of technology tools. These tools are used to gather information, document the results of this information, and analyze performance of business applications. In addition, technology tools are used to troubleshoot existing problems.

This chapter prepares you to:

- Describe the history and evolution of the Internet in general terms.

- Define terms associated with accessing information and communicating over the Internet.

- Access and navigate the Internet in different ways.

- List types of Internet resources.

- Create bookmarks for Internet sites.

- Be aware of viruses and security issues on the Internet and take steps to avoid them.

- Access Microsoft Office applications and explain their uses.

- Manage electronic mail messages.

- Manage the address book in Microsoft Outlook.

2.1 The Internet

2.2 Microsoft Office Tools

2.3 E-Mail

2.1 The Internet

The Internet is a global network of informational sites. The Internet is also referred to as the World Wide Web, or simply the Web. The Web is large number of networked computers interconnected to share knowledge, which has become an essential service catering to the business world, education environments, and our personal lives, as shown in Figure 2.1.

Figure 2.1: The Internet Caters to Businesses, Educational Institutions, and Personal Lives

Businesses use the Internet to market and sell products and services by publishing product information and troubleshooting hints. Educational institutions conduct complete courses through the Internet and may create course assignments that require Internet-based research. Personal uses of the Internet include researching medical symptoms, buying theater tickets, and finding recipes, among many others.

2.1.1 History and Evolution of the Internet

Explain the history, evolution, and future of the Internet.

The Internet began as the Advanced Research Project Agencies (ARPANET) group. ARPANET was formed in 1958 by the United States Government in response to the Soviet Union's launching of Sputnik (the first artificial satellite) in 1957. The U.S. Government wanted to lead the world in science and technology. The first network created for the ARPANET comprised four computers interconnected for the United States Department of Defense (DOD) in 1969. The four computers that first made up the ARPANET were at the University of California at Los Angeles, Stanford Research Institute (SRI), University of California at Santa Barbara, and University of Utah, at a speed of 56 Kilobits per second (Kbps).

The speed of a network connection is measured in Kilobits per second. One Kbps stands for 1000 bits per second.

ARPANET was originally designed to enable resource sharing among dissimilar computer hardware and operating systems. The common network bond created in the original ARPANET was through the networking hardware and software. ARPANET has evolved into an international public network comprising millions of computers. Today, this network is known as the Internet.

On April 30, 1995, the United States' National Science Foundation (NSF) announced that the backbone of the Internet would be privatized. Another milestone in the evolution of the Internet occurred in 1989, when Tim Berners-Lee proposed the World Wide Web (WWW) and the ability to link documents anywhere in the world.

Today, the Internet is used to share information and resources across the world. It is no longer funded exclusively by the United States government, and instead is now privately funded. Much of the expense of the Internet is incurred in maintaining its high-speed backbone. This backbone consists of the connections that private companies maintain, and which provide the Internet's infrastructure.

Internet committees have been formed to set specifications for the Internet. These committees consist of members from business, government, and educational institutions. The rapid growth and popularity of the Internet has prompted current Internet committees to look at ways of implementing an advanced addressing scheme for network connection devices in the future.

 An address is a unique number assigned to each computer that participates in a network. This address is also known as an Internet Protocol (IP). Currently, an IP address is written as a series of four numbers, each separated by a period. This addressing scheme helps to identify each computer on the network uniquely.

This addressing scheme will recognize transmissions that contain audio or video and will handle them more efficiently to reduce instances of broken transmissions. The Internet search mechanisms used today rarely reach more than five percent of the resources on the Internet. In the future, the Internet will have better means of searching the millions of networked computers and the vast wealth of information stored in them.

2.1.2 Internet Terminology

 Explain the terminology associated with accessing information and communicating over the Internet.

The Internet has developed its own terminology. The extensive use of the Internet in our daily lives requires us to be familiar with the most common Internet terms.

2.1.2.1 Using a Browser

Certain programs are used to initiate a connection between two computers. These programs require the use of a *Web browser* to access resources on the Internet and are called *client programs*. A *browser* is a program that accesses and displays files and other data available on the Internet and other networks. It provides an interface to browse the Internet and is designed to ease the task of moving between Web pages, as well as allow user customization.

Microsoft Explorer is a commonly used browser developed by Microsoft, Inc. Figure 2.2 shows the Microsoft Internet Explorer window with the site http://www.itt-tech.edu/ displayed on it.

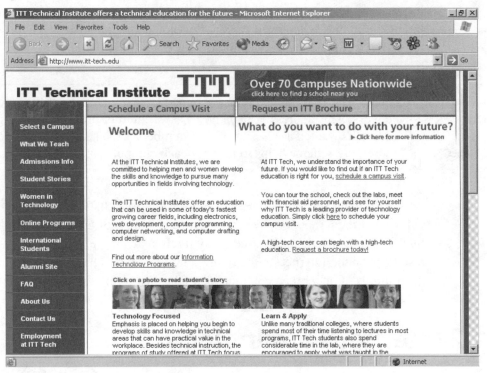

Figure 2.2: Microsoft Explorer Window

Some of the features of the Microsoft Internet Explorer window include:

- **Title bar**: This is located at the very top of the screen and contains the title of the Web document displayed. The title bar also contains the resizing and closing buttons.

- **Menu bar**: This is typically located below the title bar and contains the navigation tools used for file management (**File**), editing (**Edit**), viewing (**View**), and configuring (**Tools**), in addition to **Favorites** and **Help**.

- **Toolbars**: These provide the means for navigating between hyperlinks, searching for information, configuring favorites, and contain shortcuts for printing and sending electronic mail (e-mail) messages.

- **Address bar**: The address of the Web document or site to be displayed is provided in this bar.

- **Web page body**: This is the main area of the window and displays the text, pictures, audio, and video contained in a Web document.

■ **Status bar**: Shows the connection status and whether the connection is secure.

All browsers have the same functionality, but the look and feel of the browser window and certain features may be different. Another example of a browser is Netscape Navigator, shown in Figure 2.3.

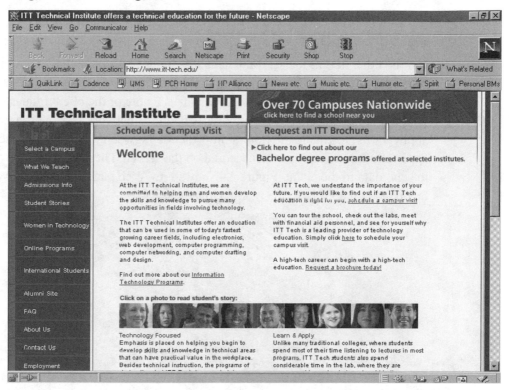

Figure 2.3: Netscape Navigator Window

2.1.2.2 Protocols and Programs on the Internet

Web page design may include *hypertext*, a program type that allows you to link documents, include images and documents, and contains other functionality that helps you interact with the Internet.

Hypertext documents may also include a small Java program called an applet or a small Microsoft program called an ActiveX control. An applet or ActiveX control embeds a program within the hypertext document. An example of an applet would be the inclusion of a running clock in the hypertext document.

Two computers are required to access Web resources: one computer acts as the client and the other acts as the server. Client/server networks comprise two or more computers. In real life, you could think of the client as an individual ordering food at a restaurant. The server at the restaurant makes a note of the client requests and returns with the prepared food. Clients and servers on the network utilize programs (called applications) to enable the flow of information between them. Clients use client applications to access resources stored on the server. The server uses server applications to send data to the client. Figure 2.4 shows how Web pages stored on a Web server can be opened on a PC, which is a client machine.

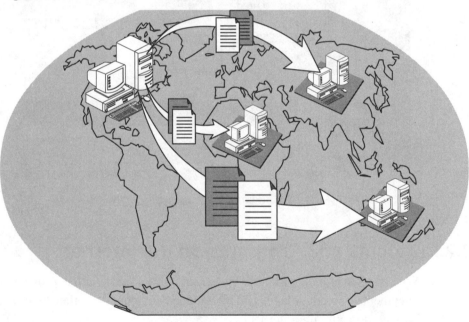

Figure 2.4: Web Pages Stored on Web Servers are Opened by Client Applications

E-mail is an example of a client/server application in which a user utilizes an e-mail client application to access mail stored on an e-mail server. Similarly, a client/server network is implemented to enable the flow of information between companies, educational institutions, and government agencies.

Example 2.1

Another example of client/server application is between an employee's PC and the company's database.

When an employee queries the company's database, the employee's PC runs a client-based application that communicates with the server application in which the database is hosted. The query is processed on the database server and the results are returned to the client.

When you browse the Internet, a Hypertext Transfer Protocol (HTTP) request is sent to a Web server that hosts Web pages.

Other programs used on the Internet are:

- File Transfer Protocol (FTP): This is used to upload and download files.
- Web log (Blog): This is a personal Web journal that can be maintained on the Internet.
- Network News Transfer Protocol (NNTP): This is used to post and read messages that pertain to a particular newsgroup.
- E-mail: This application is widely used on the Internet to receive and send messages in electronic form. E-mail is discussed in detail in Section 2.3 of this chapter.

The most common networking technology in use today is Transmission Control Protocol/Internet Protocol (TCP/IP). TCP/IP is a protocol suite that encompasses the applications used in the network. This protocol guarantees the process of information transfer by sending back an acknowledgement for every data packet that has reached its destination. Each application, from e-mail to accessing a Web site, is designed to require or send acknowledgement of completion. If no acknowledgement is received, it indicates that data transfer was not accomplished. This proves useful in critical data transfers such as a purchase being made online from an e-commerce site. Losing the customer information or billing information during the transmission would compromise the transaction integrity. TCP/IP ensures that this does not happen.

2.1.2.3 Networks and Service Providers

A computer is connected to the Internet through a Local Area Network (LAN) server or directly through an Internet Service Provider (ISP).

 Computers physically connected together across relatively short distances form a LAN. LANs exist within a single building or a single organization. Computers require a Network Interface Card (NIC) for physical connections. Some computers also use wireless technology for connectivity.

Figure 2.5 illustrates how the ISP serves as an entry point to the Internet. The ISP pays an annual fee to the private companies that maintain the Internet backbone to access the Internet; the ISP in turn provides connections to businesses, schools, and homes for an annual fee. Your educational institution provides a connection into the Internet for you. Most ISPs provide Internet access as well as e-mail and Web hosting features. Figure 2.5 shows that ISPs serve as an entry point to the Internet for businesses, schools, and homes.

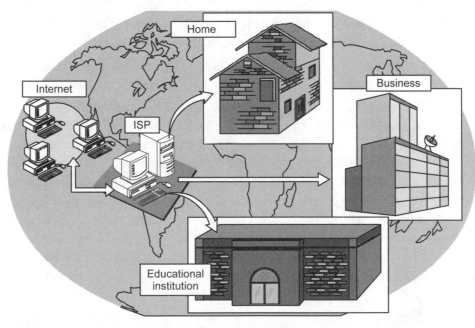

Figure 2.5: ISPs Serve as an Entry Point to the Internet for Businesses, Schools, and Homes

A home user or small business may use a standard dial-up connection, Integrated Services Digital Network (ISDN), Satellite, Broadband, or Digital Subscriber Line (DSL) connection to access the Internet. A dial-up connection utilizes the existing telephone service and requires an additional purchase of a modem. Dial-up connections provide a maximum speed of 56 Kbps for data transmission. ISDN was introduced in the mid-1980s, offers bandwidth of up to 128 Kbps, and utilizes existing telephone services. However, ISDN is limited by the telephone company offerings for the area. ISDN requires the purchase of an ISDN modem and a DSL connection at the local telephone switch.

Wide Area Networks (WAN) connections used for home and small businesses are DSL or Broadband connections.

Computers that are networked across large distances form a WAN. WAN connections may be between two geographically–distant locations.

A DSL connection makes use of existing telephone wiring but requires a DSL modem and DSL support from the local telephone company. Broadband is most often provided as an add-on to local cable broadcasting. Broadband requires coaxial or fiber optic cabling.

Coaxial cable is a type of wire that is covered by insulation and a grounded shield of braided wire. The coaxial cable is used to transmit radio signals. The shield exists to minimize radio and electrical frequency interference.

Fiber optics cables consist of strands of glass as the core. The fiber optics signal is modulated into light waves. Fiber optic signals can travel longer distances than coaxial cable and are more secure.

Large businesses or ISPs use faster WAN leased-line connections. A leased-line is a physical connection provided by a long–distance carrier that connects two locations.

2.1.3 Internet Navigation

 Describe methods used to navigate the Internet.

You can navigate the Internet by:

- Clicking a hyperlink.
- Entering the site URL in the address field of the browser.

2.1.3.1 Navigating using Hyperlinks

Web pages are created using Hyper Text Markup Language (HTML). An HTML document has a file name extension of .htm or .html. HTML documents can include text, hypertext, images, animations, video, audio, and embedded files. Examples of embedded files are an Excel spreadsheet or an online presentation that is included in the HTML document.

HTML documents support hyperlinks. Hyperlinks are links between documents that reside locally on the same computer, on other computers within the same network, or on the Internet. When you click the hyperlink, the HTML source redirects the Web page to the appropriate site.

> Example 2.2
>
> Clicking on the **Travel** hyperlink on the site http://www.yahoo.com will redirect you to the site http://travel.yahoo.com/.

2.1.3.2 Navigating Using URLs

- You can also navigate the Web by entering a valid Uniform Resource Locator (URL) in the address field of the browser. A URL contains the complete address of a Web site. It has the following four parts:

1. Protocol: Includes protocols, such as HTTP, FTP, and NEWS.

2. Domain name or IP address: Every computer on a network running TCP/IP requires a unique IP address, which is a numeric value such as 10.16.15.120. The domain name that is referenced in the URL provides a meaningful name to the IP address of the host.

3. Virtual directory: This is a location other than the default location of the Web site. The virtual directory can be located on the Web server or it can be another network resource.

4. Document: Name of the file to access at the specified location.

The various parts of a sample URL are given in Table 2.1.

Parts of a URL	Example
Protocol	http://
Domain name	www.itt-tech.edu
Virtual directory	onlineprograms
Document name	iss.html

Table 2.1: Parts of the URL http://www.itt-tech.edu/onlineprograms/iss.html

When a Web site is accessed by entering the URL, *http://www.<domain_name>*, the request is forwarded to the appropriate Web server. The Web server responds to the query by loading the home page of the Web site, unless explicit virtual directories of a document name exist. The home page is configured as the name of the HTML document to be returned to the client when they enter a Web site. The home page, similar to other HTML documents, contains images, text, and hyperlinks to other Web documents.

The Internet contains many Domain Name System (DNS) servers that host registered domain names. Computers use sets of numbers to identify other computers. The DNS server contains the mapping of the domain name to the corresponding IP address. For example, when the user queries the DNS server to resolve www.whitehouse.gov, the DNS server maps it to the IP address 152.163.197.4. The DNS name is an alias for the IP address and is much easier for users to remember.

2.1.4 Internet Resources

Describe available Internet resources and how they can be searched.

Internet resources are online versions of news, references books, and articles. Online resources offer a wealth of information about companies, educational institutions, government offices, and the private thoughts and theories of individuals. Some online references charge a one-time or annual subscription fee. Online references contain valuable information, but they may also have certain restrictions.

Any online material is copyright protected. Any use of copyrighted material must be acknowledged and permission obtained for its use.

The following precautions must be taken when utilizing online reference materials:

- Not all online information is accurate. Use more than one reliable source when doing online research.

- Online references may not be up-to-date. A nominal fee or deeper inquiry may be required to access the latest information.

- Author's credibility. If the author is not reliable, the information posted may be bogus.

- Affiliations of the author. You need to verify that the author is unbiased and is not promoting a particular product or concept due to his or her personal or professional affiliations.

- You will learn about the Internet resources in detail in Chapter 4, "Information from Electronic Sources." In the next section, you will be given an overview of these resources.

2.1.4.1 Online Databases

Online databases are public or private databases that contain product information, medical journals, or law references. Private online databases require an account and password to access the information.

Online databases are *client/server applications*. The server side hosts the database. The client requires a client-side application that is specifically designed to access that database type. Online databases on the Internet are often queried by accessing a Web site that hides the process of information retrieval from the user.

Example 2.3

The Web site http://www.amazon.com/ does not have its product database as a Web page and it is not located on a Web server. Amazon configures its Web page to include a query form to enter the product description. The Web page contains the appropriate client-side application to query the Amazon product database located on another server. The results of the query are returned to the user through another Web document.

2.1.4.2 Newsgroups and Listservs

Newsgroups and listservs are online message boards. Members are given permission to read and post to an existing thread or to start a new thread. A thread is a discussion topic. Newsgroups allow members to read or post messages directly to the online bulletin board. A listserv is used to gather the postings on a daily, weekly, or monthly basis, which are then sent as e-mail messages to registered members.

Newsgroups are client/server applications. It is a type of online database that is accessed through the client's Internet browser by changing the protocol from http: to news:. The NEWS protocol is the client-side protocol used to enter a newsgroup from within a client browser. Another more common way of accessing a newsgroup is to use a client e-mail application, such as Outlook. E-mail can be configured to enable newsgroup subscriptions.

Example 2.4

http://chat.gradschoolfairs.com/ is a discussion board site.

2.1.4.3 Commercial and Organizational Sites

Commercial and organizational sites contain product information, service offerings, troubleshooting tools, and demos that can be downloaded. Additionally, a business or organizational Web site has information related to the purchase of their products or services. The vast majority of companies have a Web site today. The features contained on the Web site are determined by the influence the Internet has on the company's profit margins. Some companies sell their services and products only through the Internet.

> **Example 2.5**
>
> Commercial Web sites, such as www.ebay.com sell products solely through their Web site. Products offered on eBay tend to sell easier when a meaningful description and a picture of the item are included. However, due to its nature, eBay does have a measurable percentage of fraudulent sales of nonexistent or incorrectly marketed items.

Commercial or organizational sites are accessed using HTTP.

2.1.4.4 Educational Resources

Educational resources are sites hosted by educational institutions that contain information about academic programs, online resources, online classes, online assignments, department information, locations, and staff information. Educational institutions are normally accessed using the .edu domain name extension.

> **Example 2.6**
>
> http://www.itt-tech.edu/ is an educational site. It is a vast resource of information that includes academic programs, admission information, campus news, and employment opportunities.

Educational institutions can also provide links to bulletin board services to be used for distance education or online assignments. Distance education provides certificate programs and undergraduate, graduate, or doctoral degrees, usually without requiring the student to enter a physical classroom.

2.1.4.5 Government Resources

Government web sites have information on local, state, or national governments. Information on government Web sites can contain agency information, online documents, telephone numbers of staff and departments, locations, and directions. Information can also be posted on current leadership policies, goals, and objectives. Most government institutions use the domain name extension of .gov.

Government institution sites are accessed using HTTP.

2.1.4.6 Blog Resources

A blog is a personal online journal that is updated often. This resource is intended for public viewing and contains non-commercial information. A blog can contain thoughts on social issues, comments about products or companies, or the author's personal philosophy. The author of a blog is referred to as a blogger. Updates made to a blog are known as blogging. Only the author of the Web log (the blog) can update it.

Web sites such as salon.blog.com have been created to assist new or current bloggers in Web log creation.

Keep the following considerations in mind when accessing a blog:

- Is the blog author of sound integrity?
- Is the blog author a subject-matter expert?
- Is the material posted on the blog up-to-date?

Blog sites are accessed using HTTP.

Figure 2.6 shows the blog site http://slashdot.org/.

Figure 2.6: The Slashdot Blog Site

2.1.5 Bookmarks and the Internet

 Describe the value of bookmarks to access the Internet.

Bookmarks are used to store Web pages you may wish to access again, thereby reducing the time required to reaccess them. Bookmarks can be organized by category. Microsoft Internet Explorer and America Online (AOL) refer to bookmarks as **Favorites**. You can create, delete, or rename the folders used to organize your bookmarks. Bookmarks are created and organized by copying the link into the appropriate category. These are saved for individual users and are associated with the user log-on account.

It is useful to maintain a private diary of these bookmarks on your hard disk. This will ensure that you have access to your favorite sites even if this list is deleted from the history or browser.

2.1.6 Security and Viruses

Describe the security features of the Internet. Explain the features of a virus and how it affects the computer and Internet access.

Internet security protects your data from malicious Internet users. If the data is not secured, unscrupulous individuals can acquire information about your identity and misuse it. As shown in Figure 2.7, various security features of the Internet include using encryption technology to make private or sensitive information less easy for dishonest individuals to access.

The data to be encrypted can include credit card numbers, telephone numbers, log-on names, passwords, and addresses.

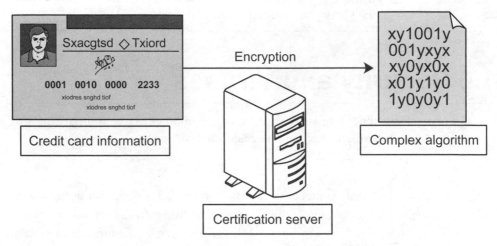

Figure 2.7: Encryption Technology

Encryption, also referred to as cryptography, involves acquiring a certificate that contains a complex encryption algorithm. These certificates are retrieved from a certificate server.

The types of encryption available today vary. Encryption can be simple or complex. A simple encryption would substitute a single character for every letter of the English alphabet. For example, every "a" is a "z," and every "b" is a "2." A more complex encryption would be where a single character is encrypted as several characters. For example, every "a" is a "1Fx4," every b is a "92km." The more complex the encryption algorithm; the more difficult it is to break the code.

Cookies are also sources of security threats. A cookie normally is a harmless file that is stored on the computer and has information on user preferences. For instance, if you are looking for pink hiking boots at an outdoors outfitter, when you access a Web site informing you about a sale on pink hiking boots a cookie stores that information on your computer as one of your preferences. As a result, the site informing you about the sale may become your home page. Unfortunately, cookies can also be used to store information about credit card numbers, user names, passwords, and telephone numbers. Unscrupulous individuals may use this information for malicious purposes.

Security threats can include integrity threats, in which an unauthorized individual modifies data. Integrity threats occur when the transmitted data is captured, modified, and retransmitted. For example, individuals may transfer your money to their account. Delay or denial threats (these need definitions) may leave your account information open, allowing unauthorized access to your account. These threats occur when the transmitted data is captured, analyzed, and then retransmitted to its original destination.

Intellectual property thefts occur when intellectual materials are used by unauthorized individuals or institutions.

Security is also breached when your computer is attacked by a hacker. A hacker is someone who writes a program to damage, view, or modify data. The program the hacker creates is known as a virus. A virus is a program hidden within legitimate code. The virus can come as an e-mail attachment and reside on your computer if it is unprotected.

An organization known as the Coordination Center (CERT) tracks down the creators of viruses and reports on existing or potential virus attacks. CERT is located at www.cert.org and contains valuable information concerning how to avoid virus attacks. CERT also makes note of what viruses are currently in existence and how to eliminate these viruses from a computer, as well as contains security practices information.

To reduce your chance of unauthorized access to your personal data or virus attacks, take the following steps:

- Update your system with the latest anti-virus software.
- Protect your computer system with a software/hardware solution designed to block unauthorized access to your computer.
- Use a secure log-on and complex password, such as Te#chn0l0g9, that is a combination of upper and lower case letters, numbers, and other characters in the password.
- Give your credit card information only to sites that use secure encryption algorithms.
- Check you credit card statements often for unknown entries.

Practice Questions

1. Which of the following actions will secure your data?
   a. Deleting the data
   b. Rewriting the data
   c. Sending partial data
   d. Encrypting the data

2. The first page opened on a Web site is known as a:
   a. home page.
   b. virtual directory page.
   c. blog page.
   d. database page.

3. The networking protocol used on the Internet is referred to as:
   a. IPX/SPX.
   b. TCP/IP.
   c. IP/TCP.
   d. Client/server.

4. Web pages are created using:
   a. HTTP.
   b. TCP/IP.
   c. HTML.
   d. WWW.

5. _____ enables you to locate data from a resource in a specific location.

   a. ULR

   b. HTML

   c. URL

   d. HTTP

6. When was Web access designed?

   a. 1957

   b. 1969

   c. 1972

   d. 1989

7. A personal journal on the Internet is a:

   a. Web site.

   b. NNTP site.

   c. Blog site.

   d. FTP site.

2.2 Microsoft Office Tools

Microsoft Office tools contain applications that help businesses, educational institutions, and individuals manage their data. As shown in Figure 2.8, Microsoft Office tools can be used to share information or create documents, spreadsheets, presentations, and databases.

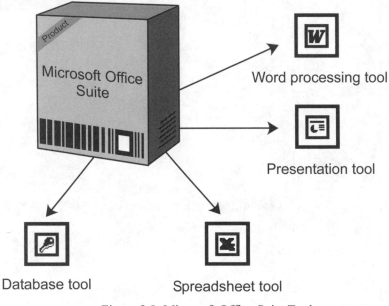

Figure 2.8: Microsoft Office Suite Tools

Microsoft offers a product referred to as the Microsoft Office Suite. The Microsoft Office Suite contains Word, Excel, PowerPoint, Access, Outlook, and FrontPage applications. You will learn how to use most of these applications in the Strategies for Technical Professionals course; in this section, however, you will learn about the uses of some of these applications.

You can always explore the features of any of these applications by using the built-in **Help** feature. This will save you from being dependent on external help, better enabling you to become an independent learner. As you explore, you will be able to tap the full potential of these applications. This will be reflected in the documents you create using them and make your work unique and impressive.

2.2.1 Microsoft Word

Explain the features and uses of the Microsoft Word application.

Word is one of the most commonly used Microsoft Office applications. Word is a document processing application in which textual information is written into a file. Word allows the creation and modification of documents used for research papers, Web pages, memos, resumes, business letters, and personal letters. Documents created with Word can be easily published on Web sites or shared through e-mail attachments with other users.

Figure 2.9 shows an example of a Word document.

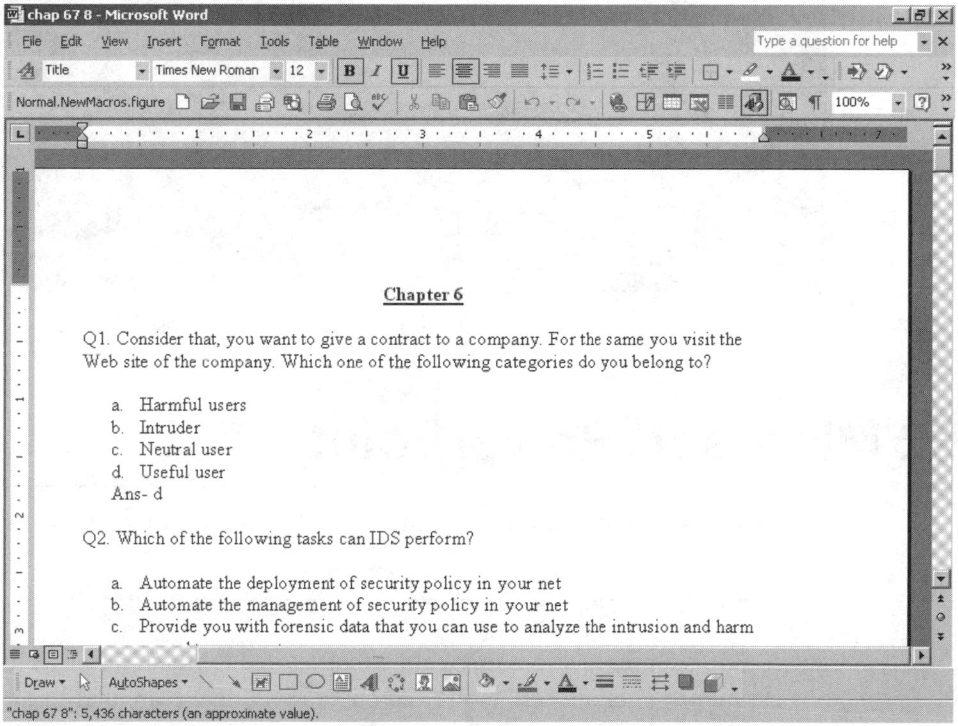

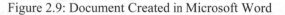

Figure 2.9: Document Created in Microsoft Word

Word provides a vast array of tools that allow for document creation and editing. Tables and images also can be easily placed into a Word document.

To start Microsoft Word from your desktop, click **Start → Programs → Microsoft Word**, as shown in Figure 2.10.

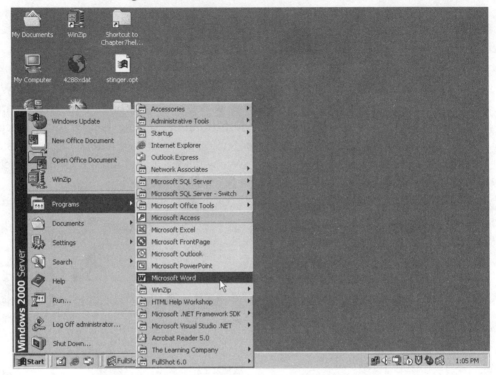

Figure 2.10: Method of Launching Microsoft Word

2.2.2 Microsoft PowerPoint

Explain the features and uses of the Microsoft PowerPoint application.

PowerPoint is a presentation application that is used to illustrate ideas to an audience. A PowerPoint presentation can be viewed on an individual computer or across a LAN, WAN, or the Internet. PowerPoint is used to create slides that can be viewed concurrently by students in a classroom or by students through an online virtual classroom. PowerPoint 2002 has the features of creating animated slides and multilingual support.

Overall, PowerPoint slides can incorporate images and graphs and provide the capability to present slideshows that can be shown at a kiosk.

A kiosk is a computer set up at a trade show or in a lobby that continuously displays a slideshow.

Figure 2.11 is an example of a PowerPoint slide using a standard template.

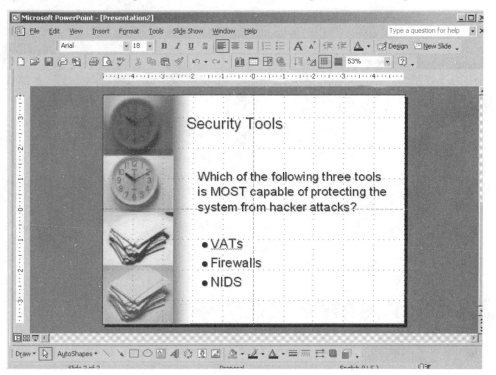

Figure 2.11: Slide Created in Microsoft PowerPoint

To launch the PowerPoint application from your desktop, click **Start → Programs → Microsoft PowerPoint**, as shown in Figure 2.12.

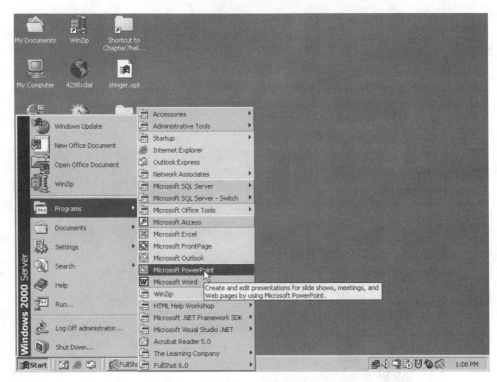

Figure 2.12: Method of Launching Microsoft PowerPoint

2.2.3 Microsoft Excel

Explain the features and uses of the Microsoft Excel application.

Excel is Microsoft's spreadsheet application, which provides a tool to manage business data. In business, Microsoft Excel is used to create spreadsheets for data analysis, schedules, and budgets. Excel is also an excellent application for managing personal finances as it provides the functionality of easily performing complex calculations on numerical data.

A wide range of documents can be created in Excel including:

- Expense reports: Business costs for an employee. These may include parking expenses, reference material purchased, or company trip expenses.
- Sales invoices: The document presented to the customer with a summary of costs incurred.
- Loan amortization: Schedule of loan payments based on the original loan value, number of payments, and interest rate.
- Timecards: Employee document used to summarize the tasks performed by the employee throughout the work day.

Figure 2.13 shows a spreadsheet that has been created using Microsoft Excel.

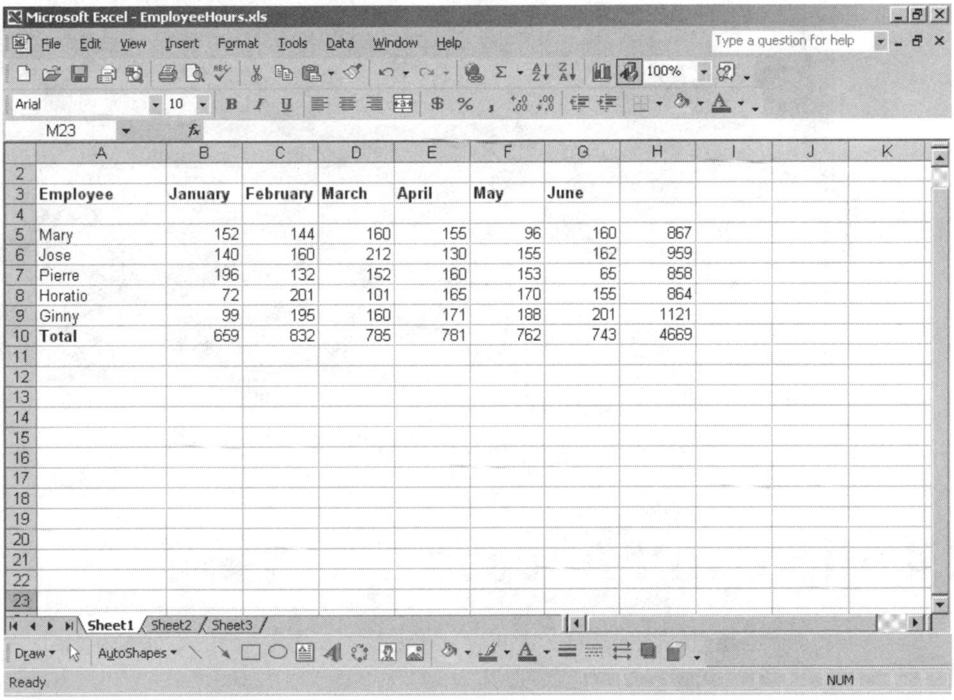
Microsoft Excel - EmployeeHours.xls
File Edit View Insert Format Tools Data Window Help
Type a question for help
Arial 10
M23
Employee January February March April May June
Mary 152 144 160 155 96 160 867
Jose 140 160 212 130 155 162 959
Pierre 196 132 152 160 153 65 858
Horatio 72 201 101 165 170 155 864
Ginny 99 195 160 171 188 201 1121
Total 659 832 785 781 762 743 4669
Sheet1 Sheet2 Sheet3
Draw AutoShapes
Ready
NUM

Figure 2.13: Spreadsheet Created Using Microsoft Excel

To start Excel from your desktop, click **Start** → **Programs** → **Microsoft Excel,** as shown in Figure 2.14.

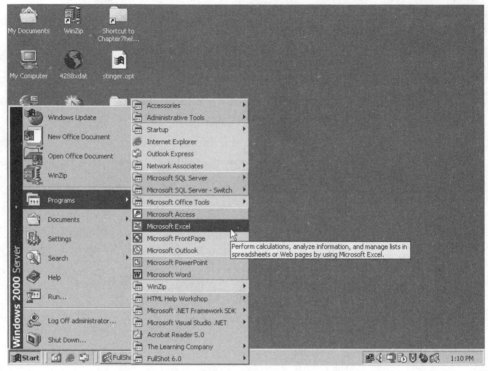

Figure 2.14: Method of Launching Microsoft Excel

2.2.4 Microsoft Access

Explain the features and uses of the Microsoft Access database.

Access provides businesses a means of quickly and easily capturing and retrieving data. Using Access, data is sorted into specified criteria for analysis. For instance, a business can save information on all the customers who bought their products, which products they bought, and the quantities they purchased in a database. Access provides a means to store the data logically and to create a report that shows which customers purchased the most products and what products they purchased. The Microsoft Access database application serves as an organized storehouse of information and is also used to keep important lists for personal or professional use. Access can be used to create interactive spreadsheets that can be regularly updated as the data changes. Such an interactive Web sheet can be ported to Web sites for easy access. Access 2002 incorporates speech recognition into the building of the database. Additionally, Access 2002 includes multi-language support.

Figure 2.15 shows an example of an Access database containing customer information.

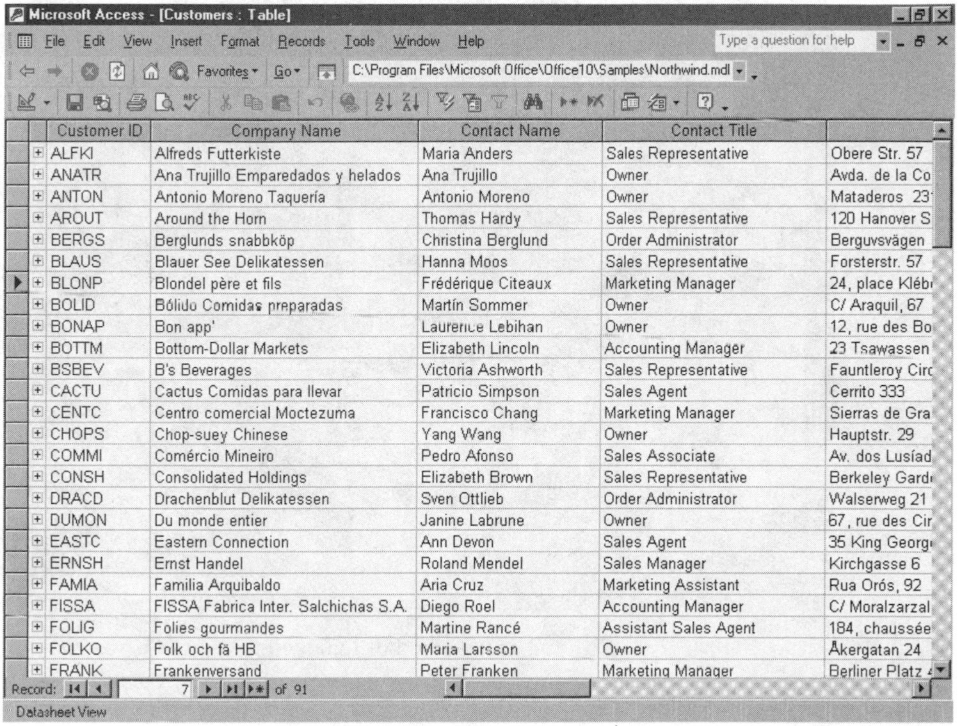

Figure 2.15: Database Created Using Microsoft Access

To launch Access from your desktop, click **Start** → **Programs** → **Microsoft Access**, as shown Figure 2.16.

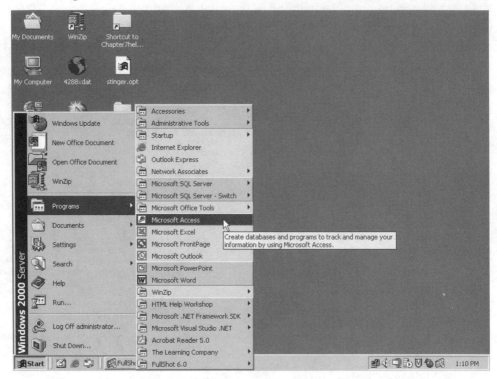

Figure 2.16: Method of Launching Microsoft Access

Practice Questions

1. Which application would be most appropriate when creating a presentation for your final project?
   a. Word
   b. Excel
   c. PowerPoint
   d. Access

2. Which application would you most likely use to plan a schedule of your automobile loan repayment?
   a. Word
   b. Excel
   c. PowerPoint
   d. Access

3. Which application would be the best choice to catalog your music so that you can sort by artist or song?
   a. Word
   b. Excel
   c. PowerPoint
   d. Access

4. Which application would you choose to write an essay for a philosophy class?
   a. Word
   b. Excel
   c. PowerPoint
   d. Access

2.3 E-Mail

E-mail has revolutionized communication. As depicted in Figure 2.17, e-mail has brought people across the globe within easy reach of each other.

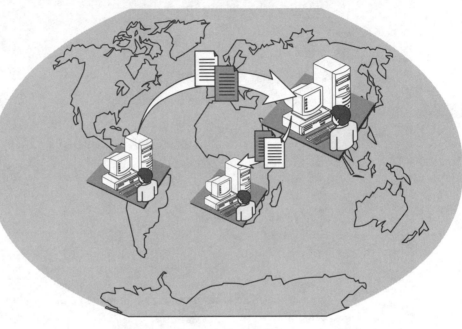

Figure 2.17: Spread of E-Mail Across the Globe

E-mail has become the primary tool of communication over the Internet. It gives you the capability to communicate with anyone who has an e-mail address and saves you the time and labor of postal mail.

In 1971, Ray Tomlinson created an internal e-mail system to send the first e-mail message across ARPANET. The original e-mail address system used in 1971 still serves as the basis of what we use today. That is:

Original e-mail address: User's log-on name@host e-mail computer

Current e-mail address: User's log-on name@host domain name

Early e-mail could contain only text; no types of graphics or attachments were allowed. Messages also could only be read in the order in which they were received. E-mail has now evolved into one of the most widely-used applications. Current e-mail systems are designed to allow sorting and searching through messages by the subject line or the content of the message. Messages are stored on an e-mail server and are opened when the user accesses them through an e-mail client application. Messages can also be sorted by subject, size, date, or author.

E-mail applications are categorized into two broad categories:

- Web-based e-mail services/applications.
- Client-server e-mail applications/services.

2.3.1 Web-Based E-Mail Services/Applications

Discuss the method of accessing Web-based e-mail services/applications.

Web-based e-mail services/applications enable accessing e-mail via any standard Web browser, such as Microsoft Internet Explorer or Netscape Navigator. These e-mail applications do not require any client applications to be installed on a user's local machine for accessing e-mail. There are many popular service providers, such as Hotmail®, Yahoo®, Mail®, and Rediff ® that provide free e-mail services. Anyone can create personal e-mail accounts (e-mail inboxes) and send/receive mails using a login id and password. Using the Internet, you can access your personal e-mail inbox from any computer at any time.

The trademarks Yahoo, Hotmail, Rediff and Mail are the property of their respective owners. You cannot use these trademarks without specific written permission of their respective owners.

Functioning

Service providers host e-mail servers on the Internet and provide personal inboxes (e-mail storage space) to all registered e-mail account holders. An easy-to-use Web-based interface enables users to access and view their personal inboxes and communicate via e-mail.

Using Web-Based E-Mail Services: Creating an E-Mail Account

To send and receive mails using a web-based e-mail service, you need to register and create an e-mail account on any e-mail service provider of your choice. You will need to perform the following tasks to create and use an e-mail account:

- Log on to the Internet
- Access service provider's Website
- Register for a new account
- Sign-in
- Send an e-mail
- View a received e-mail
- Create contacts
- Create folders

Access Service Provider's Web Site

To create an e-mail account on hotmail.com, you need to perform the following steps:

1. Open the website www.hotmail.com.
2. Click on **New Account Sign-Up** Page.
3. Type your e-mail address. Your e-mail address must include @ symbol and the domain (example: abc@ hotmail.com).

 The text before @ symbol can contain letters, numbers, and underscores (_) but no spaces or other symbols.

Register for a New Account

Next you need to provide your details on the registration page. Perform the following steps to complete the registration page:

1. Type a password and then retype it for verification.

2. The next step is to choose a secret question from the drop-down list and then next to **Secret Answer** type the answer. If you forget your password, you will need to provide this information to reset it.
3. Provide the rest of the information as requested.

Figure 2.18 shows the registration page for a Hotmail account:

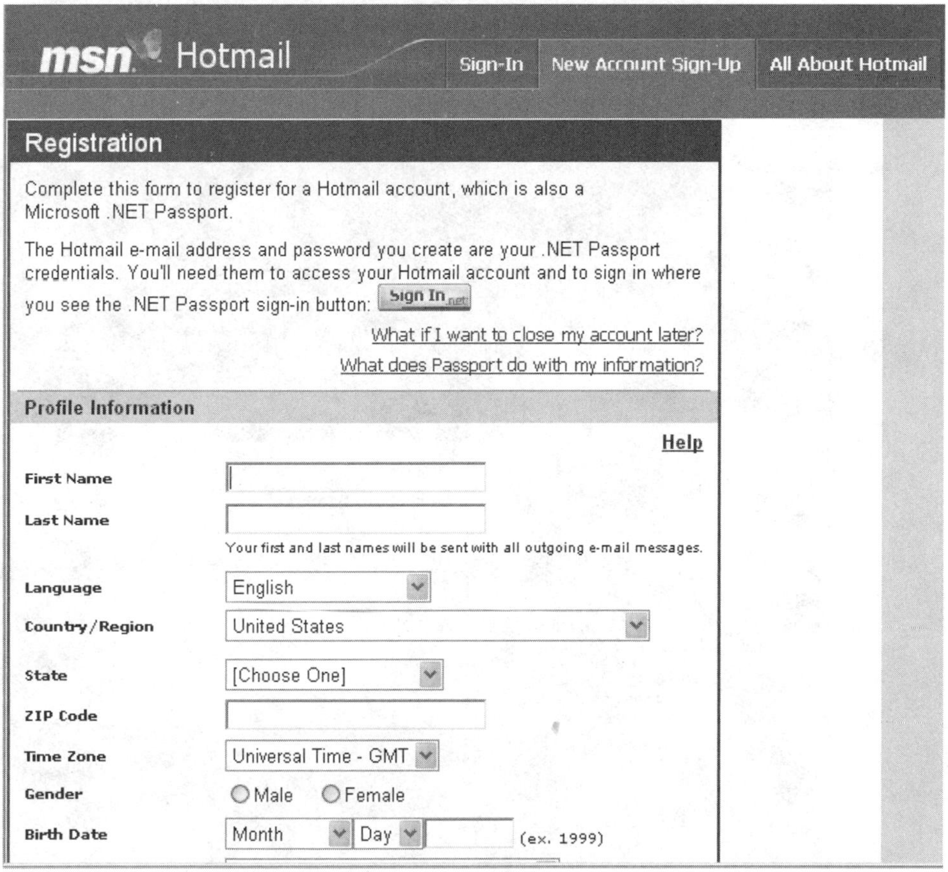

Figure 2.18: Registration Page for a Hotmail Account

Sign-In

After registration, you need to access the account. This can be done by signing into the account, or logging into it.

You need to perform the following steps to sign-in to your e-mail account.

1. Click **Sign In** at any participating site or service.

2. Type the complete e-mail address. For example, namesomeone@microsoft.com.

3. Type the password that you specified while registering for the account. Remember that your password is case-sensitive.

4. Click **Sign In**, as shown in Figure 2.19.

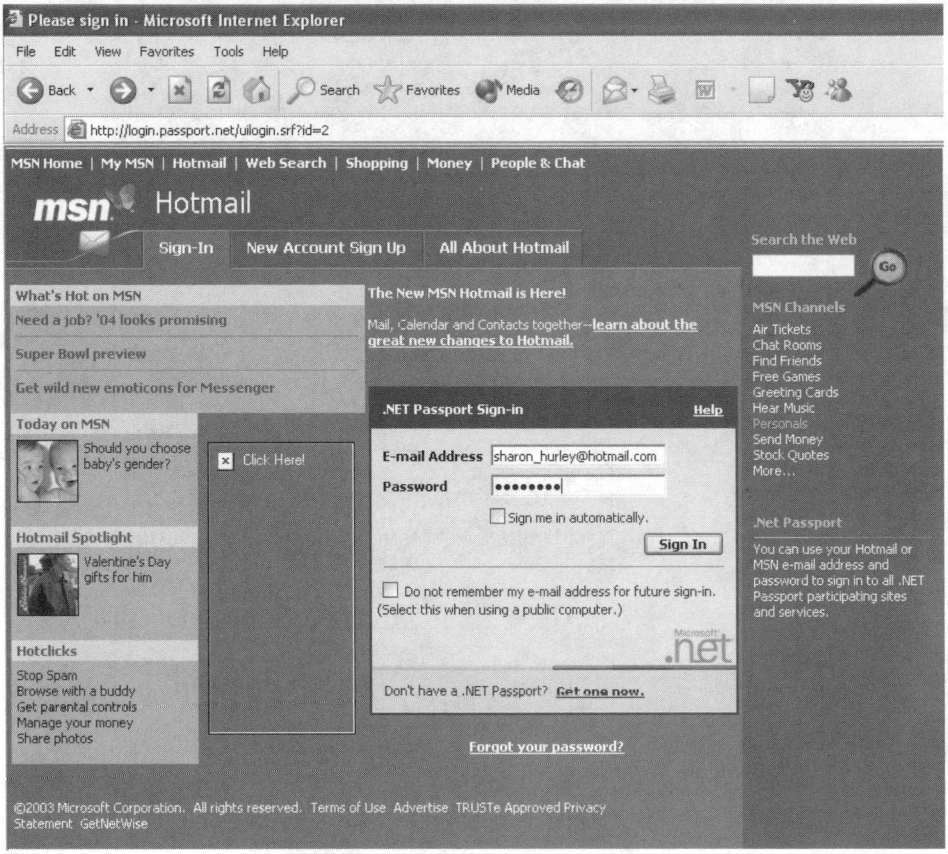

Figure 2.19: Sign-In Page for a Hotmail Account

Send an E-Mail

The **Inbox** provides a link that allows you to create a new e-mail and specify the name of the recipient to whom the mail needs to be sent.

You need to perform the following steps to send an e-mail:

1. Click **Write Message/Compose/New Message** on the navigation bar in the window displaying the Inbox. The **Write Message/Compose/New Message** screen will appear.

2. Enter the recipient(s) e-mail address(es) in the **To, CC**, and/or **BCC** fields. Addresses in the **BCC** field will not be visible by other recipients. Separate multiple e-mail addresses with a comma.

3. Type a subject for your message. The subject line will be visible in the recipients' Inbox when your message is delivered. You do not need to enter a Subject if you choose not to.

4. Type your message in the **Message Box**, as shown in figure 2.20.

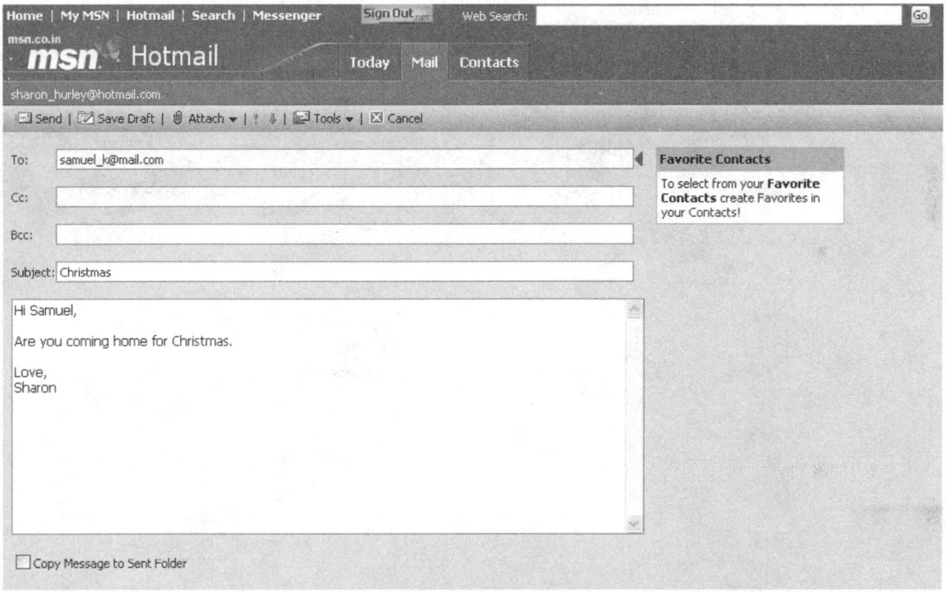

Figure 2.20: New Message Page of Hotmail Account

5. Once you have filled in at least one e-mail address and typed your message, click the **Send** button either above or below the text box.

View a Received E-Mail

Each time you login, your e-mail service will automatically check for new mail. New messages will be shown in your Inbox with the **From** field in BOLD. To check for new mail after you have logged in, you can click the **Get New Messages** or **Inbox** links on the navigation bar to the left. You can also use your browser's refresh button.

The Inbox of a Hotmail account is shown in figure 2.21:

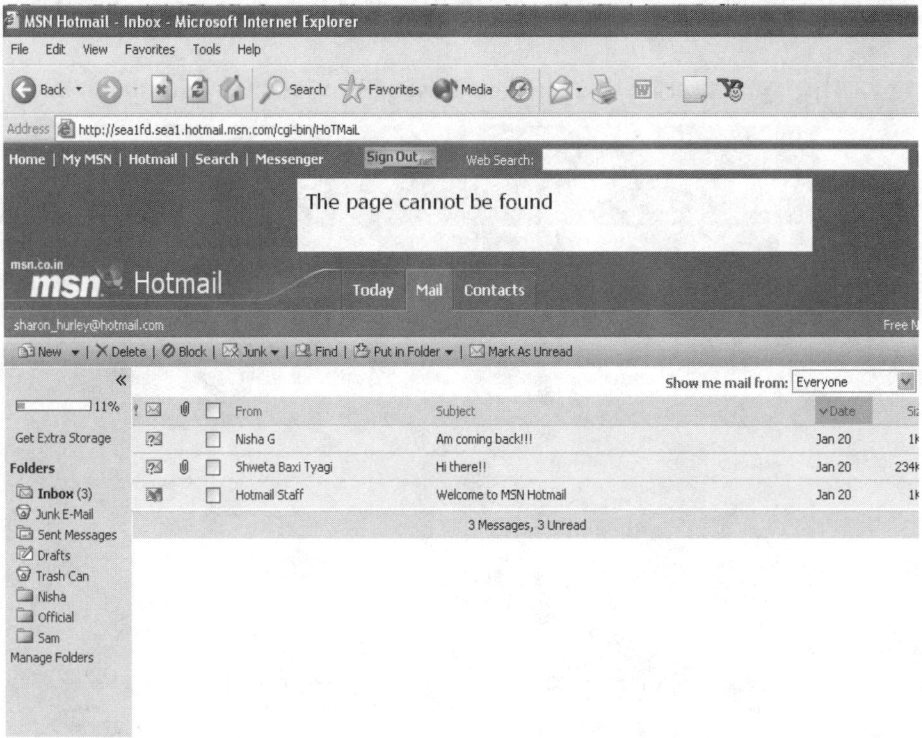

Figure 2.21: Inbox of a Hotmail Account

To read the message, you need to click on the name displayed in the **From** column.

 Most offices and educational institutions discourage employees and students from using free e-mail sites for personal communication. You are advised to check with the relevant IT authority before using them.

Create Contacts[MSOffice1]

Contacts refer to a comprehensive, online listing of your friends and associates accessible from anywhere in the world.

To add a contact, perform the following steps:

1. Click on the **Contact** menu option.

2. Enter the contact information. The e-mail address and alias name are the required fields. In addition to the required field, there are optional fields for other personal information, including name, address, phone number, fax number, and birthday.

3. Once you have finished entering the fields, click **Add Contact**.

These contacts are saved in the **Address Book** that can be used while sending e-mails to the specified people. This way you need not remember e-mail addresses of all the people you regularly correspond with.

To use the address book while sending an e-mail to a user whose name has been added to the contact list, you need to perform the following steps:

1. In the **Write/Compose** page, click the **Address Book** button next to the **To** field. This will open your **Address Book**.

2. Place a check in the appropriate box (**TO**, **CC**, or **BCC**) next to the e-mail address(es) of the recipient(s), you would like to send a message to.

3. Click on **OK** to return to the **Write Message** page.

Create Folders

You can add personal folders for organizing your e-mail.

To add a **Personal Folder**:

1. Click the **Folders** link on the navigation bar to the left.

2. Type the name of the new folder.

3. Click **Create Folder**.

To move a message from a particular folder page, select the message(s) you wish to move by clicking the checkbox(es) to the left of each message. Choose a folder from the drop-down next to the **Move To** button at the top or bottom of the screen. After you have chosen a folder, click **Move To** or **Put in Folder** and your message(s) will be moved to the selected folder.

This is illustrated in Figure 2.22, in which the user is adding the mail from Nisha G to the Nisha folder.

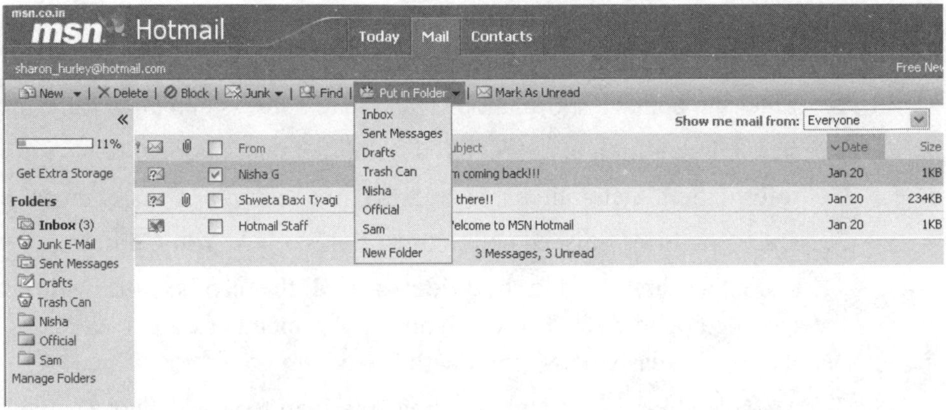

Figure 2.22: Moving Mail to Specific Folders

2.3.2 Client-Server E-Mail Applications/Services

Discuss the method of accessing client-server e-mail applications/services.

The other way of accessing e-mails is using a client-side e-mail application, such as Microsoft Outlook, Outlook Express, Lotus Mail, Eudora, and Pegasus. These e-mail applications are sold by independent software vendors, such as Microsoft, Sun Microsystems, and Lotus. To access e-mails, users need to purchase and install this software on their personal computers. Most of the Internet service providers (AT&T, AOL, Bell Pacific) provide e-mail services to subscribers that can be configured for use with these popular e-mail clients. These e-mail client applications make the task of managing e-mails very simple.

Functioning

E-mail, when accessed using client applications, works in the client-server architecture mode. The e-mail server is hosted on the Internet by the service provider. The e-mail server stores all messages sent and received by all subscribers. Individual subscribers dial into the server when they connect to the Internet and can send and receive their personal messages. All messages are then downloaded from the central server to the user's local machine and can be accessed using the client's e-mail application, such as Microsoft Outlook.

Microsoft Outlook provides a tool for organizing and managing your digital communications. Outlook includes e-mail and instant messaging along with all your day-to-day information. Day-to-day management is done using calendars, contacts, task lists, and notes. Microsoft Outlook has two major versions. The standard version, known as Outlook Express, is packaged with all Microsoft operating systems. Advanced Outlook can be purchased as a part of the Microsoft Office Suite or as a separate product.

Outlook provides a means to read, write, print, and manage e-mail. E-mails are sent to an e-mail server in which they are stored until the recipient retrieves his or her mail using an e-mail client application. Outlook provides a means of creating address lists for easy access to e-mail addresses. Outlook also allows for organization of messages through folder management.

To launch Outlook from your desktop, click **Start** → **Programs** → **Microsoft Outlook,** as shown in Figure 2.23.

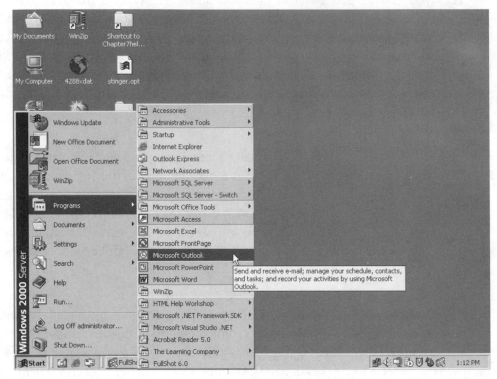

Figure 2.23: Method of Launching Microsoft Outlook

2.3.3 Managing E-Mail Messages

Explain how to manage e-mail messages.

In this section, you will learn the methods to compose, send, reply, and forward messages. Messages can include attachments and signatures. You will also learn to organize and manage e-mail messages. E-mail messages can be best managed by organizing them into multiple folders. This helps in the easy retrieval of messages.

Figure 2.24 shows the Microsoft Outlook window and its various sections.

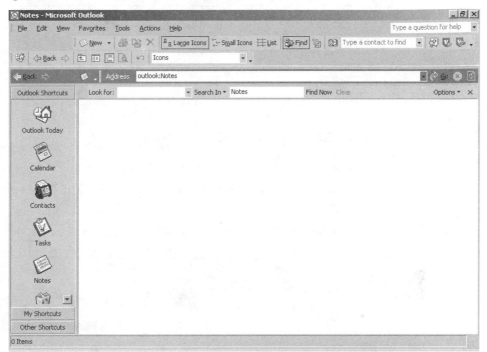

Figure 2.24: Microsoft Outlook and its Sections

The Microsoft Outlook window has the following sections:

- **Menu bar**: Used to manage e-mail messages and e-mail preferences.
- **Folder list**: Contains the standard e-mail message folders and customized folders created by you. Access to new or saved messages is done by selecting the appropriate folder.
- **Status bar**: Displays the number of items in the e-mail folder.
- **Windows sizing buttons**: Used to shrink or enlarge the screen display of Outlook.
- **Toolbar**: Provides shortcuts to send, receive, organize, and search for e-mail messages.
- **Sorting buttons**: Enable you to sort and view the messages in a folder by date, subject, or sender.
- **Message lists pane**: Displays the read and unread messages in the selected folder.
- **Message contents pane**: Shows a preview of the body of the message that is selected to view.

You can explore the ways of customizing your messages by using the **Help** feature of Outlook.

2.3.2.1 Composing and Sending Messages

To compose an e-mail message, perform the following steps:

1. Start Outlook from the Windows startup menu. Figure 2.25 displays the **Inbox** window.

2. In the **Inbox**, select **File → New → Mail Message**.

Figure 2.25: Creating a New Mail Message

The components in the **Compose Message** window include:

- **To**: Write the e-mail address of the intended recipient in this field. It is mandatory to fill this field if the message is to successfully reach the recipient. You may have more than one entry in this field.

- **Cc** (Carbon copy): You may want to send a copy of your message to others also. The persons marked in the **Cc** list need not act on the message; it is sent to keep them updated. You may also have more than one entry in this field.

- **Bcc** (Blind carbon copy): You may want to send your message to another person whose name you may not want the recipients in the **To** and **Cc**: fields to see. You may insert such entries in the **Bcc** field. You may have more than one entry in this field.

- **Subject**: Write a phrase or a brief statement indicating the intent of the message in this field.

- **Body**: Type the main body of your message here. You may also include pictures or documents in this portion of the window.

- **Attachment**: You may include a document or an executable file with your e-mail message. The names of the attached files appear in this area.

3. Compose a new e-mail message. Click the **To**: icon.

A list of e-mail addresses is displayed, as shown in Figure 2.26.

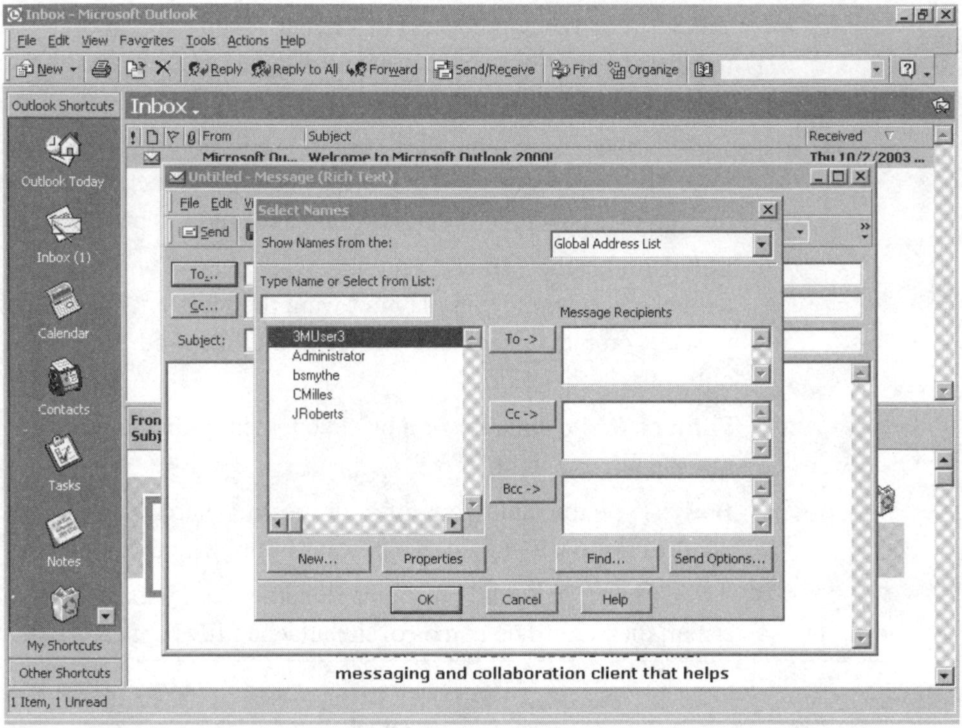

Figure 2.26: Global Address List Shows E-Mail Addresses

4. Click once on the **To**: icon and a list from the Exchange e-mail domain of mail recipients will be displayed.

5. Highlight the recipients and drag their name to the **To**:, **Cc**:, or **Bcc**: fields and then click **OK**.

6. Enter a subject in the **Subject** area, as shown in Figure 2.27.

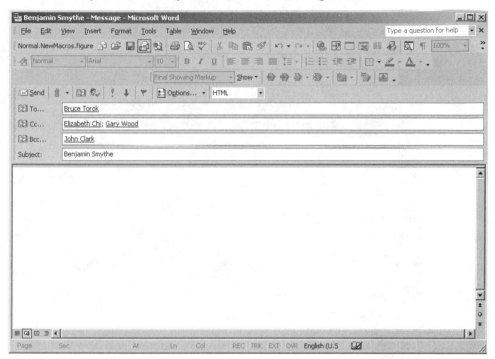

Figure 2.27: Message Window

7. Enter the **Body** of the message.
8. Click **Send** to send the message.

To add a name to the contact list of the sender of the e-mail message you are reading, press **Ctrl + k**.

After a message is read, it can be deleted, replied to, or forwarded to another recipient. To do so, perform the following steps:

1. From the **Start** menu, open **Outlook**.
2. Select the **Inbox Folder**. A list of e-mail messages is displayed.

3. You can read an e-mail message by clicking once on the message. You can **Preview** the message in the bottom half of the Outlook window even before opening the message, as shown in Figure 2.28.

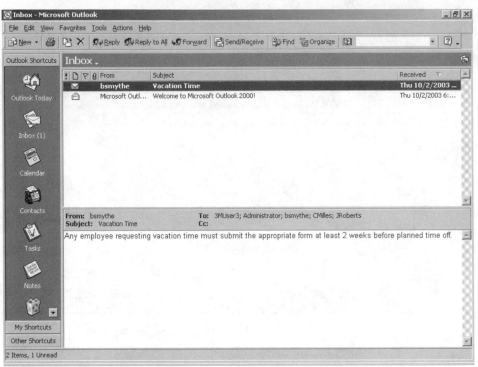

Figure 2.28: Message Preview in Inbox

4. You can reply to the sender by selecting **Reply** from the e-mail toolbar, as shown in Figure 2.29.

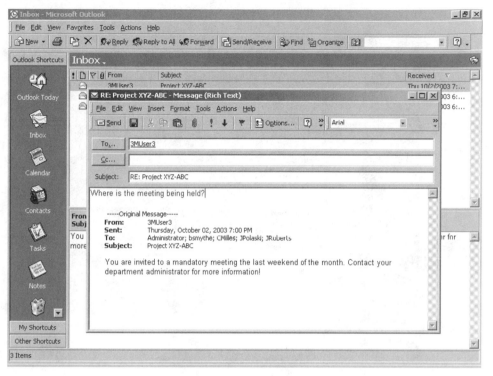

Figure 2.29: Replying to E-Mail

5. The sender's name appears in the **To**: field of the reply. Click the **To**: field to include additional recipients, as shown in Figure 2.30.

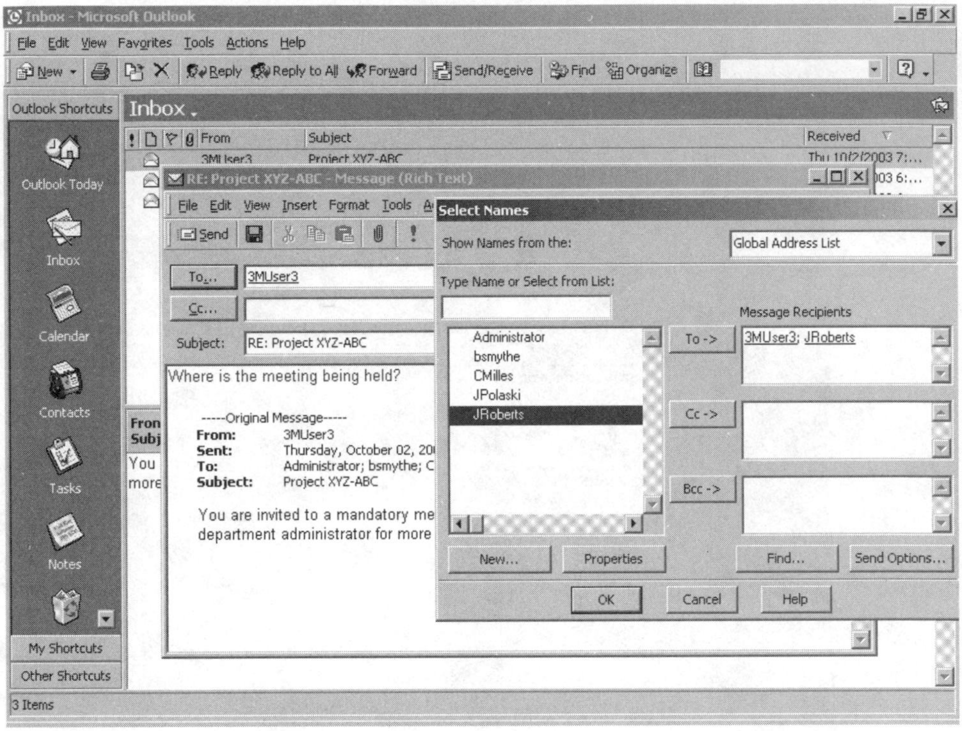

Figure 2.30: Including Additional Recipients in Reply Message

6. The **Reply to All** icon will reply to everyone listed in the **To**: and **Cc**: fields, as shown in Figure 2.31.

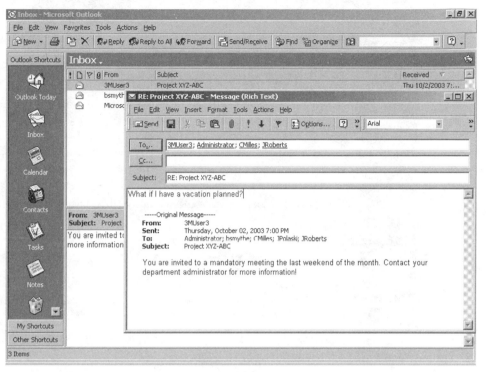

Figure 2.31: Using Reply to All Feature

7. Click **Forward** to forward the e-mail to another recipient, as shown in Figure 2.32.

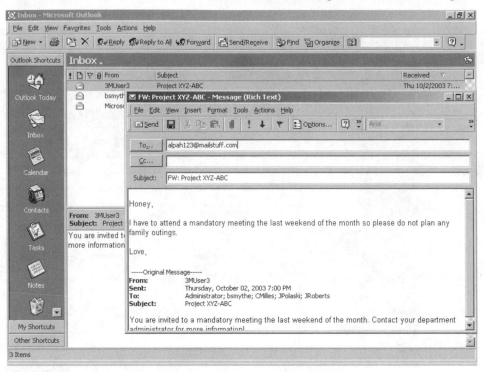

Figure 2.32: Forwarding Message

2.3.2.2 Managing Messages in Folders

Folder management in Microsoft Outlook is done to help schedule tasks, file messages, store contact information, and create online task lists. For instance, a sales representative, John, may have separate folders in Outlook for each of his customers, named after the customers. Any messages that the sales representative sends or receives from a particular customer are filed in the corresponding folder.

The standard types of folders include:

- **Calendar**: Contains schedules of meetings and appointments.
- **Contacts**: Contains customized address lists.
- **Deleted Items**: Contains any item deleted from a folder.
- **Drafts**: Contains messages that have been composed but not yet sent.
- **Inbox**: Contains messages that have been received.
- **Journal**: Tracks e-mail messages.
- **Notes**: Contains notes similar to the concept of sticky notes.
- **Outbox**: Contains messages waiting to be sent.
- **Sent Items**: Contains messages you have already sent.
- **Tasks**: Contains a personal list of tasks to be performed.

To view Outlook folders, perform the following steps:

1. Start **Outlook**.
2. If you do not see a **Folder List**, click **View → Folder List**.

The **Folder List** view appears, as shown in Figure 2.33.

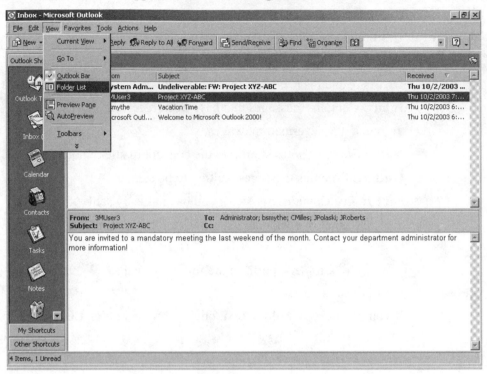

Figure 2.33: Folder View in Microsoft Outlook

To create a new personal folder, perform the following steps:

1. Right-click the **Outlook Today [Personal Folders]** folder.

2. Select **New Folder**, as shown in Figure 2.34.

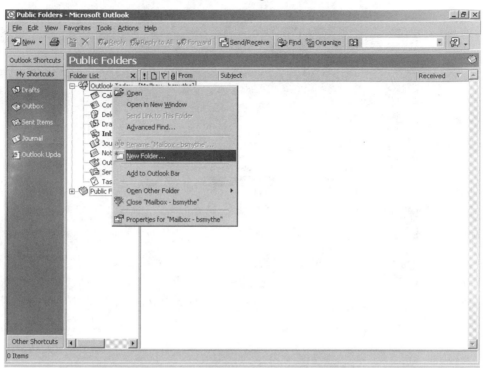

Figure 2.34: Creating New Folder

3. Enter a folder name. Select the type of folder contents from **Folder contains:** drop-down menu, as shown in Figure 2.35.

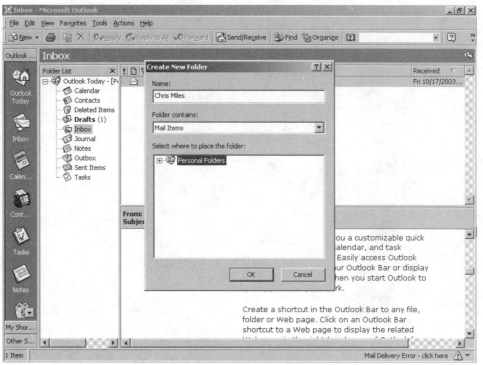

Figure 2.35: Selecting the Type of Folder Contents

4. Click **OK**.

In Outlook, folders can be renamed or deleted by right-clicking on the folder and choosing the **Rename** command.

2.3.3 Managing Address Books

 Describe address books and their usage in e-mail.

E-mail address books ease the process of sending e-mails to recipients. Each e-mail user has an individual profile and e-mail address. Outlook is run in conjunction with the Microsoft Exchange Server. The exchange server provides a **Global Address List** created by the exchange administrator, which contains all the e-mail recipients registered on the exchange server. External e-mail addresses can also be added to the **Global Address List** by the administrator.

The exchange administrator can be one or more employees assigned the responsibility of maintaining the e-mail accounts. The exchange administrator is also responsible for the general management of the exchange server.

A personal address book entry can include:

- Contact's name.
- E-mail address.
- Business and home addresses.
- Business, home, fax and, cell telephone numbers.
- Web address.
- Immediate messaging address.

The Web address is the location of the Web server associated with the contact's business or personal life. For example, if you worked for ITT Tech, your Web Server would be www.itt-tech.edu. The immediate messaging address is the address used for a live interactive chat application, such as AOL's Immediate Messaging or MSN's Immediate Message. The term immediate message implies that all participants must be logged on using an application that allows them to send messages directly to each other.

Figure 2.36 shows the form to create a **Contacts** list in Microsoft Outlook.

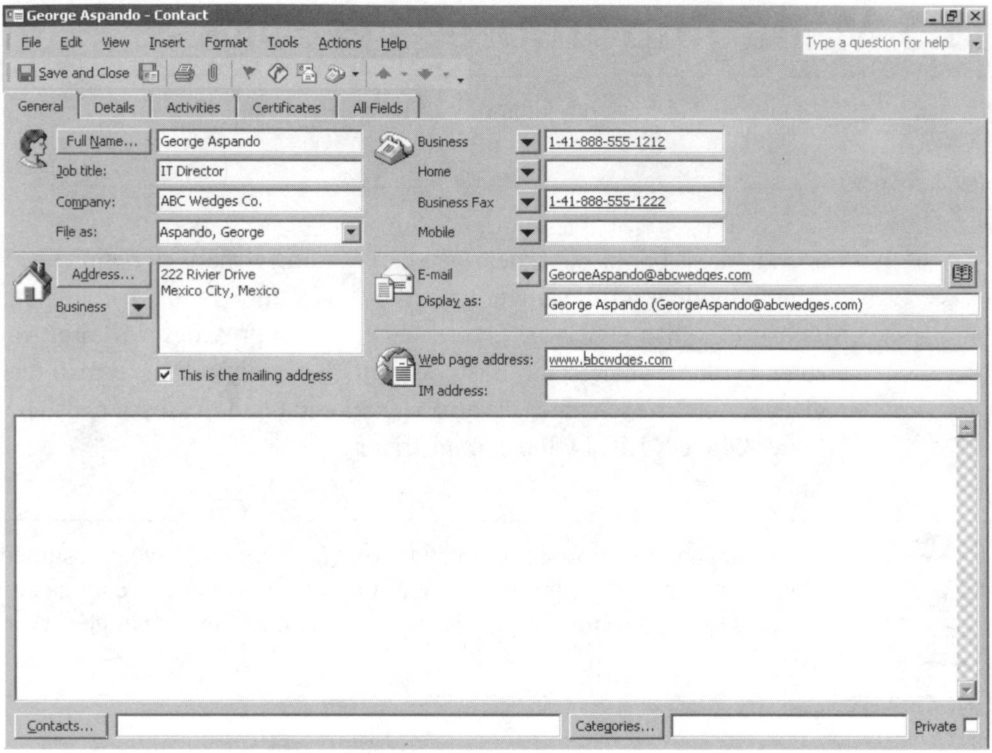

Figure 2.36: E-Mail Contact Creation Form

Use Outlook **Help** for more information about contacts in the address book.

2.3.4 E-Mail and Viruses

Explain the effect e-mail viruses can have on your computer and business.

E-mail viruses attack your computer system through attachments. The attachments contain viruses, which are executable files, with file extensions such as .exe (executable) or .vbs (Visual Basic Script). Viruses can also be sent inside a .zip file. The virus can corrupt your hard drive, delete operating system files, or damage your personal data, as shown in Figure 2.37.

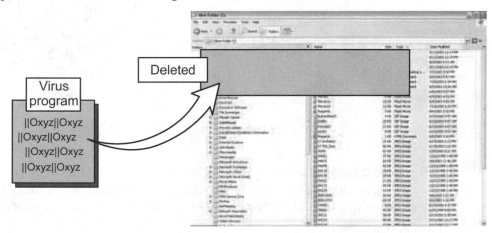

Figure 2.37: Virus May Delete Important Data

Viruses can destroy the Master Boot Record (MBR), which is read during your computer's initialization process to determine what operating system to load and where the operating files are located

You need to install an anti-virus application on your computer to protect your system against virus attacks, as shown in Figure 2.38.

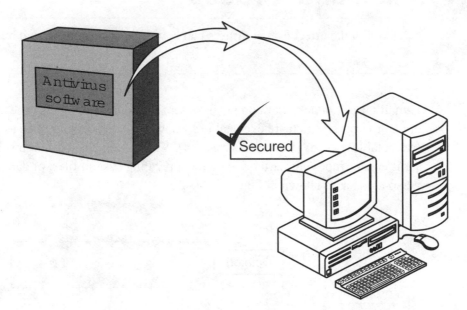

Figure 2.38: Anti-Virus Applications Secure Data

The anti-virus application will monitor all new files that are added to your computer. New files are added to your computer when you download e-mail attachments or copy from a floppy or CD-ROM. You should keep the virus program up-to-date with the latest virus fixes.

Some cautionary measures that can protect your system from e-mail viruses are:

- Never open e-mails that are from unknown senders, particularly if the message has an attachment.
- Do not run a program that you do not recognize, even if a friend or relative has sent it to you.
- Always scan attachments with anti-virus software before you download them.

Some viruses use the recipient's address list to disguise and distribute themselves. Therefore, you may receive messages with viruses from known people even though they have not sent them.

Practice Questions

1. You intend to organize a year-end party. You have much to do to organize the event successfully, including making several purchases. Which folder in your mailbox would most likely contain the details for the intended purchases for the party?
   a. Schedule
   b. Calendar
   c. Sent mail
   d. Tasks

2. Which file extensions do virus programs most often include?
   I. htm
   II. exe
   III. vbs
   IV. cat
   a. I and III
   b. II and III
   c. II and IV
   d. I and IV

3. In which field would you enter the recipient's name that you want to hide from other recipients?

   a. To:

   b. Cc:

   c. Bcc:

   d. Hide them:

Summary

In this chapter, you learned that:

- The Internet began as ARPANET. It has now grown to network computers across the world and is known as the World Wide Web (WWW).

- The Internet has begun to allow for faster and more convenient access to data, such as audio and video. Its sophistication continues to evolve.

- There are many sources of reference materials available on the Internet. Not all information is accurate, but nonetheless there is an infinite wealth of resources available at a click of the mouse.

- Some of the resources available on the Internet include:
  - Commercial and organizational Web sites
  - Online databases
  - Discussion boards (newsgroups and listservs)
  - Government Web sites
  - Educational institution Web sites
  - Blogs (weblogs)

- You can save links to your favorite Web sites as Bookmarks for later access.

- Microsoft Office tools allow you to create documents, spreadsheets, presentations, and databases. These tools include:
  - Word
  - Excel
  - PowerPoint
  - Access

- Microsoft Outlook is an e-mail client. You can send, receive, and forward messages using Outlook.

- You can create a personal address book in Microsoft Outlook to store details on your contacts.

- Security on the Internet is an important issue. Unprotected data can be damaged, causing loss to a business or an individual.

- Viruses can damage personal data as well as operating systems and applications. You can avoid viruses by using anti-virus software.

■ Viruses are often carried by e-mail, and it is therefore important to avoid them. You must scan your message attachments for viruses before you download them.

References

Book References

- Gibaldi, Joseph. *MLA Handbook for Writers of Research Papers*. New York: Modern Language Association, 2003.

- Schneider, Gary and Jessica Evans. *The Internet,* Third Edition. Boston, Ma: Course Technology—Thomson Learning, 2002.

Web Site Reference

- *ONLINE! Microsoft Education*, <http://www.Microsoft.com> (September 2003).[MSOffice3]
  http://www.microsoft.com/Education/MSITAcademy/ITAPOnlineCampus.aspx

Styles of Learning

3

Learning is the process of acquiring knowledge or skills. There are various venues for learning and several different ways in which people learn. Traditionally, people think of schooling, with a teacher as a guide, as the optimal environment for learning. However, as you begin your career, learning independently outside of a classroom is critical to your lifelong success. Understanding how you learn and determining your preferred learning style helps you to become an effective independent learner.

This chapter presents an overview of various learning styles and the overall concept of intelligence. It also discusses how an awareness of your personality traits can help you set an effective strategy for learning. Finally, it presents techniques and strategies for becoming a lifelong independent learner.

At the end of this chapter, you will be able to:

- Identify your personal learning style.

- Describe a theory of intelligence and relate it to your learning and business needs.

- Identify psychological aspects that influence independent learning.

- Develop a personal strategy for lifelong independent learning.

3.1 Personal Learning Styles

Throughout your schooling, you have probably been exposed to various techniques of teaching and learning. Reading books, watching movies or videos, listening to people explain things, and performing hands-on experiments are common methods used to teach and learn skills and concepts. Each of these methods focuses on a different way of presenting concepts and skills to students. People have natural preferences as to how they like to learn, and various teaching methods focus on these different learning preferences or styles. This section presents information on three prevalent learning styles and provides guidelines for assessing your own personal learning style.

3.1.1 Types of Learning Styles

List various learning styles.

Think about a recent experience where you had to learn a new skill. How was the information presented? How did you work with the material to master it? The way a learner works through material to learn it indicates the learner's style of learning. There are three general styles of learning:

- Visual
- Auditory
- Kinesthetic

Visual learners prefer to learn by seeing or reading. They like to read through material to understand it thoroughly. Visual learners are likely to seek out written/graphic material and take notes on a subject to enhance their learning. You would probably find a visual learner reading a set of instructions in its entirety before embarking on a project.

Auditory learners prefer to learn by hearing. They prefer to listen to explanations of concepts or procedures to understand them. Auditory learners may record lectures instead of taking notes and might seek out materials such as video and audio recordings as a preferred learning medium. You would probably find an auditory learner listening to a lecture or product demonstration.

Kinesthetic learners prefer to learn by hands-on interaction. They like to learn by doing and trying things out. Kinesthetic learners would seek simulations, laboratory work, and on-the-job training as ideal learning environments. A kinesthetic learner may begin a project without first reading or listening to detailed instructions.

Learners may prefer one of these three styles or a combination of the styles. For example, a person may prefer to try something out and then read about it in order to feel comfortable that they have learned it. In a structured setting, such as a degree program or formal training in the workplace, an instructor usually provides instruction to accommodate the different learning styles represented in the class. However, outside of formal educational situations, you are responsible for seeking instructional opportunities on your own. An awareness of your preferred learning styles helps you set a strategy for becoming an effective independent learner.

3.1.2 Assessing Your Learning Style

 Determine your personal learning style.

Determining your learning style is a matter of personal assessment. You need to have an awareness of the types of learning activities you enjoy and that are most effective for you. By reflecting on the different types of learning to which you have been exposed and comparing these with the types of activities you naturally enjoy, you can determine the learning style you prefer.

Figure 3.1 presents a sample self-survey you can use to determine your preferred learning style.

Determining Your Learning Style			
In each row, circle the description that best describes you. After completing all rows, count the number of selections you have made in each column.			
	Visual	**Auditory**	**Kinesthetic**
1	In lectures, I like to follow along on the handouts.	I prefer to listen to lectures rather than take notes or follow along.	I prefer to do lab exercises or group activities rather than attend lectures.
2	I like to read books.	I like to listen to books on tape or CD.	I prefer to dance, act, or play sports rather than read.
3	I keep in touch with friends through letters or e-mail.	I keep in touch with friends through phone calls.	I keep in touch with friends by visiting or going out with them.
4	I tend to use phrases such as "I see what you mean."	I tend to use phrases such as "That sounds good."	I tend to use phrases such as "I know how it feels."
5	I read instructions before starting a project.	I ask questions before starting a project.	I start right in on a project without reading instructions.
	Total Visual:	**Total Auditory:**	**Total Kinesthetic:**

Figure 3.1: Learning Style Assessment

Using the assessment in Figure 3.1, or a similar assessment, you can analyze where your preferences lie. You may find that your preferences are split between two or all three styles. This is natural because there are different personal characteristics that can influence how you prefer to learn. Throughout your life, your experiences and learning will help you develop your personal characteristics and give you a balanced appreciation for all learning styles.

1. You like to participate in classroom discussion groups. What type of learning style do you exhibit?

   a. Visual

   b. Auditory

   c. Kinesthetic

   d. Combination

2. During computer demonstrations, you prefer to follow the presenter by typing along. What type of learning style do you exhibit?

   a. Visual

   b. Auditory

   c. Kinesthetic

   d. Combination

3. _____ learners like to study notes.

   a. Visual

   b. Auditory

   c. Kinesthetic

   d. Combination

4. Which of the following activities would a kinesthetic learner prefer?

   a. Watching a product demonstration

   b. Attending a seminar

   c. Role play

   d. Writing an essay

5. Which of the following activities would a visual learner prefer?

   a. Watching a video

   b. Working on lab exercises

   c. Participating in a study group

   d. Building models

3.2 Theory of Multiple Intelligences

Seeking opportunities for learning that match your preferred learning style is an important strategy in independent learning. However, there is more to success in learning than simply matching your preferred learning style. Your ultimate goal is to use the knowledge that you have gained. Intelligence is defined as the ability to gain knowledge and apply it in relevant situations. In short, the desired outcome of learning is to increase intelligence, which is demonstrated by acquiring knowledge and applying it in appropriate situations.

A successful independent learner should have an awareness of the specialized abilities required for their chosen field of expertise. For example, a computer programmer should be able to apply logic and sequential thinking, physical motor skills (for typing), parsing skills, as well as other skills in a typical work situation. To be successful, a programmer should be able to recognize these different areas of intelligence and develop them as necessary to perform the job effectively.

Analyzing your personal development from the perspective of developing intelligences can help you develop a well-rounded strategy for lifelong learning. This section describes a theory of intelligences and presents suggestions for independently developing the intelligences.

3.2.1 Types of Intelligences

 Describe the theory of multiple intelligences.

In 1983, psychologist Howard Gardner developed the theory of multiple intelligences, which states that humans possess many, distinct areas of intelligence. He argued that intelligence is not just a single measure of a person's aptitude as measured by a standard IQ test. Instead, intelligence is a multifaceted aspect of a person's ability to acquire knowledge and apply it in unique situations.

Gardner developed the idea that there are several distinct intelligences, which include:

- Linguistic
- Logical-Mathematical
- Spatial
- Musical
- Bodily-Kinesthetic
- Interpersonal
- Intrapersonal

Gardner and other psychologists are also exploring additional intelligences. However, these seven are commonly accepted and incorporated into educational practice.

Linguistic intelligence focuses on language and words. It involves a capacity to learn languages and use words effectively. People with a well-developed linguistic intelligence are able to explain things, argue points of view, and influence or persuade others to accept their ideas. They are also adept at analyzing communications, either in written or oral form. Authors, poets, storytellers, lawyers, and teachers typically have a high linguistic intelligence.

Logical-Mathematical intelligence involves using numbers and logical thinking. It refers to a person's capacity to analyze, compute, think sequentially, recognize patterns, and solve problems. People with a high degree of logical-mathematical intelligence are typically rational, analytical, and take a methodical approach to life. Scientists, analysts, accountants, actuaries, chess players, and computer programmers typically have a high logical-mathematical intelligence.

Spatial intelligence refers to a potential for mastering concepts and ideas in space. It involves thinking and manipulating objects and pictures in multiple dimensions. People with a high degree of spatial intelligence can navigate through obstacles or wide spaces, orient themselves, design structures, visualize details, and create artistic works. Sculptors, architects, pilots, and inventors typically have a high spatial intelligence.

Musical intelligence involves the ability to recognize, appreciate, and perform rhythmic and melodical sequences. People use musical intelligence to sing, play an instrument, write songs, clap to the beat of a song, and recognize different tones and pitches. Composers, musicians, vocal artists, and anyone who performs to music typically have a high musical intelligence.

Bodily-Kinesthetic intelligence refers to a person's ability to use his or her body to achieve goals. It involves the ability to control body movements and handle objects in a skillful fashion. People with a high degree of bodily-kinesthetic intelligence can move with grace and power to achieve results and can translate vision into action. Body language in communication is also influenced by this intelligence. Athletes, performers, carpenters, and surgeons typically have a high bodily-kinesthetic intelligence.

Interpersonal intelligence refers to the ability to perceive intentions, motivations, and desires of other people. It involves understanding and working effectively with others. People with a high degree of interpersonal intelligence can develop strong relationships, act compassionately, negotiate, and see things from other peoples' perspectives. Sales people, social directors, politicians, leaders, teachers, actors, doctors, and nurses typically have a high degree of interpersonal intelligence.

Intrapersonal intelligence involves the ability to understand and recognize one's own feelings, desires, and abilities. It involves knowing yourself and using that knowledge to make choices and guide your life. People with a high degree of intrapersonal intelligence are self-confident, introspective, and motivated. They can make purposeful choices in their lives and take actions to improve or enrich themselves. People who work independently, are self-motivated, or are effective independent learners exhibit intrapersonal intelligence.

All these intelligences exist to some degree in every human being. Although most professions require higher degrees of some intelligence than others, all intelligences collectively help create a person's unique skills and abilities. It is never too late to develop a particular intelligence to enrich your career or personal life.

3.2.2 Mapping Intelligences to Business Needs

Describe how different intelligences can be beneficial to various business needs.

All intelligences are required in everyday life. Typically, people need to be able to read and understand language, calculate personal finances, travel from one location to another, recognize tones and sounds, use their body to perform daily tasks, relate to others, and make personal choices on a daily basis. The same is true for business. Each job function in an organization requires a combination of different types of intelligences, although at different levels of mastery. Success at a job function depends on a person's intelligence related to critical aspects of the job. Table 3.1 lists some common business needs and the intelligences related to them.

Business need	Related intelligences
Finance	Primary intelligences: logical-mathematical, interpersonal, intrapersonal Secondary intelligences: linguistic
People Management	Primary Intelligences: interpersonal, intrapersonal, linguistic Secondary intelligences: logical-mathematical, bodily-kinesthetic
Project Management	Primary intelligences: logical-mathematical, linguistic, interpersonal Secondary intelligences: intrapersonal
Human Resources Management	Primary intelligences: interpersonal, intrapersonal, linguistic Secondary intelligences: logical-mathematical, spatial
Marketing	Primary intelligences: linguistic, spatial, interpersonal Secondary intelligences: intrapersonal,

Business need	Related intelligences
	logical-mathematical, bodily-kinesthetic
Information Technology	Primary intelligences: logical-mathematical, linguistic, spatial, intrapersonal Secondary intelligences: interpersonal, bodily-kinesthetic
Legal and Contracts Administration	Primary intelligences: linguistic, logical-mathematical Secondary intelligences: interpersonal, intrapersonal
General Administrative Assistance	Primary intelligences: linguistic, logical-mathematical, interpersonal, intrapersonal Secondary intelligences: spatial

Table 3.1: Relationships Between Intelligences and Business Needs

The information in Table 3.1 presents only one viewpoint and analysis. You may find different requirements in your personal work experience. The table, however, serves as a guide for personal development and potential career preparation. Analyzing your intelligences can help you choose a career that is suitable to your strengths and also helps you plan personal development to enhance the different facets of your abilities.

3.2.3 Strategies and Techniques for Developing Intelligences

- Determine your strengths and weaknesses in the various intelligences through self-assessment.
- List the various strategies and techniques for developing intelligences.

Having an awareness of different intelligences is the first step in developing a personal strategy for learning. Once you are aware of different intelligences and their importance to your overall effectiveness, your next step is to assess your abilities with respect to them. The favored method for determining strengths and weaknesses in the various intelligences is through personal assessment.

There are various methods by which you can evaluate your intelligence. You can carry out either the assessments available in various books on multiple intelligences or the online interactivities on the Web sites discussing multiple intelligences. These interactive assessments help in determining intelligence, thereby assisting in determining your strengths and weaknesses.

To determine your intelligence, you can perform the assessment activities mentioned in any of the following books:

- *7 Kinds of Smart: Identifying and Developing Your Many Intelligences*, by Thomas Armstrong.
- *Developing Students' Multiple Intelligences*, by Kristen Nelson and Kristen Nicholson-Nelson.
- *The Best of Multiple Intelligences Activities*, by Teacher Created Materials, Inc.
- *So Each May Learn: Integrating Learning Styles and Multiple Intelligences*, by Harvey F. Silver, Richard W. Strong, and Matthew J. Perini.

The other way to determine your intelligence is by performing interactive activities on any of the following Web sites:

- http://www.engr.ncsu.edu/learningstyles/ilsweb.html
- http://www.rrcc-online.com/~psych/IntellAss.htm
- http://web.csuchico.edu/~ah24/intelligence.htm
- http://www.careerccc.org/products/cp_99_e/section1/quiz.cfm

Intelligences can be developed. You may not have an innate ability to excel at all things, but you can take steps to develop your capacity to learn and apply knowledge using each of the different intelligences. The key to developing intelligences is to find an activity that interests you. Table 3.2 presents some suggestions for activities to develop intelligences. These are merely suggestions, though you can use the list to identify additional activities that would be appealing to you.

Intelligence	Ways to develop
Linguistic	Play word games. Solve crossword puzzles. Learn vocabulary by selecting a "word of the day".
Logical-Mathematical	Solve logic puzzles.

	Play sequencing and pattern-recognition games.
	Learn to play chess.
Spatial	Take pictures or take a course in photography.
	Study maps and visualize locations.
	Take hikes or scenic drives.
Musical	Learn to play a musical instrument.
	Listen to music.
	Sing along with songs.
Bodily-Kinesthetic	Play a sport.
	Start an exercise program.
	Build three-dimensional models.
Interpersonal	Join a club or organization.
	Become a volunteer in your community.
	Play a team sport.
Intrapersonal	Maintain a journal.
	Read a personal-development or self-help book, or attend a seminar.
	Meditate or set aside personal time for quiet reflection.

Table 3.2: Activities to Develop Intelligences

Another way to develop intelligences is to practice learning techniques that focus on the different intelligences.

Table 3.3 suggests learning techniques that involve the different intelligences.

Intelligence	Learning techniques
Linguistic	Take notes and rewrite them. Discuss concepts with a study group. Read aloud.
Logical-Mathematical	Outline chapters. Create charts and graphs. Look for patterns or similarities. Analyze concepts with a study group.
Spatial	Close your eyes and visualize material. Draw diagrams.
Musical	Listen to music while studying Create rhythmic jingles or raps to summarize material.
Bodily-Kinesthetic	Use role plays to practice concepts. Complete lab exercises or participate in group activities.
Interpersonal	Join a study group. Tutor others.
Intrapersonal	Reflect on your learning. Set goals for your learning.

Table 3.3: Techniques for Learning Using Intelligences

Practice Questions

1. Which intelligence is primarily exhibited by people who participate in sports?
   a. Logical-Mathematical
   b. Interpersonal
   c. Intrapersonal
   d. Bodily-Kinesthetic

2. Pilots primarily exhibit strength in which intelligence?
   a. Spatial
   b. Interpersonal
   c. Bodily-Kinesthetic
   d. Linguistic

3. Playing chess can help develop which intelligence?
   a. Bodily-Kinesthetic
   b. Logical-Mathematical
   c. Intrapersonal
   d. Spatial

4. Keeping a journal can help develop which intelligence?
   a. Interpersonal
   b. Intrapersonal
   c. Musical
   d. Bodily-Kinesthetic

5. An awareness of body language in communication is primarily indicative of which intelligence?
   a. Bodily-Kinesthetic
   b. Linguistic
   c. Intrapersonal
   d. Interpersonal

3.3 Psychological Aspects of Independent Learning

An awareness of your preferred learning style as well as an understanding of your strong and weak intelligences can provide a foundation for independent learning. Armed with this knowledge about yourself, you can focus on aspects that you want to develop and how you want to learn them.

To enhance your effectiveness with independent learning, it is also helpful to understand how your personality characteristics can influence your learning outcomes. For example, understanding your internal levels of motivation and knowing how you tend to react to external factors can help you to plan for success in learning. This knowledge is particularly useful in helping you pursue a course as an independent learner.

This section describes the personal characteristics that are relevant to independent learning and also presents a brief overview of some common survey instruments that can help you determine your personality characteristics.

3.3.1 Qualities of Independent Learners

 Describe several personal qualities that influence independent learning.

Learning in any environment requires a certain amount of personal discipline. You must have a desire to learn and you should be able to follow the tasks required to learn the material. This may require attending classes, working through practice exercises, completing reading assignments, and working on projects. Independent learners face a greater challenge in learning than classroom learners, since they must independently seek out interactions with others to enhance their learning and exhibit a strong personal discipline and motivation to adhere to a learning plan. Personal qualities that influence independent learning include:

- Locus of control
- Emotional maturity
- Achievement motivation

Locus of control refers to your beliefs about how external events control outcomes in your life. If you fall on one end of this spectrum, you may feel that you can affect any outcome you desire in your life. Obstacles are not a problem. You can find a way to overcome them. Your achievements are a direct outcome of your actions.

At the other end of the spectrum, you may feel that external events have a great influence on the outcomes in your life. Despite your best efforts, outside circumstances will always govern your results. Obstacles are not something you overcome. Instead, they are the signposts for the twists and turns that your life will inevitably take.

If your beliefs fall toward the first end of the spectrum and you feel that you can affect outcomes you desire in your life, you have an *internal* locus of control. If your beliefs fall toward the second end of the spectrum, and you believe that external factors influence outcomes in your life, you exhibit an *external* locus of control. Figure 3.2 illustrates the spectrum of locus of control.

Internal locus of control   **External locus of control**

You control outcomes in your life   *Outside factors control outcomes in your life*

Figure 3.2: Spectrum of Locus of Control

As depicted in Figure 3.3, recognizing your personal locus of control can help you plan for success in independent learning.

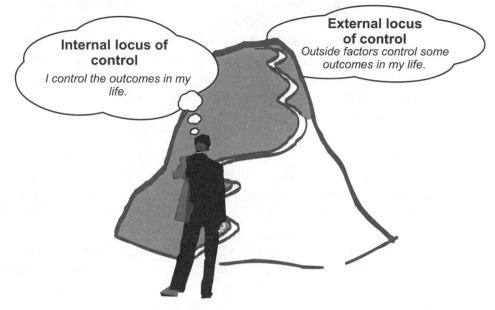

Figure 3.3: Locus of Control

If you have an internal locus of control, you will find it easier to keep to a schedule and to plan for your own learning. You take control of your outcomes and do not necessarily rely on others to tell you what steps to take. You are not likely to make excuses for not meeting expectations. If you tend toward an external locus of control, you might have to make a determined effort to stick with your learning plan. You might become easily sidetracked or might have trouble taking responsibility for your learning. To increase your success in independent learning, you should consider working with a mentor or counselor to help you recognize and overcome obstacles to your learning goals.

In an online learning environment, regularly interacting with your peers over e-mail and online discussions will prevent you from getting sidetracked. You can communicate regularly with your instructor and ask for help or tips to keep yourself focused on successfully completing the course online.

Emotional maturity refers to how you view situations and react to them. It is defined by your ability to take action, control your responses to situations, and maintain a broad perspective in terms of ideas and timeframes. Individuals with a higher degree of emotional maturity are not afraid to take action and might be inclined to take greater calculated risks than people with a lower degree of emotional maturity. Individuals with a higher degree of emotional maturity also display a more even temperament and see the big picture more often. Maturity constantly evolves. Gaining an understanding of your level of emotional maturity can help you enhance your personal effectiveness, while improving your emotional maturity can help you develop plans and overcome negative results in independent learning. A higher degree of emotional maturity enables you to become a more effective independent learner.

Achievement motivation refers to a person's internal desire to achieve results. Individuals with a higher degree of achievement motivation seek out challenging opportunities and focus on achieving results. Individuals with a lower degree of achievement motivation tend to focus more on maintaining relationships and seeking feedback than on achieving results. Successful independent learners have a higher degree of achievement motivation. They are inherently motivated by their results and can create plans and follow them with little outside guidance. Individuals with a lower degree of achievement motivation might need to develop relationships with a mentor or study group to derive the motivation required to complete the learning process.

3.3.2 Assessing Your Personality Traits

 Describe a method for assessing personality characteristics.

In addition to the qualities of independent learners, there are other personality characteristics or traits that influence an individual's effectiveness in independent or group activities. There are many viewpoints and survey instruments that describe personality characteristics.

This section describes the popular instrument, the Myers-Briggs Type Indicator. The Myers-Briggs Type Indicator is based on the work of the Swiss psychiatrist, Carl Jung. It was developed by Katherine Briggs and her daughter, Isabel Briggs Myers. Briggs and Myers built upon the work of Jung and developed the theory that there are four dimensions of personality that combine to create sixteen distinct personality types.

Figure 3.4 gives an overview of the personality dimensions and types identified by Myers and Briggs.

Myers-Briggs Personality Dimensions

Extraversion (E)—Introversion (I)

Sensing (S)—Intuitive (N)

Thinking (T)—Feeling (F)

Judging (J)—Perceiving (P)

Myers-Briggs Personality Types

ESTJ	ENTJ
ESTP	ENTP
ESFJ	ENFJ
ESFP	ENFP
ISTJ	INTJ
ISTP	INTP
ISFJ	INFJ
ISFP	INFP

Figure 3.4: Myers-Briggs Personality Dimensions and Types

The *Extraversion-Introversion* dimension of the Myers-Briggs Type Indicator refers to how a person derives energy. Extroverts (E) get their energy from being with other people or draw it from the world around them. Introverts (I) derive their energy from within themselves. Extroverts tend to seek the company of others and experience the world around them, while Introverts tend to reflect upon their own ideas.

The *Sensing-Intuition* dimension refers to what a person notices or pays attention to. Sensing (S) individuals have a preference for concrete facts and take in information through their five basic senses. Intuitive (N) individuals concentrate less on concrete facts and pay more attention to the possibilities or opportunities in a situation.

The *Thinking-Feeling* dimension describes how a person makes decisions. Thinking (T) individuals tend to make decisions based on logic and objective facts. Feeling (F) individuals tend to consider personal values in their decisions.

The *Judging-Perceiving* dimension refers to a person's preferences in lifestyle. Judging (J) individuals prefer a well-planned and organized structure, while Perceiving (P) individuals tend to be spontaneous, flexible, and carefree.

In the Myers-Briggs model, each dimension provides one preference for an individual's overall personality type. A person is:

- Either an Extrovert or Introvert
- Either Sensing or Intuitive
- Either Thinking or Feeling
- Either Judging or Perceiving

The four preferences combine to form a person's personality type. The Myers-Briggs Type Indicator consists of many questions that determine a person's personality preferences and overall personality type. Extensive information exists on the interpretation and implications for each personality type. The Myers-Briggs personality types are widely used and you can find several books or Internet resources devoted to this subject.

For more information on the Myers-Briggs Type Indicator, search the Internet.

An awareness of your personality characteristics can help you in several ways. Knowing your personality traits and tendencies can help you develop your intrapersonal and interpersonal intelligences by raising your awareness of how you tend to react in certain situations. You can make a conscious effort to improve your actions to enhance your overall effectiveness. You can also use the knowledge about your personality traits to supplement your awareness of your intelligences and preferred learning style in creating an effective personal learning plan. This is especially relevant when you pursue an online course as an independent learner.

1. The belief that you can control outcomes in your life is indicative of
    _____ .
    a. emotional maturity
    b. an external locus of control
    c. an internal locus of control
    d. achievement motivation

2. ____ is a desire to achieve results.
    a. Emotional maturity
    b. External locus of control
    c. Internal locus of control
    d. Achievement motivation

3. _____ refers to how you view situations and react to them.
    a. Emotional maturity
    b. External locus of control
    c. Internal locus of control
    d. Achievement motivation

4. The Myers-Briggs Type Indicator determines _____ .
    a. emotional maturity
    b. intelligences
    c. personality types
    d. learning styles

5. The _____ Myers-Briggs personality spectrum describes how a person derives energy.

    a. Extraversion—Introversion

    b. Sensing—Intuition

    c. Thinking—Feeling

    d. Judging—Perceiving

3.4 Maximizing Your Learning

Understanding the dimensions and characteristics of your personality, assessing your strong and weak intelligences, and gaining an awareness of your preferred learning style creates a foundation on which you can approach your learning. The final key to success in learning is to develop personal strategies for seeking and following opportunities to learn. Creating a learning plan is a critical factor to your success in lifelong independent learning. Establishing good learning habits and seeking feedback arc also important. This section presents the techniques and strategies that you can use to maximize your learning throughout your lifetime.

3.4.1 Strategies for Learning

 Describe strategies that can help you to become a successful lifelong independent learner.

When thinking about learning, most people consider attending a course offered by a school, university, or professional training organization. Their focus on learning is typically limited to time spent in formal courses or educational programs. However, becoming a successful lifelong independent learner requires thinking beyond these norms. Lifelong learners continuously maintain their learning and seek out various learning opportunities. Their learning moves outside the classroom and many different situations become learning opportunities.

Becoming a successful lifelong independent learner requires you to develop varied strategies for learning. The following list provides suggestions for strategies and activities that can help you to learn and maintain new skills and knowledge outside of a traditional classroom setting.

- Read newspapers and trade journals—In addition to news on current events, many newspapers contain information on businesses, technology, and learning opportunities. Trade journals also provide a valuable resource to keep your knowledge in specialized fields up-to-date.

- Build and maintain a professional and personal network of friends and business associates—A network is one of the most important tools for any professional.

Relationships within your network can help you broaden your knowledge and open new career opportunities.

- Join a professional organization—Professional organizations can provide you an opportunity to broaden your professional network, learn about the latest developments in your field, and hear different perspectives on popular topics.

- Seek a mentor—Working with a mentor can be a rewarding experience. Mentors can help you develop plans and strategies, provide feedback, and give you valuable career guidance.

- Make a personal commitment to developing yourself—Create personal learning plans or establish a contract with yourself to focus on personal development. You are in control of your own destiny with respect to lifelong independent learning.

3.4.2 Good Habits for Learning

 List several habits that contribute to positive results in learning.

Throughout your schooling, you have probably adopted study habits that help you succeed in learning. These habits include procedures for effective note taking, study processes, and planning and time management skills. There are several other habits that can contribute to positive results in independent learning. These include:

- Proactively seeking opportunities for learning—Once you leave formal schooling and begin your career, you will need to seek out opportunities for learning. Taking proactive steps toward learning helps you keep your skills up-to-date and develop new skills in a timely manner.

- Organizing your learning—Create plans and carefully consider opportunities for development. Know the purpose for each development opportunity you undertake so that you can evaluate its effectiveness and make appropriate plans for further development.

- Reflecting on your learning—Take time to think about the skills and knowledge you gain and your intent for learning. Reflecting on what you learned, how you learned it, and how much you enjoyed the learning experience will help you choose appropriate future learning opportunities and enhance your overall personal development.

■ Continuously assessing your skills and knowledge—Lifelong learning never stops. Assessing your skills and knowledge continuously will enhance your ongoing learning results.

3.4.3 Creating a Learning Plan

 Create a learning plan for successful learning that is appropriate for your learning style.

A learning plan is essential to an organized approach toward lifelong learning. The plan provides a structure for you to follow in assessing your skills, determining which areas you want to focus on for development, creating a plan of action, and evaluating the results of your learning. Figure 3.5 shows a process for creating a learning plan.

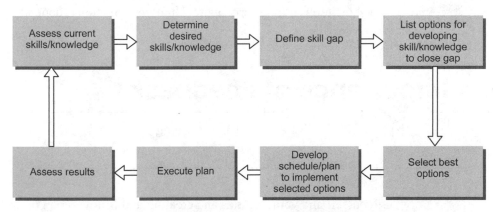

Figure 3.5: Process of Creating a Learning Plan

A typical learning process would include:

1. Assessing your current skills and knowledge: Knowing your current capabilities is critical to developing a plan for improvement.

2. Determining your desired skills and knowledge areas: You need to set a target for your development.

3. Determining the gap that exists between your current level of proficiency and your desired level of proficiency: This gap defines what you need to learn, or the skills you need to develop.

4. Generating a list of options for developing the required skills and knowledge: Look beyond traditional classroom learning in developing your possible options.

5. From the list of possible options, selecting the best development activities: Generate a list of criteria to use in evaluating the options. Be sure to consider your personal learning style preferences as part of the evaluation criteria.

6. Developing a detailed plan and schedule for implementing your chosen learning activities: This is your action plan.

7. Executing the plan and completing your learning activities.

8. Assessing your results: Measure your skill and knowledge levels and compare it to your target. Reflect on how you enjoyed your learning activities. Re-evaluate your assumptions about your learning style and make any necessary adjustments.

9. Preparing to begin the process again: Lifelong learning is a continuous process.

To maximize your learning, you should perform this process on a periodic basis. You may take a short-term or long-term approach to your planning, depending on your objectives for learning.

3.4.4 Importance of Feedback

 Explain why feedback is critical to learning.

Knowing yourself and your abilities and creating and following an organized plan for personal development will position you well for success in lifelong learning. However, these elements alone will not ensure your success as a learner. Feedback is an essential element of learning. Feedback helps you:

■ Clarify and confirm your understanding of material.

■ Obtain input on your strengths and weaknesses.

■ Gain insight on different perspectives and points of view.

Feedback can come in several forms.

Table 3.4 outlines some feedback mechanisms that can help you enhance your learning.

Feedback Method	Description
Ask questions	Asking questions helps you clarify your understanding of topics.
Seek advice	Seeking advice from your instructor, a mentor, or peers provides you different perspectives or points of view.
Take tests/quizzes; Answer practice questions	Your results provide you immediate feedback on the effectiveness of your learning.

Table 3.4: Feedback Mechanisms for Learning

Practice Questions

1. Which of the following is true?

   Statement A: Strategies for successful learning include reading newspapers and trade journals, seeking a mentor, and maintaining a professional network.

   Statement B: Lifelong learners typically focus on earning degrees through formal programs.

   a. Statement A is true but Statement B is false.

   b. Statement A is false but Statement B is true.

   c. Both statements are true.

   d. Both statements are false.

2. Which of the following are considered good habits for learning?

   I. Effective note-taking

   II. Proactively seeking opportunities for learning

   III. Continuously assessing skills and knowledge

   a. I and II

   b. I and III

   c. II and III

   d. I, II, and III

3. The difference between your desired level of proficiency and your current level of proficiency is called _____.

   a. a skill gap

   b. a target level of proficiency

   c. feedback

   d. continuous assessment

4. Taking a test is a form of _____.

   a. lifelong learning

   b. feedback

   c. planning

   d. mentoring

Summary

In this chapter, you learned:

- A learning style describes how you prefer to learn. There are three prevalent learning styles: visual, auditory, and kinesthetic.

- Intelligence is the capacity to learn and apply skills or knowledge.

- The intelligences include linguistic, logical-mathematical, spatial, musical, bodily-kinesthetic, interpersonal, and intrapersonal. Gardner and other psychologists are exploring additional intelligences as well.

- Different career tracks or business needs require strengths in different intelligences.

- Mapping career fields or business needs by required intelligences can help you select an appropriate career and aid you in creating a personal development plan to achieve your career goals.

- A plan for developing intelligences includes a self-assessment on strengths and weaknesses and identifying development activities that are appealing to you.

- You can also develop intelligences by practicing learning techniques that involve the different intelligences.

- Personal qualities that influence independent learning include locus of control, emotional maturity, and achievement motivation.

- The Myers-Briggs model determines personality based on four dimensions: Extraversion–Introversion (E-I), Sensing–Intuitive (S-N), Thinking–Feeling (T-F), and Judging–Perceiving (J-P). These dimension characteristics combine to form sixteen different personality types.

- Maximizing your learning involves developing strategies for learning, establishing good habits for learning, creating a learning plan, and seeking feedback.

References

- Armstrong, Thomas. *7 Kinds of Smart: Identifying and Developing Your Many Intelligences*. New York, NY: Penguin Group, 1993.

- Gardner, Howard. *Intelligence Reframed: Multiple Intelligences for the 21st Century*. New York, NY: Basic Books, 1999.

- Davis, James R. and Adelaide B. Davis. *Managing Your Own Learning*. San Francisco, CA: Berrett-Koehler Publishers, Inc. 2000.

- Hirsh, Sandra Krebs and Jean M. Kummerow. *Introduction to Type in Organizations: Individual Interpretive Guide*, Second Edition. Palo Alto, CA: Consulting Psychologists Press, Inc. 1990.

- Nelson, Kristen, and Kristen Nicholson-Nelson. *Developing Students' Multiple Intelligences*.

- *The Best of Multiple Intelligences Activities*, by Teacher Created Materials Inc.

- Silver Harvey F., Richard W. Strong and Matthew J. Perini. *So Each May Learn: Integrating Learning Styles and Multiple Intelligences*.

Information from Electronic Sources

4

The Internet provides a vast array of information for personal, educational, and business use. Locating and validating relevant information on the Internet is important to succeed both personally and professionally. In addition, proper use and citing of the information is essential. This chapter presents techniques and guidelines to locate information on the Internet effectively and to use it properly.

This chapter prepares you to:

- Identify types of resources found on the Internet.
- Locate information on the Internet.
- Use techniques to refine Internet searches.
- Validate and evaluate information found on the Internet.
- Download information from the Internet.
- Avoid plagiarism and libel when using electronic sources.
- Cite electronic references.

4.1 Types of Resources

The Internet has many different components for information and communication. To effectively use this information and capability, you first need to understand the types of resources that are available. The common Internet resources are online references, online databases, newsgroups and listservs, commercial sites, and educational sites. This chapter provides information about how to use common Internet resources for your research effectively.

4.1.1 Online References

Describe the nature of reference resources on the Internet.

Online references is a general category that encompasses traditional print-based reference material found on the Internet in electronic format. Encyclopedias, dictionaries, journals, and newspapers are among the references that can be found online. Research can be made much easier by using online reference material.

Online reference material may either be available for free or there may be a nominal charge to access the material. Online references are available on "pay-per-use" basis. The text of the same resources is also available on electronic media (CD-ROMS). When searching for information in online reference material, remember the following:

- Some online reference material that is available for free may not be the latest version available or may not contain sufficient information. You will have to judge whether the information is sufficient for your needs.

- Online reference material, whether free or associated with a charge, is protected by copyright. Although you may have paid a fee to access the material, you are still obliged to cite it appropriately in your work. Section 4.7 presents information on citing resources.

- The information found in online reference material is verified for accuracy most of the time.

The ITT Tech Virtual Library contains links to online references in the **Periodicals** and **Reference Resources** links on the Main Menu.

4.1.2 Online Databases

 Explain the value of using an online database to research a topic.

Online databases are public databases that can be accessed on the Web. Online databases provide you access to a great depth of related information on topics, such as law, businesses, regulatory matters, various fields of research, news, and so on. Similar to other online reference resources, the information may or may not be available for free. You may need to register and obtain a member account to access a database. Figure 4.1 shows an online database http://www.amazon.com/.

Figure 4.1: An Online Database

Remember the following about online database resources:

- Specific topics in the database are not accessible through standard searches. You may need to subscribe to the database to search its contents.

- Information in the databases is usually specialized and unique. Databases can be a rich source of information.

- Although there may be a charge associated with accessing a database, it is not necessarily a guarantee that the information is absolutely current. You may find that some inherently dynamic information does not reflect current updates. For instance, data regarding a company's management team may change, but that change may not be immediately updated in the site database. However, information from an online database is generally more reliable than information found in other public domains. Remember to look out for tags with time-stamps stating information updated on dd/mm/yy.

The ITT Tech Virtual Library has links to online research databases in the **Periodicals** link of the Main Menu.

4.1.3 Newsgroups and Listservs

Explain the uses of Internet Newsgroups and Listservs.

Newsgroups and listservs can be described as online discussion boards. They are a means for people to post their opinions or information on any topic and also for people to find opinions or information on any topic. These are truly open forums for communication once you have subscribed to the service.

Newsgroups are similar to online bulletin boards. They contain postings and responses on many different topics. You can use a newsgroup to find information on a topic or to ask for information. Noted experts on a topic may participate in a newsgroup. Alternatively, a participant in the newsgroup may be able to point you to an expert or help you to locate valuable information.

Listservs are e-mail messages that are sent to subscribers of a list. They are similar in content to newsgroups, but the medium for accessing them is through e-mail instead of a browser. Listservs have the advantage that they are sent to subscribers. Therefore, subscribers are regularly reminded to view the information. However, there is still no guarantec that subscribers will pay attention to the e-mail or participate.

Figure 4.2 shows a discussion board site:
http://chat.gradschoolfairs.com/webx?14@@.ee73db9.

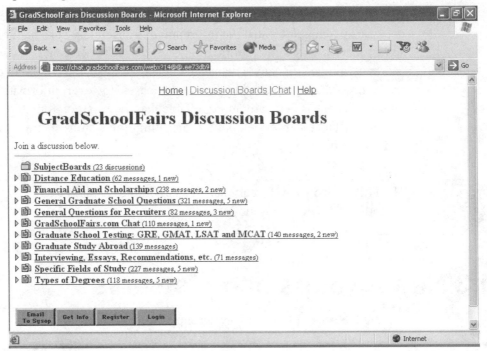

Figure 4.2: Discussion Board Site

Remember the following when using information from a discussion board, newsgroup, or listserv:

▪ Always be careful to verify the accuracy of the information.

▪ It may be difficult to determine the identity of a respondent by the e-mail address. Be cautious about the information. If you are looking for experts, verify their identity and credentials.

▪ Information you gather may not be original. Try to determine the origin of information you find on discussion boards.

Information from these discussion boards can provide a quick overview of the scope of a topic or lead you to valuable sources of information. This is networking in action in both the technological and behavioral arenas.

4.1.4 Commercial Sites

Describe the uses, benefits, and precautions to be kept in mind while using commercial sites as sources of information.

Researching various applications, vendors, and companies is vastly simplified using the Internet. Commercial sites, identified by .com in their Web address, contain a wide range of information. Some of this information may be suitable for research; however, you may find that much of the information is aimed at marketing and advertising. It is worth exploring these sites, partially because they may contain valuable information or links, but mostly because they are so prevalent that you will not be able to avoid them.

A Web site of a company promoting its products and services is very useful to professionals in making business decisions. These serve different purposes for different people, which are:

- Information for information seekers
- A tool for the marketing department of the organization
- An image-making tool for the public relations department of the organization

Today, a company without a Web site is considered to have diminished credibility in the marketplace. Using a company's Web site, you can quickly learn all about the organization's products and services, the locations of company offices, the senior management of the company, and sometimes lists of its other companies or customers. At times, you can find valuable articles that address research or trends associated with company products or services. However, remember that the information provided on these sites is aimed at encouraging people to purchase products and services from the company. Some objective information may be provided, but generally you may find that most information on the site is biased toward promoting the company's products.

Sites that sell books, such as www.amazon.com, can be useful in researching books on particular topics. You can view descriptions of the book to get an idea of the general content and how particular topics are covered. You may also be able to view parts of the book, such as the preface, table of contents, and chapter excerpts. In many cases, people who have read the book post their opinions on it, which you may find useful in deciding whether to purchase the book. Do not hesitate to explore books offered for sale on commercial sites. You can gain valuable information on contents and perhaps even decide to order a book online that provides exactly what you need.

Figure 4.3 shows a commercial site http://www.ebay.com/.

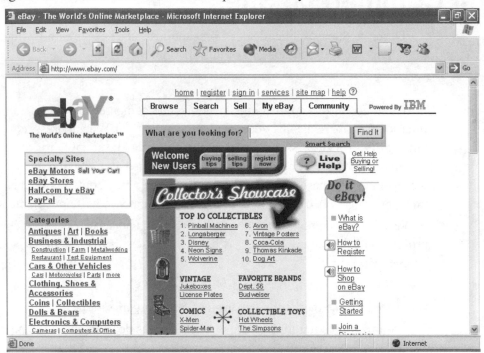

Figure 4.3: Ebay's Commercial Site

When reviewing information from a commercial site, consider the following:

- While many of these sites may contain useful information, they may also be biased toward one particular product or philosophy.

- These sites can be extremely valuable in researching potential vendors or software applications. Professionals may want to do business only with a company that has a company Web site.

- Almost anyone can create a .com site. Therefore, verify the information provided before you use it.

The ITT Tech Virtual Library contains links to some commercial sites in the **Reference Resources** link on the Main Menu.

4.1.5 Educational Sites

Describe the uses, benefits, and cautions of using educational sites as sources of information.

Sites related to educational institutions can provide a wealth of useful information. After all, the institutions are dedicated to research and learning. Therefore, it is logical that their Web sites would provide plentiful tips, tools, and information suitable for research.

Educational institution sites are generally recognized by .edu in the Web address portion of the URL. For example www.itt-tech.edu is the site of the ITT Technical Institute. The home pages of these sites generally provide pointers to a vast array of information about the institution. Much of this information is aimed at enticing students and other interested parties to explore the benefits of attending the college or university. While browsing the site for information, you can use the site map or index to quickly identify areas of information. Some sites also include a search feature that will help you locate the required information.

Figure 4.4 shows the educational site http://www.itt-tech.edu/.

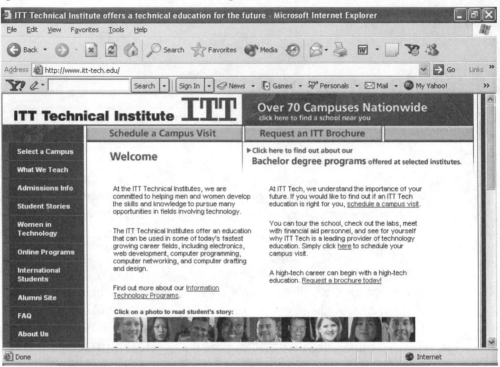

Figure 4.4: ITT's Educational Site

When using information from educational institution sites, remember the following:

- The information that is provided is most often targeted at prospective students. It may or may not be applicable to your specific requirement.

- If you are a student at the educational institution or are looking for information on universities/schools/colleges, the site may be the first place for you to look for information. The site may provide information and links that will be useful for your specific assignments or program requirements.

There are many educational sites referenced in the ITT Tech Virtual Library. Some tutorials and reference links point to other educational sites.

4.1.6 Government Sites

Describe the uses, benefits, and cautions in using government sites as sources of information.

Government sites, usually identified by .gov in their Web address, are sponsored by government agencies. These can be related to federal, state, or local departments of government or specific government services. You can find interesting facts and valuable information on government sites.

There is a wide variety of government sites. Many sites provide necessary forms and instructions, such as tax forms, and provide access to common services, such as renewing a driver's license. Other sites provide access to archives and general laws.

Figure 4.5 shows a government site http://www.senate.gov.

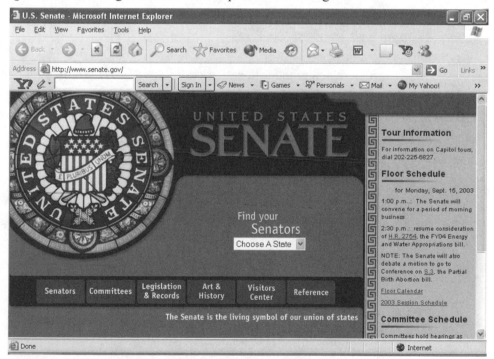

Figure 4.5: The United States' Senate Government Site

When using government sites, it is helpful to keep in mind that:

- Many governmental agencies are still working toward making all appropriate information available to the public on the Internet, but there is still a long way to go. You may not find all public information on a government site.

- Because of the vast amount of information on government Web sites, you may find it useful to spend some time familiarizing yourself with a particular site before beginning your research.

- Government sites can be a great resource for you to learn more about issues at all governmental levels, which will help you to become a more involved citizen.

 The ITT Tech Virtual Library contains links to government sites in the **Reference Resources** section.

Practice Questions

1. Which of the following options is FALSE for online reference material?

    Online reference material _____.

    a. can be used extensively if you have paid for it.

    b. has probably been verified for accuracy.

    c. may not be current.

    d. is sometimes also available on a CD, which can be ordered from the site providing the same reference material.

2. How would you normally find out which topics are available in an online database?

    a. Through a standard Internet search

    b. From a listing on an educational site

    c. Using a search linked to the database

    d. By word-of-mouth

3. _____ are e-mail messages that are sent to subscribers.
   a. Newsgroups
   b. Spam
   c. Listservs
   d. Online references

4. Which of the following statements is TRUE about commercial sites?
   a. There is no need to verify information from a .com site since it is sponsored by a company.
   b. Commercial sites can be valuable sources of research information.
   c. Commercial sites are used only for commercial transactions.
   d. Commercial sites must be sponsored by commercial entities.

5. Which of the following statements is FALSE?
   a. Education sites are accessible only to students attending the institution.
   b. Educational sites usually provide information for students as well as people interested in finding out more about the institution.
   c. Educational institution sites contain .edu as part of their Web address.
   d. An educational institution site may have a search engine that searches for specific information on the site.

6. What type of Internet site may provide tax forms and instructions?
   a. Online database
   b. reference
   c. Government
   d. Commercial

4.2 Locating Information

After learning about the types of resources available to you on the Internet, you can focus on finding what you need. With the vast amount of information available, there are also a number of different ways to locate the relevant information. This section provides an overview of how to locate information quickly.

4.2.1 Quick Searching

Search for a topic on the Internet by typing keywords in the **Address** field.

Your Internet experience may have been limited to simply accessing sites through URLs and clicking links from there. Alternatively, you may have tried searching but had little success in finding what you need. This section presents some techniques you can use to find information quickly. Searching the Internet is an iterative process. You might need to try several different methods and iterations to find what you need.

The simplest and sometimes the most direct way to find a topic on the Internet is to try typing a word or phrase directly in the address field of your browser. This usually launches a basic keyword search and in an instant you will probably see search results displayed in your browser window. This is accomplished by a search engine. A search engine is a software program that searches resources on the Internet and then gathers and reports information that is related to the specified keyword. The most relevant hits are usually displayed at the top of the list (depending on what relevant means to the search engine and not necessarily to you). This method of searching can usually get you started and can also provide you to clues toward refining your search.

4.2.2 Common Search Engines

Describe some common search engines on the Internet.

There are a few general types of search engines on the Internet.

■ Some search engines use a variety of methods to search the vast span of the Web site-by-site. These engines rely on specialized methods for crawling to different sites and cataloging what they consider to be relevant information. Figure 4.6 shows the first page of a search engine http://www.google.com/.

Figure 4.6: First Page of the Google Search Engine

■ Other search engines are known as Meta search engines. Meta search engines do not search the Web directly; rather, they employ other search engines to do the searching and then organize and present the results to you. These engines can give you greater coverage in your search. Figure 4.7 shows a Meta search engine http://www.metagopher.com/ that employs other search engines to present results.

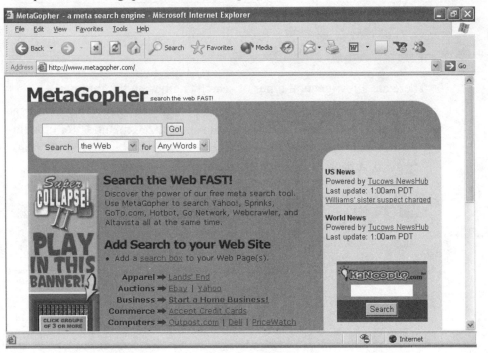

Figure 4.7: First Page of the MetaGopher Search Engine

■ There are also search engines that are specific to certain Web sites. These engines are tuned to find information specifically within the site to which they are dedicated. They can help you to quickly narrow down to specific information on a site once you locate a site that seems to have what you need.

Conducting searches and selecting a preferred search engine from the wide array available is a matter of personal preference. The following list provides some criteria to consider while selecting a search engine that you intend to use often:

■ Quality of results: Do your queries generally return useful results? Do you get links to the types of information you are looking for?

■ Ease of use: Is the syntax for specifying search strings intuitive? Is the online help complete, accurate, and helpful?

■ Ease in refining results: Does the search engine make it easy for you to narrow down and search for results that are similar to a given result?

Try different search engines several times before selecting your favorites. Remember it often takes several attempts and perhaps several different search engines to find what you need.

4.2.3 Simple Searches

Search for a topic on the Internet using a basic search.

After you select a search engine, there are several techniques you can use to improve your efficiency and effectiveness in searching. The following list provides some tips for conducting effective searches:

■ Start simple. Use one or two keywords and see what results you get. Starting off with a long list of keywords or a complicated search string may be unproductive.

■ If your results are completely unexpected, check your spelling. You may have inadvertently typed something incorrectly.

■ Think carefully about the type of information you need and select keywords strategically. Use words that most closely and uniquely describe the information you are looking for.

■ Review the Help associated with the search engine to ensure that you are specifying words and phrases in the most effective manner.

Usually, a few iterations of a basic search are required to produce a short list of relevant sources for your information.

Practice Questions

1. Which of the following statements is FALSE for search engines?
   a. Some search engines use several different search engines to perform a search, then organize and present the results to you.
   b. Some search engines are specific to certain Web sites.
   c. Most search engines will give you the same results.
   d. Search engines make determinations about how relevant results are to your request.

2. Which of the following statements is TRUE about online search techniques?
   a. Search engines use a built-in spell checker to correct wrong spellings in keywords.
   b. Typing keywords in the Address field of your browser can be an easy way to search the Internet.
   c. Search engines are very good at simple searches, but make it difficult to drill down and search for specific information.
   d. General search engines will search the entire Internet for information.

4.3 Refining Your Search Results

In your search for information, you may have encountered some common outcomes. You received too much information or not the right information. How can you narrow or broaden your search effectively to find the information that you seek? This section describes how to use Boolean operators and wild cards to provide more detail in your searches. The section also explains how to use common advanced search features and techniques to refine your results further.

4.3.1 Boolean Operators

 Use Boolean operators to refine search results.

Before launching into detail about using Boolean operators, you may be wondering where the term "Boolean" comes from. The term is named after George Boole (1815-1864), an English mathematician who is well known for his work in logic and algebra. Boolean operators, the most common of which are AND, OR, and NOT, help you refine your searches by looking for specific combinations or exclusions of words. Many search engines provide support for using these operators to further define search strings.

Check the Help text provided with a search engine to determine which Boolean operators are supported and to determine the correct syntax for using them.

Table 4.1 lists the Boolean operators and suggestions for using them.

Boolean operator	Suggested uses
AND	Used to narrow your search. Only instances containing both terms are returned.
OR	Used to broaden your search to include different terms. Instances containing one or the other or both terms are returned.

Boolean operator	Suggested uses
NOT	Used to narrow your search to exclude certain terms.

Table 4.1: Boolean Operators

The syntax for the Boolean operators differs among search engines. For example, some search engines use a minus sign (-) for NOT and a plus sign (+) for AND. In addition, some search engines might use the AND operator by default, so it is not necessary to specify it. Finally, some search engines may only allow Boolean operators in advanced searches. It is a good practice to decide on a few favorite search engines that you are likely to use most often and become familiar with their features and syntax. This will make your searching more effective.

Some search engines provide additional support for combining operators using parentheses. This can provide you the benefit of additional precision in your search, but it also adds to the complexity of the search string. If this feature is available, make sure you understand what you are seeking.

4.3.2 Wild Cards

Use wild cards to expand search results.

As the term implies, wild cards are used to represent any character or word. You may use a wild card in some situations. These include instances when you:

- Are not sure of the exact spelling of a word
- Want to save keystrokes
- Know only a few words of a title
- Want to find all variations of a word

The asterisk (*) is the most common wild card and it represents any series of characters. This wild card can be a valuable tool when you are not sure of the exact spelling or phrase you are searching for. This powerful wild card can also return many more results than you were expecting.

While the asterisk is a common wild card, different search engines support different wild cards. Always check the Help provided with your search engine to see which wild cards are supported and how they are interpreted.

You should be aware that some search engines do not require the explicit use of a wild card. These search engines automatically assume wild cards and search for partial strings. Other search engines search only for the exact string specified. First, try your search without a wild card. If you do not get results, try using a wild card. Remember, searching is a complex process. You may not find what you want on the first try.

4.3.3 Advanced Search and Other Helpful Techniques

Use an advanced search feature to refine search results.

Many search engines provide an advanced search feature to help you refine your searches. Typically, advanced features allow you to search on particular criteria, giving you an opportunity to search for specific characteristics of data. Searching within a specified timeframe is one common search criteria that may appear in an advanced search. Some other advanced search features may also allow you to restrict your search to certain file types or to certain languages.

Figure 4.8 shows a screen shot of an advanced search page http://altavista.com/web/adv.

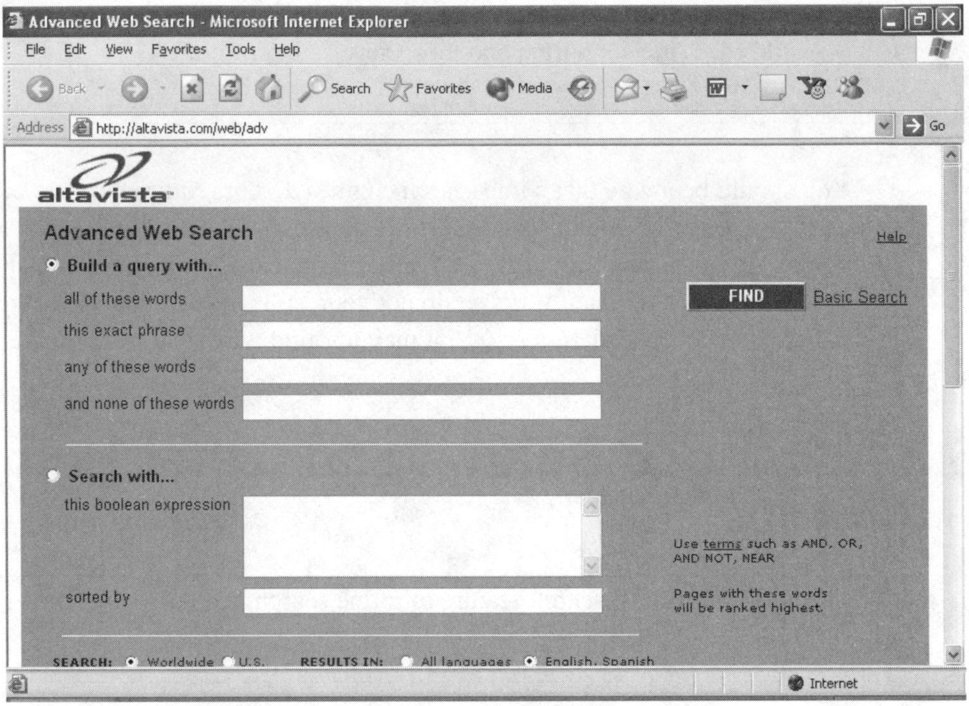

Figure 4.8: Advanced Altavista Search Screen

In addition to using advanced search features that may be available, there are a few techniques that you can use to refine your searches:

- Try to think of synonyms of the keywords you are using in your search to increase your chances of finding the best information.
- Look for additional keywords on pages of information that are close to your target. Use those keywords and any synonyms to refine your search.
- Try using quotation marks around a key phrase related to the information you are seeking. Generally, search engines look for the specific phrase contained within quotation marks. This helps you narrow in on important words and phrases.
- Try your search on a few different search engines. Each engine works a little differently and returns different results.

Searching the Internet is more a skill than an art. Think of the information you are searching for as the center of a target. Approach it from several different angles and you will be more likely to encircle it completely and find a wealth of information that suits your needs.

1. Which of the following is NOT a Boolean operator?
    a. AND
    b. NOT
    c. OR
    d. NEITHER

2. Which of the following characters is the most common wild card?
    a. *
    b. ^
    c. ?
    d. &

3. Which of the following statements is TRUE about advanced search features?
    a. All advanced search features require you to use quotation marks around keyword phrases.
    b. Some advanced search features allow you to search for results in a particular language.
    c. All advanced search features accept standard syntax for Boolean operators.
    d. Most search engines share the same engine for advanced searches.

4.4 Validating and Evaluating Information

Now that you have found the information you were searching for, how do you know if the retrieved information is accurate or trustworthy? How do you know if it is really what you need? It is important to validate the information, you gather over the Internet, as depicted in Figure 4.9.

Figure 4.9: Validate Any Information Gathered over the Internet

This section provides some criteria and guidelines you can use to assess whether the information you have found is credible and usable.

4.4.1 Criteria for Evaluation

List criteria that can be used to evaluate information.

Deciding to use data found on the Internet is essentially no different than making a major purchasing decision. You need to determine the qualities and characteristics of the data that are important to your needs and then assess the data against those criteria to determine if the data is right for you. Before beginning to create a list of criteria for evaluating data, it is useful to consider some of the problems that may occur with data on the Internet. An awareness of these problems will help you determine the criteria you want to focus on during your evaluation.

Table 4.2 outlines some common potential problems with data on the Internet.

Problem	Description
Outdated information	Data on the Internet is not always maintained or updated. Just because you do not find current information on a Web site does not mean that updated information does not exist.
Inaccurate or invalid information	Some information may be incorrect. Be careful of this on discussion boards, in e-mail messages, and on personal Web sites.
Ambiguity	You may find data or conclusions on the Web that are not backed up with original source information, which makes it difficult to interpret the information accurately.
Bias	Some information may be biased toward promoting a particular product or point of view.
Indirect reference	Some information you find may not be direct from the source. You may be reading a second-hand or third-hand interpretation of a fact or concept, which may make it difficult to track the veracity of the information.

Table 4.2: Common Problems with Electronic Data

Remember that the Internet is an open forum. It is easy to publish information and controls are not always in place to verify the accuracy of information. It is up to you to take precautions to verify your data.

With potential problem areas in mind, you can begin to create a list of criteria to use in evaluating information. Suggested areas to consider include:

- Credentials of the author: Is the author a recognized expert in the field, a student studying the field, a professional with experience in the field, or a rank amateur? Do not automatically disqualify information from rank amateurs, but do verify it.

- Objectivity: Assess the source of the information to determine whether any type of bias exists. Is the information from a commercial Web site that is trying to persuade people to purchase a particular product or service? Bias should not necessarily disqualify the information, however, you should be diligent in searching differing viewpoints on information that could be potentially biased.

- Date: Look at the publication date or the date the Web site was last modified to determine the age of the information.

- Source: Factor the likelihood that information from the Web site has not been verified or reviewed before publishing. For example, you can have more confidence in information from an online journal than information from a discussion board. While both sources may be accurate, information from the discussion board should probably undergo more scrutiny before you make a decision to use it. This is because it may not have been thoroughly verified prior to posting.

- Concurrency with other sources: Are the facts similar to other facts on the topic? If you see any data that seems out of the ordinary, you should scrutinize it further before using it.

Always consider the criteria that you will use to evaluate information. It will help you to be more efficient in gathering quality information and give you more confidence in your research.

4.4.2 Validation Strategies

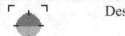 Describe several steps you can take to validate information and data.

Once you have determined the criteria you will use to validate your data, there are several strategies you can use to gather the information you need for validation. These strategies are:

- Create a checklist: Decide the criteria on which you want to validate the data and create a checklist. You can determine which criteria to weigh more heavily than others and then use the checklist to evaluate your sources of information.

- Ask for validation: If you are not sure how to interpret data or you want to be sure that your interpretation is correct, send an e-mail message to the author or sponsor of the Web site. Alternatively, you could also ask for validation on a discussion board or send an e-mail message to a known expert in the field.
- Look for information in several sources: Validate the concurrency of the information by checking several related sources for similar information.
- Research the author's credentials: Try to determine if the author is an expert in the field. Does he or she have a degree in the field? Is he or she a member of a professional organization? Does he or she speak at industry or trade conferences? Has he or she written other papers on the topic? These are just some ways to determine an author's credibility. You may also think of other ways.
- Common sense and instinct: Step back and perform a reality check. Follow your instincts. If you are uneasy about using a source of data, even after employing some of the strategies discussed, do not use it.

Practice Questions

1. Which technique would be most helpful in validating potentially biased information?
   a. Research the author's credentials
   b. Check the publication date of the information
   c. Use your common sense and instinct
   d. Look for similar information in other sources

2. Which of the following techniques would NOT be useful in validating information from electronic sources?
   a. Use a checklist
   b. Use your instinct
   c. Send email to the author
   d. Search for keywords in the text

4.5 Downloading Information

Most Web sites provide an interesting and interactive way for you to explore a topic. However, there are several types of Internet resources that provide information that is appropriate for downloading to your computer. You may be downloading program code, a plug-in for your browser, templates for documents you need to create, artwork, or research articles. These resources may be on a standard Web site or on a special type of site for downloading. This section describes how to download information found on the Internet to your computer.

4.5.1 Downloading from Web Sites

 Describe how to download files or copy information from a Web or FTP site.

The Internet is a valuable resource for many activities. You probably have come across several files that you would like to copy, or download, to your computer.

You might need to download a file because:

- You would like additional functionality for an application you are running, for example a plug-in for your browser.
- You need critical updates to an application on your system, for example virus definitions or security patches.
- You need a template or other documents for your work.
- You would like to have a copy of the document, information, or artwork on your computer for easy access.

Downloading is a fairly straightforward process. To download a file, perform the following steps:

1. Click the icon or link associated with the file.
2. Answer any questions that may be presented to you.
3. Specify the location on your computer where you want to store the file.

You may not be required to complete all three steps. Sometimes, downloads are completed automatically when you click the link to the file.

There are special sites, called FTP sites, that are dedicated to downloading files. FTP stands for File Transfer Protocol. It is a means of transferring files from one computer to another that has been in existence since pre-Internet times. FTP basically uses a different protocol to transfer files than the Internet. You will recognize an FTP site by the indication of ftp, instead of http, in the protocol field of the URL. FTP may provide a more efficient way to transfer some large files. The process for downloading from an FTP site is similar to the three-step process described in the previous paragraph. A simple specialized application is usually required to handle the download to your computer, but this might be available through your browser.

Example 4.1 is a sample of a specialized application that is used to upload and download files.

Example 4.1

WS_FTP Pro is an example of an FTP client program. It has a drag-and-drop interface, which allows users to transfer files securely between locations such as home and office or client and vendor. Figure 4.10 shows the interface of the application with an upload in progress.

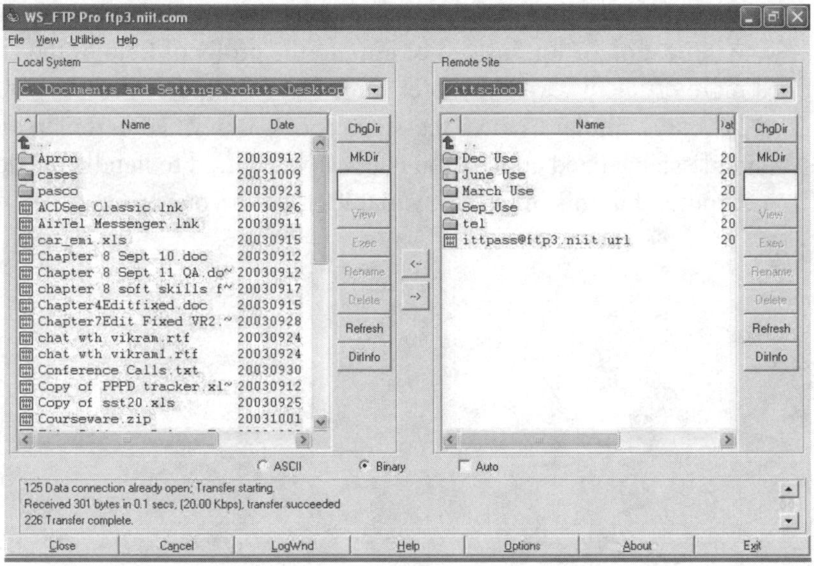

Figure 4.10: WS_FTP Client Program Interface

If you find it difficult to download files from an FTP site, check for Help associated with the site for some pointers and guidelines.

4.5.2 Cautions about Downloading

 List some issues to be aware of while downloading files to your computer.

Downloading files from the Web is a convenient way to get access to critical application files and useful reference materials. Do not let the ease of obtaining the information overshadow the diligence you must exercise in ensuring that you are using the information properly and safely. Consider the following when downloading files to your computer:

- Make sure that you understand your restrictions and obligations with respect to using the files. If there is a licensing agreement associated with the download, ensure that you abide by it before downloading the file.

- Take care to scan the file for viruses before placing it on your computer. Alternatively, ensure that the files are from a trusted source before you download them.

There is a natural temptation to use information verbatim when it exists in a readily–usable format on your computer. When necessary, ensure that you cite the source of the information properly in order to avoid plagiarism.

The topics of plagiarism and citing references are covered in sections 4.6 and 4.7.

Practice Questions

1. Which of the following statements is TRUE?
   a. Information that is available to be downloaded can be used freely without citing the source.
   b. All downloaded files go to a special "download" folder on your computer.
   c. You may need to accept a licensing agreement before downloading some files.
   d. You cannot edit or modify files that your download.

2. FTP stands for:
   a. First Try Protocol
   b. File Transfer Protocol
   c. File Transmission Prefix
   d. Fast Transfer Protocol

4.6 Cautions: Plagiarism and Libel

In some cases, you may be downloading data that is used in applications for which you have a license, such as updated virus definitions for your virus protection software. In such situations, you have agreed to licensing terms for use of the data or information and your responsibilities for proper use of the information have been specified. However, most of the information that you find on the Internet does not fall into this category. You may be using information from an online reference, such as an encyclopedia, or you may be citing a person's ideas or opinions. In such situations, you need to take care that you use and cite the information properly to avoid problems. You also may be commenting on a person's ideas, either on a Web discussion forum or in your research work. Just as you need to take care that you cite information properly, you also need to take care that you do not harm a person's reputation in your comments about his or her work. This section defines two potential problem areas, plagiarism and libel, and describes steps you can take to avoid them.

4.6.1 Plagiarism

Define plagiarism and explain how to avoid it.

Plagiarism is generally defined as presenting someone else's words or ideas as your own. The concept is usually learned early in grade school when students write their first research papers and are cautioned against copying information directly from encyclopedias or books. The concept broadens throughout your learning as you begin to do research that is more complicated and to consult expert research and opinions on theoretical topics. You need to ensure that you do not present someone's unique ideas as your own.

Before the days of electronic information, it was a somewhat arduous task to plagiarize information word-for-word. True, the temptation to copy an article verbatim always existed, but in the old days, you had to retype the information. In today's world of electronic information, words are easily copied into documents with a few short keystrokes. With this temptation at your fingertips, you must be especially cautious about plagiarism.

Figure 4.11: Avoid Plagiarism

How can you avoid plagiarism? The following list provides several suggestions for ensuring that you do not fall into the trap of plagiarism:

- Remember that all published information, whether in electronic or print format, is copyright protected. That means that some entity owns the rights to the use of the material. Therefore, you must credit the sources of your work. In some cases, you may also need to ask permission to use the work in your project.

- Take the time to understand the material you are researching, and then synthesize it and present it in your own words. Cite references to your sources within the text wherever necessary, such as when using ideas that are unique to a certain source.

- When you have contacted an expert for information, always be sure to cite the source of the ideas and information you are presenting, even if the information you gathered was from a conversation.

- Where practical, point readers to a URL to access information, instead of attempting to "reinvent the wheel" yourself and risking plagiarism.

- Ensure that you appropriately cite and gain permission for using artwork or diagrams. It is very appealing to simply cut-and-paste diagrams or artwork from the

Web into your documents. Do not use artwork unless you are certain that you have appropriate permission. Cite the source as required.

 Some sites such as http://www.edutie.com/ provide the facility to check a material for plagiarized content. You can enroll on the site and submit the material for a plagiarism check. The checked documents are posted in your account with a rating on plagiarized content. You can submit limited number of documents for a free plagiarism check. You can check more documents for plagiarism by paying a fee. Explore the Internet for more sites offering plagiarism check services.

4.6.2 Libel

 Define libel and slander and explain how to avoid them.

Slander is defined as making a false oral statement.
Libel is defined as making false statements that are damaging to a person's character or reputation.

Figure 4.12: Take Great Care to Avoid Slander or Libel

You may be wondering how you could fall into this trap in the context of using online information. True, the opportunities for plagiarism are far higher than the opportunities for libel. The opportunities to share or publish opinions online are plentiful in the context of e-mail or on discussion boards. However, you need to be cautious of publishing statements that could be false and harmful to a person's reputation.
In the context of online research, you need to take care to avoid libel when you are working with information that is directly attributed to a person. You need to take care

that you do not make any statements that are false and could damage the person's professional reputation. Be especially cautious in e-mail transmissions and postings to discussion boards. Take care that you do not make libelous statements yourself or repeat libelous statements that others have made.

The following list provides some suggestions for avoiding libel:

- When working directly with experts, ask thorough questions and ensure that you understand the information that the expert provides you. Ensure that you have permission to use the information. Do not publish false information that could directly or indirectly undermine a person's credibility.

- Avoid publishing personal judgments about a person's work that are not backed by established facts.

- Avoid relying on second-hand opinions and judgments about an expert's work.

- Do not make unsubstantiated damaging statements about corporations, educational institutions, or individuals that can be distributed electronically.

By using good personal judgment and common sense, you can avoid potential instances of libel.

Practice Questions

1. You find a research paper on the Web that includes an algorithm for sorting that is identical to one in a textbook you are using. There is no reference to a resource for the algorithm. This is:

   I. Plagiarism

   II. Libel

   III. Neither plagiarism nor libel—the information is acceptable.

   a. I only

   b. II only

   c. III only

   d. I and II

2. You read a research paper that includes the same section headings in the same order as a textbook on the same topic. This is:

I. Plagiarism

II. Libel

III. Neither plagiarism nor libel—the information is acceptable

a. I. only

b. II. only

c. III. only

d. I and II

3. You make untrue damaging remarks about a startup Internet company on a discussion board. This is:

I. Plagiarism

II. Libel

III. Neither plagiarism nor libel—the remarks are acceptable

a. I only

b. II only

c. III only

d. I and II

4.7 Citing Electronic Sources

Using information found on the Internet is no different than using printed information. While using information you researched it is necessary to cite its source. This section describes how to cite information you found on various Internet resources.

4.7.1 Internet Sites

Describe the information needed to cite an Internet site source.

As you noticed in your search on the Internet, information is available in many different formats and styles. You can find information in various formats, including standard Web sites, in electronically published articles, or in white papers. Because of the wide variety of sources of information, the format for citing these references can vary. The standards used in citing print information sources may not be available to you. However, there is a recommended standard to follow while citing an Internet site source. The citation should include:

- Author's name
- Description of the page or document you are referencing
- URL
- Date on which you accessed the material

When providing a URL, copy the URL from the browser address window and paste it into your document. This will help avoid typographical errors.

There are many different styles that are generally accepted for citing references. Some of the more popular styles include:

- APA style
- MLA style
- Chicago style

APA refers to the American Psychological Society, MLA refers to the Modern Language Association, and Chicago style refers to the style outlined in the *Chicago Manual of Style*.

The APA style is commonly used in social sciences, while the MLA style is used in the humanities and literature. The Chicago style is widely used in sciences and is a common reference for writing term papers and theses. Ensure you know the style format your instructor expects you to use in your research papers. All styles have recommendations for citing electronic information. Here are some examples using Chicago style.

Example 4.2

A reference to a glossary of terms found on a commercial vendor Web site accessed August 3, 2003.

Eva Kaplan-Leiserson, "Glossary," American Society for Training and Development, 2002, http://www.learningcircuits.org/glossary.html, (3 August 2003)

Example 4.3

A reference to a message posted to a discussion board accessed on August 3, 2003.

Jim Buyens, "Re: Entering an HTML Link," 2 August 2003, http://communities.microsoft.com/newsgroups/default.asp?icp=prod office&slcid=US, (3 August 2003).

Example 4.3

A reference to an informational article posted on a commercial Web site accessed on August 3, 2003.

Kevin Oakes, with Raghavan Rengarajan, "A Primer on Technology Driven Learning", May 2003, http://home.click2learn.com/en/downloads/A_Primer_on_Technology2. pdf (3 August 2003)

A link to the style manuals is available in the ITT Tech Virtual Library. From the main menu, select **Reference Resources**. Scroll down the page to the section on Style Manuals. This section has multiple links to styles of citing references.

Remember that when using Internet site resources, you may not have much of the traditional detail for citing references available to you. Do your best to provide as much detail as possible and to provide a URL that points directly to the information you are citing. Provide the date of access because information on Web sites changes frequently.

4.7.2 Online Reference Sources

Describe the information needed to cite an online reference source.

As discussed in the previous topic, citing general information found on Web sites can be tricky because traditional bibliographic information may not be available. When using online reference sources, such as online journals or databases, you may be relieved to note that much of the traditional information for citing references is usually available.

When citing online reference sources, ensure that you have most of the following information:

- Author's name
- Date of publication
- Title of book, journal, or article
- Relevant page numbers and other similar information about the source
- Date you retrieved the information
- URL

Some of this information may not be available or relevant for your source, but do your best to supply as much information as possible.

The following examples show specific entries for some online reference resources:

> **Example 4.5**
>
> A reference to an online book accessed on August 3, 2003.
>
> David Fox and Mitchell Waite, "Computer Animation Primer," 1984, http://www.atariarchives.org/cap/, (3 August 2003).

> **Example 4.6**
>
> A reference to an article from an online news service accessed on August 3, 2003.
>
> Dave Marash, "Rise Up: Emotional, Financial Needs Challenge Rcbuilding of World Trade Center Site," abcnews.com, 2 August 2003, http://abcnews.go.com/sections/nightline/Nightline/ntl_
>
> marash_wtc_030802.html, (3 August 2003)

> **Example 4.7**
>
> A reference to an article in an online encyclopedia accessed on August 3, 2003.
>
> "Artificial Intelligence," Microsoft Encarta Online Encyclopedia, copyright 2003 Microsoft Corporation, http://encarta.msn.com/encnet/refpages/RefArticle.aspx?refid=76156711 8, (3 August 2003)

Remember, always cite your references to avoid plagiarism. Citing sources also provides a means for readers to explore further resources or topics on their own.

Practice Questions

1. What information is NOT generally used in citing information from electronic sources?

    a. Author's name

    b. Publisher name and location

    c. Date of access

    d. Date of publication or copyright

2. In the following citation of an online book, what is the date when the information was published?

    David Fox and Mitchell Waite, " Computer Animation primer," 1984, http://www.atariarchives.org/cap/, (3 August 2003).

    I.   August 3, 2003

    II. 1984

    III. The publication date is not given

    a. I only

    b. II only

    c. III only

    d. I and II

3. What style is commonly used for citing sources in the humanities?

    a. MLA

    b. APA

    c. Chicago

    d. HMA

4. What style is commonly used for citing sources in social sciences?
   a. MLA
   b. APA
   c. Chicago
   d. HMA

Summary

In this chapter, you learned:

- Effectively locating and validating relevant electronic information is important for personal and professional success.

- There are many sources of information available on the Internet. Some of these sources that are useful for research purposes include:
  - Online reference sources such as encyclopedias and journals
  - Online databases
  - Discussion boards (newsgroups and listservs)
  - Commercial sites
  - Educational sites

- Locating information on the Internet is an iterative process. You can easily search the Internet by typing keywords in the address field of your browser. Many search engines provide specialized capability to help you locate information.

- Several advanced search techniques can help you refine your search activities. These techniques include making use of Boolean operators and wild cards in search strings and taking advantage of advanced features of a search engine.

- It is important to validate information you find on the Internet before you use it. Techniques such as creating a checklist of assessment criteria and checking for similar data in other sources are useful strategies for evaluating the quality and accuracy of information.

- Downloading files from a Web site to your computer is usually accomplished in a few simple clicks. Take care to ensure that you use the files responsibly.

- Always cite sources for information you may use and avoid making false statements that may damage a person's reputation. These precautions will help you avoid plagiarism and libel.

- Several styles for citing electronic resources are generally accepted. Gather as much information about your sources as you can and follow the style guide recommended by your instructor.

References

Book References

- Basch, Reva and Mary Ellen Bates. *Researching Online for Dummies*, Second Edition. New York, NY: IDG Books Worldwide. 2000.
- Berkman, Robert I. *Find It Fast*, Fifth Edition. New York, NY: Harper Resource. 2000

Web Site Reference

- Bedford / St. Martin's ONLINE! Citation Styles, <http://www.bedfordstmartins.com/online/citex.html> (01 August 2003).

Word Processing Tools

5

Word processing tools are used to record and present information in a well-formatted document. You can embed images and links to other files in your document. You will learn to use Microsoft Word for word processing in this chapter. In addition to learning the basic features of a word processor, you will learn about other features, such as hyperlinks offered by Microsoft Word.

At the end of this chapter, you will be able to:

- Edit text in a document.

- Format paragraphs in a document.

- Apply bullet and numbering formatting to lists.

- Apply borders and shading to text.

- Insert headers and footers with relevant information.

- Save and print a document.

- Create, format, edit, and align tables in a document.

- Insert Clip Art into a document.

- Create hypertext links in a document.

- Save a document as a Web page and view it on the Web.

- Track changes and insert comments while reviewing a document.

- Use the Help feature to discover and apply additional features or troubleshoot a document.

5.1 Basic Word Processing Techniques

5.2 Techniques for Working with Tables

5.3 Additional Word Features

5.1 Basic Word Processing Techniques

Word processing allows you to place information in a document for sharing, saving, or reporting. Word processing applications have replaced handwritten notes and typewriters. Unlike handwritten or typed documents, documents created in a word processing application can be edited and saved easily for later access. You can enter text, embed pictures and tables, and add colors to documents using word processing. You also can have text in different sizes and styles in your document.

This chapter assumes that you have a basic understanding of Microsoft Word. If you do not feel comfortable with your knowledge of Microsoft Word, it is strongly suggested that you refresh your basics by completing an online tutorial.

You can access the Microsoft Word online tutorial from the ITT Tech Virtual Library, by logging on to the virtual library at http://www.itt-techlibrary.com/. Then from the main menu, select the **Learning Guides** link. Under Online Tutorials, scroll down and select **Microsoft Office 2000 Tutorials**. Select **Word** from the list of Office Programs. Click the **Begin the Word tutorial** link to begin.

Refer to Word **Help** whenever you need more information about a feature.

A menu displays a list of commands. Most menus in Microsoft Word are located on the Menu Bar, the toolbar at the top of the screen, as shown in figure 5.1.

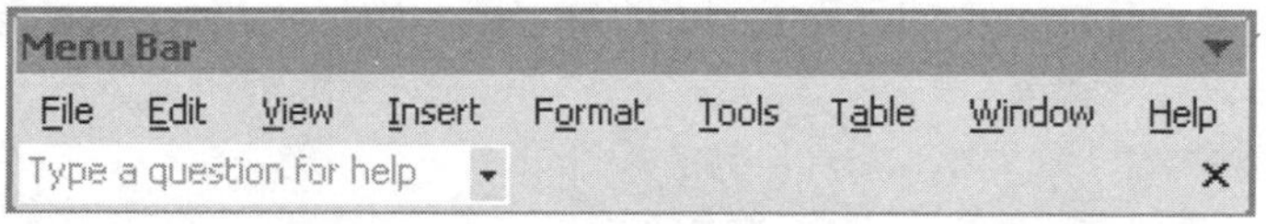

Figure 5.1: Menu Bar in Microsoft Word

Toolbars can contain buttons and menus. You can see the name of the toolbar when you detach it from other toolbars.

You can customize the number of toolbars you would like to be displayed in the Microsoft Word window. To do so, perform the following steps:

1. Click **Tools → Customize**. This opens the Customize dialog box.

2. Click the **Toolbars** tab. The list of available toolbars is displayed.

3. Select or clear the appropriate check boxes based on the toolbars to be displayed, as shown in Figure 5.2.

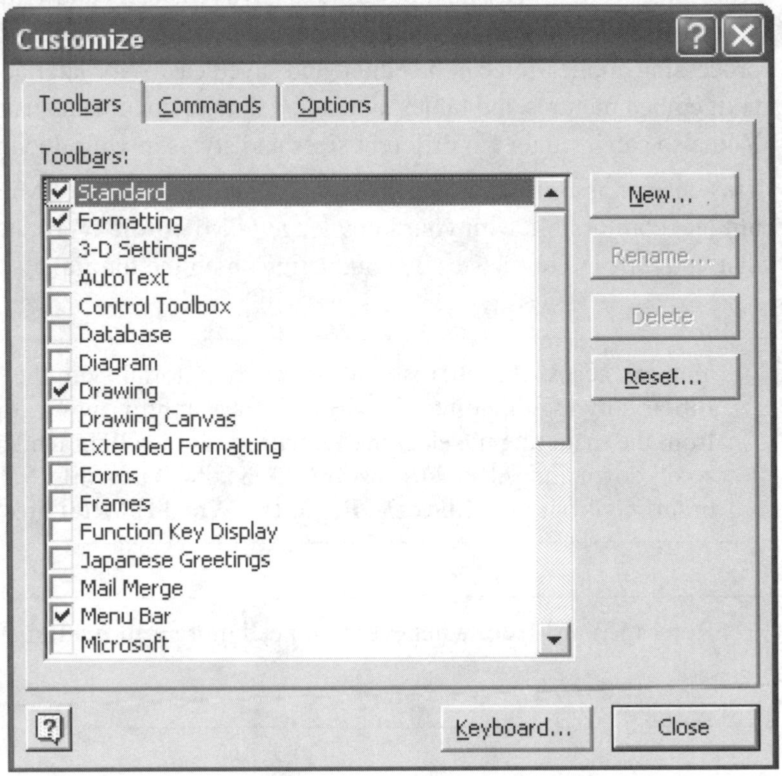

Figure 5.2: Customize Dialog Box—Toolbars Tab

4. Click **Close**. The selected toolbars will be displayed in the window.

5.1.1 Editing Text

Edit text in a Word document.

You can edit documents using the editing capability in word processing. You can add, delete, and modify text. You can edit text in your Microsoft Word document using the:

■ Edit menu in the Menu Bar

■ Standard toolbar

To edit text using the **Edit** menu options, highlight the text and click the appropriate command in the **Edit** menu. To edit text using the Standard toolbar, highlight the text and click the icon of the command you wish to perform. You will be guided through such an exercise later in this section.

While you can add, delete, and modify text using the **Edit** menu, it also provides other options. Explore the menu and use Word Help to learn about the other capabilities of Word.

Some of the commands in the **Edit** menu can also be performed by using a combination of keyboard keys. Such a combination of keys is referred to as hot keys or shortcut keys. For example, you can perform the **Paste** command by pressing the "Ctrl" and "V" keys. Explore the hot keys for other commands by using Word Help.

Figure 5.3 shows the Standard toolbar in Microsoft Word.

Figure 5.3: Standard Toolbar in Microsoft Word

In case you cannot see the Standard toolbar in the Word window, you can invoke it from the **View** menu in the Menu Bar. Select **View** → **Toolbars** → **Standard** to make the Standard toolbar visible.

Table 5.1 shows the icons in the Standard toolbar and their functions.

Icon	Function
	Creates a new blank document.
	Opens a document. You can choose a document from the History, My Documents, Desktop, Favorites, and My Network Places folders or browse to a particular folder and open a document.
	Saves the current document to the last saved location.
	Launches the Compose page of the default e-mail application to enable you to e-mail your current document.
	Launches the search feature to enable you to search for files on your PC.
	Prints the document to the current default printer.
	Allows you to preview the document as it would appear printed.
	Performs spelling and grammar checks on the document.
	Cuts the highlighted selection to be moved to another location or to be discarded.
	Copies the highlighted selection to another location, leaving the original highlighted selection intact.
	Pastes the selection to the location pointed to by the cursor.
	Copies the format from the selected item to another item.
	Undoes the typing. Includes a drop-down menu with recent edits.
	Redoes the typing. Reverses the undo action.
	Displays the tables and borders toolbar.
	Inserts a table in the document.

	Inserts a Microsoft Excel spreadsheet. You will learn more about spreadsheets in Chapter 7.
	Inserts columns.
	Displays or hides the drawing toolbar.
100% ▾	Enlarges or reduces the size of the current document. You can select the extent of magnification or reduction from the drop-down menu.

Table 5.1: Components and Functions of the Standard Toolbar in Microsoft Word

Many features of the toolbar remain hidden until used. Additionally, a toolbar selection that is not used frequently may become hidden.

Text, pictures, tables, or any other item in a Word document can be moved within the same document or to a different document. When a selection is moved, it is cut and no longer exists in its original location. The cut selection is placed in a temporary storage area known as the **Clipboard**. The Clipboard is emptied when you log off or shut down the computer.

Another edit command is **Copy**. This command creates a copy of the selected text, picture, table, or other item in the document and places it on the Clipboard. It leaves the original item intact.

The **Paste** command is used to insert the items placed on the Clipboard at the appropriate location in the document.

Any item in a document can be deleted. After you highlight the item, you can delete it by:

- Selecting **Edit** → **Delete** from the Menu Bar.
- Selecting **Edit** → **Cut** from the Menu Bar.
- Using the **Delete** key on your keyboard.

Consider the sample text given in Figure 5.4.

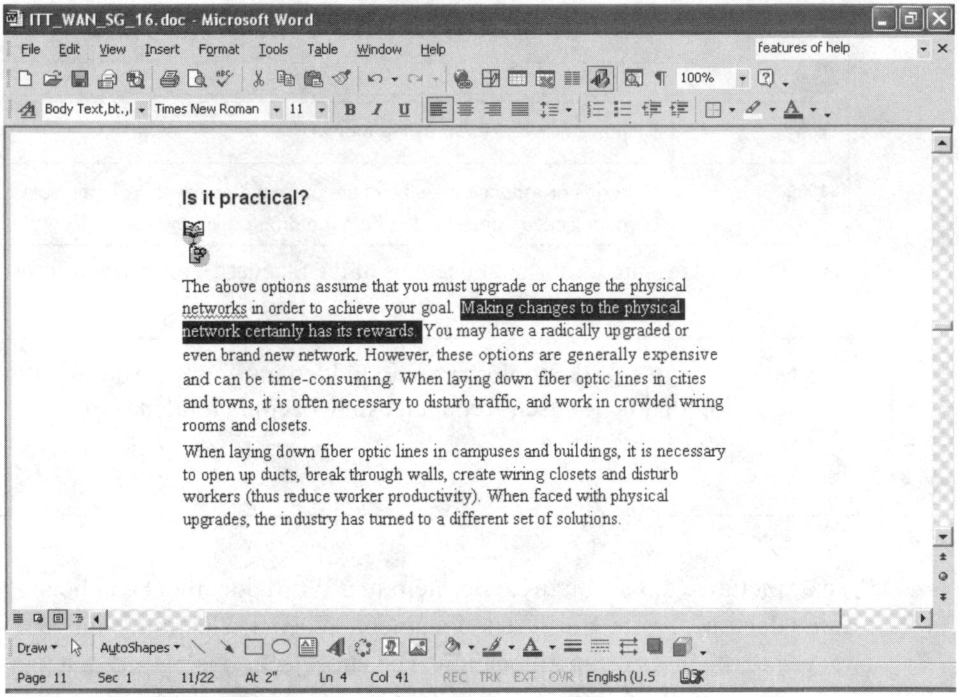

Figure 5.4: Sample Text to be Edited

You need to:

▪ Move the highlighted text to the end of the first paragraph.

▪ Delete the second paragraph.

▪ Copy the graphic icon to the end of the first paragraph.

To do this, perform the following steps:

1. To move the highlighted text select **Edit → Cut**.

2. Move the cursor to the end of the first paragraph and then select **Edit → Paste**.

The line of text can be seen at the end of the first paragraph, as shown in Figure 5.5.

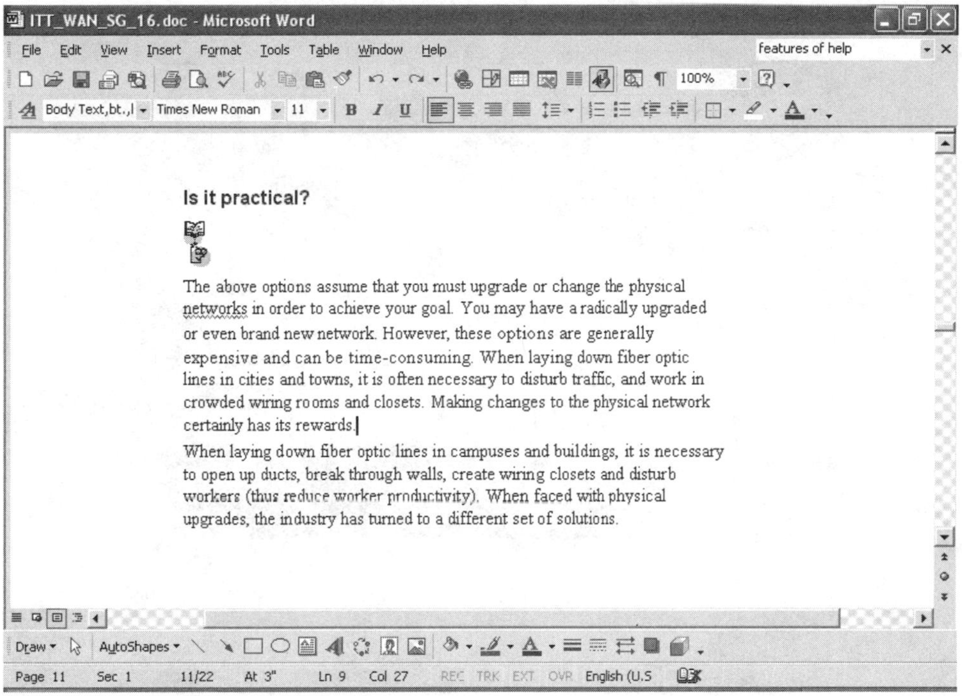

Figure 5.5: Highlighted Text Has Been Moved

3. Select the second paragraph, as shown in Figure 5.6.

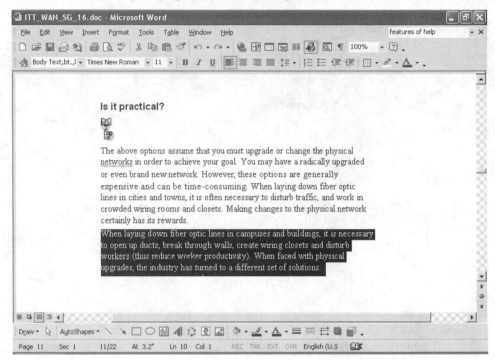

Figure 5.6: Highlighted Text for Deletion

4. Select **Edit → Delete**. The selected text is deleted, as shown in Figure 5.7.

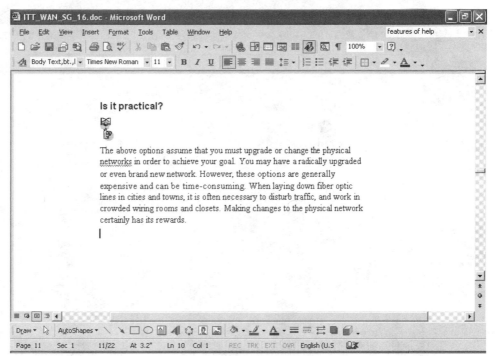

Figure 5.7: Text Deleted

5. Select the **Graphic** icon, as shown in Figure 5.8.

Figure 5.8: Highlighted Graphic Icon

6. Select **Edit → Copy**.

7. Move the cursor to the end of the first paragraph and then select **Edit → Paste**. As seen in Figure 5.9, a copy of the graphic icon is pasted at the end of the paragraph.

Figure 5.9: Edited Text with the Copied Graphic Icon

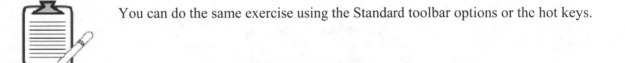

You can do the same exercise using the Standard toolbar options or the hot keys.

5.1.2 Formatting Text

 Apply formats to text in a Word document.

You can modify or format your text using the:

- Format options in the Menu Bar
- Formatting toolbar

To format text using the **Format** menu, highlight the text and click the appropriate command in the Format menu.

To format text using the Formatting toolbar, highlight the text and click the icon of the command that you wish to perform. Figure 5.10 shows the options in the Formatting toolbar.

Figure 5.10: Formatting Toolbar

Table 5.2 shows the components of the Formatting toolbar and their functions.

Icon	Function
A	Enables you to set the style and formatting for text.
Body Text	Specifies the style of the selected text.
Times New Roman	Specifies the font of the selected text.
11	Specifies the font size of the selected text.
B	Makes the selected text **bold**.
I	Makes the selected text *italics*.
U	Makes the selected text underlined.
	Aligns the selected text to the left, center, right, or justified.

Icon	Function
	Adjusts the spacing between lines of text.
	Converts the selected lines of text into a numbered list.
	Converts the selected lines of text into a bulleted list.
	Decreases or increases indent of the selected text.
	Inserts a border on the outside of the selected text.
	Sets a color around selected text to highlight it. You can choose a color from the palette of colors.
	Sets a color to the selected text to differentiate it from the surrounding text. You can choose a color from the palette of colors.

Table 5.2: Formatting Toolbar Components and Functions

Hot keys also exist for some of the Formatting toolbar options. For example, you can make your text bold by selecting the text and then pressing the "Ctrl" and "B" keys. Explore the hot keys for other commands by using Word Help.

Fonts determine the look of the text. Font choices include choosing the size and style of the font.

5.1.2.1 Formatting Paragraphs

Formatting can also be applied to complete paragraphs. Paragraph formatting affects the look of the paragraph by determining its:

■ Alignment: Specifies where data is located with reference to the paragraph. Options include right-justified, left-justified, and centered.

■ Indentation: Specifies the number of empty spaces before the first letter of the paragraph.

- Spacing: Specifies the amount of space between the lines in a paragraph. Options include single, one-and-a-half, double, or other configurable spacing.

- Pagination: Specifies whether a new page is automatically started when the amount of space allocated to the page is filled. Page breaks can also be manual.

You can access the paragraph formatting menu by selecting the **Format → Paragraph** menu option. Figure 5.11 shows the indent and spacing options available for paragraphs.

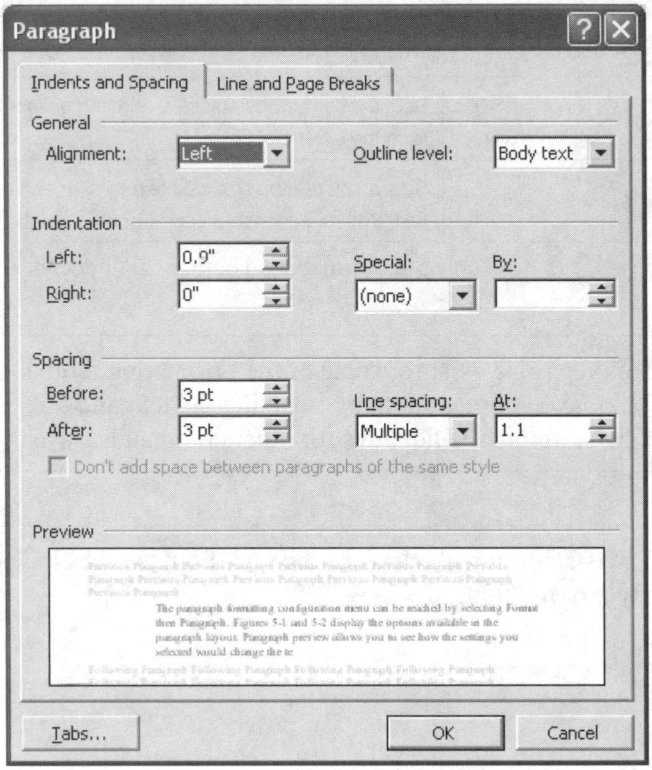

Figure 5.11: Indent and Spacing Options for Paragraphs

Figure 5.12 shows the line and page break options available for paragraphs.

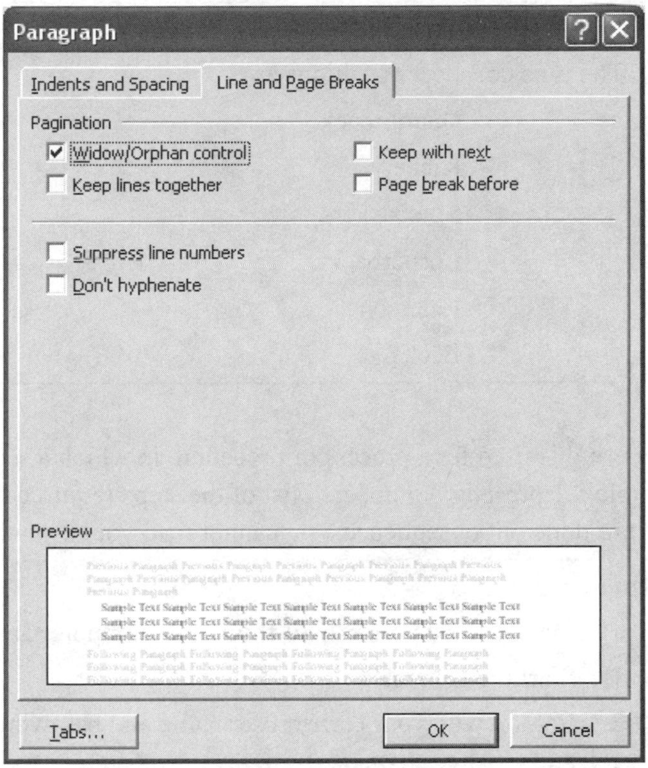

Paragraph [?] [X]

Indents and Spacing | Line and Page Breaks

Pagination
☑ Widow/Orphan control ☐ Keep with next
☐ Keep lines together ☐ Page break before

☐ Suppress line numbers
☐ Don't hyphenate

Preview

Tabs... | OK | Cancel

Figure 5.12: Line and Page Break Options for Paragraphs

 Paragraph preview window shows you a preview of your selected settings on the paragraph.

5.1.2.2 Bullets and Numbering

Bullets and numbering are used to organize the presentation of a list or procedural steps in a document. Bullets are applied to unordered lists in which there is no step-by-step sequence or procedure. They are used to describe the features of a product or process.

Example 5.1 shows a bulleted list of player positions in soccer.

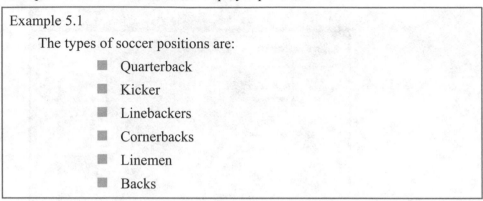

Example 5.1
    The types of soccer positions are:

- Quarterback
- Kicker
- Linebackers
- Cornerbacks
- Linemen
- Backs

Numbering is used for a process or procedure in which a sequence of steps is important. Example 5.2 presents a numbered list of the steps required to read your e-mail. If any steps are done out of sequence, you cannot read your e-mail.

Example 5.2
    The steps to read your e-mail from your computer are:

1. Start the computer.
2. Log on with your correct user name and password.
3. Open your e-mail application.
4. Click the e-mail message that you want to read.

You can click the Bullets or Numbering icons in the Formatting toolbar to create bullet lists or numbered lists respectively. You can also select the **Format → Bullets and Numbering** option from the Menu Bar to create a list.

By default, the bullet style is a filled-in circle but this can be customized. To customize the bullet style, perform the following steps:

1. Highlight the selection for which you want to insert bullets.
2. Select **Format → Bullets and Numbering**.
3. Select the **Bulleted** tab.
4. Select a bullet type and then click **OK**.

Figure 5.13 shows the standard bullet styles.

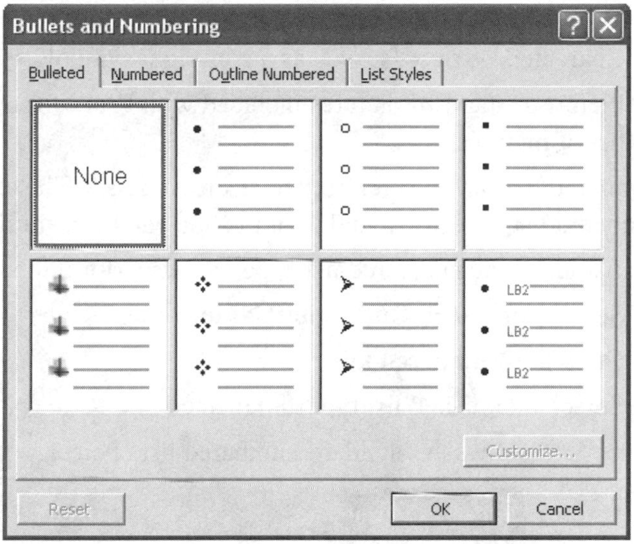

Figure 5.13: Bullets and Numbering Dialog Box—Bulleted Tab

5. Click **Customize** to choose the appearance of your bullets from the available styles. Figure 5.14 show the **Customize Bulleted List** dialog box.

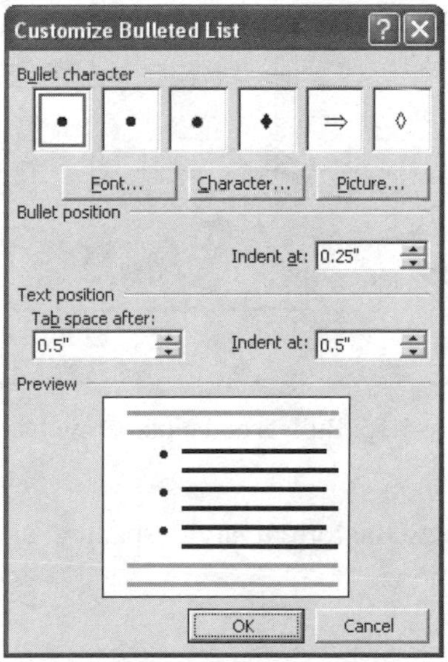

Figure 5.14: Customize Bulleted List Dialog Box

You can customize bullets in the following ways:

- Font—Type, style, and size.
- Character—Symbols, such as a copyright symbol, stylus, or heart.
- Picture—Standard pictures included with Word for bullets or imported from your list of pictures.

Numbered lists are also referred to as ordered lists. The style of numbering in a numbered list is set by default, but this too can be customized.

To customize the numbered list appearance, perform the following steps:

1. Select **Format → Bullets and Numbering**.
2. Click the **Numbered** tab.
3. Select a numbered list type and then click **OK**.

Figure 5.15 shows the standard numbered list choices.

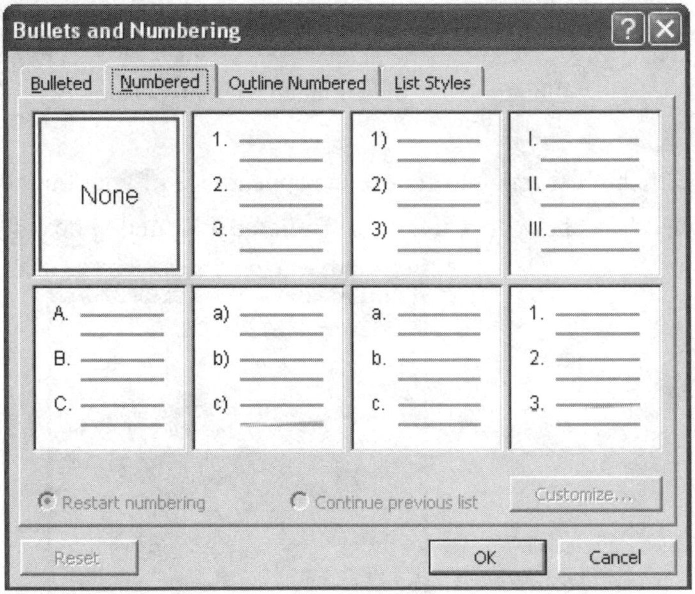

Figure 5.15: Bullets and Numbering Dialog Box—Numbered Tab

You can customize the format, style, spacing, and appearance of the numbered list from the available options.

Figure 5.16 shows the customizing options available for numbered lists.

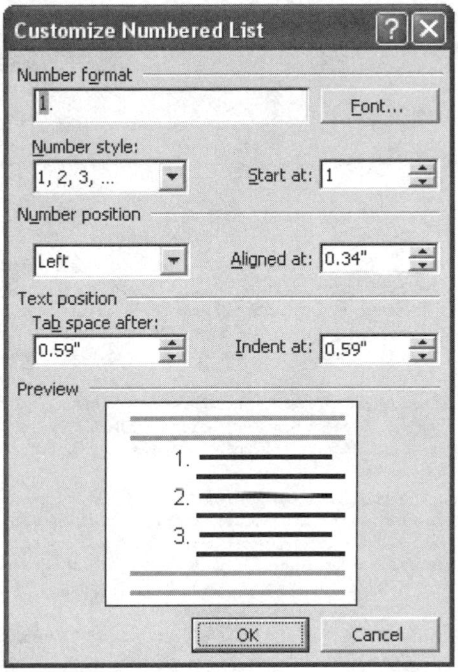

Figure 5.16: Customize Numbered List Dialog Box

Consider the text given in Figure 5.17. To improve the presentation of points in the paragraph, you can convert it to a bulleted list.

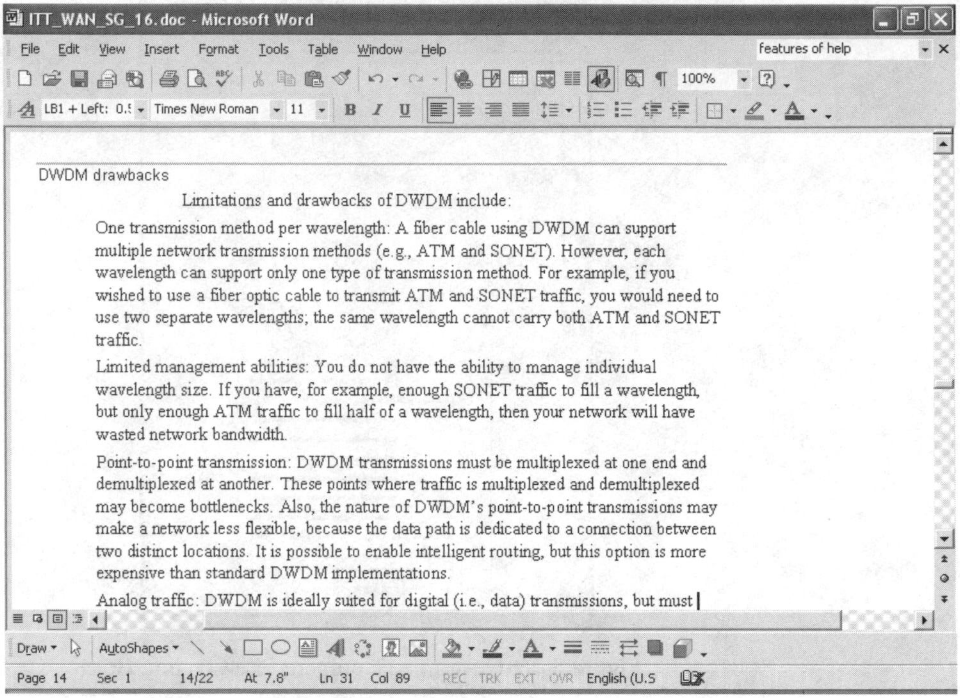

Figure 5.17: Sample Text with Points Merged in a Paragraph

To create a bulleted list for the text in Figure 5.17, perform the following steps:

1. Select the text to be presented as a single bulleted point.
2. Select **Format → Bullets and Numbering**.
3. Select the **Bulleted** tab and then choose a style of bullets.

The formatted text is shown in Figure 5.18.

The formatted text is shown in Figure 5.18.

```
ITT_WAN_SG_16.doc - Microsoft Word                                    _ □ X

File   Edit   View   Insert   Format   Tools   Table   Window   Help        features of help       ▾ ×

 □ 📂 🖫 🖨 🖳  🖨 🔍 ✖  ✂ 📋 🖺 ✑  ↺ ▾ ↻ ▾  🖳 🖽 🔲 🖾 ☰ 🗾 🔍 ¶ 100% ▾ 🖹 .

🄰 LB1          ▾  Times New Roman ▾ 11 ▾  B  I  U  ▐▀ ▀ ▀ ▀ ⁀▾  ⁝⁝ ⁝⁝ ⁇ ⁇  □ ▾ ℒ ▾ 🄰 ▾ .

            push in to connect and pull out to disconnect the wire.

       DWDM drawbacks

            Limitations and drawbacks of DWDM include:

            ▪  One transmission method per wavelength: A fiber cable using DWDM
               can support multiple network transmission methods (e.g., ATM and
               SONET). However, each wavelength can support only one type of
               transmission method. For example, if you wished to use a fiber optic
               cable to transmit ATM and SONET traffic, you would need to use two
               separate wavelengths; the same wavelength cannot carry both ATM and
               SONET traffic.

            ▪  Limited management abilities: You do not have the ability to manage
               individual wavelength size. If you have, for example, enough SONET
               traffic to fill a wavelength, but only enough ATM traffic to fill half of a
               wavelength, then your network will have wasted network bandwidth.

            ▪  Point-to-point transmission: DWDM transmissions must be multiplexed
               at one end and demultiplexed at another. These points where traffic is
               multiplexed and demultiplexed may become bottlenecks. Also, the
               nature of DWDM's point-to-point transmissions may make a network|
               less flexible. because the data path is dedicated to a connection between

Draw ▾ ⌖  AutoShapes ▾ ＼ ＼ □ ○ 🖾 🔷 ⚙ 🖾 🖾  ◊ ▾ ℒ ▾ 🄰 ▾ ☰ ☰ ⇄ ■ 🗊 .

Page 14    Sec 1    14/22    At 7.4"   Ln 29  Col 66   REC TRK EXT OVR  English (U.S  🗔
```

Figure 5.18: Points Arranged as a Bulleted List

 Use Word Help for more information about bullets and numbering.

5.1.2.3 Borders and Shading

Borders and shading are used to emphasize text in a paragraph or table. The borders and shading options can be implemented if you want to emphasize some information. To apply borders or shading, perform the following steps:

1. Select the text to format.

2. Select **Format → Borders and Shading**. This opens the **Borders and Shading** dialog box with the Borders, Page Border, and Shading tabs.

3. Choose the appropriate tab and set your format requirements.

Figure 5.19 shows the Borders and Shading dialog box.

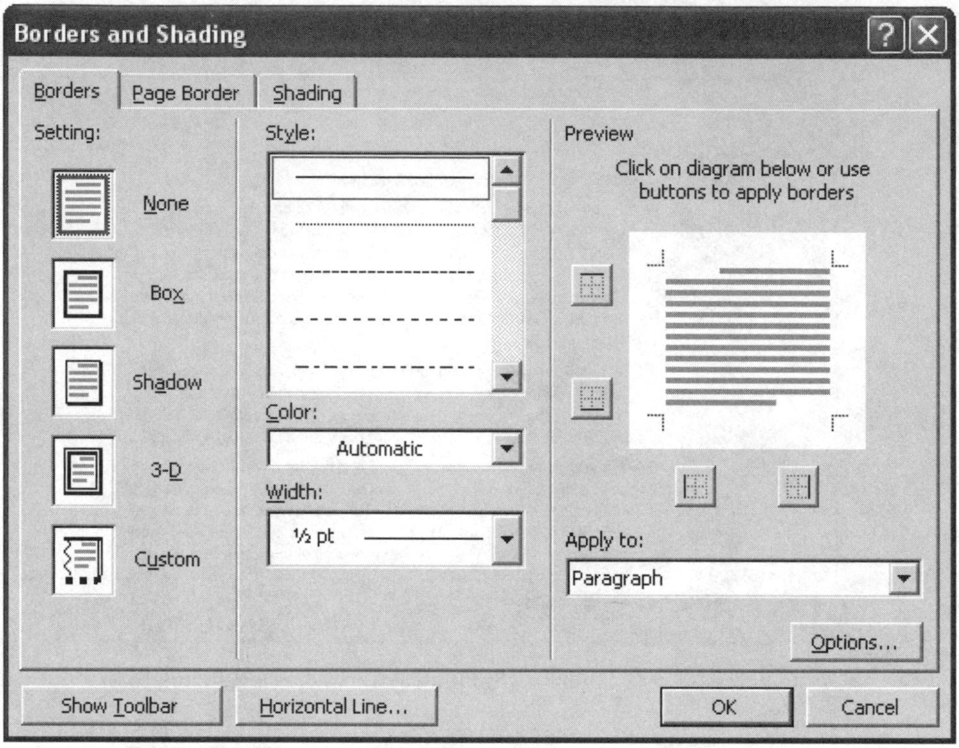

Figure 5.19: Borders and Shading Dialog Box with Borders Tab

4. Click **OK**.

You can also use the **Tables and Borders** toolbar to format. Select **View** → **Toolbars** → **Tables and Borders** to display the toolbar, as shown in Figure 5.20.

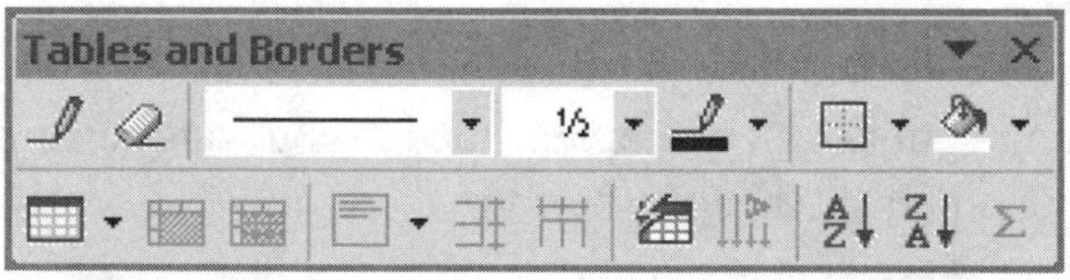

Figure 5.20: Tables and Borders Toolbar

Consider the sample text given in Figure 5.21. To make this text more readable and to add emphasis at the right places, you must format it.

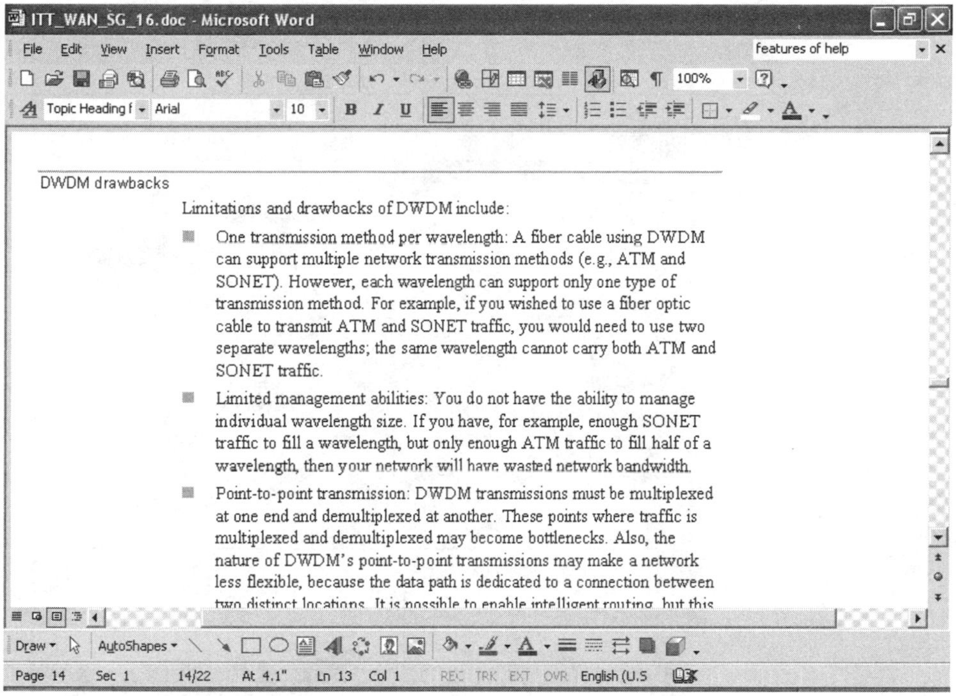

Figure 5.21: Sample Unformatted Text

To add emphasis to the title text, increase its font size and make it bold. You can also enclose it within a border. Finally, highlight the bulleted list points in a different color.

To format the sample text, perform the following steps:

1. Select the title text.
2. Select **Format → Font**.

3. Choose **12** in the Size list box and **Bold** in the Font style list box, as shown in Figure 5.22.

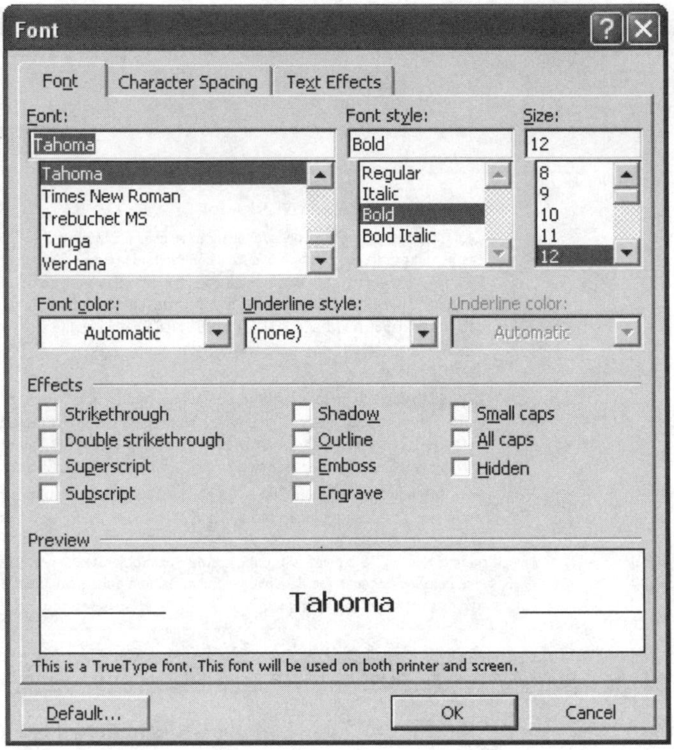

Figure 5.22: Font Dialog Box

4. Click **OK** to set the title font.

5. Select **Format → Borders and Shading**. Choose a border style from the Borders tab. The formatted text appears, as shown in Figure 5.23.

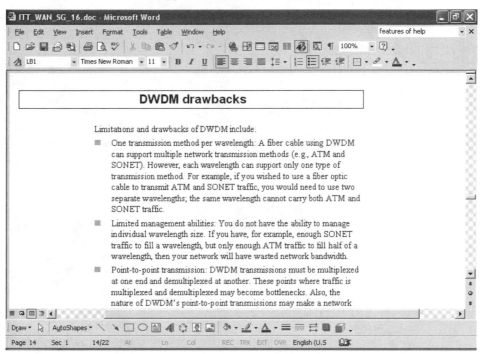

Figure 5.23: Bold and Bordered Title in Text

6. Select the bulleted text to highlight.
7. From the Formatting toolbar, click the **Highlight** icon.

8. From the palette that opens, select a color for the highlight. The formatted list appears, as shown in Figure 5.24.

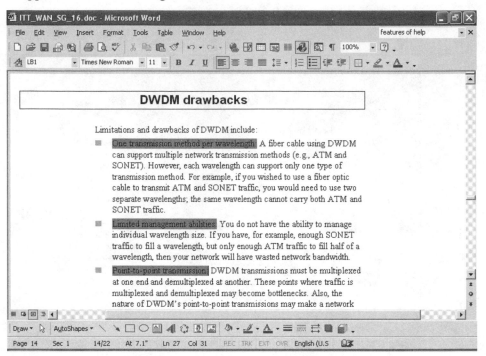

Figure 5.24: Highlighted Points in a List

5.1.3 Headers and Footers

Insert headers and footers containing relevant information into a document.

Headers and footers are used to display some document-related information at the top or bottom of the pages in your document. For example, your instructor may require every page of your assignment to be numbered or the assignment topic to be displayed on each page. The topmost line on the page is the header and the bottommost line on the page is the footer.

Relevant information that commonly occurs in headers and footers includes:

▪   Page numbers

- Date
- Document name
- Company name or logo
- Copyright protection statement
- Author name

Page numbers, when included in the header or footer, can be configured to number the pages in the document automatically.

To insert or change a header or footer, perform the following steps:

1. Select **View → Header and Footer**. The **Header and Footer** toolbar appears, as shown in Figure 5.25.

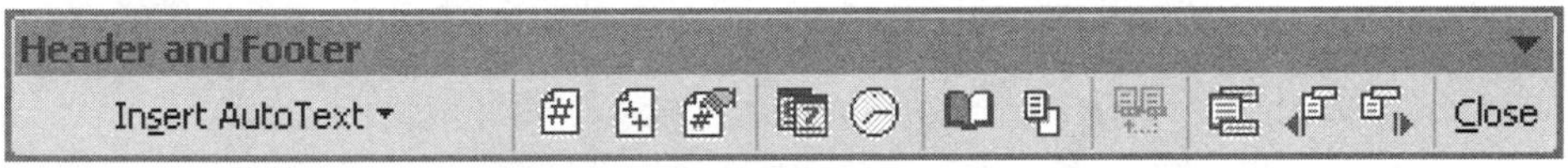

Figure 5.25: Header and Footer Toolbar

2. Configure the header or footer using the toolbar.
3. Click **Close**.

You can also specify even and odd numbered pages to have different headers and footers. This is useful in documents that you want to print like a book. You may want the document title to appear on each even page, and a different title, such as the most recent subheading, to appear on each odd page.

Figure 5.26 shows an example of pages in a book in which the name of the chapter appears in different locations on the odd and even pages.

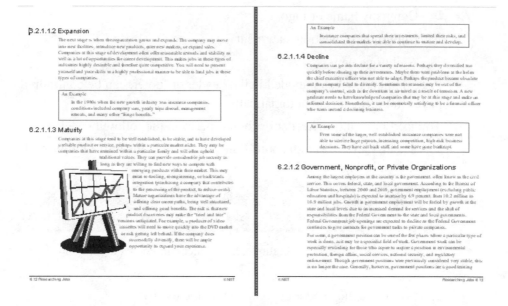

Figure 5.26: Different Footer Settings for Odd and Even Pages

5.1.4 Saving and Printing

Save and print a document.

After creating a new Word document or while editing an existing document, it will be necessary for you to save your work to a permanent storage media, such as the local hard drive, floppy disk, network drive, or a writeable CD or DVD device. If your work is not saved, it will be permanently lost when you close the application or shut down the system. Although saving is a simple task, you have to be careful about the location and the format in which you save the document.

You may be required to print your document in order to submit a hardcopy of it to your instructor, or you may want to review your document by reading through a hard copy and then editing later.

Saving Your Document

To save a newly-created document in the default Word 2000 format, perform the following steps:

1. Select **File → Save As**. Figure 5.27 displays the Save As dialog box that opens.

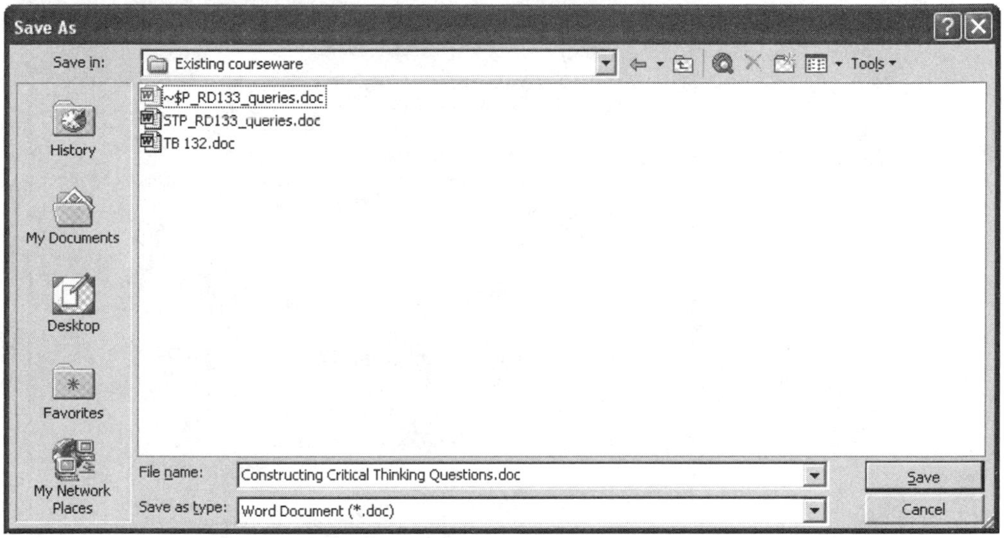

![Save As dialog box showing Save in: Existing courseware with files ~$P_RD133_queries.doc, STP_RD133_queries.doc, TB 132.doc; File name: Constructing Critical Thinking Questions.doc; Save as type: Word Document (*.doc)]

Figure 5.27: Save As Dialog Box

2. In the **Save in** drop-down list, browse to the folder in which you want to save the document.

3. Ensure that the default Word 2000 format, Word Document (*.doc), is selected in the **Save as type** list.

4. Type a name for the file and then click **Save**. This leaves the file open and saves it to the selected location.

You can save a modified document in its existing location by:

- Pressing the **Ctrl** and **S** keys.
- Selecting **File → Save**.
- Clicking the **Save** icon on the Standard toolbar.

If you enable AutoRecovery, Word periodically saves your documents. Word uses the AutoRecovery feature to recover your document if a problem occurs during editing.

Word automatically opens the same document with the word, "Recovered" suffixed to the name of the document. To enable Word to create recovery files at regular intervals, perform the following steps:

1. Select **Tools → Options**. Figure 5.28 displays the Options dialog box that opens.

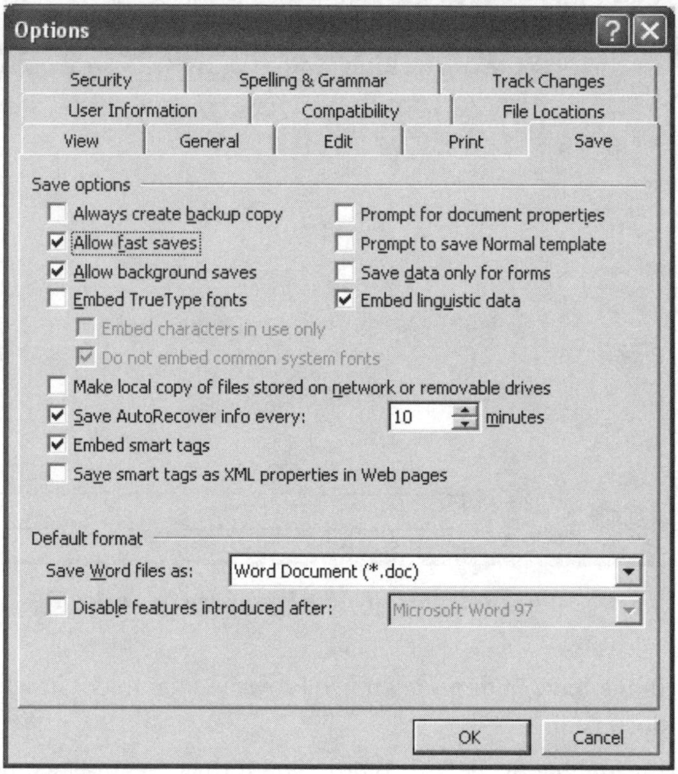

Figure 5.28: Setting the AutoRecovery Feature in Word in the Options Dialog Box

2. Click the **Save** tab.

3. Ensure that the **Allow fast saves** check box is clear.

4. Ensure that the **Allow background saves** and the **Save AutoRecover info every**: check boxes are selected.

5. Set the **Save AutoRecover info every spin box** to a minimum of 10 minutes, as shown in Figure 5.28.

6. Click **OK** to close the dialog box.

When you reboot your computer after a Word application failure, open the Word application first. Select **File → Save As** to save the recovered document with a new name and then continue your work.

Printing Your Document

You can print your document by clicking the Printer icon in the Standard toolbar or choosing the **File → Print** menu option. The Printer icon enables you to print using the default printer, however, you may occasionally want to print to another printer.

To redirect your document to another printer, perform the following steps:

1. Select **File → Print**. Figure 5.29 shows the Print dialog box with a drop down list of available printers.

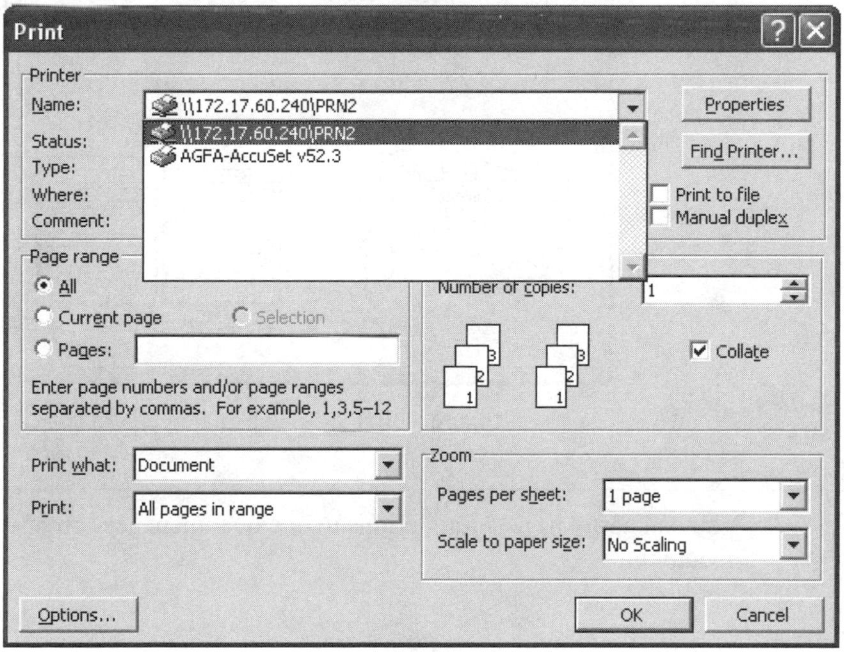

Figure 5.29: Print Dialog Box

2. The default printer is selected in the Name drop-down list. You can select any printer from this drop-down list.
3. Click **OK** to print the document.

Before you print your document, you can set its layout by using the **Page Setup** dialog box, as shown in Figure 5.30. Select **File → Page Setup** to open the **Page Setup** dialog box. You can use this dialog box to ensure that the changes are applied across the entire document.

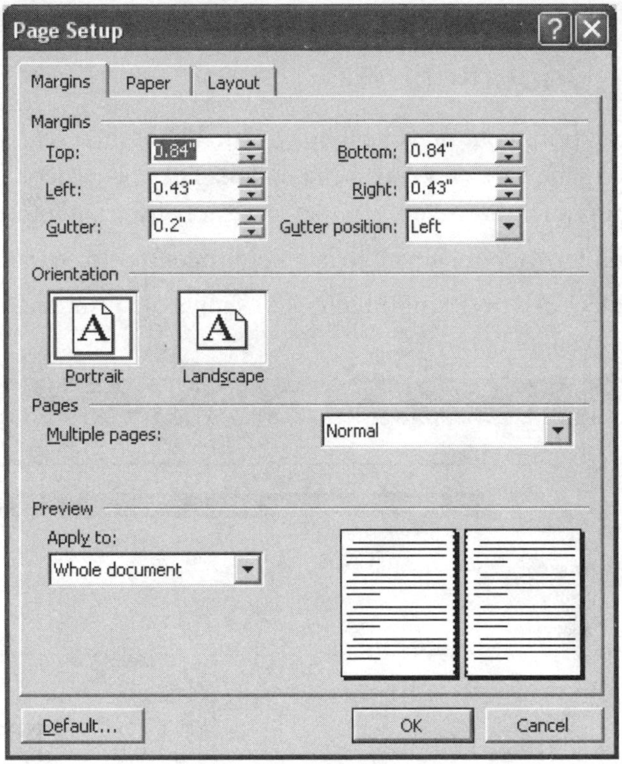

Figure 5.30: Page Setup Dialog Box

 You can apply page setup options to one document section or to an entire document.

Table 5.3 lists the three tabs in the Page Setup dialog box along with the available options.

Tab	Options
Margins	Options in this tab enable you to specify the top, bottom, left, and right margins of a page. These margins are specified in terms of their distance from the edge of the paper.
Paper	Options in this tab give you a choice of standard paper sizes. You can also specify a custom size. In addition, you can set the direction in which the printer will print the document, such as Portrait and Landscape.
Layout	Options in this tab help you to set the finer details in a more complex document. These details include defining sections and odd and even page characteristics.

Table 5.3: Options in the Page Setup Dialog Box

You may want to set other print options before your document gets printed. As shown in Figure 5.31, you can use the Print dialog box to set print options.

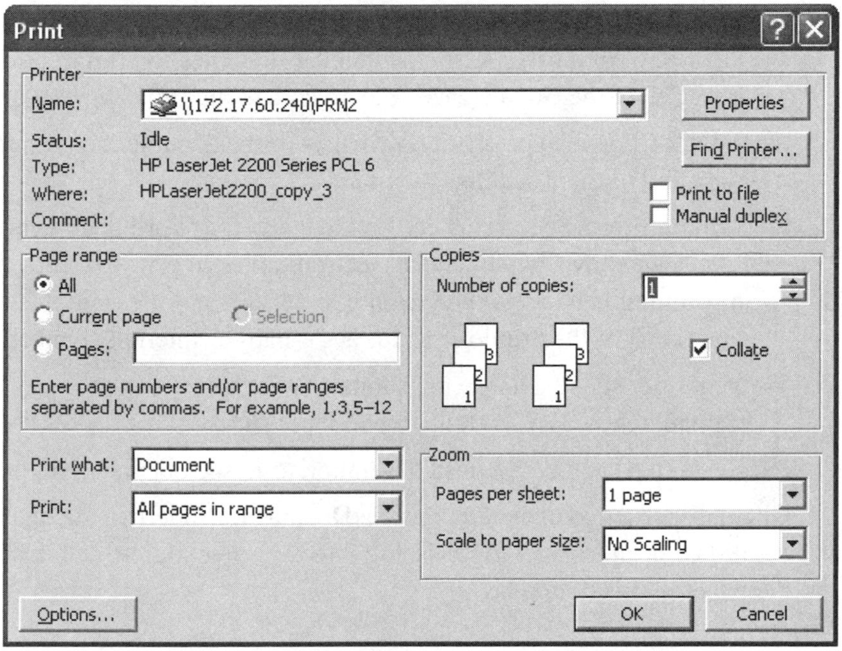

Figure 5.31: Print Dialog Box

The Print dialog box contains the following main options:

- Name: Use this drop-down list to select the printer.
- Page range: If you do not want to print all pages, select the Current page option or type the range of page numbers you want to print in the Pages text box. You may also select a piece of text and choose to print only that selection.
- Print what: Use this drop-down list to print other parts of a document, such as document properties, comments, or styles. The default option is Document.
- Print: Use this drop-down list to specify whether you want to print all pages in the specified range or print only odd or even pages.

 Notice that, by default, the printer is set to print all the pages of the active document.

- Copies: Use this to specify the number of copies to print in the Number of copies box. Select the Collate check box to collate multiple copies.
- Zoom: Choose to print multiple pages of the document on a single sheet of paper with and without scaling.
- Print to file: Select this check box to convert a Word document to a Postscript print file. This allows you to create electronic files to give to print vendors. The quality of printing is better when you directly print from files and it is also easy to submit your work if the printing vendor has e-mail or Internet connectivity.
- Pages per sheet: Choose the number of document pages to print on one sheet. Valid numbers include 1, 2, 4, or 16 pages per sheet.
- Scale to page size: Choose this option to fit the document on the print paper.

Click Properties to open the printer's Document Properties dialog box. You can set additional print choices for finishing effects, paper source, and document alignment on the paper in this dialog box.

Figure 5.32 shows the printer's Document Properties dialog box.

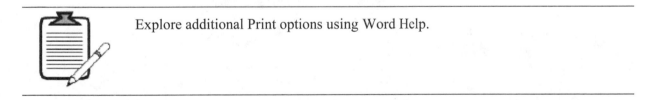

Figure 5.32: Printer Document Properties Dialog Box

Explore additional Print options using Word Help.

It is useful to preview a document before you print it. You can view the document on the screen to check for formatting, layout, and colors, and overall to see how the document will appear printed. You can use the Zoom setting, reduce the size to ten percent and view multiple pages together.

To preview the document before printing, perform the following steps:

1. Click the **Print Preview** button on the Standard toolbar. Figure 5.33 shows the preview of a single page of a document.

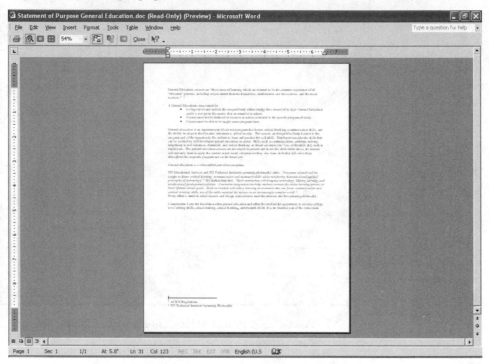

Figure 5.33: Print Preview of a Single Page

2. Click the **Multiple Pages** icon on the Print Preview toolbar and then select the appropriate option to view multiple pages on the screen, as shown in Figure 5.34.

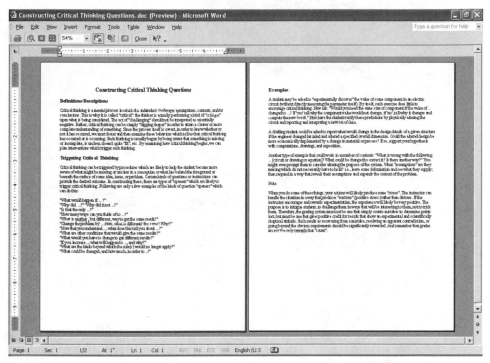

Figure 5.34: Print Preview of Multiple Pages

Print Preview also offers the **Shrink to Fit** feature. If the last page in a document contains just a few lines of text, click the **Shrink to Fit** button to force the last few lines onto the previous page. This feature actually alters the font size to reduce the document by one page.

1. Identify the keyboard sequence that enables you to move data between locations?
   a. Ctrl + V
   b. Ctrl + C
   c. Ctrl + M
   d. Ctrl + X

2. You want to print a table that has 10 columns and 3 rows. Which Orientation option in the Page Setup dialog box is best suited to print this table?
   a. Portrait
   b. Landscape
   c. Vertical
   d. Horizontal

3. Which of the following is true?
   Statement A: A bullet can consist of a pound sign.
   Statement B: A picture cannot serve as a bullet.
   a. Statement A is true, Statement B is false.
   b. Statement A is false, Statement B is true.
   c. Both statements are true.
   d. Both statements are false.

4. Footers should NOT contain:
   a. A bulleted list
   b. Page number
   c. Name of the author of the document
   d. Date

5. Which of the following does not help you emphasize text in your document?
   a. Shading
   b. Border
   c. Bold font
   d. Font size 2

6. When writing down the directions to your favorite restaurant, how will you present the information?
   a. Using a numbered list
   b. Using a table
   c. Using a paragraph
   d. Using a bulleted list

7. Which of the following is true when you cut a selected piece of text?
   a. The text is removed from its original location until pasted.
   b. The text exists in its original location even after cutting.
   c. copy of the text can be seen in its original location while the original text is deleted.
   d. The text is permanently deleted and there is no way to recover it.

5.2 Techniques for Working with Tables

Tables are used to organize data in rows and columns. A table produces a better visual effect than do single ordered or unordered lists.

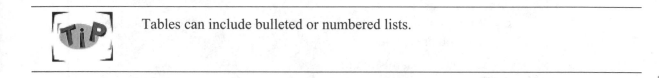

Tables can include bulleted or numbered lists.

A table is made up of a series of cells created as a result of the intersection of rows and columns. Tables can contain text, images, characters, or lists.

You can use a table to present and compare data. For example, consider that you are purchasing a new car and want to compare the price, horsepower, mileage, and seating capacity of several sports cars. The data for the selected cars is shown in Table 5.4.

Model	Price	Horsepower	Mileage (City/Highway)	Seating capacity
Able ZX	$32,500	180@5500	21/29	4
Campy X2x	$33,620	215@5700	18/27	2
Forage Mouse	$28,705	305@5800	17/25	4
Harry Hustler	$32,600	240@8300	20/26	2

Table 5.4: Comparison Between Sports Car Brands

The same information can also be written as a paragraph. However, a quick glance at the table gives all the information necessary for comparison without having to read through lengthy text.

Tables may have cells of differing lengths. You can use a variety of colors and fonts in different cells.

5.2.1 Inserting Tables

Create a table in a document.

Microsoft Word provides a variety of standard formats that can be used to create or modify a table. You can also draw your own table. Tables can be colorful and have visible or invisible separator lines.

To insert a table, perform the following steps:

1. Select **Table → Insert → Table.** Figure 5.35 displays the Insert Table dialog box that appears.
2. Select the number of rows and columns to include in the table.
3. Select the desired table style.
4. Click **OK** to create the table.

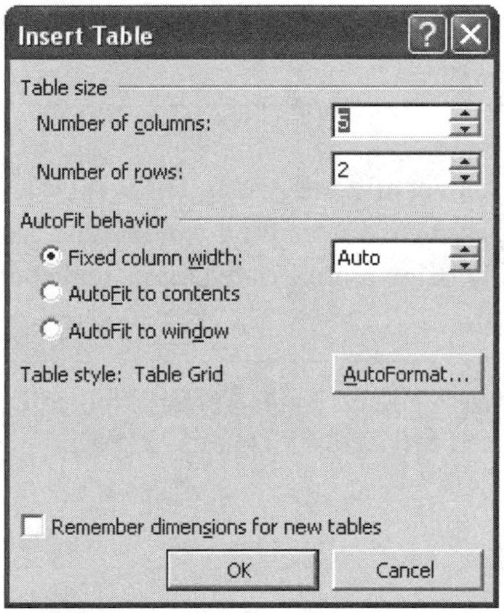

Figure 5.35: Insert Table Dialog Box

You can draw the table using the icons in the **Tables and Borders** toolbar.

You can open the **Tables and Borders** toolbar from the **Table** menu by selecting **Table → Draw Table**.

A third way of drawing a table is by using the **Insert Table** icon in the Standard toolbar. Manually drawing a table allows you to vary the design of the cells and define the depth and width of the area in which the data will be placed.

Refer to Word Help for more options and information about inserting tables in Word documents.

5.2.2 Formatting Tables

Apply automatic or manual formatting to a table.

An important aspect of table management is table formatting. The format of the table defines its appearance. Formatting can include configuring the table with or without border lines, choosing appropriate colors, and specifying the distances between cells.

You can use a Create Table Wizard to create a table. Explore Word Help to learn how you can invoke and use this Wizard.

When the Create Table Wizard is used, you can choose the initial table format. After creating the table, you may decide that the table format does not correctly represent the information and that you prefer another style. To modify the table format in the Word document, perform the following steps:

1. Select the table to format.

2. Select **Table → Table AutoFormat**. Figure 5.36 shows the Table AutoFormat dialog box that appears.

3. Choose from the list of available table styles. You can preview the style in the Preview pane of the dialog box.

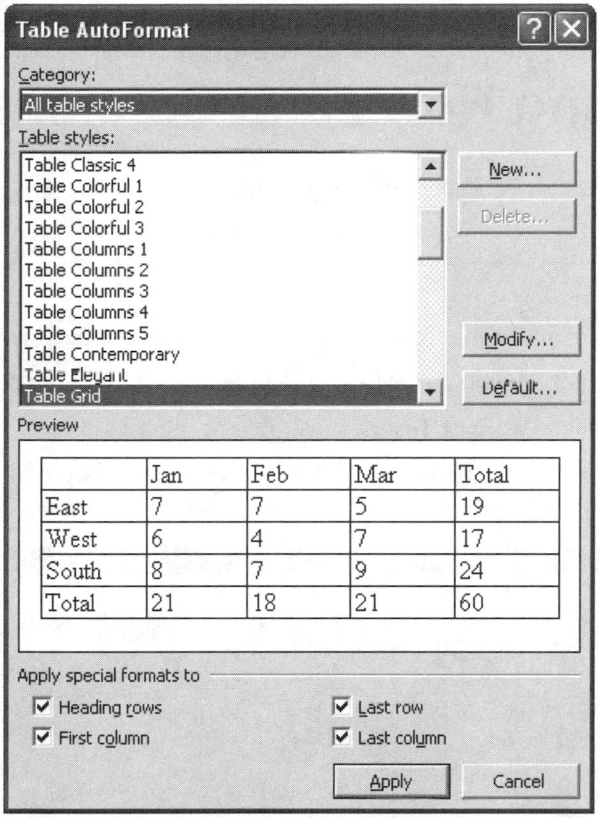

Figure 5.36: Table AutoFormat Options

4. Click **OK** to apply the previewed format to the selected table.

To resize a table, perform the following steps:

1. Right-click once on the table.

2. A resizing box appears at the bottom right of the table. Drag the box using the mouse to decrease or increase the table size. All cells are proportionally moved.

An individual column or row can be resized by selecting a cell. Place your mouse pointer on the bar above, below, or to either side of the cell and then drag the bar to increase or decrease the size of the cell.

5.2.3 Adding Rows and Columns

Add rows and columns to a table.

To insert additional rows or columns to the table, perform the following steps:

1. Select the cell closest to where you want to add the row or column.
2. Select **Table → Insert**, as shown in Figure 5.37.
3. Select from the Rows Above, Rows Below, Columns to the Left, or Columns to the Right options. To add more rows or columns, repeat steps 2 and 3.

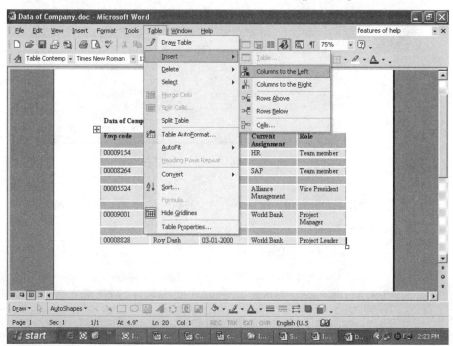

Figure 5.37: Adding Rows or Columns

5.2.4 Deleting Rows, Columns, Cell, and Tables

Delete the rows, columns, cells of a table, or the entire table.

You may need to delete an entire table or individual rows or cells to remove redundant data. To delete a table, perform the following steps:

1. Click anywhere on the table to be deleted, as shown in Figure 5.38.

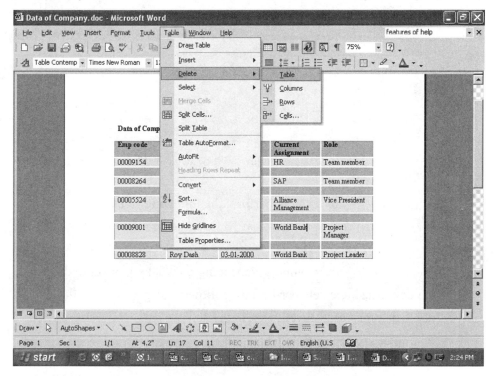

Figure 5.38: Selecting Table for Deletion

2. Select **Table → Delete → Table**. The selected table is deleted, as shown in Figure 5.39.

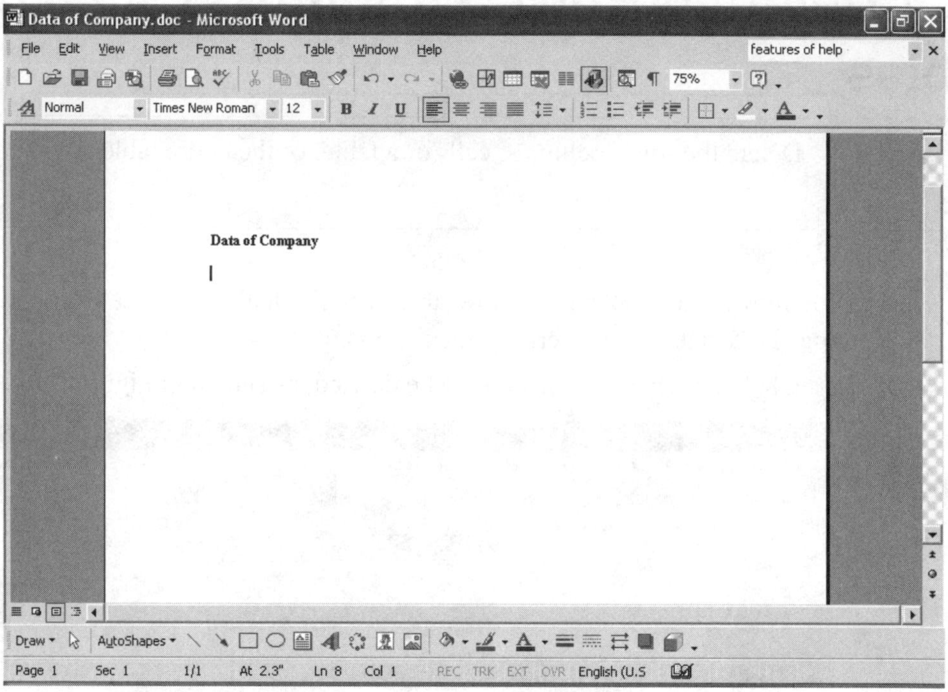

Figure 5.39: Selected Table is Deleted

To delete a row or column, perform the following steps:

1. Click the row or column that you want to delete.

2. Select **Table → Delete**.

3. Select Rows or Columns, depending on what you want to delete.

To delete a single cell, perform the following steps:

4. Click the cell that you want to delete.

5. Select **Table → Delete → Cells**.

6. Choose one of the following depending on how you want the cell to get deleted:

   ▪ Shift cells left

   ▪ Shift cells up

   ▪ Delete entire row

   ▪ Delete entire column

5.2.5 Aligning Tables

 Align tables in a document.

You can align the table with reference to the text in the document. For example, you may want the table to be displayed centered below the text above it. Table alignment can be set to left-justified, centered, or right-justified, as shown in Figure 5.40.

To align a table, perform the following steps:

1. Click the table to select it.
2. Select **Table → Table Properties**. Figure 5.40 shows the Table Properties dialog box that appears.
3. Choose one of the Alignment options in the Table tab.

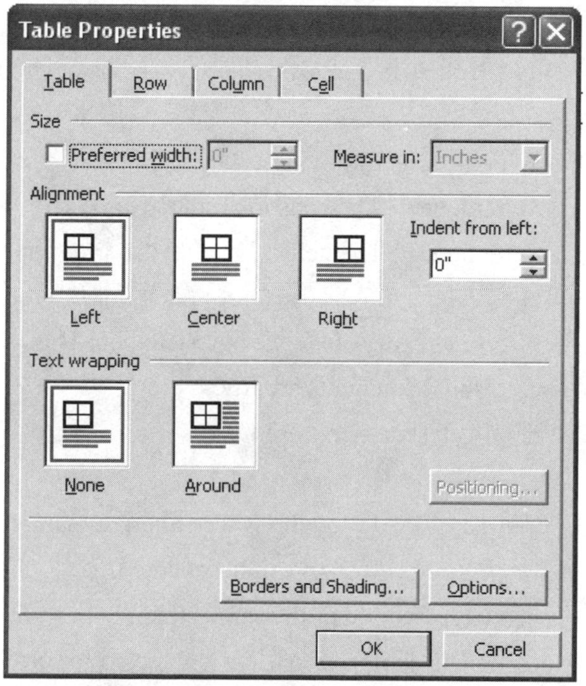

Figure 5.40: Table Properties Dialog Box

Aligning a table does not affect the contents of the individual cells. Use Word Help for more information on aligning tables.

Practice Questions

1. Which of the following is true?

   Statement A: One cell in a table can contain pictures while another cell in the same table can contain only text.

   Statement B: Cells can be individually deleted.

   a. Statement A is true, but Statement B is false.
   b. Statement A is false, but Statement B is true.
   c. Both statements are true.
   d. Both statements are false.

2. Which of the following is true?

   Statement A: The cells in a table can be individually resized.

   Statement B: The cells in a table can only include text.

   a. Statement A is true, but Statement B is false.
   b. Statement A is false, but Statement B is true.
   c. Both statements are true.
   d. Both statements are false.

3. Which of the following is true about a manually-drawn table?

   a. Varied cell sizes can be selected.
   b. Cells will be of the same size.
   c. Cells do not have to be connected to form a table.
   d. A large table is easier to create, if manually drawn.

5.3 Additional Word Features

You can enhance the appearance and usability of your Word document by inserting Clip Art images or hyperlinks. Clip Art is a collection of usable graphics that can be inserted into a document. Word documents can be saved as Web documents to be published on Web sites. Hypertext links to Web sites can be included in Word documents. Word enables you to track the changes that you make while reviewing your document. In addition, you can accept or reject changes in another review round before you finalize your document. You can also insert comments while reviewing a document. This section also discusses the Help feature in Word.

5.3.1 Clip Art

Insert Clip Art into a document.

Clip Art allows you to create greater visual impact in your Word document. The process of adding Clip Art to a document in a Word 2002 document has changed from that in Word 2000 and its older versions.

The Microsoft Web server contains more that 135,000 pieces of Clip Art, animations, sounds, and photos that you can freely download and use in your documents.

If your version of Word is older than Word 2002, use Help to learn how to insert Clip Art. To determine the Word version you are running, select **Help → About Microsoft Word**.

5.3.1.1 Inserting Clip Art

To insert Clip Art in your Word document, perform the following steps:

1. Select **Insert → Picture → Clip Art**. The Insert Clip Art pane is displayed in the Word window, as shown in Figure 5.41. You can search for Clip Art in the various search fields that are available. For example, you may choose "books" as the Search criteria.

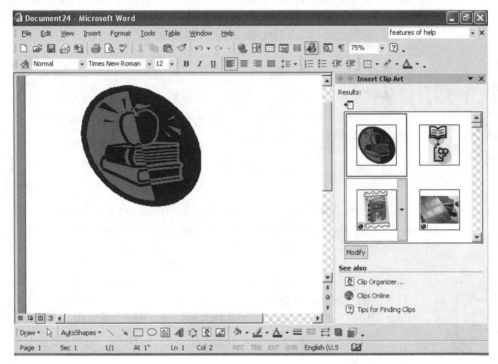

Figure 5.41: Insert Clip Art Pane

2. Click the Clip Art image to be inserted and then drag it to the correct place in the document.

You can also search for appropriate Clip Art in the following general categories:

■ All collections: Includes all categories of Clip Art.

■ All media file types: Includes Clip Art, photographs, movies, and sounds.

Additional Clip Art can also be acquired from numerous online Web sites.

Clip Art can be organized for your own reference. For example, you can start a Clip Organizer named "Friends" that contains photographs of friends to use as Clip Art.

5.3.1.2 Resizing Clip Art

After the Clip Art has been selected and inserted in the document, it can be resized. To resize any piece of Clip Art, perform the following steps:

1. Click on the Clip Art to select it. As seen in Figure 5.42, a border with square handles appears around the picture.

2. Place the mouse pointer on any of the 8 squares in the outline of the Clip Art.

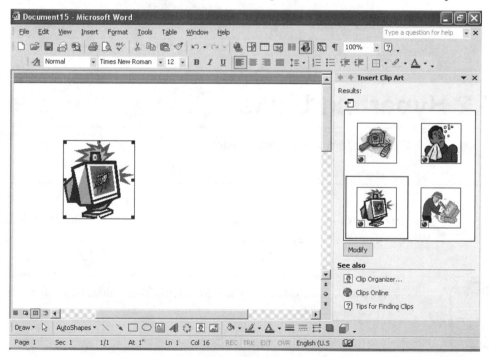

Figure 5.42: Clip Art Sample in Word

3. Hold the left mouse button down and drag the square in to reduce or drag it out to enlarge the picture. Figure 5.43 shows the Clip Art image enlarged.

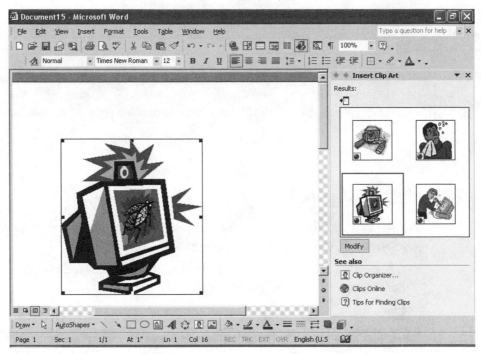

Figure 5.43: Enlarged Clip Art

5.3.2 Hypertext Links

Create hypertext links in a document.

Hypertext links in a Word document enable you to move from the linked text in the Word document to the location of the link.

A hyperlink is automatically added when a Web address, such as www.itt-tech.edu, is typed in.

Hyperlinks can connect to:

- Web sites
- E-mail addresses
- Location in the same document or another document

Figure 5.44 shows an example of text as a hyperlink to a Web site. Hyperlinks appear underlined in the document. You can click the hyperlink to go to the specified location.

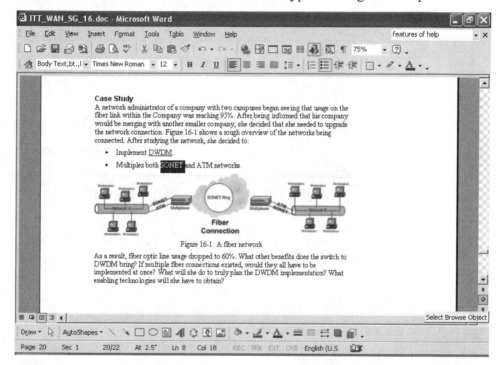

Figure 5.44: Document with Hyperlinks

To create a hyperlink with the text SONET, perform the following steps:

1. Select the text to convert into a hyperlink.
2. Select **Insert → Hyperlink.** The Insert Hyperlink dialog box is displayed.

The text that you wish to convert into a hyperlink is displayed in the **Text to display** field, as shown in Figure 5.45.

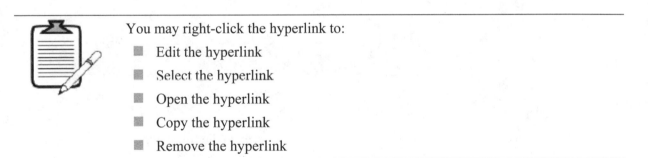

Figure 5.45: "Insert Hyperlink"[MSOffice1] Dialog Box

3. Enter the hyperlink address in the **Address** field. This address is the location where you will be taken upon clicking the hyperlink.

You may right-click the hyperlink to:

- Edit the hyperlink
- Select the hyperlink
- Open the hyperlink
- Copy the hyperlink
- Remove the hyperlink

5.3.3 Web Usage

 Save a document as a Web page and use it on the Web.

You can save your document as a Web page. It can then be accessed through your browser instead of through Word.

To save a document as a Web page, perform the following steps:

1. Select **File → Save As**.
2. In the Save As type drop-down list, choose **Web page (*.htm, *.html)**. The document be saved as a Web page.

 After you have saved your document as a Web page, the Web administrator can place it on a Web server.

5.3.4 Reviewing Documents

 Track changes and insert comments while reviewing a document.

After you create the document, it is always advisable to review it before considering it finished. In addition, your instructor may want to let you see the changes made while reviewing the document you submit. You can add comments and view the tracked changes to the document while reviewing. Tracked changes and added comments are referred to as *markups*.

You can use the **Reviewing** toolbar to toggle between *tracking* and *not tracking* changes while reviewing. Figure 5.46 shows the tracking options in the Reviewing toolbar.

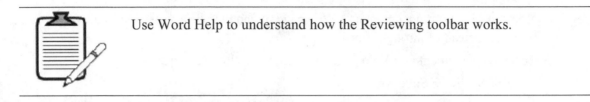

Figure 5.46: Reviewing Toolbar

 Use Word Help to understand how the Reviewing toolbar works.

To track changes while editing, perform the following steps:

1. Open the Word document that you want to review.
2. Select **Tools → Track Changes**. The changes you make to your document will be tracked in a different color.

Figure 5.47 shows a document with changes tracked in a different color.

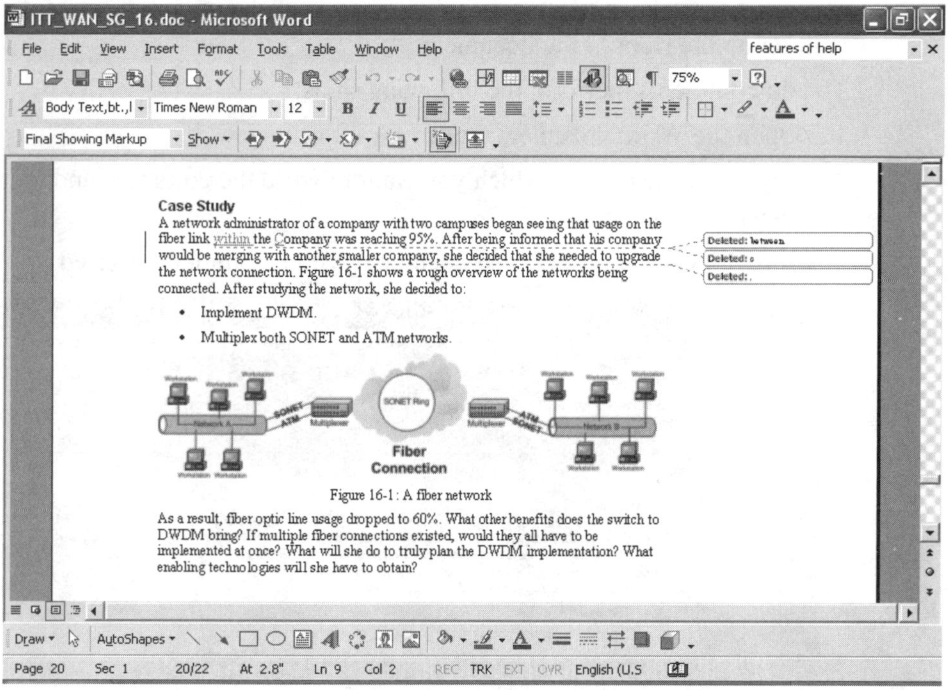

Figure 5.47: Document with Changes Tracked

When tracking is enabled, TRK appears in the status bar at the bottom of the document. You can also double-click TRK in the status bar to toggle between tracking and not tracking changes while reviewing.

The color and format used to track changes can be modified. Changes tracked on a Web document will appear on the Web page. Use Word Help for more information on these features and others.

To turn off tracking, select **Tools → Track Changes**. TRK appears dimmed in the status bar when tracking is turned off.

Comments are used for notes by the author or reviewer. For example, your instructor may want to add comments when reviewing your document. Comments appear as a balloon on the right of the document.

To add comments, perform the following steps:

1. Open the Word document that you want to review.

2. Highlight the text for which you want to write the comment and then select **Insert → Comment**.

Figure 5.48 shows a reviewed document with a comment inserted.

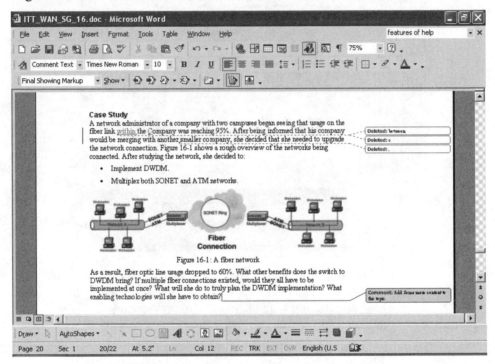

Figure 5.48: Reviewed Document with Inserted Comment

 You can also include voice comments. Use the Word Help for more information on this comment feature.

5.3.5 Using Help

 Use the Help feature to discover and apply additional features or to troubleshoot your document.

Help is the one of the most valuable resources available when using Word. You can access the Word Help menu by clicking **Help** on the Menu Bar.

The Help screen has three tabs:

- Contents: Lists the Help categories.
- Answer Wizard: Allows to enter the information to search.
- Index: Offers alphabetically-organized Help content.

Figure 5.49 displays the Word Help Contents menu.

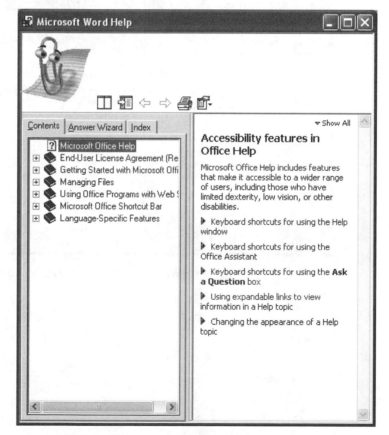

Figure 5.49: Word Help—Contents Tab

You can enter a keyword, word, or series of words in the **What would you like to do?** text box in the Answer Wizard tab, and then click **Search** to get the list of topics in which the search phrase is present.

Figure 5.50 shows the Answer Wizard tab.

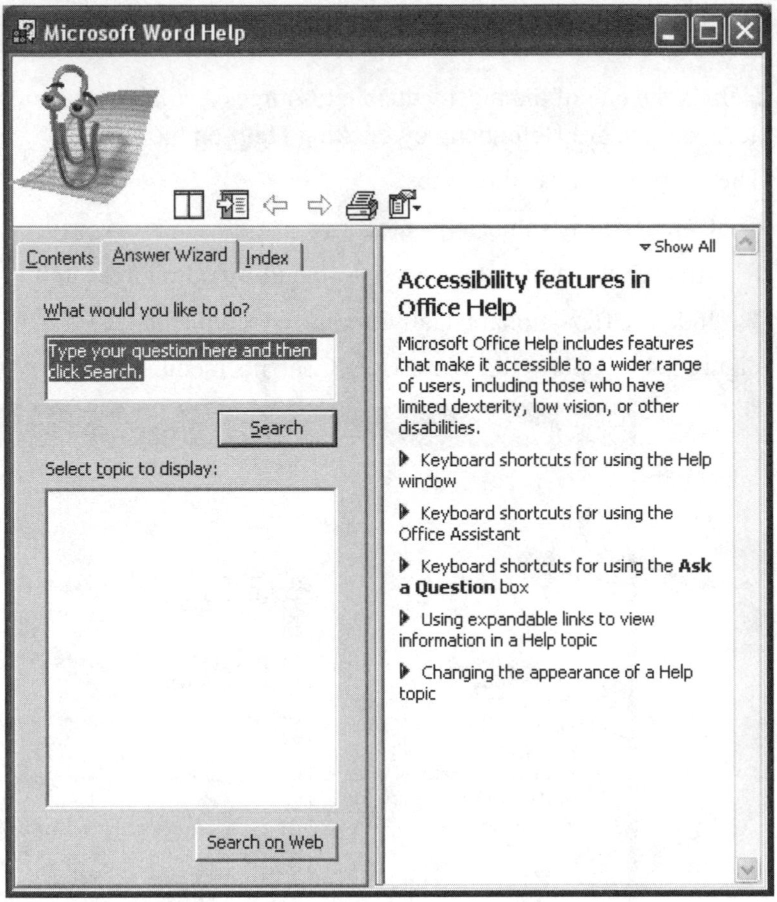

Figure 5.50: Word Help—Answer Wizard Tab

Help can be searched by alphabetized keywords using the Index tab, as shown in Figure 5.51.

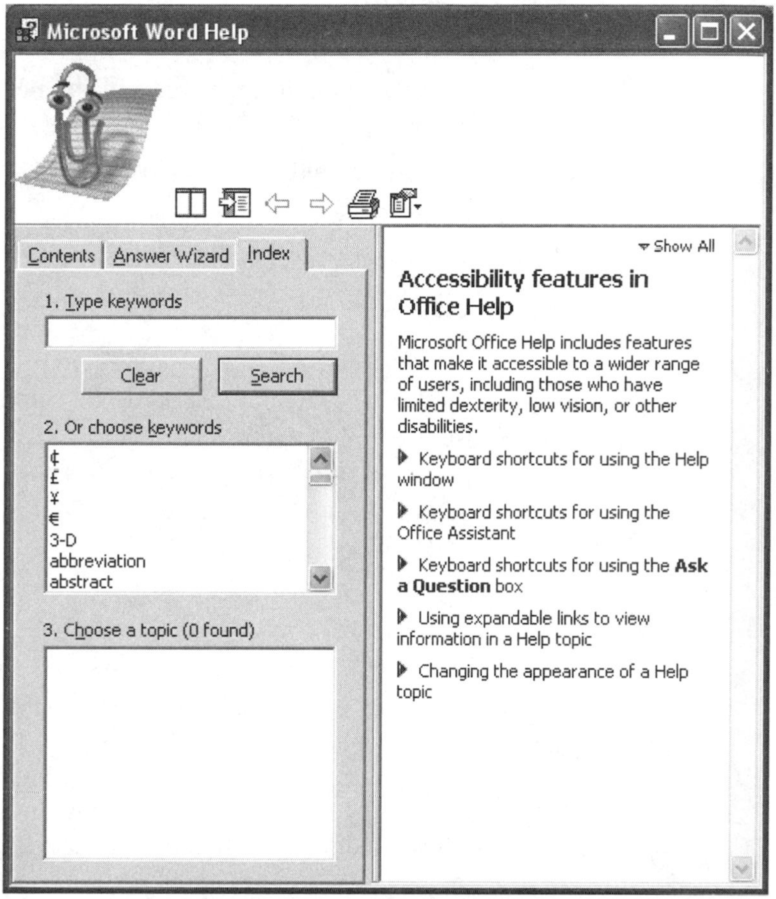

Figure 5.51: Help—Index Tab

You can also use the **Office Assistant** for Help. When enabled, it can be seen as an animated character that offers help as you work on your document. The Assistant is shared by all Microsoft Office programs. The Office Assistant answers your questions, offers tips, and provides help on a variety of features, including some Wizards. The Assistant can suggest Help topics that are relevant to the specific task you are performing even before you request them.

Practice Questions

1. To convert your document into a page readable on the Web, what step will you perform?
    a. Save the document with the .doc extension.
    b. Save the document with the .htm extension.
    c. Print the document.
    d. Cut and paste the document to the server hosting the page.

2. You are sure that the track changes feature is not set when ___ is dimmed and disabled in the bottom status bar.
    a. OVR
    b. REC
    c. EXT
    d. TRK

3. A hyperlink to a networked destination is not available when _____.
    a. network access is not available.
    b. network access is available.
    c. the site or e-mail address specified by the hyperlink is available.
    d. you are not logged on to your e-mail account.

4. Which of the following is true?
    Statement A: Clip Art can be resized after it is placed on the document.
    Statement B: Free Clip Art is available on the Internet.
    a. Statement A is true but Statement B is false.
    b. Statement A is false but Statement B is true.
    c. Both statements are true.
    d. Both statements are false.

5. You are an independent learner. If you wanted to know how to change the color of text when tracking changes while reviewing a document, what would you do?

a. Seek help from a working professional who uses Word.

b. Use Word Help.

c. Ask a peer by sending an e-mail.

d. Ask your instructor.

Summary

In this chapter, you learned:

- Microsoft Word is a powerful data processing application. It enables you to create, edit, and share information as a document.

- Word has many features that can be used to emphasize the information presented. These include:

    - Bullets

    - Tables

    - Borders

    - Shading

    - Font styles

- Word documents can contain hyperlinks to Web sites, e-mails, or other locations within the same or another document.

- Word documents can be converted into Web pages by saving them as .html or .htm files.

- The review features in Word include the provisions of tracking changes and adding comments.

- The Word Help feature enables you to learn more about available features. Additionally, you can use the Help feature to explore features in a newer version of the application.

Reference

- *ONLINE! Microsoft Education*, <http://www.microsoft.com> (September 2003)
  http://www.microsoft.com/Education/MSITAcademy/ITAPOnlineCampus.aspx

Presentation Tools

6

Presentations are valuable tools for classroom teaching, selling products and concepts, and conducting meetings and seminars. In this chapter, you will learn about Microsoft PowerPoint. It is a simple, yet powerful tool used to create effective presentations. You can deliver the presentations personally or through a medium such as the Web. You can create your presentation using a built-in template and enhance its appeal by inserting animations and hyperlinks.

This chapter prepares you to:

- Describe the best practices for creating online presentations.

- Add and modify text for a presentation.

- Describe the features and components of templates in Microsoft PowerPoint.

- Explain how to access and modify the slide master template.

- Draw and arrange shapes in a presentation.

- Use transition effects between the slides of a presentation.

- Create animation effects on a slide.

- Create slide shows.

- Add hyperlinks in a presentation.

- Use the PowerPoint Help feature to discover and apply additional features or troubleshoot your presentation.

6.1 Developing a Presentation

6.2 Working with Templates in Microsoft PowerPoint

6.3 Creating Transitions and Animation

6.4 Additional PowerPoint Features

6.1 Developing a Presentation

PowerPoint allows you to create powerful visual aids that draw the attention of the audience and clearly and precisely explain the topic of discussion. Information is presented in the form of a slide show. Slides may or may not be accompanied by the presenter's narration. In this section, you will learn the best practices to develop an online presentation. You also will learn the procedure to add and modify text to a slide and arrange items on a slide.

This chapter assumes that you have a basic understanding of Microsoft PowerPoint. If you do not feel comfortable with your knowledge of Microsoft PowerPoint, it is strongly suggested that you refresh yourself by completing an online tutorial.

You may access the Microsoft PowerPoint online tutorial from the ITT Tech Virtual Library. Log on to the virtual library at http://library.itt-tech.edu/. From the main menu, select the **Learning Guides** Link. Under **Online Tutorials**, scroll down and select **Microsoft Office 2000 Tutorials**. Select **PowerPoint** from the list of Office Programs. Click the **Begin the PowerPoint tutorial** link to start the tutorial.

Additional PowerPoint tutorials are available on the Microsoft Web site http://www.microsoft.com/downloads. In the **Product/Technology** section, select **PowerPoint** from the drop-down menu. Enter **PowerPoint** in the Keywords section tutorial and then click **Go**.

You can find additional online PowerPoint tutorials using a Web search application to search for the keywords "PowerPoint Tutorial." An example of a site for a PowerPoint tutorial returned by a search engine is: http://www.electricteacher.com/tutorial3.htm

Refer to PowerPoint Help whenever you need more information on a feature or to learn how to use the feature.

Similar to other Microsoft Office products, such as Microsoft Word, PowerPoint has the Menu Bar, Standard toolbar, and Formatting toolbar. However, some of the options in these menus may be specific to PowerPoint.

Explore the PowerPoint toolbars and their options. Use PowerPoint Help to learn the use of these options.

6.1.1 Characteristics of Online Presentations

Describe best practices for online presentations.

The success of your presentation lies in being able to create and retain the audience's attention and make them listen to and understand the salient points in your presentation. You need to decide in advance the desired result of the presentation. This section discusses some of the best practices to follow for online presentations to be successful.

A number of factors can impact the design and features of your presentation. Therefore, before creating a presentation, you need to find answers to the following questions:

- Who is the audience and what is their familiarity with the topic being discussed?
- What are the audience's interests?
- What will the size of the audience be?
- What will the size of the room be in which the presentation will be shown?
- What will the lighting in the room be?
- What is the equipment available to display the presentation? What is the configuration of the following:
  - Monitor size
  - Projection device
  - Screen resolution (crispness of the display)
- Will transition be used between slides?
- Will animation be used?
- Should the slides be created to evoke discussions based on the slide topics?

- Is the goal of the presentation to teach or to motivate?
- Is the presentation unmanned'?

Apart from the presentation logistics, you need to ensure your presentation is effective enough to make an impact. The points to keep in mind when creating slides are discussed next. As shown in a Figure 6.1, slides need to be consistent and blend in an appealing manner with respect to:

- Color schemes
- Backgrounds
- Font sizes, styles, and colors
- Bullet and numbering formats
- Templates

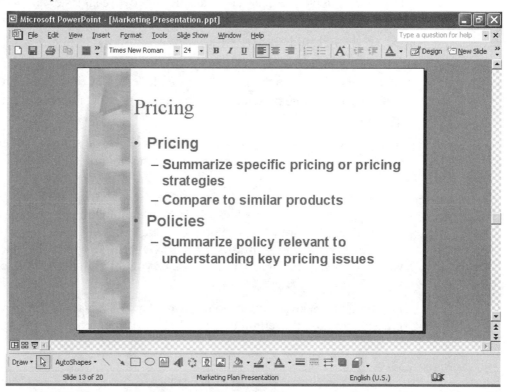

Figure 6.1: A Well-Planned PowerPoint Slide

Some key points to be considered when creating slides are:

- Introduce the main points first: List the main topics discussed in the presentation on the first slide. This prepares the audience for the overall agenda of the presentation.

- Place content on the slide: A slide should have clear key points. Avoid putting too many points on each slide. A cluttered slide is unappealing and distracts the viewer from the main content.

- Give a suitable slide title: The slide title should be crisp. Preferably, it should not exceed one line.

- Use graphics wisely: While graphics enhance the appeal of your slides, it is advisable to keep graphics limited and simple. Ensure that you do not use redundant graphics, as they can be very distracting.

- Use effects in the presentation: Transitions between slides or animations on slides can also enhance the appeal of the presentation. However, ensure that you do not use a poor style of transitions or animations.

- Present points as lists: If a particular slide title contains multiple points, it is advisable to list down the key phrases. Include details of the information in the **Notes** portion of the presentation. This can be used by the presenter to elaborate on the points on the slides.

- Summarize the key points of the presentation: The last slide of the presentation can summarize the key points discussed in the presentation.

If you have never created a PowerPoint presentation before, you can use the AutoContent Wizard in PowerPoint to create a presentation. To start the wizard, select **File → New Presentation → AutoContent Wizard**. The Start screen of the wizard opens. AutoContent Wizard guides you through the steps to create the various slides of the presentation.

For more information on how to use AutoContent Wizard to create a PowerPoint presentation, use PowerPoint Help.

6.1.2 Creating a Master Slide

Create a master slide for your presentation.

PowerPoint has three main views:

- Normal: Useful while creating slides.
- Slide Sorter: Useful to view all the slides together and sort them.
- Slide Show: View the presentation as a full-screen slide show.

There is also a Master view that helps you to control the appearance of a presentation universally. The settings defined in this view control the font, background, and layout of the slides in your presentation. Before putting any information into your presentation slide, you need to create the master slide.

From the Menu Bar, select **View → Master → Slide Master** to open the Slide Master View window, as shown in Figure 6.2.

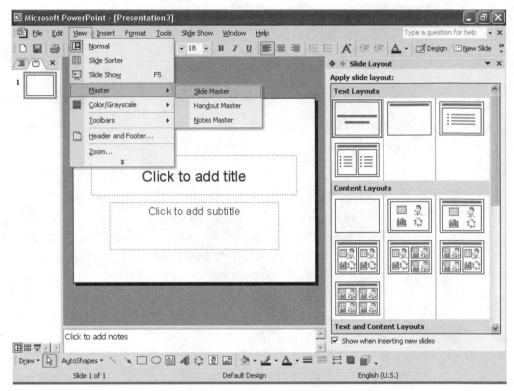

Figure 6.2: Creating the Slide Master

 To close the slide layout options displayed on the right, click the **Close** button in the upper-right corner of the pane.

To set the background of the master slide, perform the following steps:

1. In the Slide Master View window, select **Format → Background**. The Background dialog box appears, as shown in Figure 6.3.

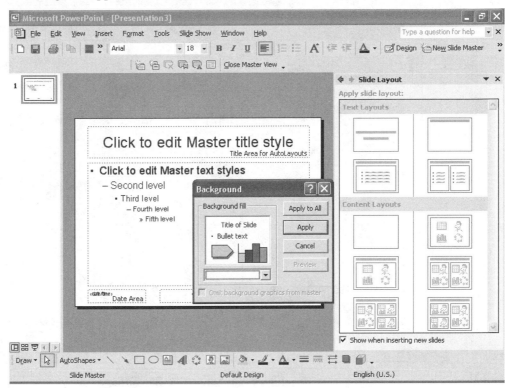

Figure 6.3: Setting the Background for the Slide Master

2. Choose the background color from the **Background Fill** drop-down menu, as shown in Figure 6.4.

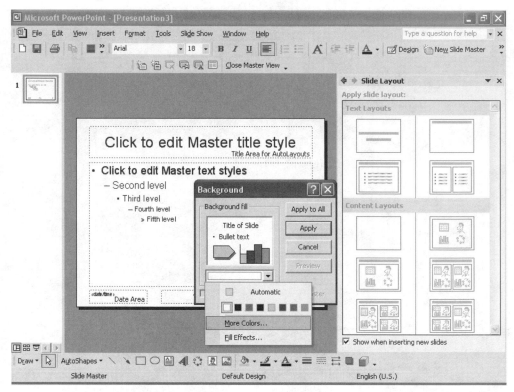

Figure 6.4: Setting the Background Color

You can select the **More Colors** option or the **Fill Effects** option to choose additional colors and shadings.

3. Click **More Colors** to open the Colors dialog box. Click the **Standard** tab to display the standard colors, as shown in Figure 6.5.

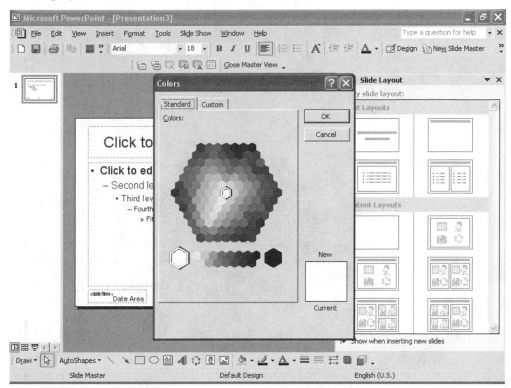

Figure 6.5: Standard Color Spectrum

4. Click a **color** for the slide master background. The box on the lower-right of the screen shows the selected color and current background color, as shown in Figure 6.6.

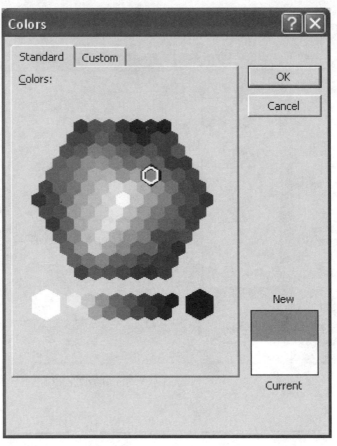

Figure 6.6: Comparing the Selected Colors

5. Click **OK**. The selected color is shown in the background of the Background Fill area of the Background dialog box, as shown in Figure 6.7.

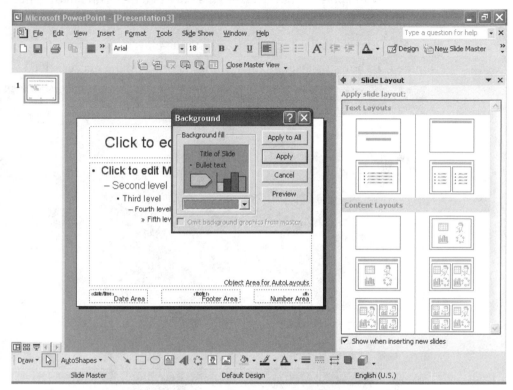

Figure 6.7: Preview of the Selected Background Color

6. Next, you can click:

■ **Apply to All** to replace the existing background for all slides.

■ **Apply** to apply the new background only to the existing master slide.

■ **Cancel** not to apply the background at all.

■ **Preview** to view the slide master with the chosen background.

Figure 6.8 shows the background settings applied on the master slide.

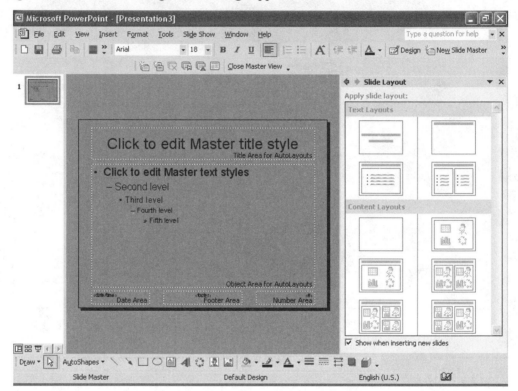

Figure 6.8: Applied Background Color Results

You can also customize the default font, style, and size in the slide master.

To change font features, perform the following steps:

1. Select **Format → Font**. The Font dialog box appears, as shown in Figure 6.9.

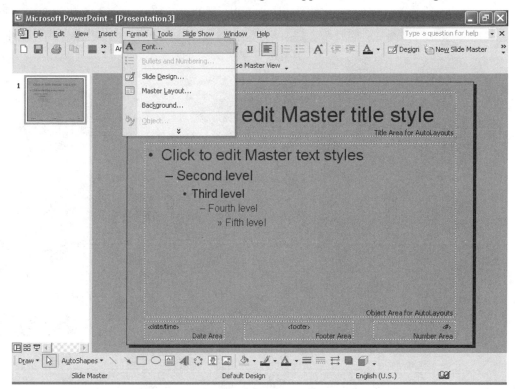

Figure 6.9: Selecting Font Format Option

As shown in Figure 6.10, the various sections in the Font dialog box are:

▓ Font: You can select the required font from the list of fonts available.

▓ Font style: This contains a list of the various font styles, such as:

- Regular

- Bold

- Italic

- Bold Italic

▓ Size: You can select the required size from the list of sizes.

▓ Color: You can select the required font color from this drop-down list.

▓ Effects: This contains a set of check boxes that you can select to set various text effects, such as underlines, shadows, and embossing.

2. To format the font for a particular level, first highlight the text selection on the slidemaster. Then select **Format→Font** and define your settings. For instance, as displayed in Figure 6.10, **Arial, Regular, 18,** and **black** have been selected.

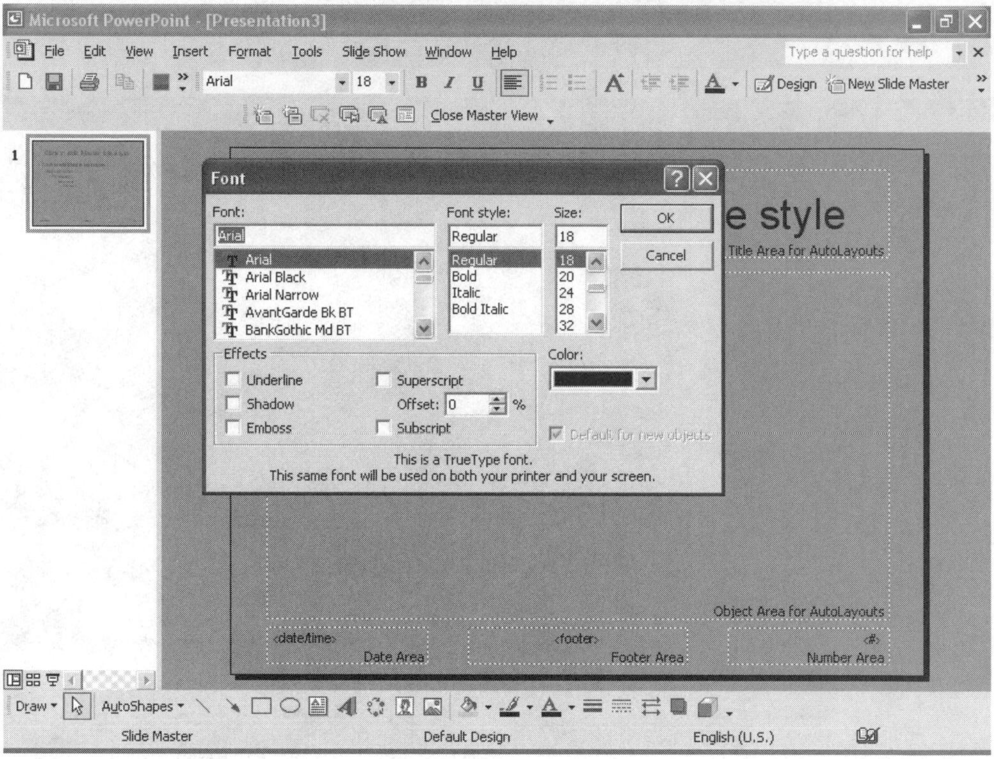

Figure 6.10: Font Dialog Box Options

3. After setting preferences on the Master Slide, click **OK** to return to the Normal view.

    You can see the effect of your settings in the Normal view, as shown in Figure 6.11.

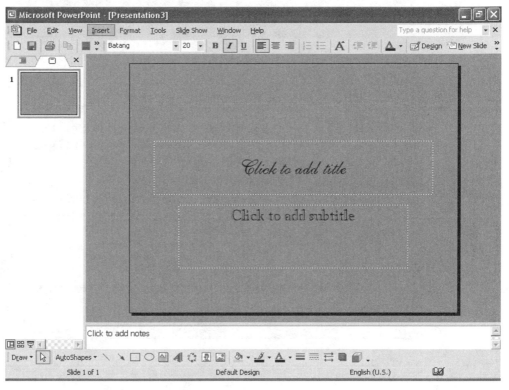

Figure 6.11: Modified Fonts Reflected in Slide Master

6.1.3 Working with Slide Text

 Add and modify text in a presentation.

After the slide master is created, you need to add text to each slide. Most slides contain a heading, with the exception of the title slide and slides exclusively used for graphics. The slide heading should describe the information in the body of the slide.

Figure 6.12 shows a sample slide with text.

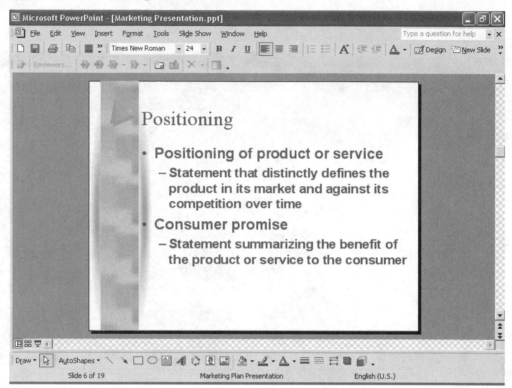

Figure 6.12: Slide Header and Body

The information needs to be presented in each slide as keywords and phrases and not long sentences. There are times when a sentence may be used, for example, when displaying a quote on a slide. Otherwise, the text in the slides is used to present information or to open a discussion.

A slide may include relevant graphics along with text. Graphics should be inserted to improve the appearance of the slide or reiterate a point in the text.

A slide typically contains bulleted points that are discussed by the presenter. Figure 6.13 shows a sample slide with bullet points.

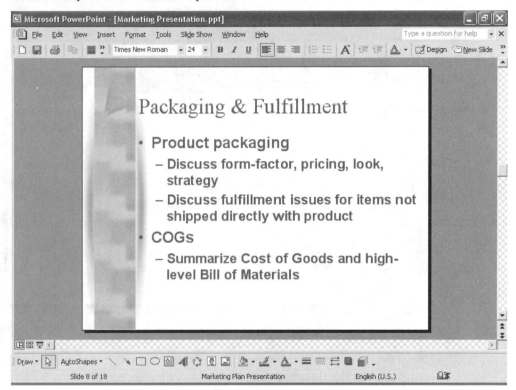

Figure 6.13: Slide with Bullet Points

A slide may contain a series of processes to be executed in a particular order. Such a slide would require a numbered list, as shown in Figure 6.14.

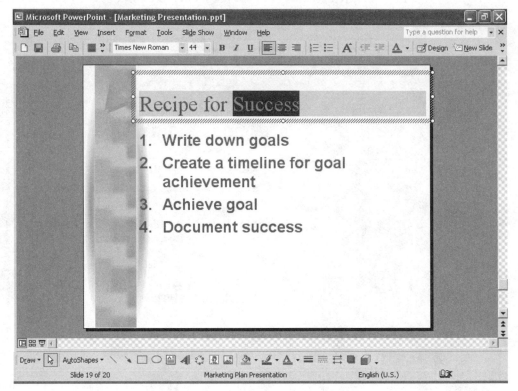

Figure 6.14: Slide with a Numbered List

 Care should be taken to keep the slide uncluttered. A slide is used to present the highlights of a topic and should not contain everything about the topic.

You can enter the detailed text of your presentation in the Notes section in the Normal view. These serve as speaker notes.

To view the notes section along with the slide text, select **View → Notes Page**, as shown in Figure 6.15.

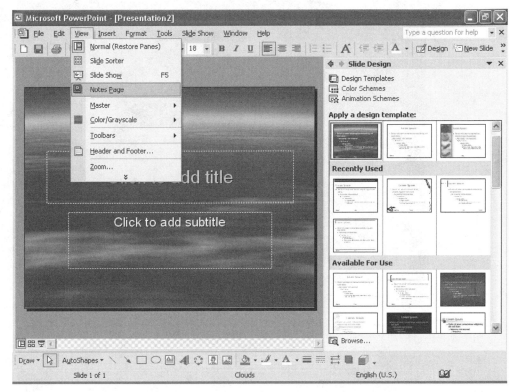

Figure 6.15: Accessing the Notes Page

As shown in Figure 6.16, the Notes Page section is now displayed.

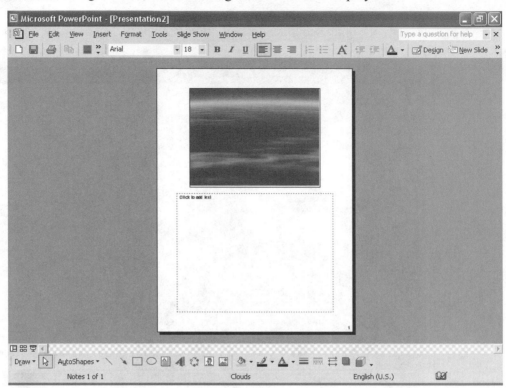

Figure 6.16: Slide with Notes Page

After you have created your slides and speaker notes, you may need to modify them. PowerPoint allows you to view all the slides in your presentation in the Slide Sorter view.

1. To open the Slide Sorter view, select **View** → **Slide Sorter**, as shown in Figure 6.17.

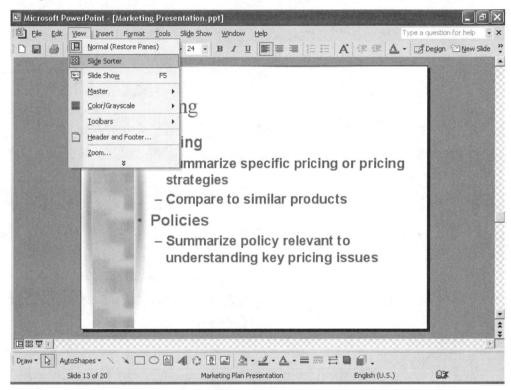

Figure 6.17: Accessing the Slide Sorter

Figure 6.18 shows the Slide Sorter view.

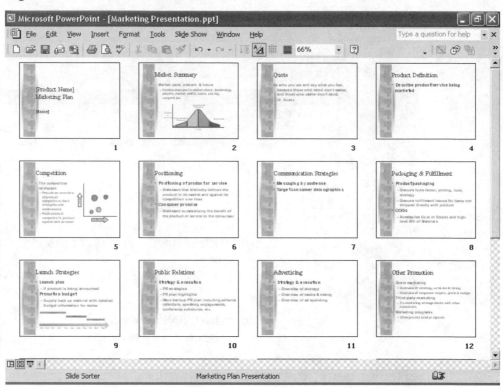

Figure 6.18: Slide Sorter View

2. Double-click the slide to be modified, as shown in Figure 6.19.

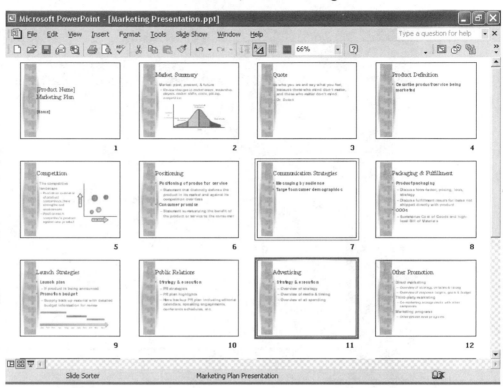

Figure 6.19: Selecting a Slide from the Slide Sorter

The selected slide will be displayed in the Normal view, as shown in Figure 6.20. You can now make changes to the slide.

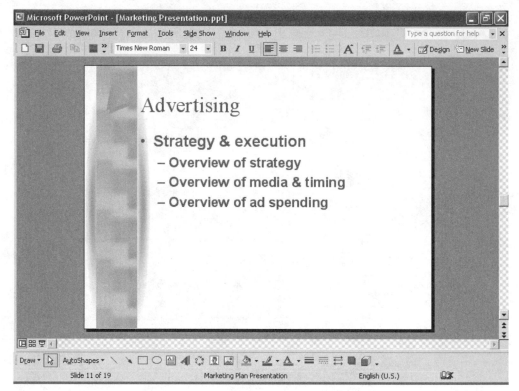

Figure 6.20: Slide Selected for Modification

You can add documents created in other Microsoft Office applications to your presentation. For example, you can import an Excel chart into a PowerPoint presentation. Presenting numeric data in the form of charts or graphs make the presentations more effective and easier to understand.

6.1.4 Using Drawing Tools

 Draw and arrange shapes in a presentation.

You can create and edit drawings in PowerPoint slides by using the **Drawing** toolbar. The **AutoShapes** option in the Drawing toolbar contains some common shapes that you can add to a presentation.

 If the Drawing toolbar is not visible, select **View → Toolbars → Drawing** to display it.

From the Drawing toolbar, you can use AutoShapes to insert:

- Lines
- Connectors
- Basic Shapes
- Block Arrows
- Flowchart
- Stars and Banners
- Callouts
- Action Buttons

Other AutoShapes choices are also available. Explore these choices using PowerPoint Help to find out their potential uses for your presentation.

The various options in the Drawing toolbar are shown in Figure 6.21. You can also see the Basic Shapes options in the Drawing toolbar.

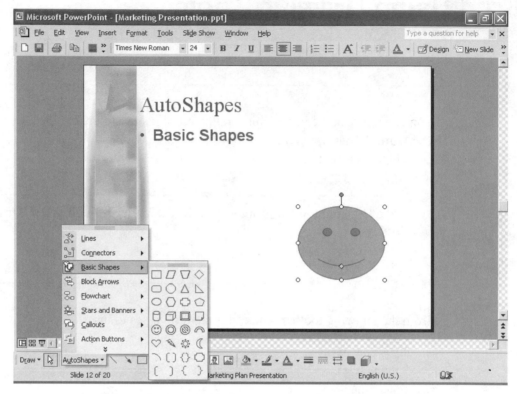

Figure 6.21: Basic Shapes Options in the Drawing Toolbar

The **Action Buttons** option in AutoShapes is used to perform an action from within the PowerPoint slide. As shown in Figure 6.22, the Action Buttons options include:

- Redirect to another slide or Web site
- Add sound
- Add a movie
- Proceed to the online Help feature

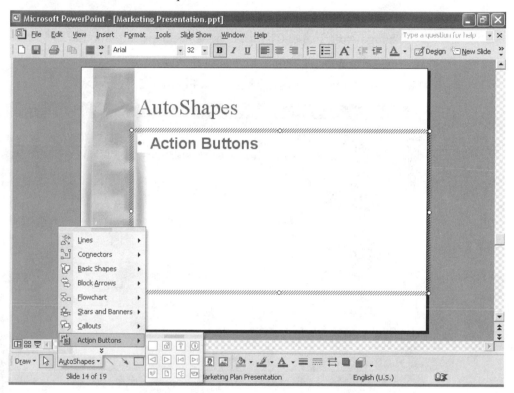

Figure 6.22: Action Buttons Options in the Drawing Toolbar

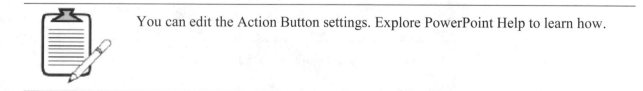

You can edit the Action Button settings. Explore PowerPoint Help to learn how.

The **Draw** icon in the Drawing toolbar offers choices to arrange items on a slide. The various options are:

- ▣ Order: Changes the order of items on the slide.
- ▣ Grid and Guides: Adds a grid to guide placement of text.
- ▣ Nudge: Moves a selected item by a small amount.
- ▣ Align or Distribute: Aligns within the slide.
- ▣ Rotate or Flip: Rotates or flips a selected AutoShape.
- ▣ Change AutoShape: Changes one AutoShape into another.
- ▣ Set AutoShape Defaults: Sets default AutoShape.

The various Draw options are shown in Figure 6.23.

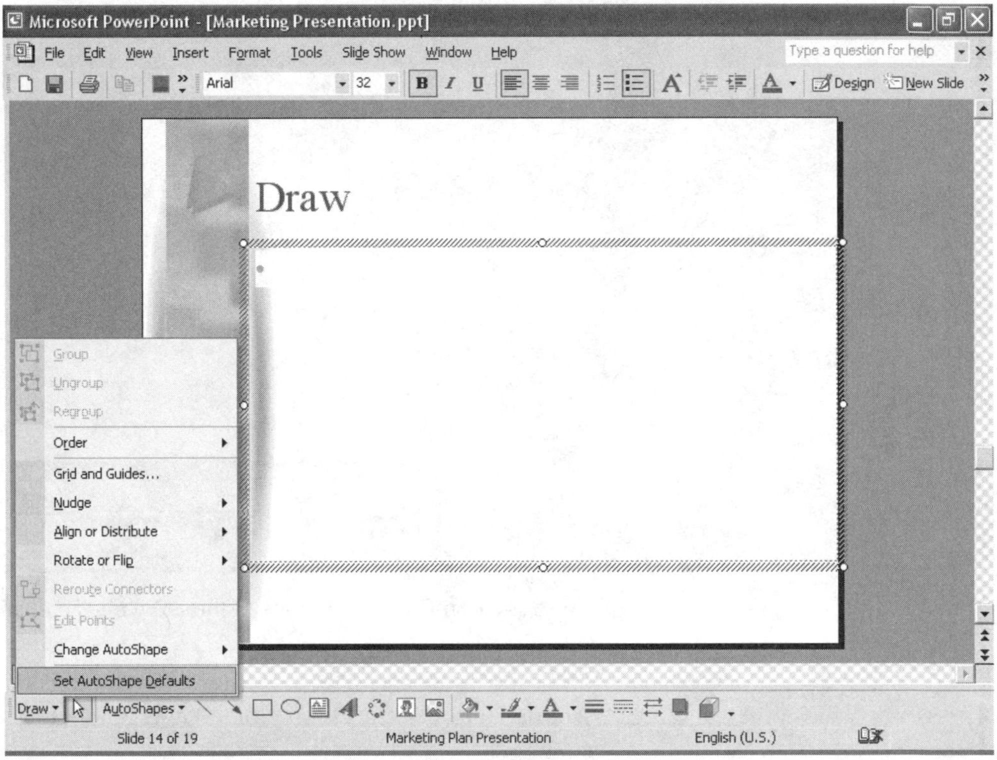

Figure 6.23: Draw Options in the Drawing Toolbar

 For more information on drawing and arranging shapes in a presentation, use PowerPoint Help.

Practice Questions

1. Which of the following is true?

   Statement A: The more information on a slide, the more effective it is.

   Statement B: PowerPoint presentation is a useful tool to present ideas.

   a. Statement A is true but Statement B is false.
   b. Statement A is false but Statement B is true.
   c. Both statements are true.
   d. Both statements are false.

2. Which of the following cannot be added in a PowerPoint slide using the AutoShapes option in the Drawing toolbar?

   a. Line
   b. Stars
   c. Shading
   d. Block Arrows

3. Before creating a presentation, it is important to know the _____.

   I. size of the device used to display the presentation.
   II. size of the room.
   III. favorite colors of the audience.
   IV. loudness of the presenter's voice.

   a. I only
   b. I and II
   c. II and III
   d. III and IV

4. Which one of these is the best practice to follow when creating slides?
    a. Use small fonts.
    b. Use black background and navy blue text.
    c. Insert one bullet per page.
    d. Use a font size and style that is easily viewable by the audience.

5. Which of the following is an AutoShape option?
    a. Stars
    b. Captions
    c. Shading
    d. Quotes

6. When using a PowerPoint presentation in a lecture, which of the following would improve it?
    a. Cluttered slides
    b. Discussion questions in the slide show
    c. No graphics
    d. A dark background image with a foreground font in black

6.2 Working with Templates in Microsoft PowerPoint

A template is a standard design format that provides consistent style to a document. For example, a company letterhead acts as a template for the official letters written by the staff of the company. PowerPoint provides you with various templates that can be used to apply specific styles to a presentation. A template gives your presentation a more professional look. In addition to using the default templates provided by PowerPoint, you can create your own templates or modify existing ones. You can also use the Slide Master to define your own template.

In this section, you will learn about the various template features and how to apply templates to a PowerPoint presentation.

6.2.1 Template Features

Describe the features and components of templates in Microsoft PowerPoint.

PowerPoint templates constitute a blueprint for a presentation. When you create a new PowerPoint presentation, several design templates for the presentation are displayed. You can use a template to customize a presentation. The format and color scheme of a template are predetermined.

A presentation typically has a specific style that is applied across all slides to maintain consistency. Aspects of style include features such as color scheme, font style, headers, and footers. It is difficult and time-consuming to apply the same style individually to each slide. A template therefore saves time and lends consistency to your presentation.

When you open a blank presentation, a basic presentation design is offered. To add a more appealing format to the document, click **From Design Template** in the Slide Design column on the right, as shown in Figure 6.24.

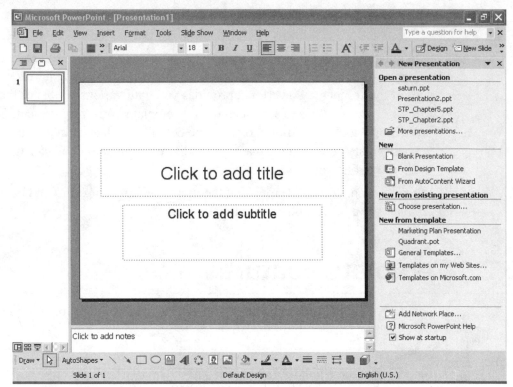

Figure 6.24: Opening a New PowerPoint Presentation

A selection of design templates is displayed, as shown in Figure 6.25. PowerPoint provides a limited number of design templates.

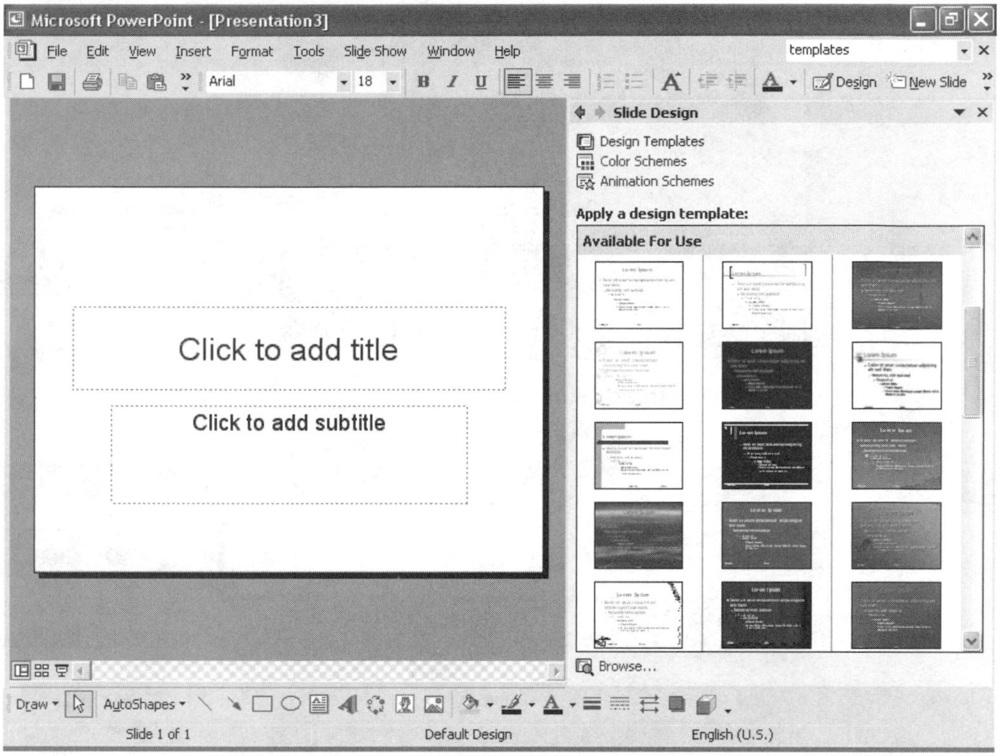

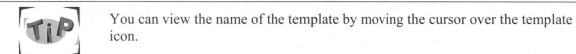

Figure 6.25: Design Templates Options

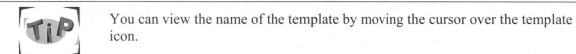 You can view the name of the template by moving the cursor over the template icon.

Click a **template** to add the template design to your presentation, as shown in Figure 6.26.

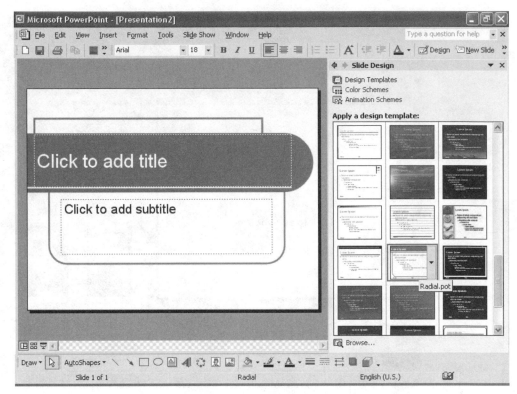

Figure 6.26: Applying a Template

You can now add the content to the slides with the selected design template.

 Additional templates can be found on the Microsoft Office Web site http://office.microsoft.com/templates/.

6.2.2 Creating a Slide Master Template

Explain how to create your own template using the Slide Master.

PowerPoint provides a slide, called Slidc Master, which you can add to any presentation. Slide Master stores elements and formats of style that must appear on each slide in the presentation. Any change made to Slide Master affects the presentation globally. The Slide Master contains configuration features for a template, including:

- Font size
- Color
- Placeholders, including locations of titles, subtitles, and bullets
- Background design
- Animation
- Slide transitioning

You may add these features according to your requirements, or, you may add an available design template in PowerPoint, to your Slide Master.

Now that you have learned how to add slide elements to a Slide Master, we will turn to how to add a design template to a Slide Master.

To add a design template to your Slide Master, perform the following steps:

1. Select **View → Master**. As shown in Figure 6.27, the following options are displayed:

■ Slide Master: Enables you to define master settings for all slides.

■ Handout Master: Enables you to define master settings for handouts.

■ Notes Master: Enables you to define master settings for the notes section.

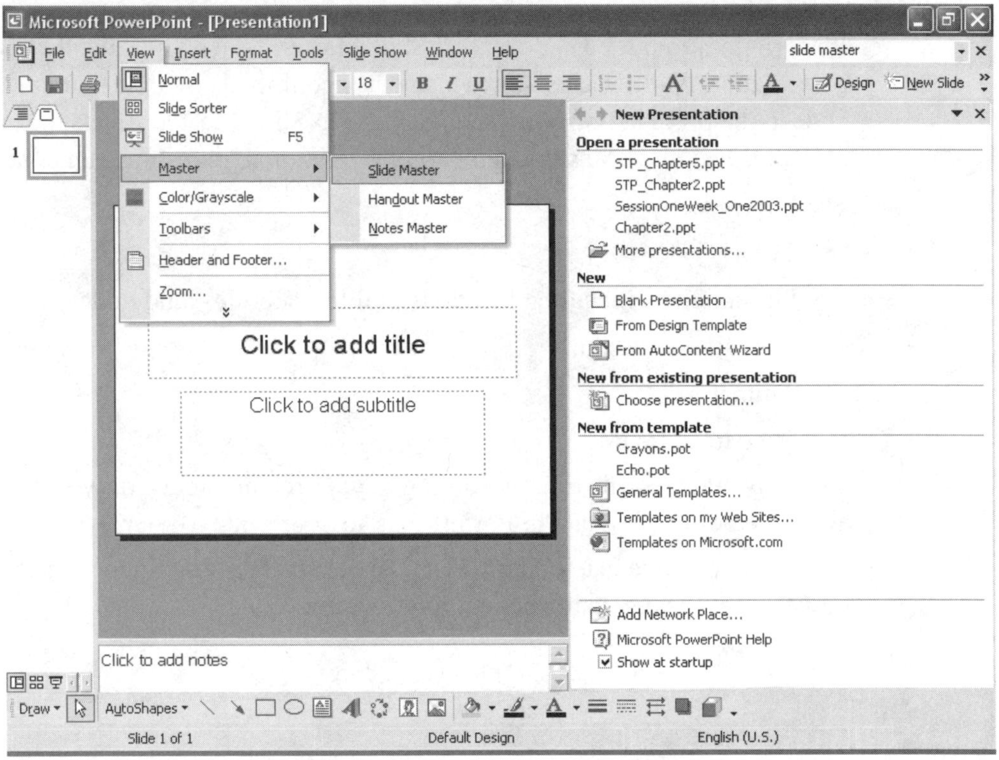

Figure 6.27: Accessing the Slide Master

When a new presentation is created, all elements in Slide Master are set to default values, as shown in Figure 6.28. You can change these values to customize your presentation by selecting the elements and modifying their characteristics, such as font and color. You can also add objects universally, such as text boxes and Clip Art, to a presentation by adding them once to a Slide Master.

As discussed earlier, you can modify the Slide Master to include:

▪ Bullets

▪ Numbering

▪ Font size

▪ Colors

▪ Font style

▪ Background

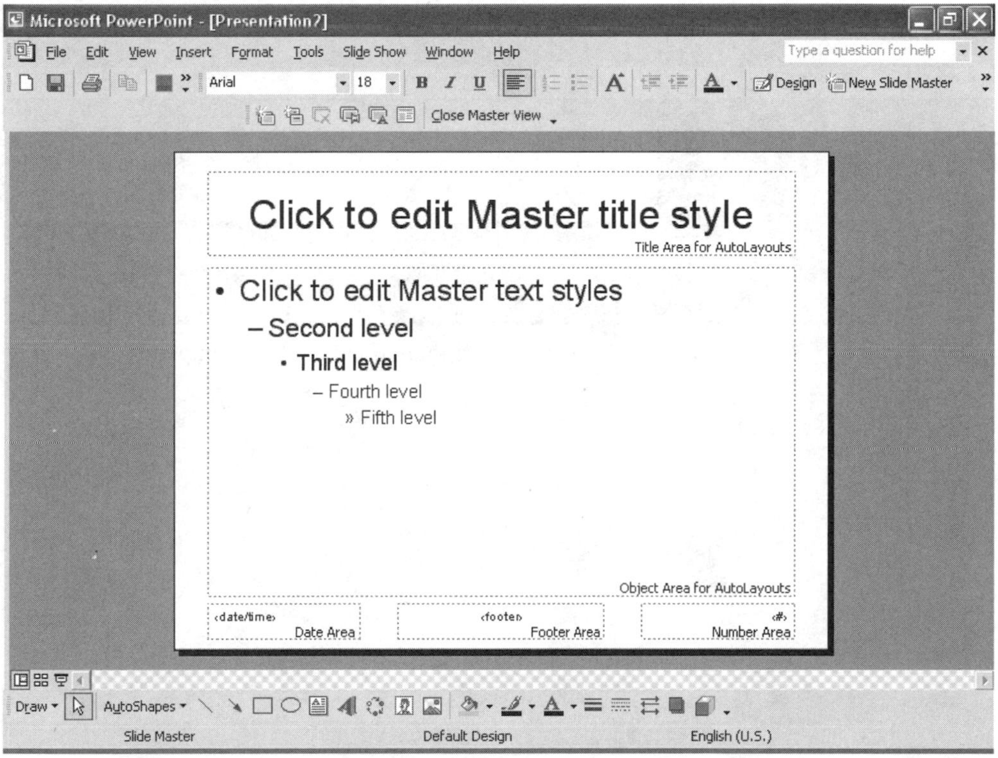

Figure 6.28: Default Slide Master

To add a design template to the Slide Master, perform the following steps:

1. Select **Format → Slide Design**, as shown in Figure 6.29.

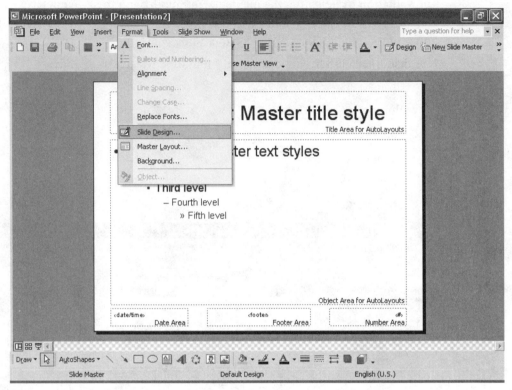

Figure 6.29: Adding Templates

2. Select the design template you wish to apply to the Slide Master, as shown in Figure 6.30.

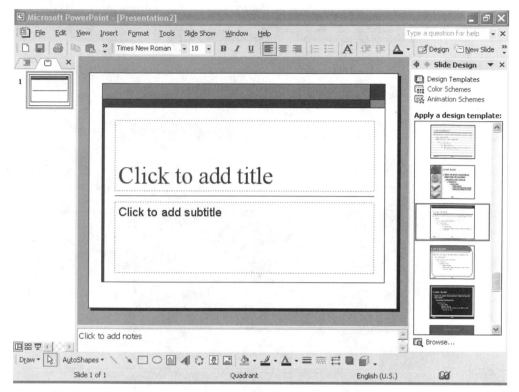

Figure 6.30: Applying a Template to the Slide Master

Multiple masters can be created for a single PowerPoint document. To add an additional slide master, perform the following steps:

1. Select **Insert → New Slide Master**, as shown in Figure 6.31.

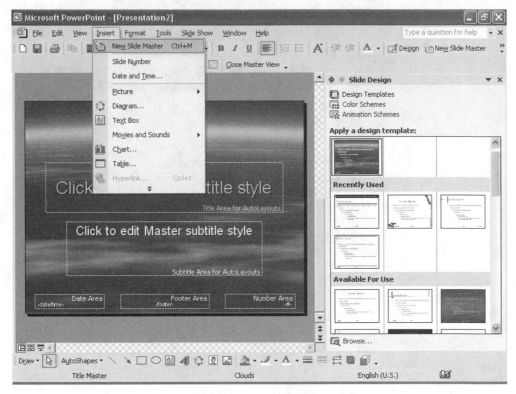

Figure 6.31: Adding a New Slide Master

2. Select the **template** and **format** of the new Slide Master, as shown in Figure 6.32.

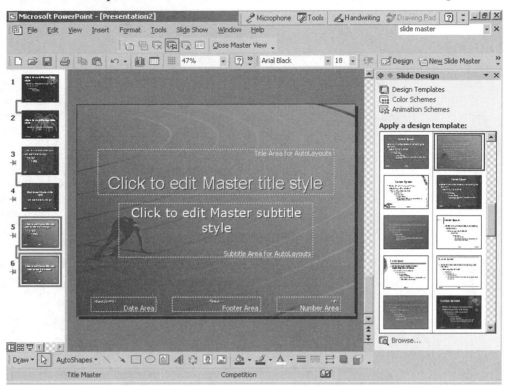

Figure 6.32: Additional Slide Master

You may need to delete a Slide Master.

1. To delete the slide master, select **View → Master → Slide Master**, as shown in Figure 6.33.

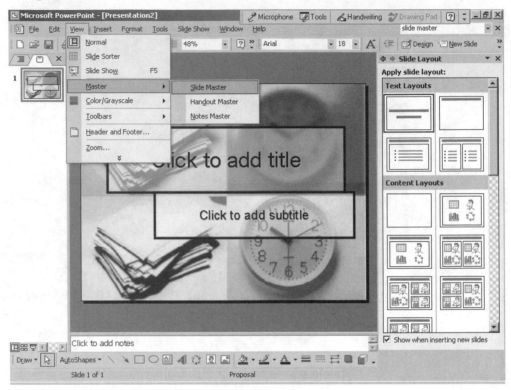

Figure 6.33: Selecting the Slide Master for Deletion

2. Right-click the master to be deleted and then select **Delete Slide**, as shown in Figure 6.34.

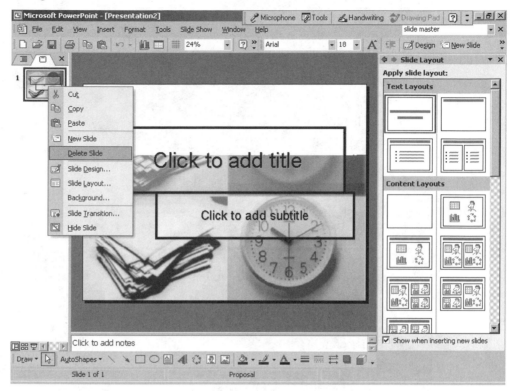

Figure 6.34: Deleting a Slide Master

 Use the PowerPoint Help feature for more information about Slide Masters.

1. Templates serve as a _____ for a presentation.
   I. wizard.
   II. graphic.
   III. blueprint.
   a. II only
   b. III only
   c. I and II
   d. II and III

2. When you start creating a new PowerPoint presentation, the default slide created does NOT contain _____.
   I. font style
   II. shading
   III. pictures
   IV. text
   a. I and II
   b. II and III
   c. I, II and III
   d. I, II, and IV

3. How many masters can be configured for a single presentation?
   a. None
   b. One
   c. Two
   d. No known limit

4. PowerPoint would be the appropriate application for which of the following?

   a. Creating a resume.

   b. Balancing your check book.

   c. Determining an auto loan payback period.

   d. Enhancing a presentation on a research project.

5. When you are unsure about a particular feature of PowerPoint, what would be your best course of action?

   a. Do nothing, do not use the feature.

   b. Use a Web search engine to find information about the feature.

   c. Use the PowerPoint Help feature.

   d. Go to the Web site www.PowerPointQuestions.org.

6. Which of the following statements is true about a PowerPoint Slide Master?

   a. A master can be modified at any time.

   b. Only one master is allowed per document.

   c. A master must be created during the initial document creation.

   d. A master must have color.

7. Which of the following can a PowerPoint Slide Master contain?

   I. Bullets and numbering

   II. Fixed font size

   III. Footer

   a. I and II

   b. I and III

   c. II and III

   d. I, II, and III

6.3 Creating Transitions and Animations

Sound and video effects can make a presentation come alive for the audience. You can make a presentation more attractive and interesting by adding transitions and animation to it, or by adding sound, video, or animated pictures from either a file or Clip Art gallery. PowerPoint also allows you to control the time, speed, and style of animated objects in your presentation.

If a presentation is being used for a *kiosk*—a computer that is not manned and has a continuously-running PowerPoint slide presentation—it is important that the movement between slides is not too fast or too slow. Each slide can be individually configured to allow for a variety of animations, such as fading in, fading out, coming in from the left of the page, or starting from the bottom of the page. You can add animation to objects located on either the Slide Master or on a specific slide.

6.3.1 Transitions Between Slides

 Use transition effects between the slides of a presentation.

Transitioning controls the movement between slides when performing a slide show. A presentation may be more effective if transitioning of the slides is added. The transition of fading in or out of a slide may make the slide show more interesting. Adding sound to the slide show can add impact if there is no accompanying lecture.

To set slide transitions, perform the following steps:

1. Select **Slide Show → Slide Transition**, as shown in Figure 6.35.

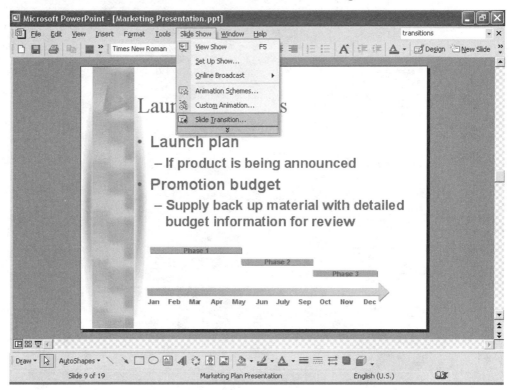

Figure 6.35: Selecting the Slide Transition Option

The various slide transition options are displayed on the extreme right pane, as shown in Figure 6.36.

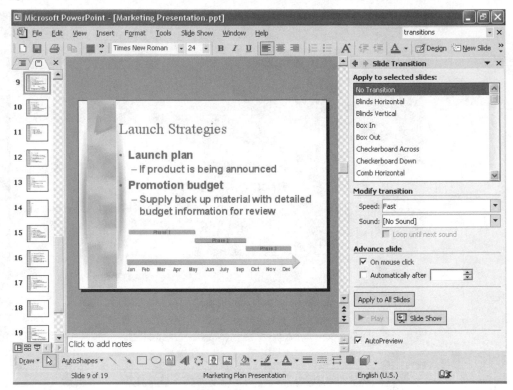

Figure 6.36: Slide Transition Options

Some of the slide transition options include:

- No transition (default)
- Blinds Vertically
- Blinds Horizontally
- Box In
- Box Out
- Checkerboard Across
- Checkerboard Down

2. Select a transition option and press **Play** to test the transition, as shown in Figure 6.37.

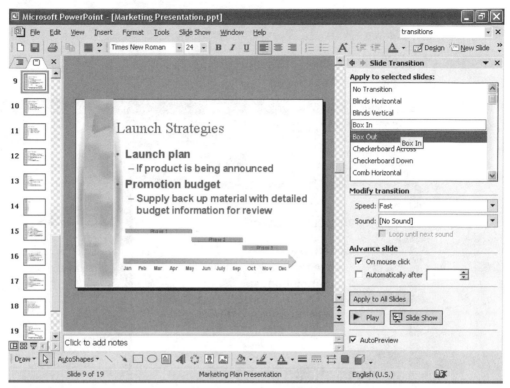

Figure 6.37: Testing Transitions

Always test the effect of transitions before you finalize your settings. Not all transitions in a presentation may be appropriate for the content and context of your presentation.

Transition speeds can be modified to make the movement between slides faster or slower using the **Speed** option in the Modify transition section, as shown in Figure 6.38. Speed options include:

- Slow
- Medium
- Fast

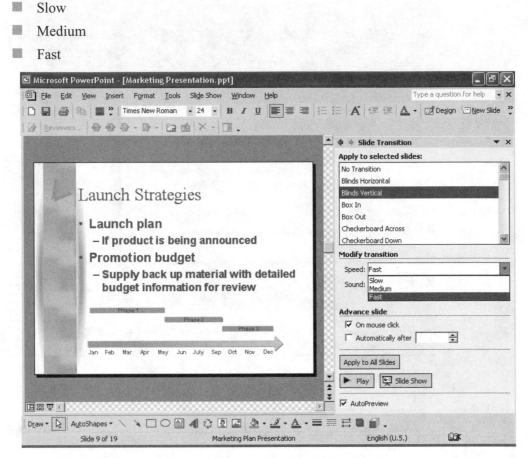

Figure 6.38: Setting the Transition Speed

Sound can also be added to the presentation using the Sound option in the **Modify transition** section, as shown in Figure 6.39. Any type of .wav (Wave sound file) can be added.

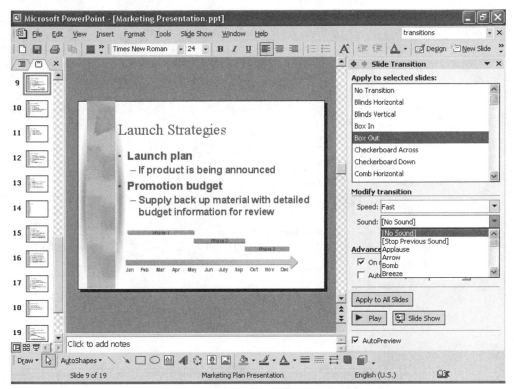

Figure 6.39: Setting the Transition Sound

After selecting the transition method, speed, and sound, choose **Apply to All Slides** and then select **Slide Show** to view the results. Figure 6.40 shows the slide show that is created with customized settings for slide transition and sound.

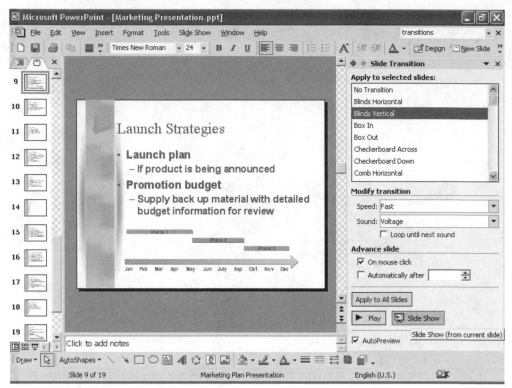

Figure 6.40: Slide Show

6.3.2 Animations

Create animation effects on a slide.

Animation is added to a slide show to capture the audience's attention. To add animations to a slide, select **Slide Show → Animation Schemes**, as shown in Figure 6.41.

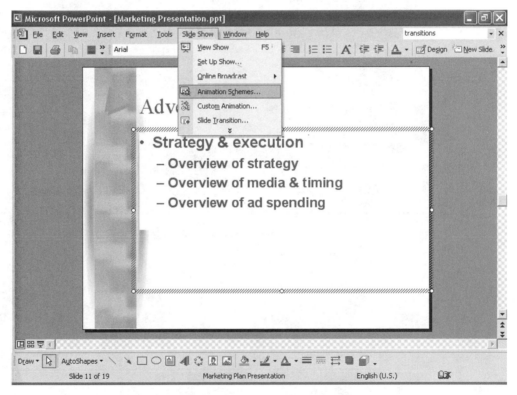

Figure 6.41: Adding Animations

The Animation Schemes options appear in the extreme right pane, as shown in Figure 6.42.

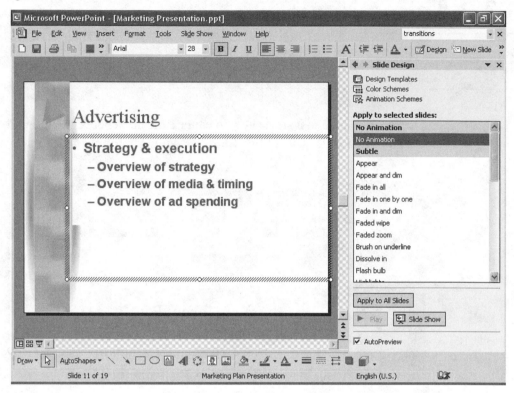

Figure 6.42: Animation Schemes Options

As shown in Figure 6.43, click the required animation option to select it. The current slide immediately shows the effect of the animation. The animation will only be applied to the current slide. Click **Apply to All Slides** to apply the animation for the entire presentation.

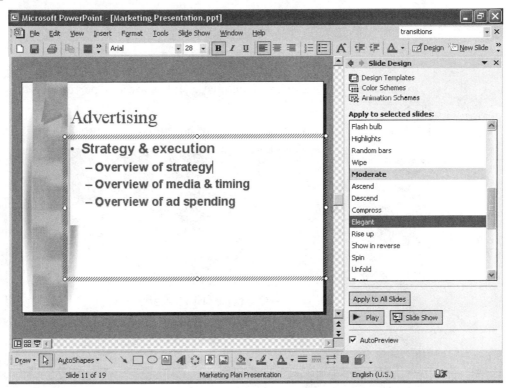

Figure 6.43: Elegant Animation Option

6.3.3 Slide Shows

Create manual and automatic slide shows.

You can configure manual and automatic slide shows by performing the following steps:

1. Select **Slide Show → Set Up Show**, as shown in Figure 6.44.

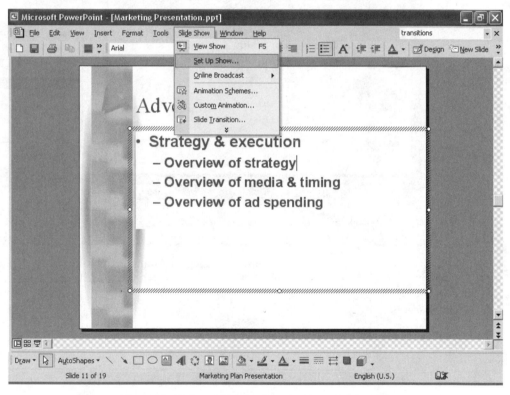

Figure 6.44: Invoking the Set Up Show Dialog Box

The **Set Up Show** dialog box is displayed, as shown in Figure 6.45.

Figure 6.45: Set Up Show Dialog Box

The slide show options include:

- Show type
    - Presented by speaker (full screen)
    - Browsed by an individual (window)
    - Browsed at a kiosk (full screen)
- Show slides
    - All slides
    - Selected slides
- Show options
    - Loop continuously until "Esc"
    - Show without narration

- Show without animation
- Advance slides
  - Manually
  - Using timings, if present
- Pen color—select color of the pen that is displayed during the slide show.
- Multiple monitors—If multiple monitors are present, choose the PowerPoint display monitor for the slide show to appear on.
- Performance—If advanced graphics hardware is available to provide better resolution, enable the **Use hardware graphics acceleration** check box.
- Slide show resolution.

2. Define settings for your slide show.

3. Select **OK** to accept slide show configurations that are suitable for your requirements.

To start the slide show presentations select **View → Slide Show**. The slide show starts, as shown in Figure 6.46.

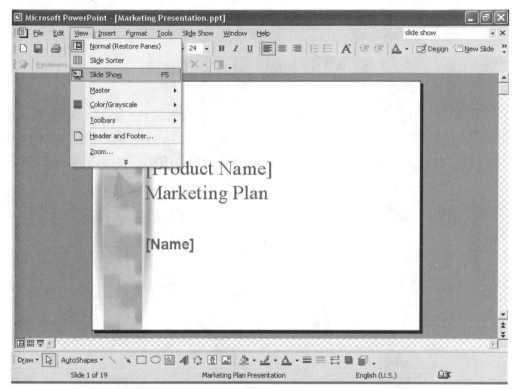

Figure 6.46: Starting the Slide Show

 You can also start the slide show by pressing the **F5** key.

If one of the full screen options was chosen, the slide show is displayed on the entire monitor, as shown in Figure 6.47.

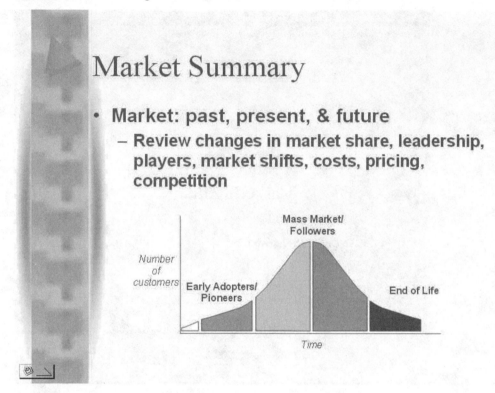

Figure 6.47: Full Screen Slide Show

Practice Questions

1. The movement between slides in a kiosk is controlled through which of the following?

    a. Animation

    b. AutoShapes

    c. Templates

    d. Transitioning

2. Which of the following statements is true about animation in PowerPoint?

    a. Animation can be applied to one slide only.
    b. Animation must be applied to all slides or none in a presentation.
    c. Animation controls the movement between slides.
    d. Animation is not available in PowerPoint.

3. Identify the file type that can be used to incorporate sound in a PowerPoint slide show?

    a. .doc
    b. .ppt
    c. .vaw
    d. .wav

4. Which of the following statements is true about a PowerPoint slide show?

    I. A slide show can only run manually.
    II. A slide show can only run automatically.
    III. A slide show can run manually as well as automatically.

    a. I only
    b. II only
    c. III only
    d. I and II

6.4 Additional PowerPoint Features

PowerPoint has some additional features that make it a valuable tool for conveying your ideas. Additional features, such as the capability to add hyperlinks to slides, make your presentation very effective. The presenter can click the hyperlink and the presentation is directed to the location specified in the link.

A necessary and powerful PowerPoint feature is Help. Whenever you are in doubt about a PowerPoint feature, you can use the Help feature.

6.4.1 Hyperlinks

 Create hyperlinks in a presentation.

Hyperlinks can be used to redirect the presenter to another location from within the slide show.

To create a hyperlink in a presentation, perform the following steps:

1. Open a PowerPoint slide and then select **Insert → Hyperlink**, as shown in Figure 6.48.

Figure 6.48: Inserting a Hyperlink into PowerPoint

This opens the **Insert Hyperlink** dialog box, as shown in Figure 6.49.

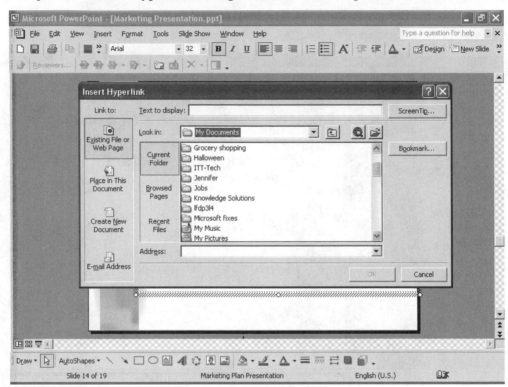

Figure 6.49: Insert Hyperlink Dialog Box

2. Enter the text to display as the hyperlink on the slide in the **Text to display** text box, as shown in Figure 6.50. After choosing the hypertext to display, choose a **location** to link to. Locations include:

▪ An existing file or Web page

▪ A place in the current document

▪ A new document

▪ An e-mail address

In this example, the hypertext on the slide is ITT-tech and the link location is the Web address http://www.itt-tech.edu, as shown in Figure 6.50.

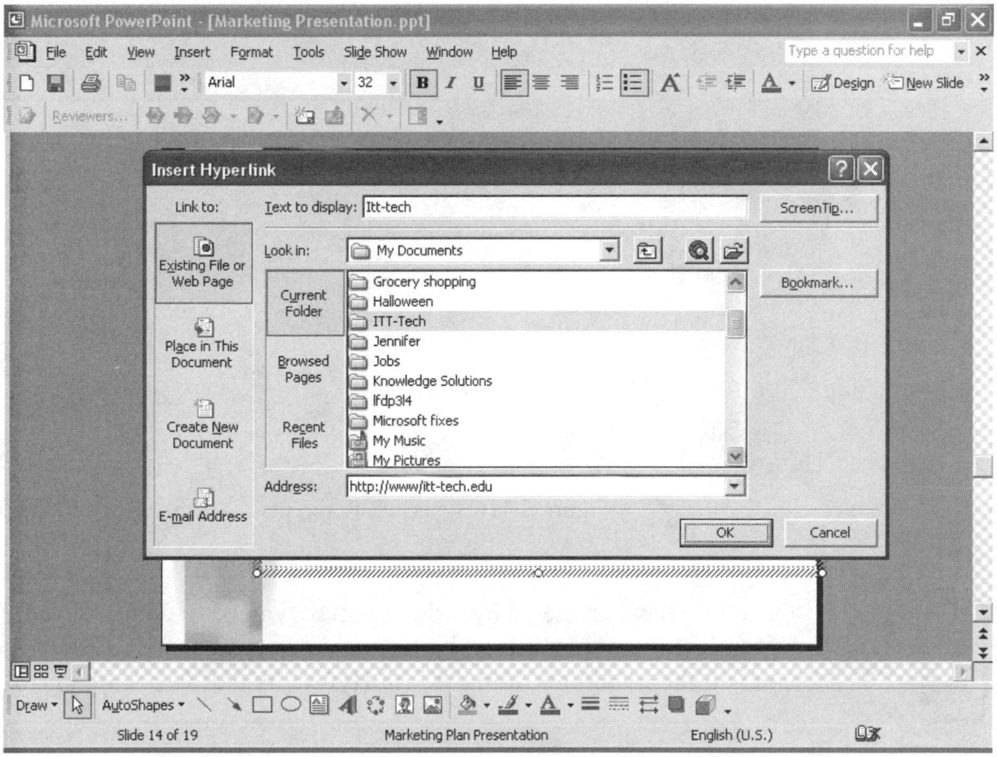

Figure 6.50: Inserting a Hyperlink

3. In the slide show, click once on the **hyperlink** to be redirected to the address specified, as shown in Figure 6.51. You are redirected to the location specified in the Insert Hyperlink dialog box.

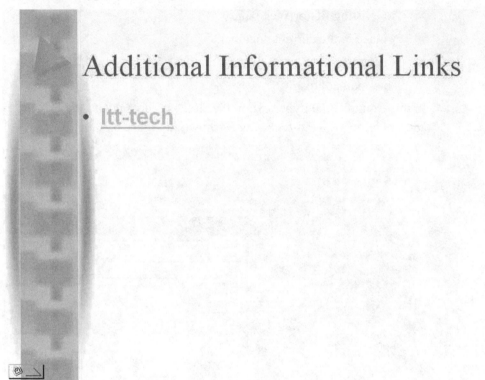

Figure 6.51: Hyperlink Redirects to the Specified Location

Once you have created a hyperlink, you may need to edit it. To edit a hyperlink, right-click the **hyperlink** in the Normal view, and choose **Edit Hyperlink**. You can edit the hyperlink from the Edit Hyperlink dialog box that is displayed.

6.4.2 Using Help

 Use PowerPoint Help to learn and apply additional features or troubleshoot your presentation.

The **Help** feature in Microsoft PowerPoint is very useful. You can use it to explore features that you may not have studied about or learn about features added to a newer version of the application. You can also utilize Help to troubleshoot your presentation.

 The Help feature in Microsoft PowerPoint is similar to that of Microsoft Word's.

To access Help in PowerPoint, perform the following steps:

1. From the Menu Bar, select **Help → Microsoft PowerPoint Help**, as shown in Figure 6.52.

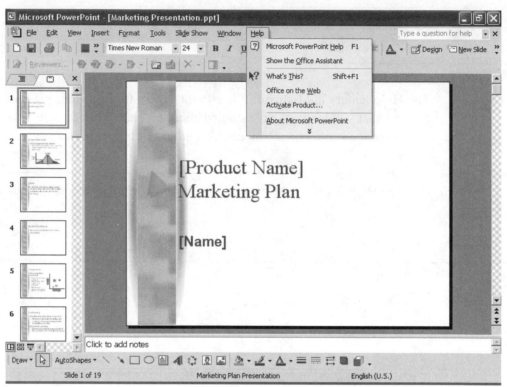

Figure 6.52: Accessing PowerPoint Help

The various Help options are shown in Figure 6.53.

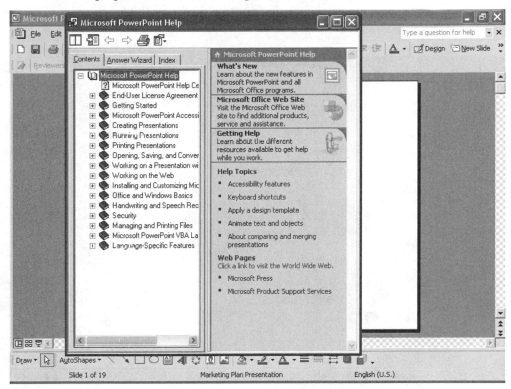

Figure 6.53: Help Options in PowerPoint

The three tabs in PowerPoint Help are:

- Contents
- Answer Wizard
- Index

The **Contents** tab categorizes the various Help options, as shown in Figure 6.54. For instance, you can choose the **Running Presentations** option to learn how to set up a presentation.

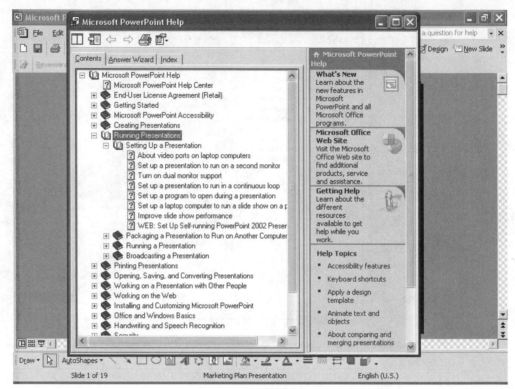

Figure 6.54: Contents Tab in PowerPoint Help

The **Answer Wizard** tab has the option of framing a question and searching for help on related keywords. The Answer Wizard tab is shown in Figure 6.55.

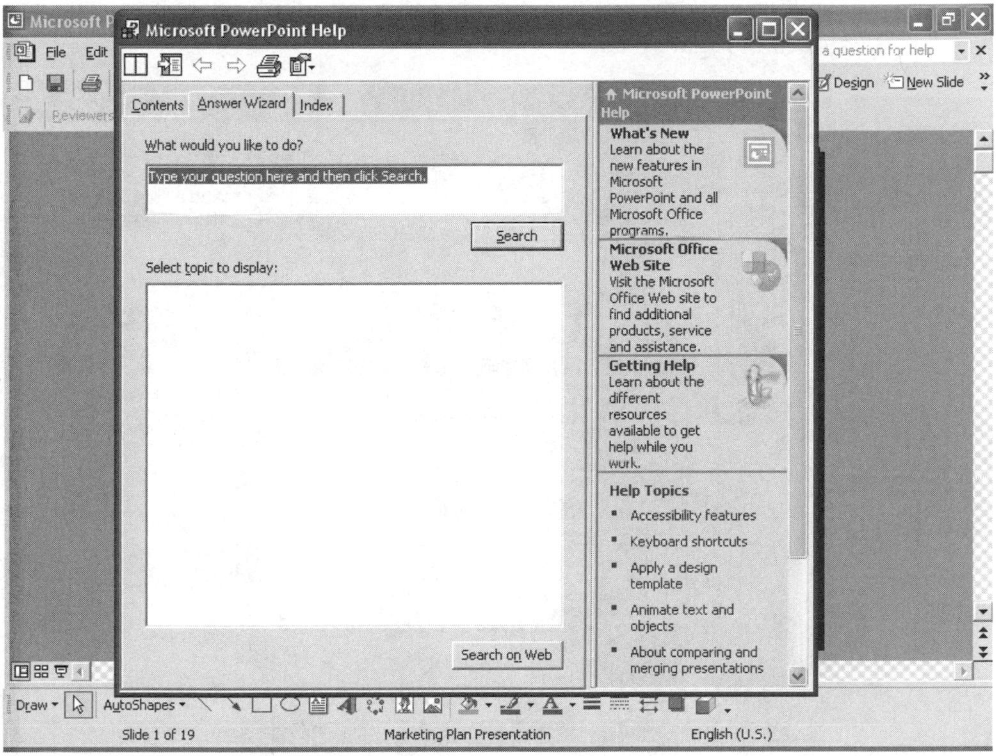

Figure 6.55: Answer Wizard Tab in PowerPoint Help

You can enter a keyword or question in the **What would you like to do?** text box and click **Search**. All related topics will be listed in the **Select topic to display** area. You can then click on a topic in the list and relevant information appears in the next pane, as shown in Figure 6.56.

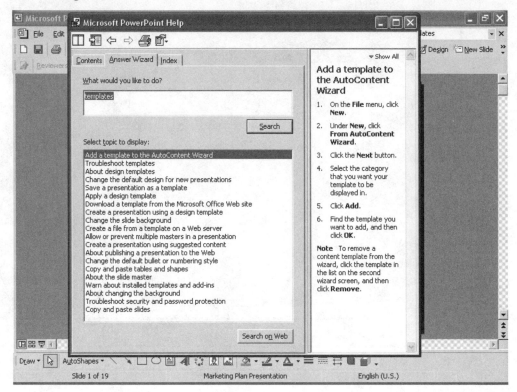

Figure 6.56: Answer Wizard Query in PowerPoint Help

The **Index** tab offers a selection of keywords from which you can choose to display help information. You can also enter the keywords in the **Type keywords** text box and then click **Search** to display the related topics. The Index tab is shown in Figure 6.57.

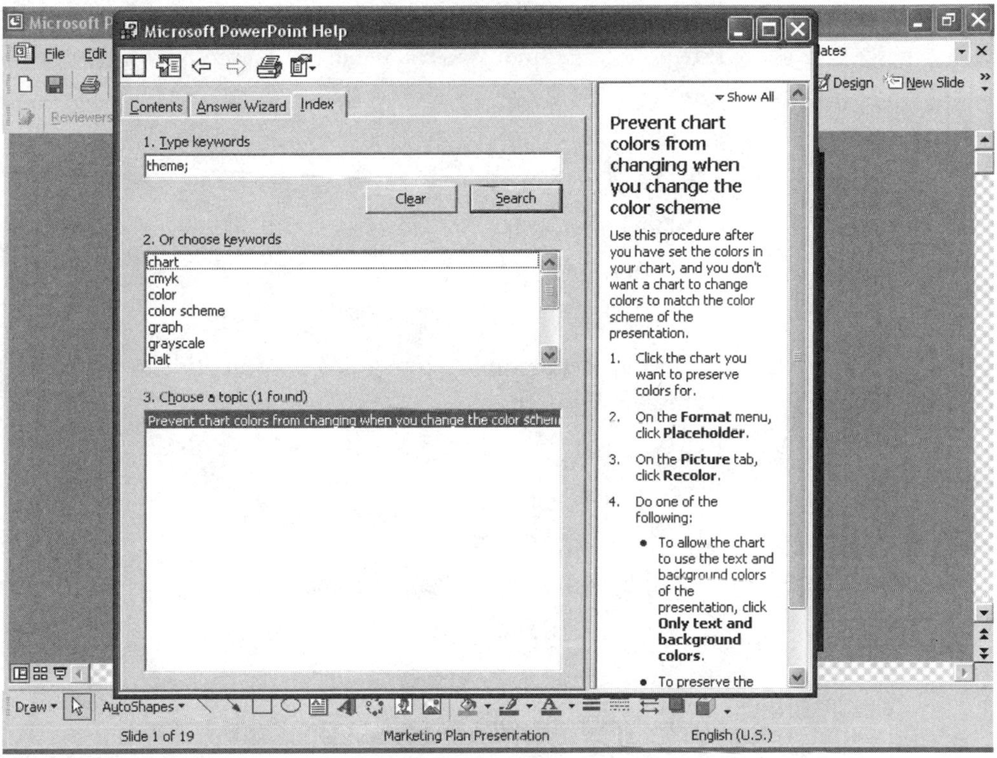

Figure 6.57: Index in PowerPoint Help

PowerPoint is a powerful tool. You can use this tool to create presentations that convey your ideas effectively. To do this, you should be comfortable exploring PowerPoint Help frequently. This will help you to create distinctive presentations by exploring and applying the features of this application. It will also make you a lifelong independent learner who uses technology to advance his or her career.

Practice Questions

1. PowerPoint Help provides a means to search by which of the following?
   a. Graphics
   b. Keywords
   c. Document name
   d. Author

2. Hyperlinks can redirect from a PowerPoint slide to which of the following locations?
   I. Web site
   II. Recent file
   III. Local CD-ROM device
   IV. Slide within the current document
   a. I, II, and III only
   b. II, III, and IV only
   c. I, III, and IV only
   d. I, II, III, and IV

3. Where would you find information on how to apply a template?
   a. Animation schemes
   b. Help
   c. Transitions
   d. Spelling

4. Which of the following statement is true about hyperlinks in a PowerPoint slide?

I. Hyperlinks are always underlined.

II. Hyperlinks are never underlined.

III. Hyperlinks are the same color as all other text in the document.

IV. Hyperlinks are a different color than all other text in the document.

a. I and IV

b. I and III

c. II and III

d. II and IV

Summary

In this chapter, you learned:

- PowerPoint is a powerful application to create online presentations.
- PowerPoint templates can be applied to a presentation to generate visually appealing slides.
- The slide master is used to provide consistent:
  - Font formats
  - Background colors
- The best practices to be followed when creating a slide presentation are:
  - List the main topics discussed in the presentation on the first slide.
  - A slide should have clear key points. Avoid putting too many points on each slide.
  - The slide title should be crisp. Preferably, it should not exceed one line.
  - Keep graphics limited and simple.
  - Transitions between slides or animations on slides can also enhance the appeal of the presentation. However, ensure that you do not use a style of transition or animation not in keeping with your topic.
  - If a particular slide title contains multiple points, it is advisable to list down the key phrases. Include details of the information in the Notes portion of the presentation.
- PowerPoint slides can be created, modified, and deleted in a presentation.
- The drawings that can be added to a slide include:
  - Arrows
  - Connectors
  - Flow charts
  - Callouts
  - Action Buttons

- Slide transition can be controlled by setting:
  - The amount of time between slides
  - How the new slide arrives in the presentation
  - The sound to be added
- Animation can be added to a single slide or all slides.
- Slide shows can be automated or manual.
- Hyperlinks can be added to a slide to direct the presenter to:
  - existing files or Web pages
  - a place in the current document
  - a new document
  - e-mail addresses

Reference

- *ONLINE! Microsoft Education,*
  http://www.microsoft.com/Education/MSITAcademy/ITAPOnlineCampus.aspx

Spreadsheet and Database Tools

7

This chapter describes how to use the spreadsheet and database tools in the Microsoft Office suite. The spreadsheet tool in the Microsoft Office suite is called Microsoft Excel and the database tool is called Microsoft Access. You can use Excel to prepare schedules, budgets, and purchase orders by using built-in mathematical functions. Access helps to organize and sort data in a convenient and retrievable format.

This chapter prepares you to:

- Enter data and perform basic calculations in a spreadsheet.
- Apply functions in a spreadsheet.
- Create charts and graphs in a spreadsheet.
- Format the spreadsheet.
- Save and print a spreadsheet.
- Design a summary spreadsheet and insert a hyperlink to another spreadsheet.
- Save a spreadsheet as a Web page and use it on the Web.
- Use the Excel Help feature to discover and apply additional features or troubleshoot your spreadsheet.
- Create a database and database forms.
- Query a database and generate database reports.
- Use the Access Help feature to discover and apply additional features or troubleshoot your database.

7.1 Basic Techniques of Working with Spreadsheets

7.2 Introducing Interactive Features of Spreadsheets

7.3 Features of Databases

7.1 Basic Techniques of Working with Spreadsheets

Spreadsheets function as tools for gathering numerical values and calculating their results. For example, a spreadsheet can be used to create a budget. You can specify the data of monthly expenses, including rent, gas, automobile insurance, and dining out, in a spreadsheet and configure the spreadsheet to automatically add up the values. A change in value of any item would be automatically taken care of in the result. Assume you have configured the spreadsheet to display a sum of expenses for food and washing. The sheet for the total value would automatically update an increase in the expense value for food.

In Microsoft Excel, a book of spreadsheets is referred to as a workbook. When you open Excel, you open a workbook that can contain up to 255 worksheets. A worksheet is organized into cells by columns and rows. Data is entered into these cells.

A tab at the bottom of the window identifies each worksheet, which is also referred to as a sheet. When you open Excel, only three sheets show, but you can easily add sheets when required.

You can use worksheets to store important business data and to analyze this data for future use. However, you need to organize the data within worksheets and manage multiple worksheets within workbooks to ensure that the data is presented effectively. This includes adding rows and columns to your worksheets. In addition, you might also need to add, rename, and move worksheets within a workbook.

Just as in a Word document, an Excel Workbook displays the Menu Bar and other toolbars on top of the window. To view the list of toolbars available in Excel, select **View → Toolbars**.

The **Standard** toolbar and **Formatting** toolbar are available in Excel too. However, some of the options in these toolbars may be specific to Excel, as shown in Figure 7.1 and Figure 7.2.

Figure 7.1: Formatting Toolbar in Excel

Figure 7.2: Standard Toolbar in Excel

For instance, the Formatting toolbar in Excel has additional icons for formatting the numerical data to be depicted as currency or percentage. Refer to Table 7.1 for these additional icons and their functions.

Icon	Function
	Merge and Center icon merges the selected cells in the worksheet and centers the data within the merged cell. When you merge cells containing multiple values, only the value in the upper left cell is retained in the merged cell.
 $	Currency Style icon enables you to insert the currency style of Dollar for numeric values.
%	Percent Style icon enables you to represent a numeric value as a percentage value.
 ,	Comma Style icon enables you to insert a comma into a numeric value.

Table 7.1: Additional Icons in Excel Formatting Toolbar and Their Functions

The Standard toolbar in Excel has additional icons for adding and sorting data. Refer to Table 7.2 for these additional icons and their functions.

Icon	Function
 Σ ▾	AutoSum icon performs simple calculations, such as sum and average of selected numerical data. You can use the drop-down menu to select more functions in Excel.
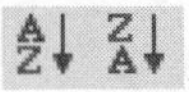 A↓Z Z↓A	Sort Ascending and Sort Descending icons sort selected data in an

Icon	Function
	ascending or descending order.
	Chart Wizard icon guides you through the steps of creating a chart in Excel.

Table 7.2: Additional Icons in Excel Standard Toolbar and Their Functions

Additionally, Excel also has a Formula Bar as shown in Figure 7.3.

Figure 7.3: Formula Bar in Excel

Refer to Table 7.3 for the components of this bar and their functions.

Component	Function
Formula Bar field	Displays the contents of the selected cell. In addition, when formulas or functions are applied to a selected cell, this bar displays those formulas or functions.
Tick symbol	Can be clicked to complete the process of entering the data in a cell.
Cross symbol	Cancels the data entered in a selected cell and leaves the cell blank.
Symbol fx	Invokes the Insert Function dialog box if the numeric value entered in the selected cell is data. You can then use the dialog box to apply a function to the numeric value in the cell. If the value in the selected cell is a formula, you invoke the Function Arguments dialog box when you click the symbol fx.

Table 7.3: Formula Bar Components and Their Functions

Excel performs calculations automatically. Both formulas and functions help you to automate the process of performing mathematical calculations. Charts and graphs allow numeric data to be presented visually.

In this section, you will learn to enter and sort data into worksheets, perform calculations using formulas and functions, copy or move cells, format, save, and print worksheets.

This chapter assumes that you have a basic understanding of Excel. If you are unfamiliar with the basics of spreadsheets, it is advised that you increase your familiarity with spreadsheets before proceeding.

You may access a Microsoft Excel online tutorial from the ITT Tech Virtual Library. Log on to the Virtual library at http://library.itt-tech.edu/. From the Main Menu, click the **Learning Guides** link. Under the Online Tutorials, scroll down and select **Microsoft Office 2000 Tutorials**. Select **Excel** from the list of Office Programs. Click the link **Begin the Excel tutorial** at the top.

Excel tutorials can also be found on the Internet. You may use a search engine and enter the keywords "Excel Tutorial." Alternatively, you can access a tutorial on Excel at the Web site http://www.microsoft.com/education/?ID=Excel2002Tutorial.

7.1.1 Entering Data in Spreadsheets

Enter data in worksheets.

The interface to enter data in Excel is called a worksheet. The task of adding data into these worksheets is known as data entry. The data entered in a worksheet can be a combination of a descriptor for a value and the value itself. If a spreadsheet contains a list of dollar figures with no corresponding descriptors of what the values represent, it will not be of much use. In this topic, you will learn to create a simple worksheet and add data to it.

When you open Microsoft Excel, a blank worksheet is displayed by default, as shown in Figure 7.4. To the right of the worksheet is displayed the **New Workbook** menu. It can be used to:

■ Open an existing workbook.

■ Create a new blank workbook.

■ Create a new workbook by using an existing worksheet format.

■ Create a new worksheet from a template.

To create a new blank workbook, perform the following steps:

1. Select **New → Blank Workbook**.

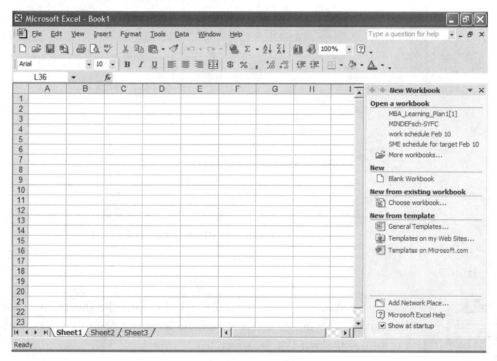

Figure 7.4: Opening a New Spreadsheet

Observe the layout of the Microsoft Excel workbook, as shown in Figure 7.5. The white area where data can be specified is the current worksheet, called Sheet1 by default. You can see the tabs of the other two default sheets at the bottom of the window.

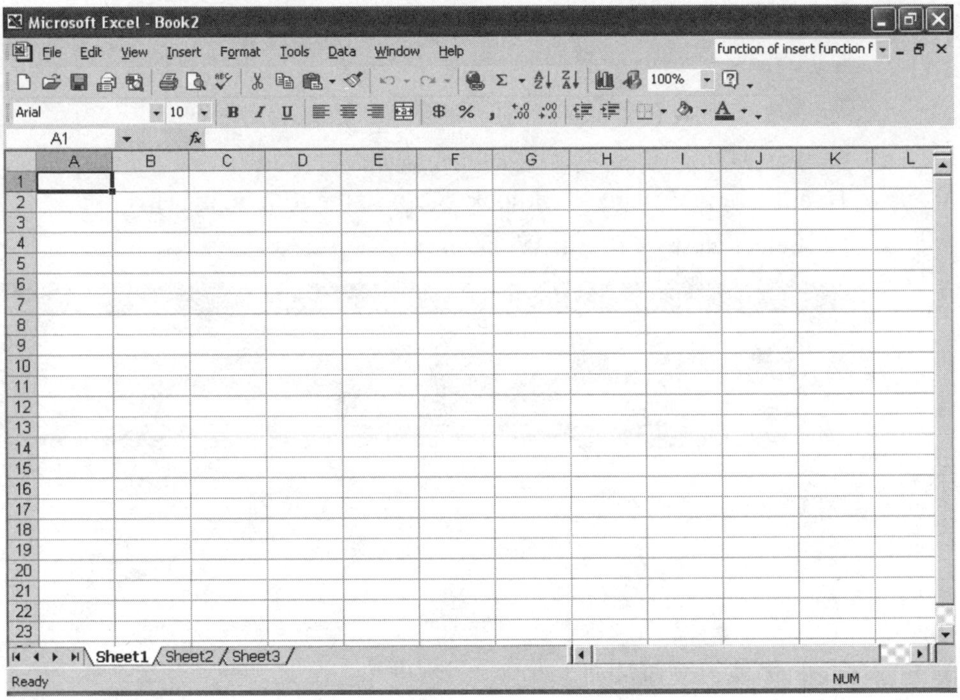

Figure 7.5: Blank Workbook Creation

You can rename the worksheets by right-clicking the sheet name in the tab at the bottom of the window and selecting the **Rename** command. You can then customize the name of the sheet.

In a worksheet, the columns are labeled alphabetically and the rows are labeled numerically. When entering data in the very first cell of the worksheet, you would be selecting Column A and Row 1, also referred to as cell A1. An identifier such as A1 is the address of the cell and is called the Cell Reference. To refer to a cell, enter the column letter followed by the row number.

By default, a worksheet can have a total of 256 columns (A through IV) and 65536 rows (1 through 65536). These letters and numbers are called Row and Column headings.

2. To enter data into the worksheet, you can click a cell and enter the data. Data can be textual or numeric. In Figure 7.6, a list of grocery items and their prices have been entered in the worksheet. The title of this list is My First Spreadsheet.

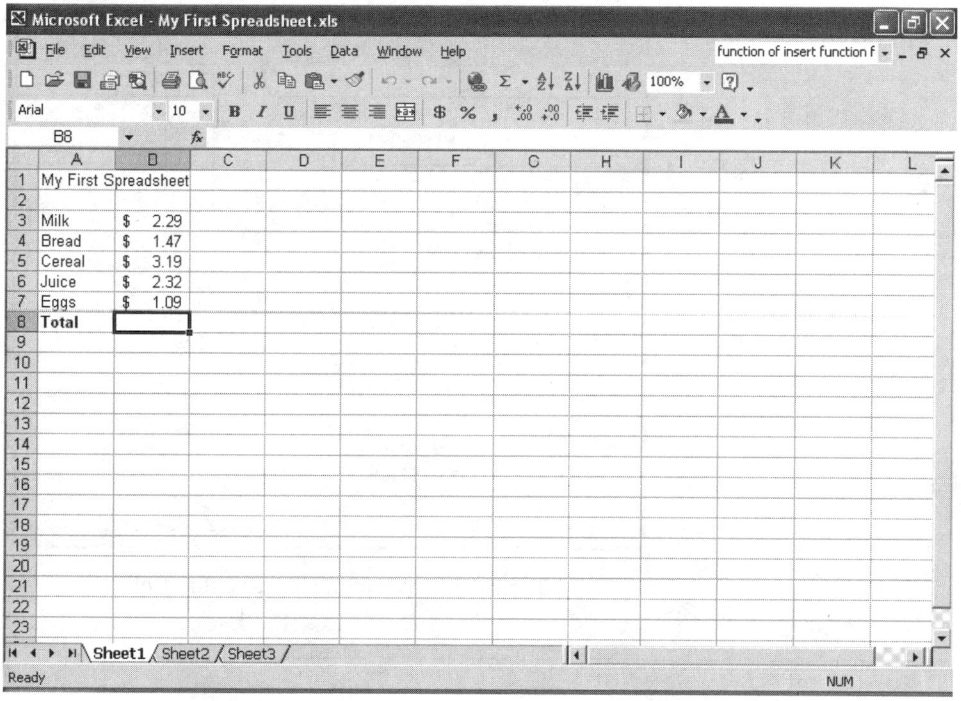

Figure 7.6: Entering Text and Numeric Data in an Excel Worksheet

When you enter data in a cell, it may overlap or carry forward into another cell. For example, Figure 7.6 shows the text, My First Spreadsheet. This text was entered in cell A1 but it occupies two cells, A1 and B1.

You can wrap the text within a cell. For this, right-click the cell where data was entered (in this example A1) and select the **Format Cells** option. Select the **Alignment** tab in the Format Cells dialog box, as shown in Figure 7.7. In the Text Control area, check the **Wrap text** check box and click **OK**. The text will now wrap into multiple rows within the cell A1.

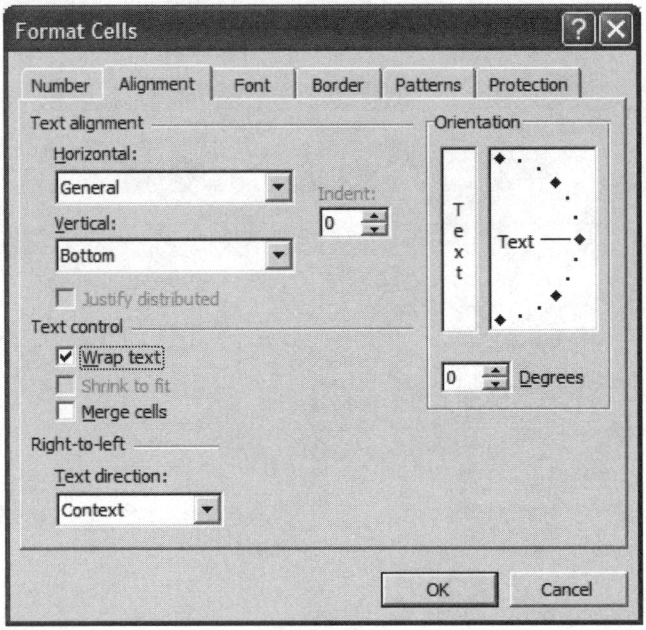

Figure 7.7: Wrapping Text Within Cells

7.1.2 Using Formulas and Functions

Use formulas and functions to perform basic calculations on data, such as sum and product.

A worksheet can be configured to calculate the data provided in the sheet. Both formulas and functions in Excel help you automate the process of performing mathematical calculations. Selecting the data and applying a formula or a function can perform both simple and complex calculations of data.

A formula is a mathematical instruction. It is inserted in a worksheet cell to perform a particular operation on the specified data. You can use formulas and functions to perform mathematical calculations, such as addition, subtraction, multiplication, and division.

A formula or function applied to one cell can be used for other cells as well. Right-click the cell with the original formula or function and select **Copy**. Highlight the other cells where the same formula or function is to be applied, and select **Paste**.

Alternatively, you may drag the black rectangular border around the selected cell with the original formula or function, by the black square or the Fill Handle, over the remaining cells. This replicates the formula or function in the other cells. The Fill Handle around the cell is shown in Figure 7.8.

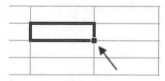

Figure 7.8: Fill Handle Around a Cell

Using Formulas

All formulas have the following characteristics:

- Formulas begin with the equal (=) sign. The equal sign helps Excel to distinguish a formula from other text, numbers, or information contained in a worksheet cell.

- Formulas inserted in worksheet cells can be copied to other cells. This feature enables you to create a formula once and use it at multiple locations within the worksheet.
- Formulas can contain Cell References.

When you specify cell references in formulas, the latter use the values in these cell references to calculate results. If you change the values in these cell references, the result of the formula will automatically update.

You can create a formula by using different methods but the basic steps are the same. You can type a formula in a worksheet cell or in the Formula Bar. After typing the formula in a cell, press **Enter** or click the **tick icon** on the Formula Bar to mark the creation of the formula.

Consider Figure 7.9 showing the price of grocery items. If you need to add the price of all the items and display the result at the bottom of the list, perform the following steps using a formula:

1. Click once on the cell in which you want to create a formula. In this case, you will click cell **B8**.

Note that the original cell location appears in the Formula Bar. Instead of clicking the cell, you can also type the cell address in the Formula Bar.

2. Type =**sum(** in the cell B8.
3. To add the values of cells B3 to B7, first click cell **B3**.
4. Press **Shift** and then click Cell **B7**. The range of cells from B3 to B7 is selected.

5. Type).

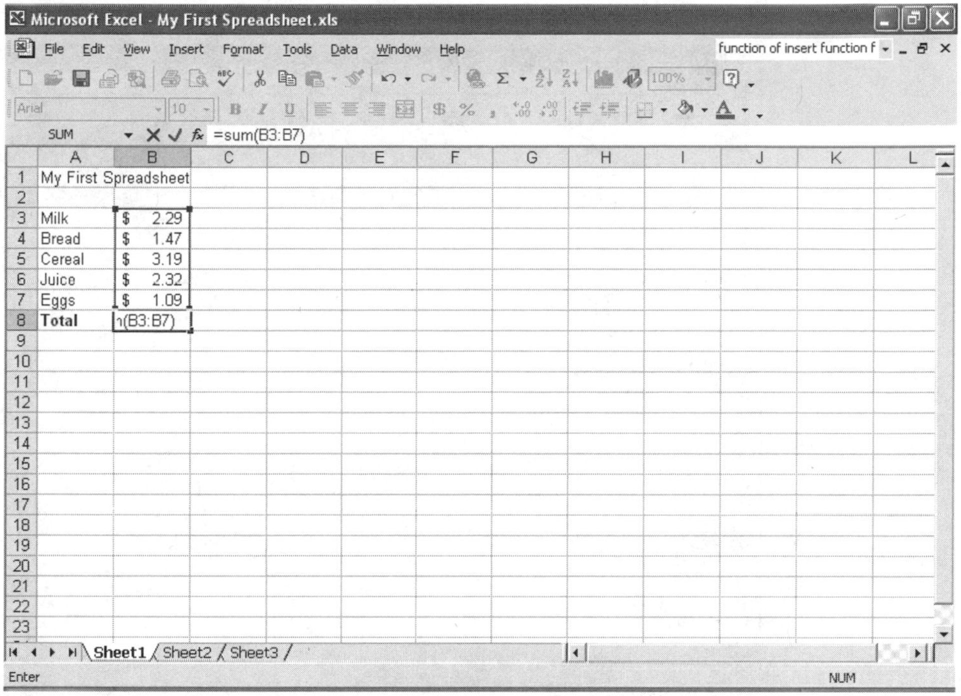

Figure 7.9: Performing Addition by Using a Formula

6. Press **Enter**. The result of the calculation is displayed in cell B8, as shown in Figure 7.10.

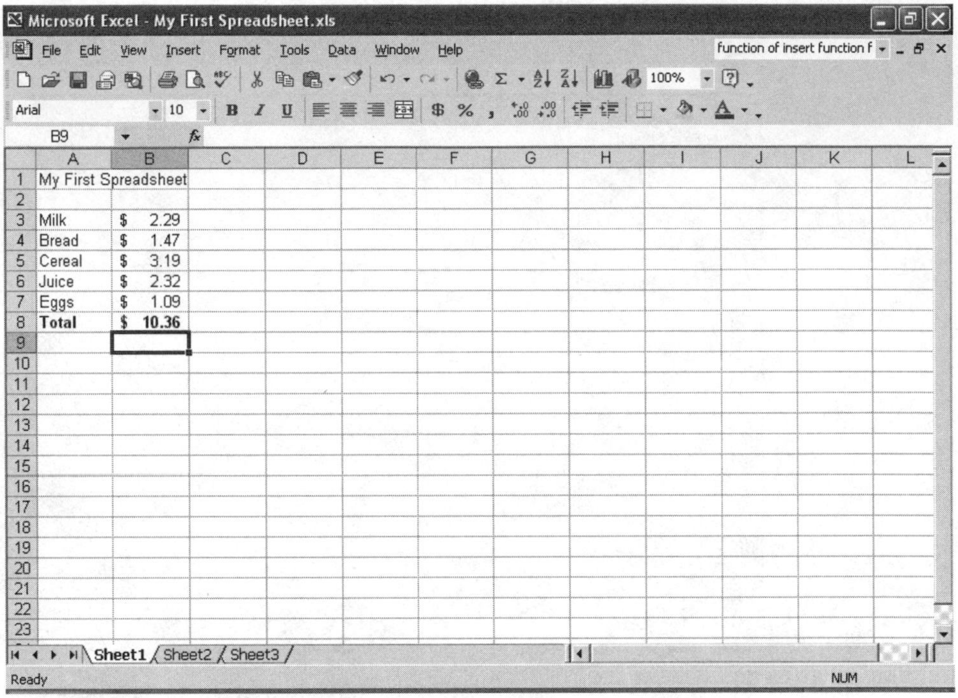

	A	B	C	D	E	F	G	H	I	J	K	L
1	My First Spreadsheet											
2												
3	Milk	$ 2.29										
4	Bread	$ 1.47										
5	Cereal	$ 3.19										
6	Juice	$ 2.32										
7	Eggs	$ 1.09										
8	**Total**	$ **10.36**										

Figure 7.10: Displaying the Result of Excel Formula Calculations

When you press **Enter**, the cell below the one that contains the formula becomes the active cell by default.

If you click the **tick icon** on the Formula bar to complete the creation of a formula, the cell containing the formula remains active.

Ensure that you do not click another worksheet cell to complete the creation of a formula. This is because every cell that you click after typing = is added to the formula.

If you change the values in these cell references, the result of the formula will also change. For instance, if you change the value of cell B3, the result is recalculated and updated automatically, as shown in Figure 7.11.

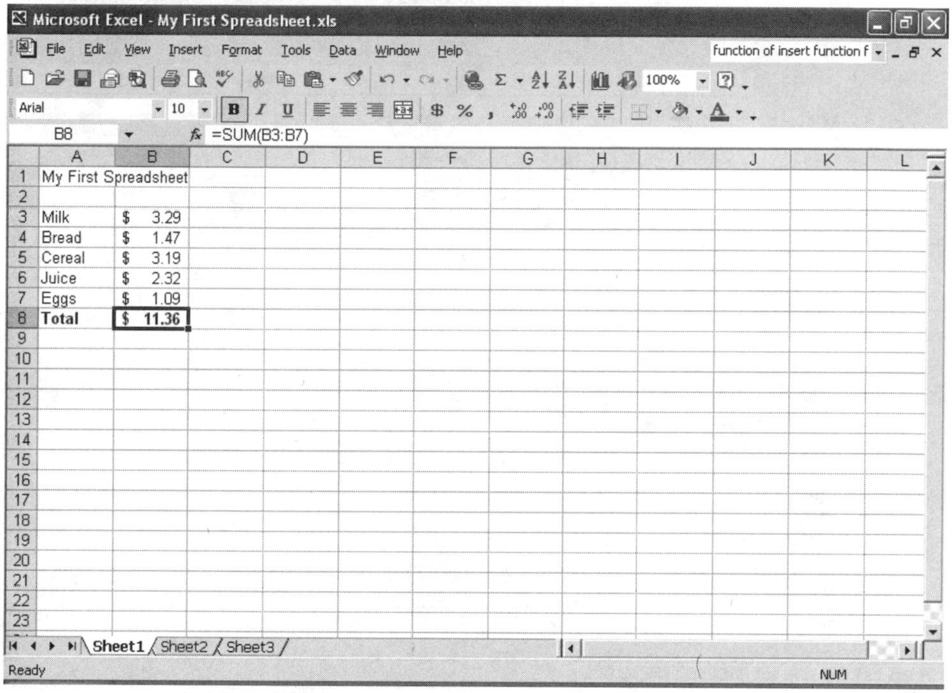

Figure 7.11: Automatic Recalculation

Other calculations can also be performed in a worksheet. As shown in Figure 7.11, you may need to multiply quantities of items to be purchased along with their prices. The product is to be displayed in column C.

Perform the following steps for this calculation:

1. Highlight the cell **D3** where the formula result will be displayed.

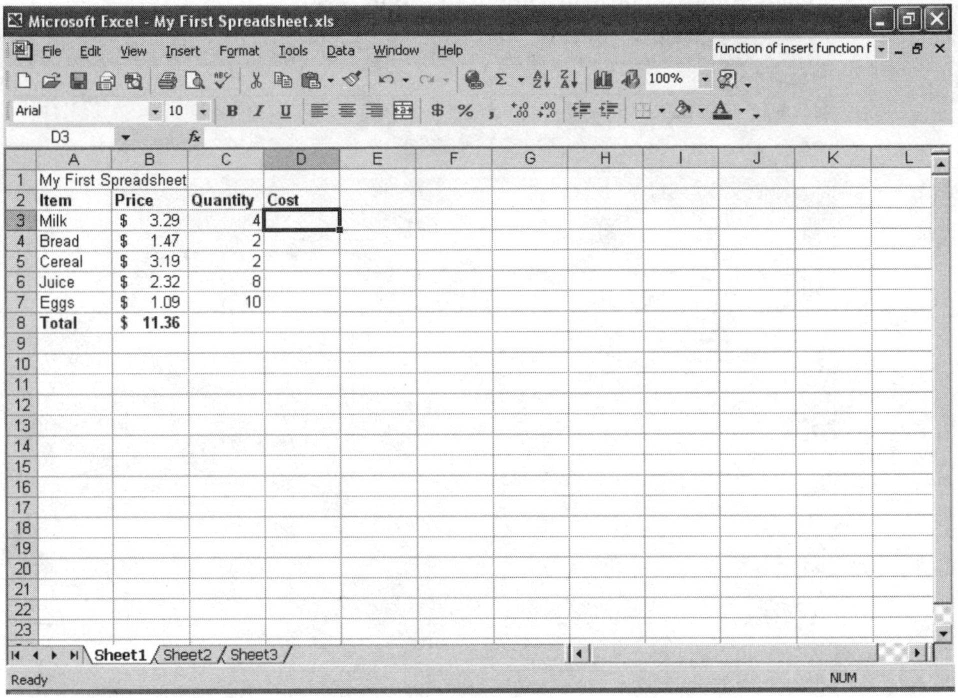

Figure 7.12: Determining Product

2. Type **=Product(** in this cell.
3. Press the **Shift** key and select cells **C3** to **B3**. The cell range can be seen as part of the formula in the Formula Bar.

4. Type **)**.

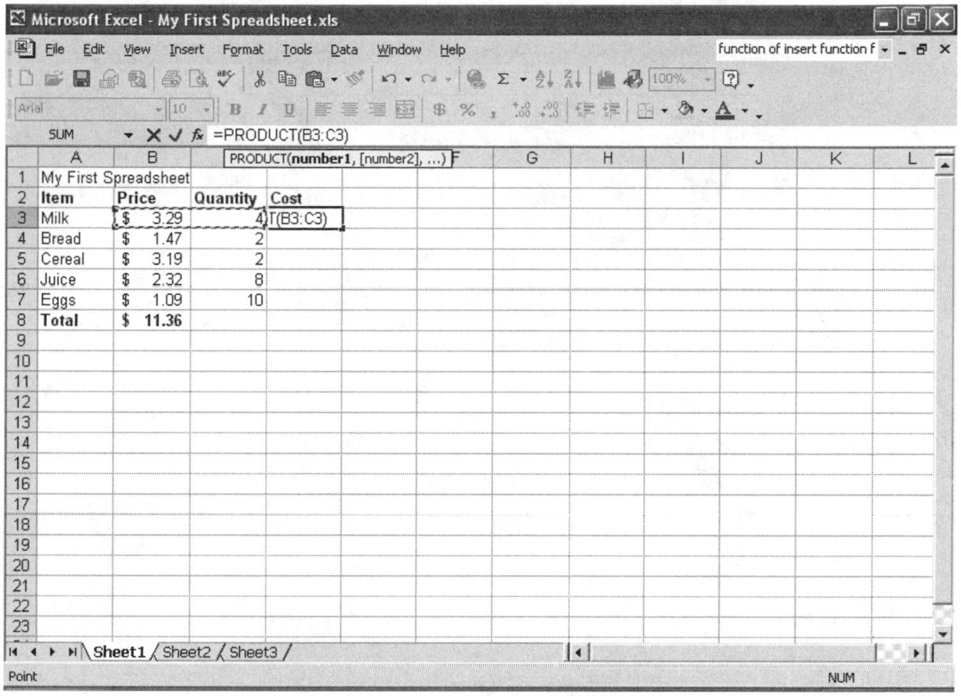

Figure 7.13: Applying a Multiplication Formula in Excel

5. Press **Enter**. The result is displayed in the destination cell D3, as shown in Figure 7.14.

	A	B	C	D
1	My First Spreadsheet			
2	**Item**	**Price**	**Quantity**	**Cost**
3	Milk	$ 3.29	4	13.16
4	Bread	$ 1.47	2	
5	Cereal	$ 3.19	2	
6	Juice	$ 2.32	8	
7	Eggs	$ 1.09	10	
8	**Total**	**$ 11.36**		

Figure 7.14: Result of a Product Formula

You can hide formulas used in your worksheet. Hiding formulas enables you to conceal the calculation methods used in your workbook from users who might be sharing the workbook with you.

Explore Excel **Help** to learn how you can hide formulas. Explore Excel Help to learn and apply other formulas on data.

Using Functions

A *function* is a ready-to-use calculation tool that is available in Excel and can be incorporated in a formula. Functions perform a specific operation on selected data. Worksheet functions can process a variety of tasks ranging from general arithmetic operations to complex calculations and intricate statistical tests.

Excel provides the following types of functions:

- Text
- Math and Trigonometric
- Date and Time
- Logical
- Information
- Statistical
- Financial
- Lookup and Reference

For example, SUM is a worksheet function. You can use the SUM function in the formula =SUM(C3:C7) to calculate the sum total of the values in the cell range C3 to C7, as shown in Figure 7.15.

There are two parts of every function—the *name* and the *argument*. The name is used to refer to the function. In the above example, SUM is the name of the function. The arguments in a function specify the input data on which the function operates. In the example mentioned earlier, C3:C7 is the argument that specifies the input data for the SUM function. Excel provides several categories of functions.

To perform calculations, you can directly type a function in the destination cell. You can also use the mouse to select a cell range that can act as the argument for a given function.

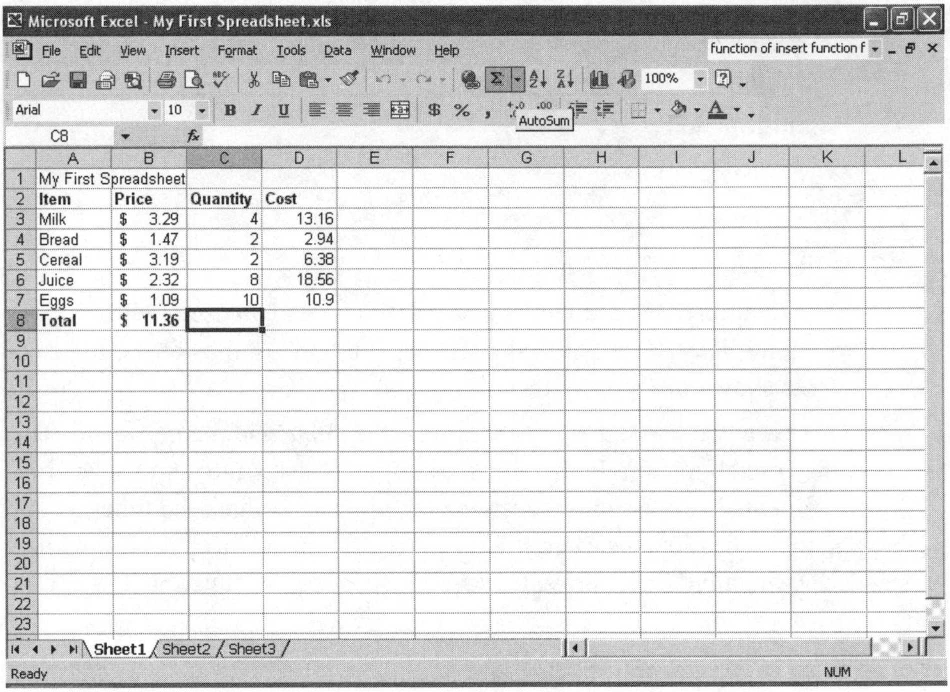

Figure 7.15: Using the AutoSum Icon

For example, if you want to calculate the total quantities of all items in the grocery list, as shown in Figure 7.15, perform the following steps:

1. Select the destination cell in which you want to store the total quantity.

2. Click the **AutoSum** icon on the Standard toolbar to select the cells with values to be added automatically, as shown in Figure 7.16.

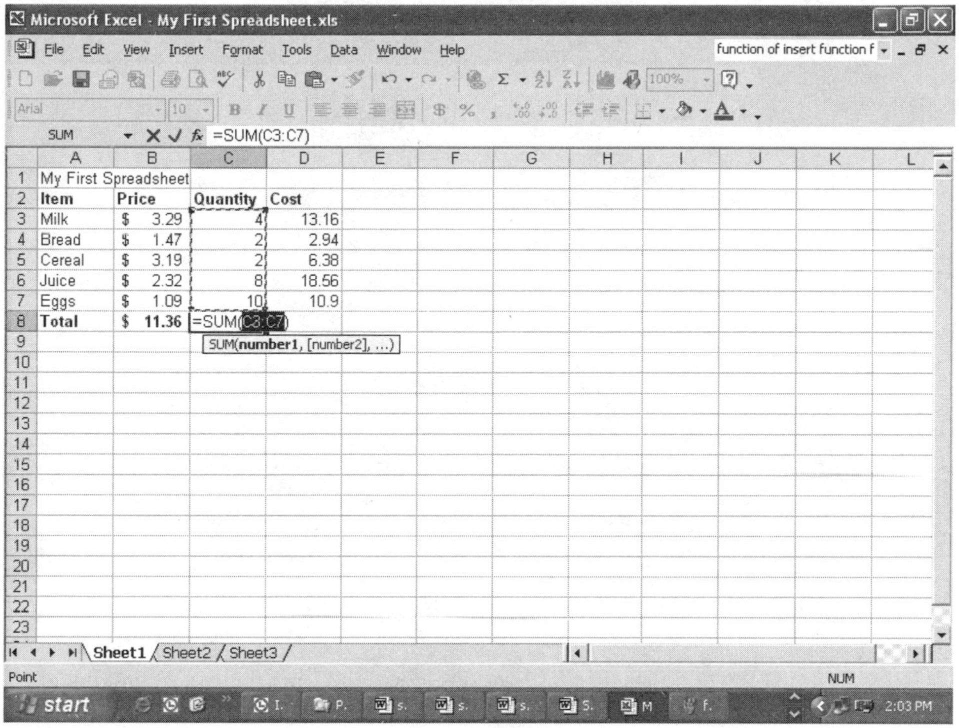

Figure 7.16: Cells Selected Automatically

3. Press **Enter**. The result is displayed in the destination cell, as shown in Figure 7.17.

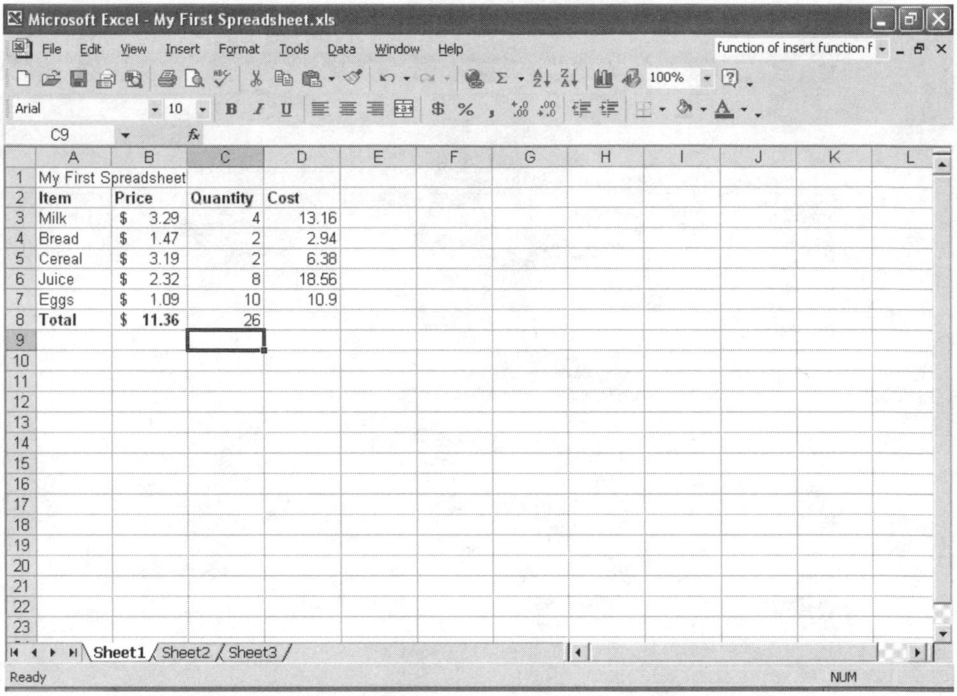

Figure 7.17: Addition Result Using the AutoSum Function

7.1.3 Sorting Data

Sort data by specifying criteria.

Text as well as numerical data can be sorted in ascending or descending order in Excel. You can sort or arrange a list in a logical order, ascending or descending in alphabetic order, or in numeric order.

Excel uses the following rules while sorting a list in ascending order:

- Blank cells are always placed at the end of a sorted list.
- Numbers are sorted from the smallest negative to the largest positive number.
- Alphanumeric data is sorted left to right.
- Text, including text with numbers, is sorted in alphabetical order.

These rules are reversed when the sort operation is performed in the descending order.

To sort data based on a single column, perform the following steps:

1. Select the area to be sorted, including the column headers.

 If a list contains totals at the bottom or at the right of the list, do not include the totals in the area to be sorted.

2. Select **Data → Sort** and the selected area will be highlighted. The Sort dialog box, as shown in Figure 7.18, appears.

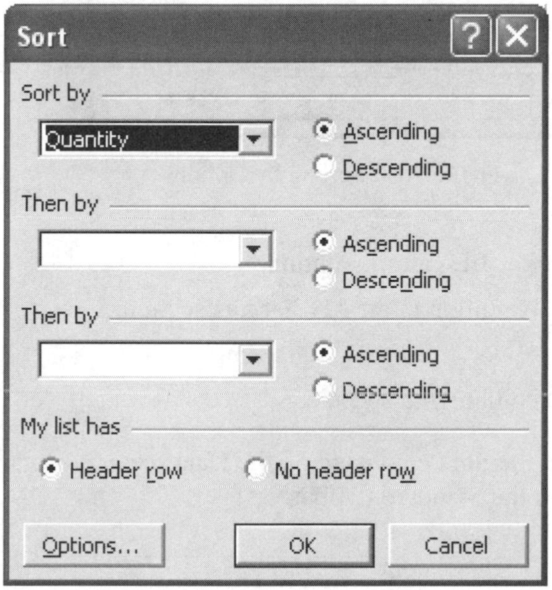

Figure 7.18: Sort Dialog Box

3. Select the columns that you want to sort from the **Sort by** list.

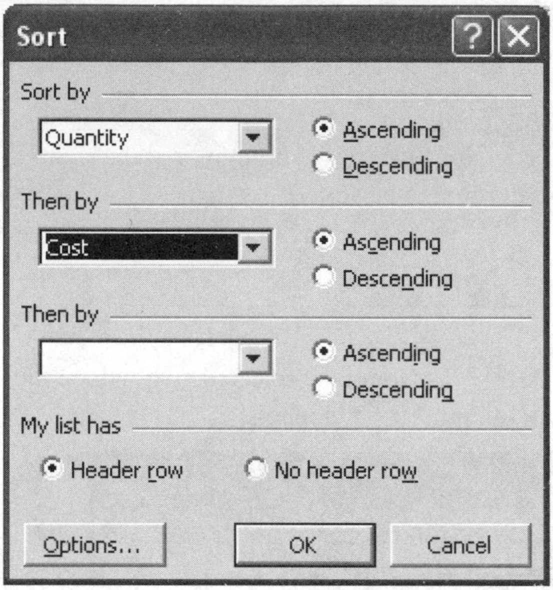

Sort ? X

Sort by
Quantity ▼   ⦿ Ascending
               ○ Descending

Then by
Cost ▼   ⦿ Ascending
               ○ Descending

Then by
[   ] ▼ ⦿ Ascending
               ○ Descending

My list has
⦿ Header row   ○ No header row

Options...   OK   Cancel

Figure 7.19: Sorting by Options

4. Click the **Ascending** or **Descending** option.
5. Click the **Header row** option in the **My list has** section.
6. Click **OK**.

The list is sorted by the column you specify.

In addition to using the **Sort** command on the Data menu, you can use the Sort buttons available on the Standard toolbar.

If you select an isolated column or row to sort, you will receive a warning message, as shown in Figure 7.20.

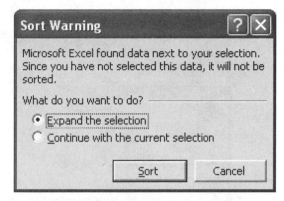

Figure 7.20: Sort Warning Dialog Box

In the **Sort Warning** dialog box, click the **Expand the selection** option to include the entire table or click the **Continue with the current selection** option. Though you can sort just one column without affecting the other rows or columns, it might affect the integrity of your table.

If you want to sort a table by more than one criterion, you can specify additional requirements in the Sort dialog box, as shown in Figure 7.21. Often, you may need to sort a row rather than a column. Consider the following procedure:

1. Select the area to be sorted.

Select **Data → Sort** and click **Options** in the **Sort** dialog box. This opens the **Sort Options** dialog box, as shown in Figure 7.21.

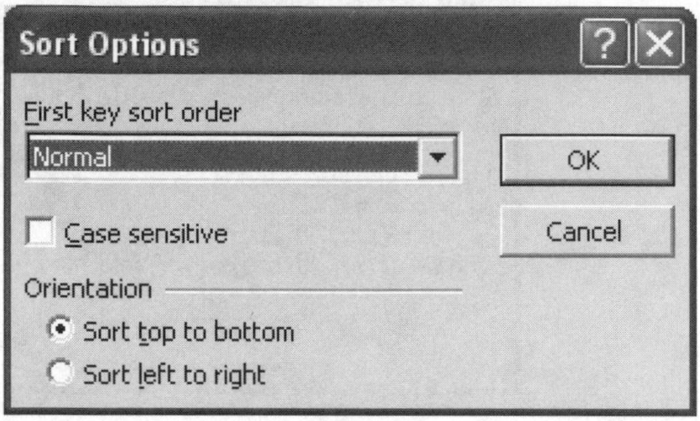

Figure 7.21: Sort Options Dialog Box

2. Select the **Sort top to bottom** option and click **OK**.

3. Select the row number or row label, now available in the Sort by box, on the basis of how you want to sort the table.

4. Select the **Descending** option in the **Sort by** section and click **OK**. The result of sorting a row is displayed.

If you need to return a sorted list to the original state, add a numeric column to the table before sorting. You can now sort the table by the additional numeric column to return the sorted list to the original state.

7.1.4 Inserting Rows, Columns, and Cells

Insert rows, columns, and cells in worksheets.

Excel allows you to insert rows, columns, and cells. You can insert either a single row or multiple rows, columns, or cells.

Inserting Rows

To insert a row, click any cell in the row above which you want to insert a new row and select **Insert → Rows**, as shown in Figure 7.22.

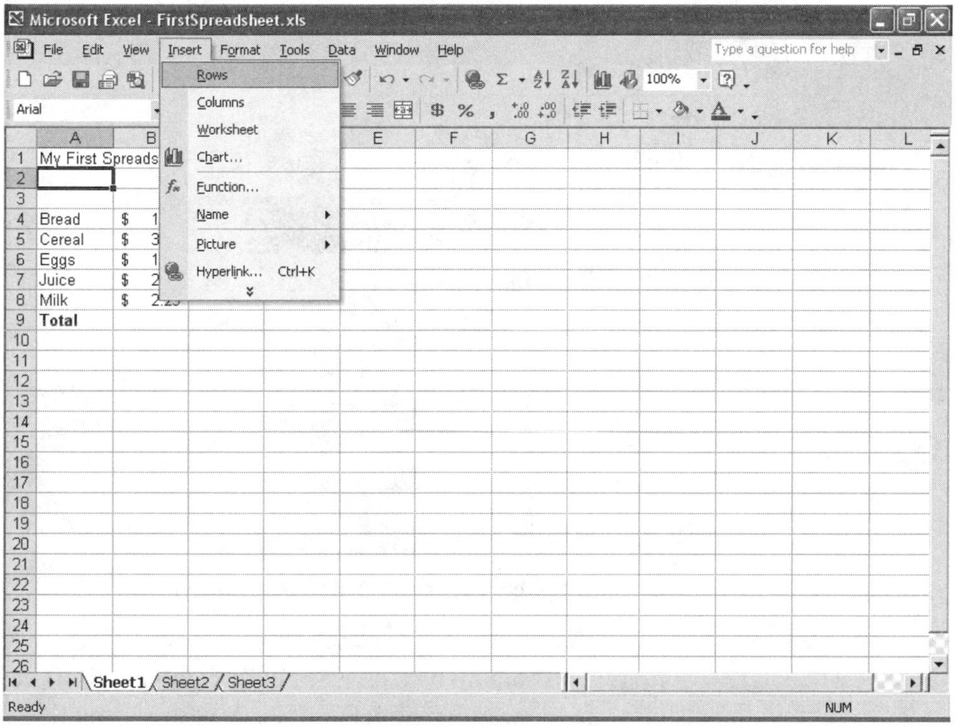

Figure 7.22: Adding Rows

Alternatively, you can select the row above which you want to insert a new row, press the **Ctrl**, **Shift**, and "+" keys, select the **Entire row** option, and click **OK**.

Inserting Columns

You can also insert columns in a worksheet to accommodate more data. To insert a column, perform the following steps:

1. Click a cell in the column to the left of which you want to insert multiple columns.
2. Select the same number of cells in columns that you want to insert to the right of the currently selected cell. For example, if you want to insert two new columns to the left of column D, select cells in columns D and E.
3. Select **Insert → Columns**.

Inserting Cells

You can insert blank cells in worksheets to the left of or above a selected cell. To insert a single cell, perform the following steps:

1. Select a cell.
2. Select **Insert → Cells**.

The Insert dialog box appears, as shown in Figure 7.23.

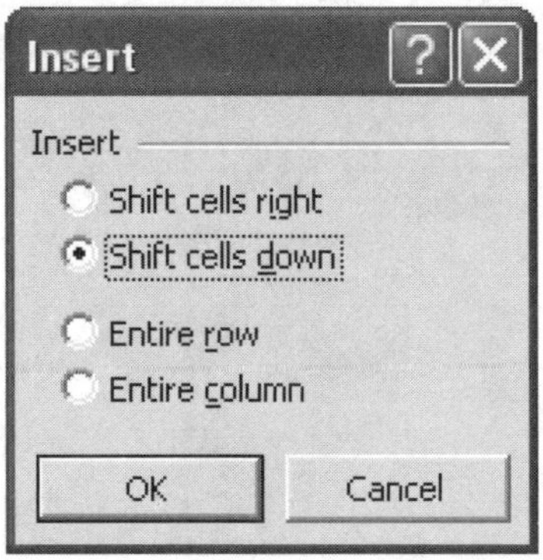

Figure 7.23: Insert Dialog Box for Cells

The top two options in this dialog box are **Shift cells right** and **Shift cells down**. The first option enables you to insert a new cell to the left of the currently selected cell. The second option enables you to insert a new cell above the selected cell. The **Shift cells down** option is selected by default.

3. Click OK to insert a new cell.

7.1.5 Copying and Moving Cells

 Copy and move cells in excel.

Excel allows you to copy or move cells. You can copy or move single cells or many cells.

Copying Cells

You can copy a cell by using:

- The drag-and-drop method
- The Edit menu

To copy the contents of cells B3 to B8 by using the drag-and-drop method, perform the following steps:

1. Select cell **B3**.
2. Place the pointer at the border of cell **B3** and press the **Ctrl** key. The pointer will change, as shown in Figure 7.24.

	A	B	C	D	E
1					
2	Product ID	Quarter	2001	2002	2003
3	T001	Q1	$60,000	$65,000	$62,050
4	T001	Q2	$10,235	$17,500	$15,550
5	T001	Q3	$31,000	$32,350	$29,100
6	T001	Q4	$40,000	$35,765	$42,345
7					
8	T002		$10,770	$12,000	$11,550
9	T002		$39,000	$35,670	$37,205
10	T002		$23,120	$25,450	$27,100
11	T002		$12,000	$11,450	$13,000

Figure 7.24: Selecting Cell

3. With the **Ctrl** key pressed and cell B3 selected, drag to cell B8, as shown in Figure 7.25.

	A	B	C	D	E
1					
2	**Product ID**	**Quarter**	**2001**	**2002**	**2003**
3	T001	Q1	$60,000	$65,000	$62,050
4	T001	Q2	$10,235	$17,500	$15,550
5	T001	Q3	$31,000	$32,350	$29,100
6	T001	Q4	$40,000	$35,765	$42,345
7					
8	T002		$10,770	$12,000	$11,550
9	T002	B8 9,000		$35,670	$37,205
10	T002	$23,120		$25,450	$27,100
11	T002		$12,000	$11,450	$13,000

Figure 7.25: Dragging Selected Cell

To copy a cell by using the **Edit** menu, perform the following steps:

1. Select the source cell.
2. Select **Edit → Copy** or press the **Ctrl** and **C** keys.

 You can use the **Shift** key to copy multiple cells. Press the Shift key and select the first and the last cell in the range. All interim cells also get selected by default. You can then press the Ctrl and C keys to copy the cells.

---

3. Select the destination cell.
4. Select **Edit → Paste** or press the **Ctrl** and **V** keys.

Moving Cells

You can move cells to rearrange the existing data in a worksheet. Similar to copying cells, you can use the drag-and-drop method or the Edit menu to move cells from one location to another in a worksheet.

To move a cell by using the drag-and-drop method, perform the following steps:

1. Select the source cell.
2. Place the pointer at the border of the cell.
3. Drag the cell to the desired location.

To move a cell by using the Edit menu, perform the following steps:

1. Select the source cell.
2. Select **Edit → Cut** or press the **Ctrl** and **X** keys.
3. Select the destination cell.
4. Select **Edit → Paste**.

7.1.6 Working with Charts

Explain how to create charts and convert them to another chart type to use them for relevant purposes.

The appeal and effectiveness of worksheets can be increased by converting data into charts or graphs. Data is often easier to analyze when presented in a graph or chart format.

Excel allows you to create many types of charts and graphs, including the following:

- Bar/column graphs and clustered bar/column graphs
- Pie charts
- Line graphs
- Area graphs
- Scatter diagrams
- Surface charts
- Radar charts
- Bubble charts

You can learn about these types of charts as you create a chart using the Chart Wizard, as shown later in this chapter. The Chart Wizard presents a brief description of a chart type as you select it from the list of chart types.

It is important first to establish the purpose for which the chart is to be used, as this purpose will determine which type of chart you choose. Sometimes you may need to present data as charts for multiple purposes. In such a situation, you may present your data as multiple types of charts.

Before creating a chart or graph, it is necessary first to collect the data and place it in the Excel worksheet. Once labels for the data and their values are entered into the worksheet, the Excel Chart Wizard can be used to create a chart.

Creating Charts

Let us consider sample data of employees' work hours that needs to be presented as a chart. Perform the following steps to create a clustered column graph using the Employee Hours worksheet, as shown in Figure 7.26.

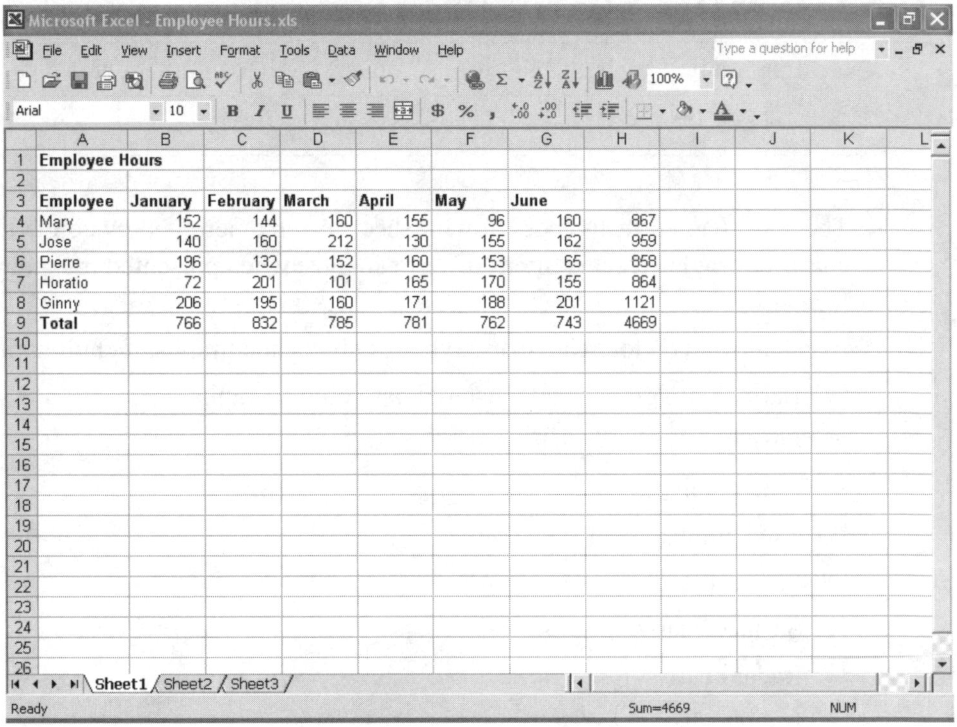

	A	B	C	D	E	F	G	H
1	**Employee Hours**							
2								
3	**Employee**	**January**	**February**	**March**	**April**	**May**	**June**	
4	Mary	152	144	160	155	96	160	867
5	Jose	140	160	212	130	155	162	959
6	Pierre	196	132	152	160	153	65	858
7	Horatio	72	201	101	165	170	155	864
8	Ginny	206	195	160	171	188	201	1121
9	**Total**	766	832	785	781	762	743	4669

Figure 7.26: Employee Hours Worksheet

As shown in Figure 7.25, select the range of data to be placed into the chart. Highlight the block of cells B4 through G8.

From the Menu Bar, select **Insert → Chart**. The screen shown in Figure 7.27 appears.

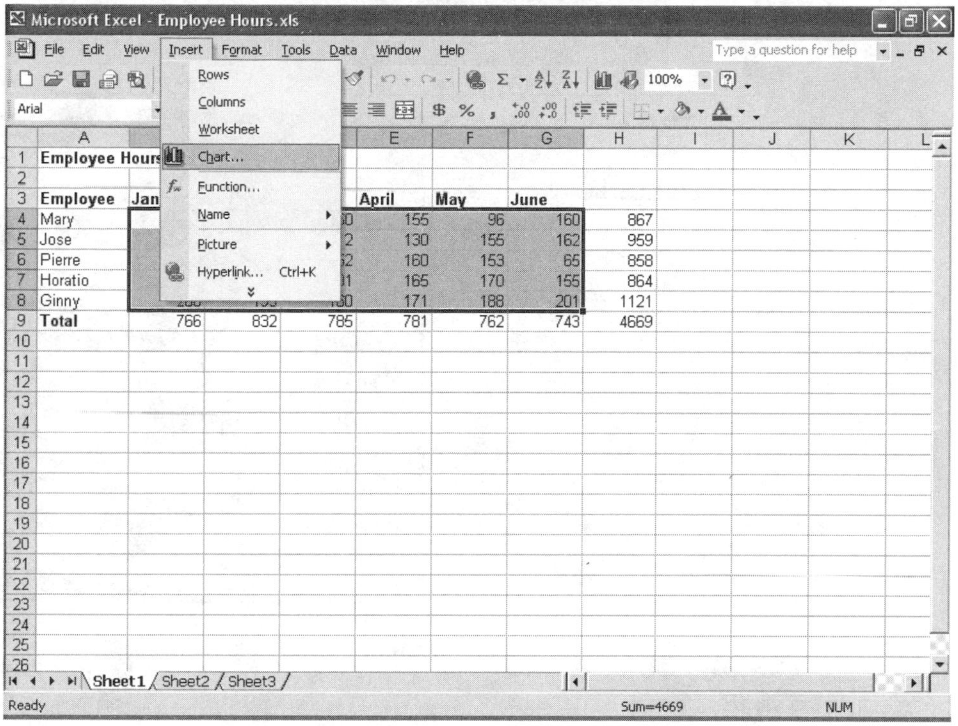

Figure 7.27: Selecting the Chart Option

The Chart Wizard is displayed, as shown in Figure 7.28. Choose the **Column** chart type from the list of chart types. A brief description of the selected chart type is displayed. Click **Next.**

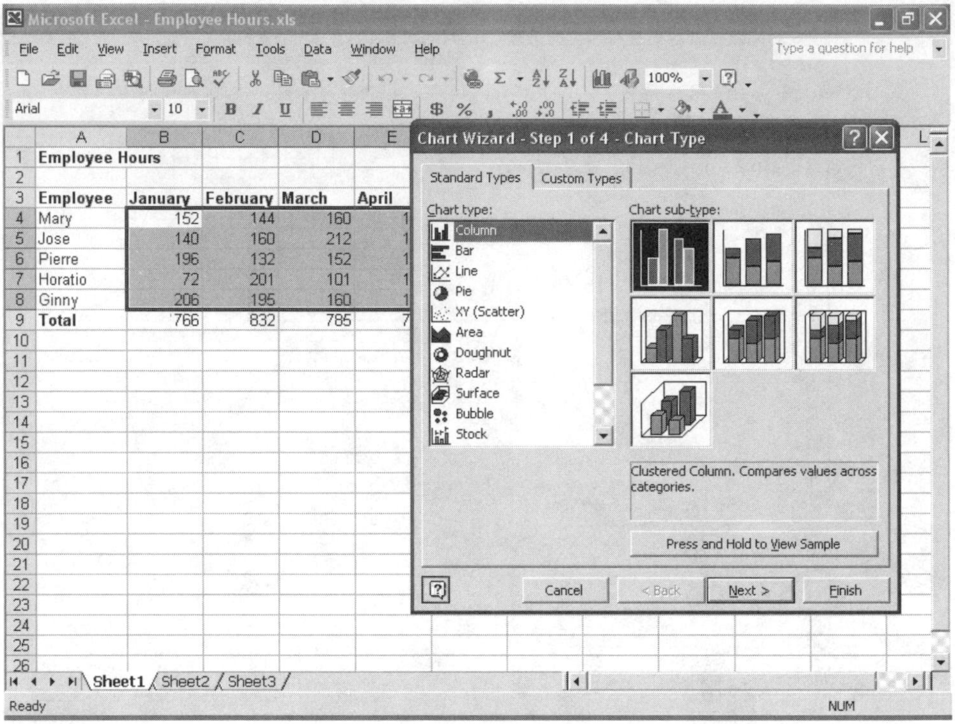

Figure 7.28: Selecting a Chart Type

To preview the results of a chart type selection, highlight a chart type and click the **Press and Hold to View sample** button.

The **Data Range** selection dialog box is displayed, as shown in Figure 7.29. Select the rows or columns that will be represented in the graph. A preview of the resulting graph is also displayed. Click **Next** to continue.

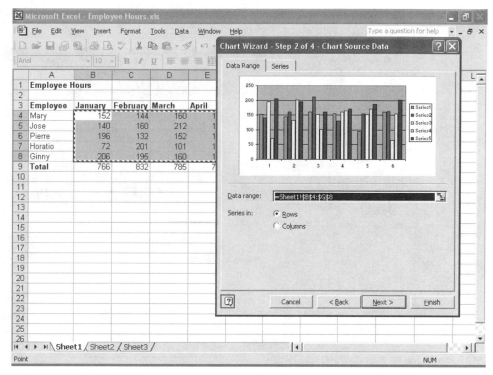

Figure 7.29: Selecting the Data Range

Select the **Series** tab to assign labels to each row or column in the graph. This is dependent on the previous menu selection. Labels can be entered for the rows or columns depending upon what you selected in the **Data Range** view. In this example, rows selected have information on employees. **Series1** represents **Mary**, **Series2** represents **Jose**, and so on, as shown in Figure 7.30.

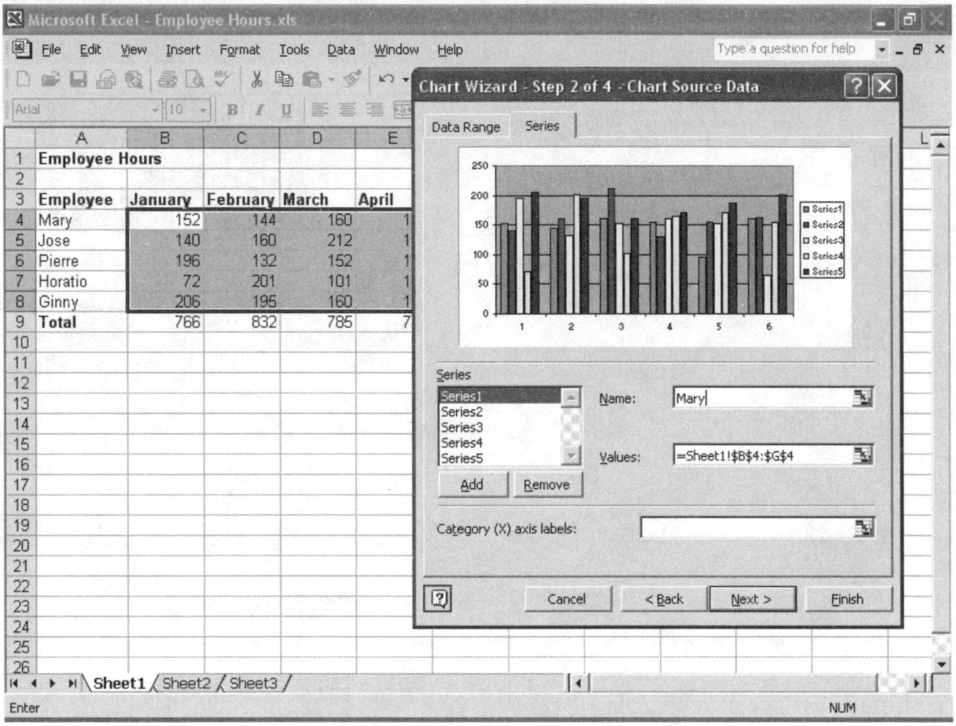

Figure 7.30: Assigning Names to a Series

Once the names are entered appropriately for the rows or columns, select **Next** to set the **Titles**, as shown in Figure 7.31.

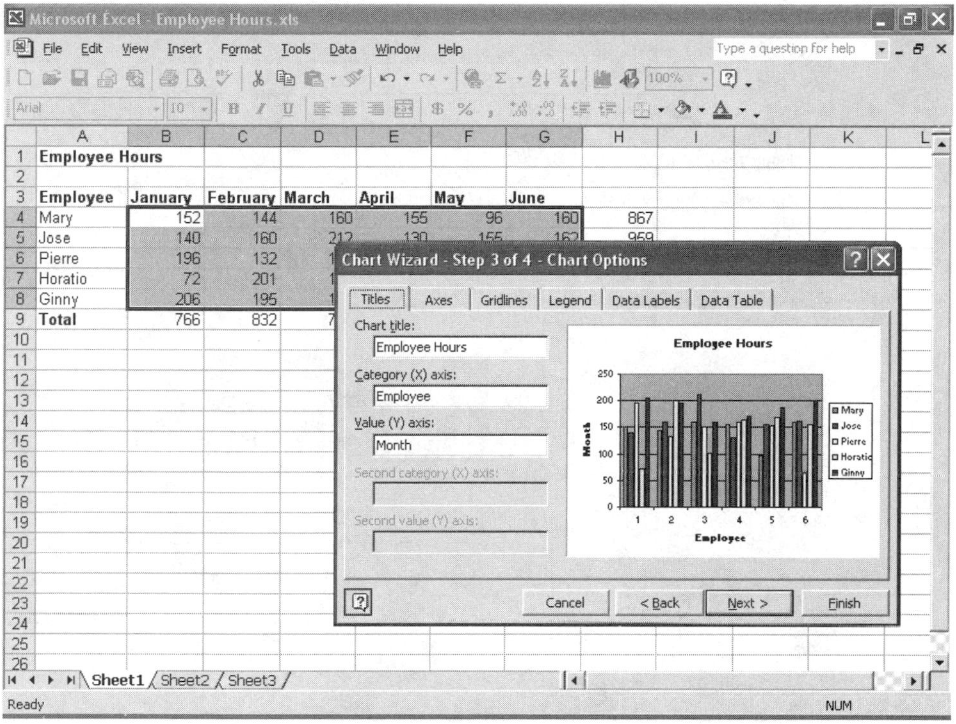

Figure 7.31: Assigning Chart and Axis Labels

Titles are comprised of the name of the chart, name of the X-axis, and name of the Y-axis.

Click **Finish** to complete the process of creating the chart. The finished chart is displayed, as shown in Figure 7.32.

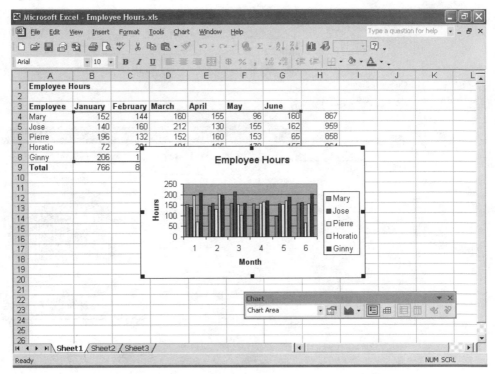

Figure 7.32: Data Represented as Column Graph

Additional chart types can be created through the Chart Wizard. However, you may need to select data in a different manner for different chart and graph types. Explore Excel Help for more information.

Converting Charts

Once a chart is created, it can be converted to another type of chart. In the example of the Employee Hours worksheet, you may want to see the work hours of employees as a pie chart. You then need to convert the column graph into a pie chart.

To convert an existing chart type to another type, perform the following steps:

1. Right-click the existing chart and click once on **Chart Type**, as shown in Figure 7.33.

Another way to invoke the list of chart types is to select the **Chart** from the Menu Bar and select a **Chart Type**.

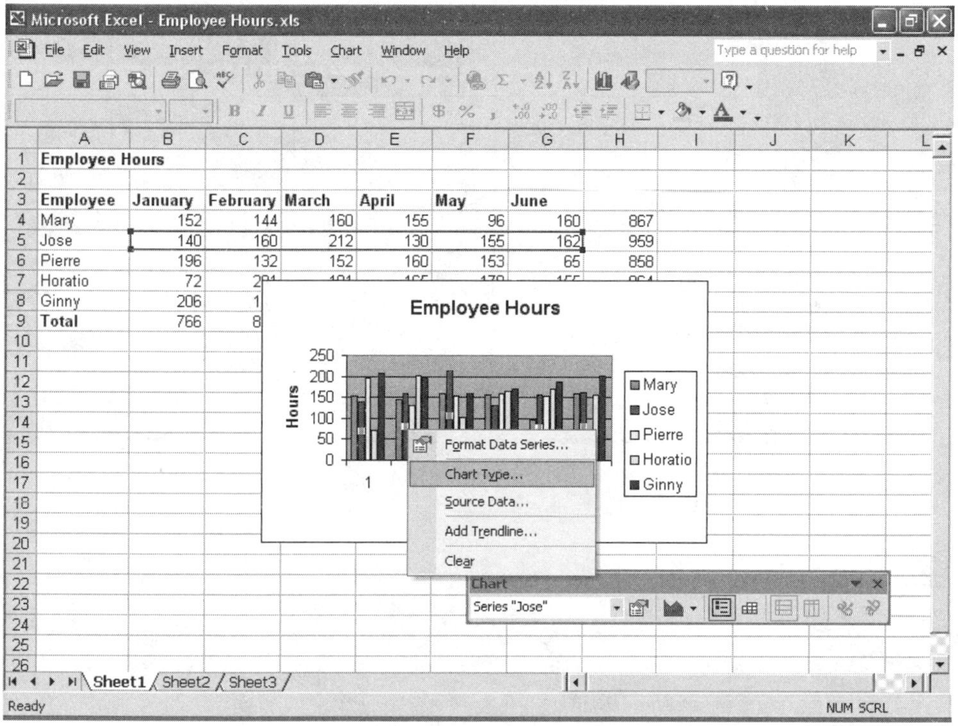

Figure 7.33: Selecting the Chart Type

2. Descriptions of other standard and custom types of charts are displayed, as shown in Figure 7.34. Select **Pie** to view its description.

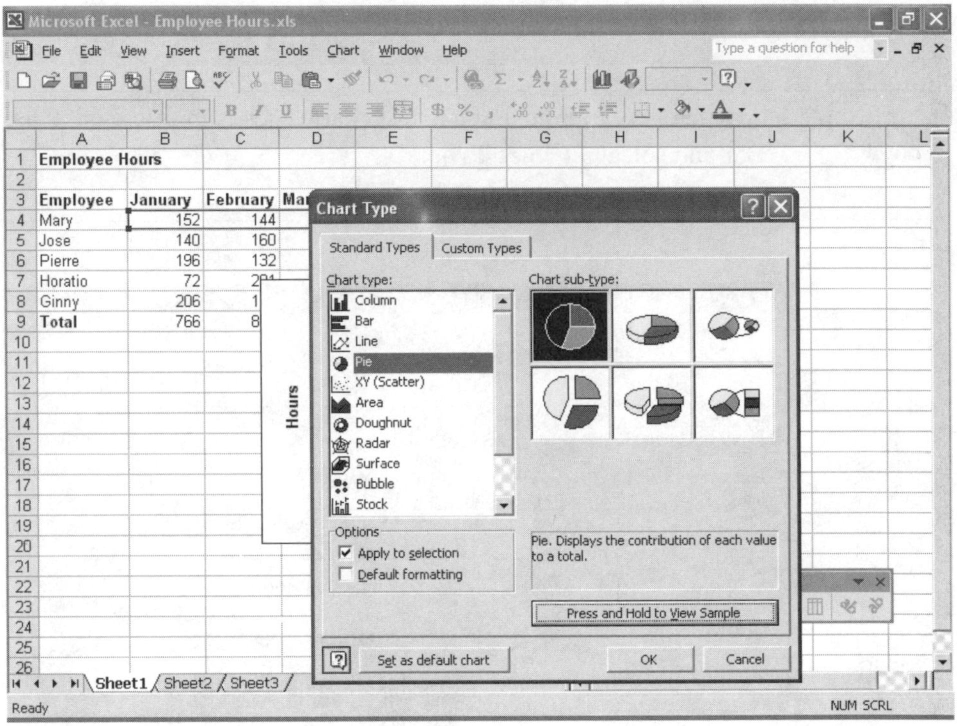

Figure 7.34: Standard Chart Types

3. Select **OK** to change the chart type to **Pie**. The data is now displayed as a Pie chart, as shown in Figure 7.35.

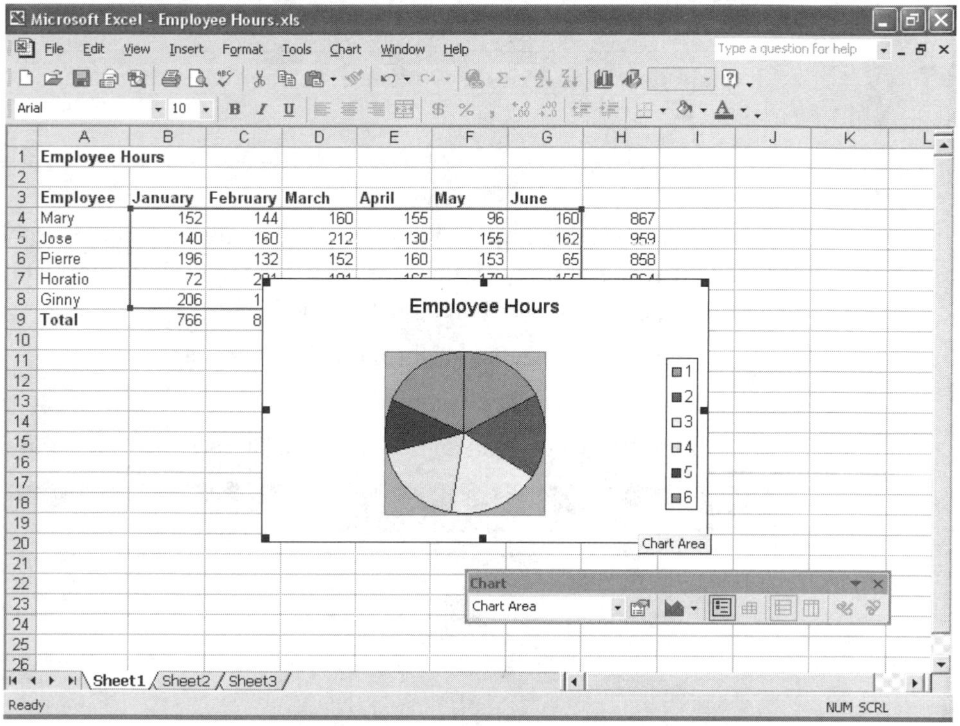

	A	B	C	D	E	F	G	H
1	Employee Hours							
2								
3	Employee	January	February	March	April	May	June	
4	Mary	152	144	160	155	96	160	867
5	Jose	140	160	212	130	155	162	959
6	Pierre	196	132	152	160	153	65	858
7	Horatio	72						
8	Ginny	206						
9	Total	766						

Employee Hours

Figure 7.35: Employee Hours Pie Chart

A chart can be deleted by clicking once on the chart and pressing the **Delete** key.

7.1.7 Formatting the Worksheet

Explain how to format the worksheet to improve its appearance.

It is possible to modify any of the worksheet settings in Excel to enhance its appearance and make it easier to use. Text can be made bold and italicized. Additionally, color of the cell, text, or graph bars can be modified.

To modify the color of cells, perform the following steps:

1. Highlight the cells to be colored.
2. Select the **Fill color** icon and choose a color, as shown in Figure 7.36.

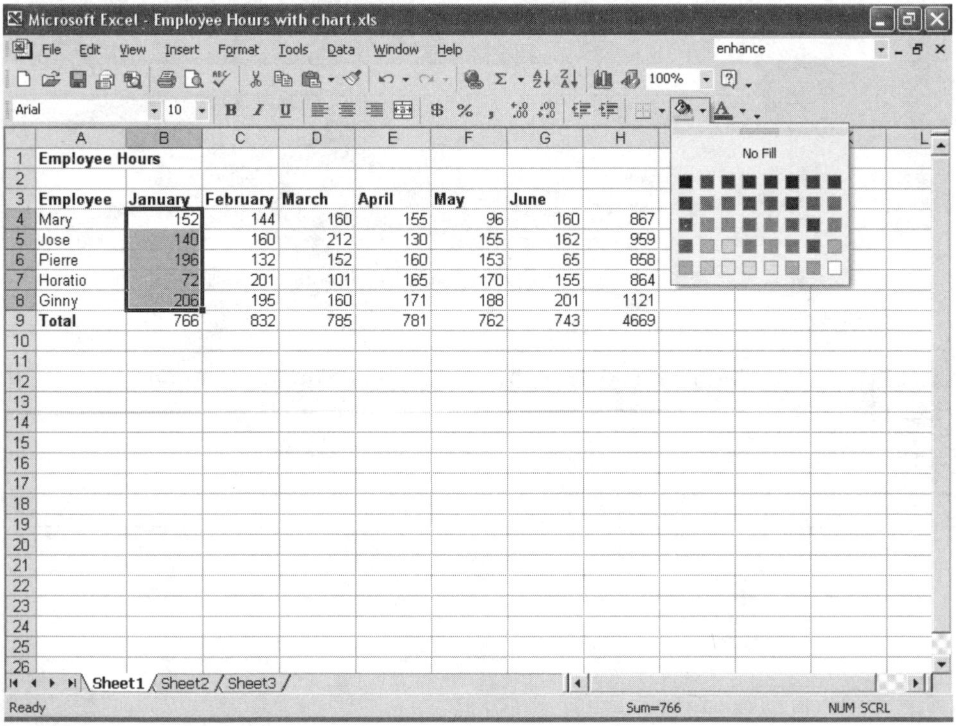

Figure 7.36: Adding Color to Cells

As shown in Figure 7.37, rows and columns can have different colors to enhance the visual impact of the worksheet.

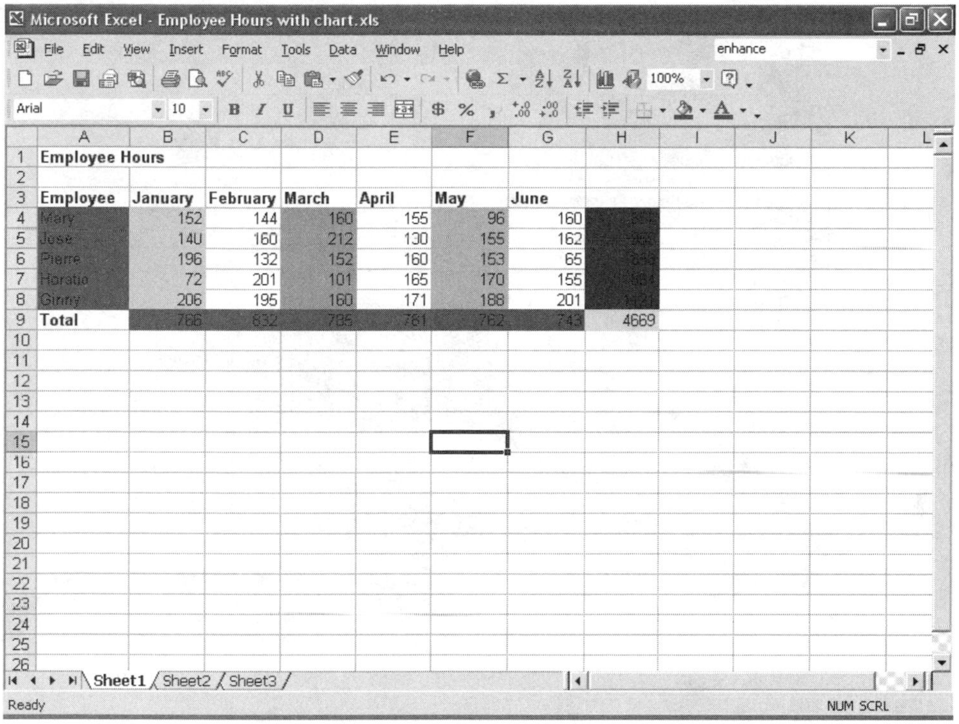

	A	B	C	D	E	F	G	H
1	Employee Hours							
2								
3	Employee	January	February	March	April	May	June	
4	Mary	152	144	160	155	96	160	
5	Jose	140	160	212	130	155	162	
6	Pierre	196	132	152	160	153	65	
7	Horatio	72	201	101	165	170	155	
8	Ginny	206	195	160	171	188	201	
9	Total	766	832	785	781	762	743	4669

Figure 7.37: Colored Rows and Columns

Charts and graphs can also be visually enhanced by adding or modifying their default colors. To modify the colors of the graph bars, perform the following steps:

1. Right-click the chart and select **Chart Options**.

If the Chart toolbar is not visible, select **Insert, Toolbars**, and check the box for **Chart**.

2. Choose each bar of the graph by its **Series** name. Select the **Format Data Series** icon and choose the new color, as shown in Figure 7.38.

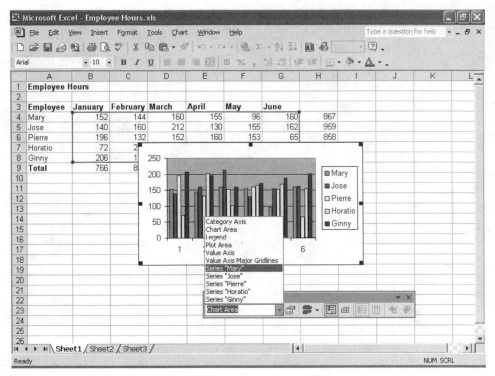

Figure 7.38: Modifying Series

A sample of the selected color is displayed, as shown in Figure 7.39.

3. Click **OK** to apply the color.

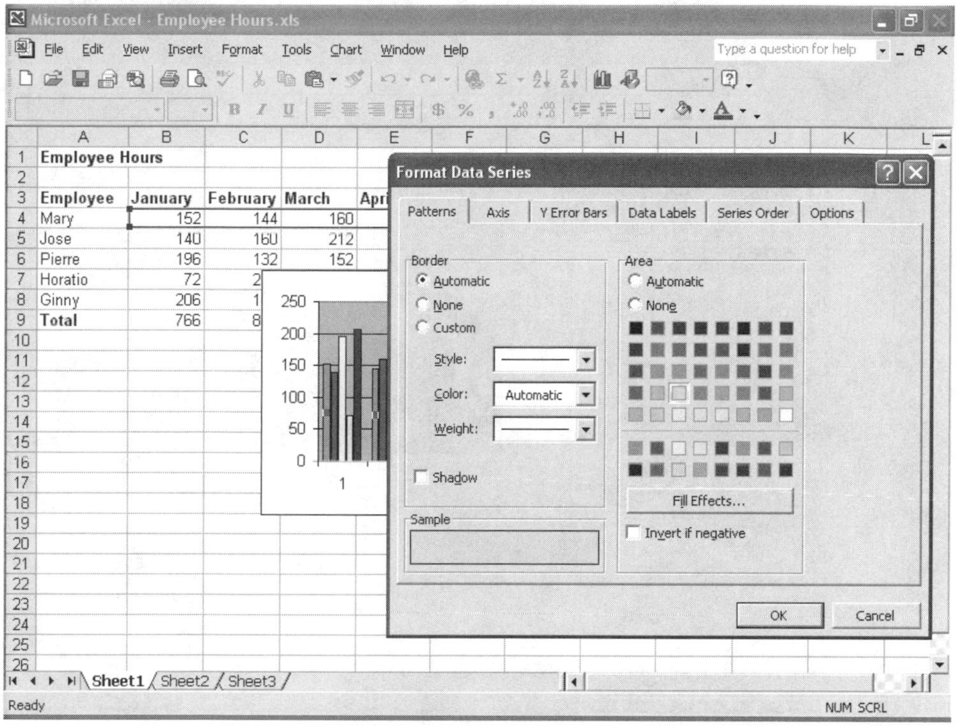

Figure 7.39: Series Color Options

4. Similarly, select each series individually and assign it the color of your choice. The bar colors will show different colors, as shown in Figure 7.40.

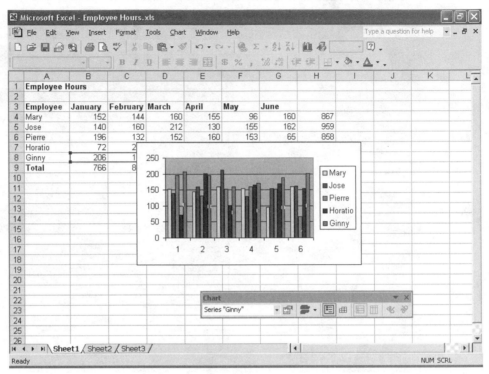

Figure 7.40: Changed Series Colors

You can also modify the legend color and chart area color. However, adding too much color to every feature in a spreadsheet is not advisable as it will often divert attention from data or significant data may lose prominence.

You can also change the size of your chart. To change the size of the chart in the worksheet, click once on the chart and use any of the 8 small black squares (also called resize handles) surrounding the chart to manually increase or decrease the chart size.

Cells can also contain Clip Art for greater visual appeal. Perform the following steps to add Clip Art to your worksheet.

1. Click the area in the worksheet where you want to add the Clip Art.

2. Select **Insert → Picture → Clip Art,** as shown in Figure 7.41.

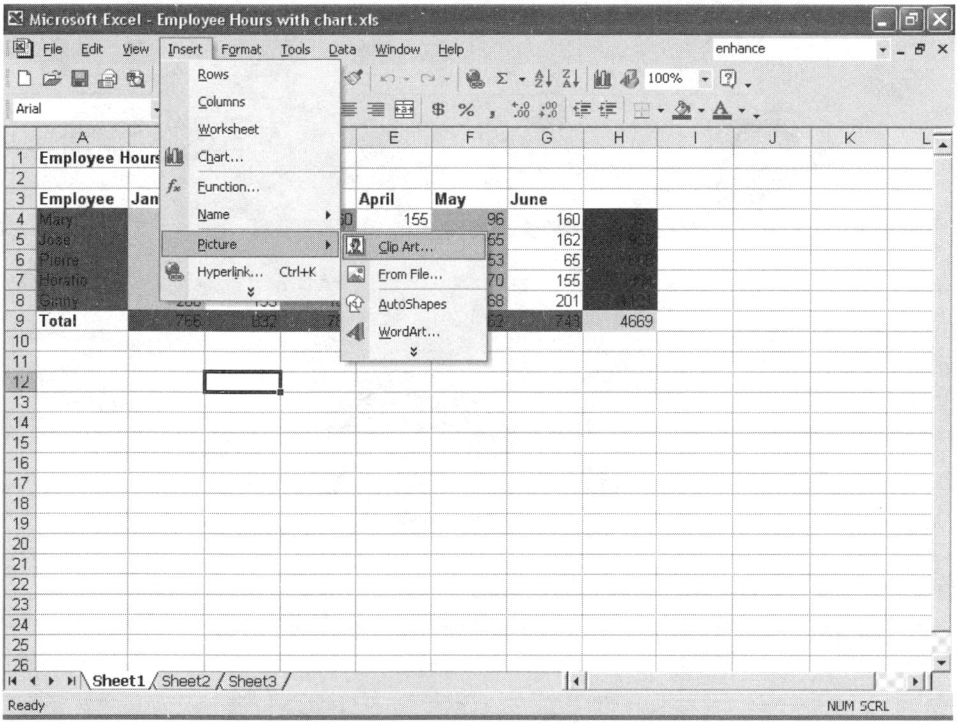

Figure 7.41: Inserting Clip Art

3. Enter a topic to search in the Clip Art or search online for more Clip Art options.

Microsoft has an extensive online library of available Clip Art. Access the site http://www.microsoft.com/homepage/ms.htm. Enter the keywords Clip Art in the Search field on the home page and you can download Clip Art of your choice.

4. After finding the Clip Art of your choice, click once on the picture to place it in the worksheet. The picture is displayed in your worksheet, as shown in Figure 7.42.

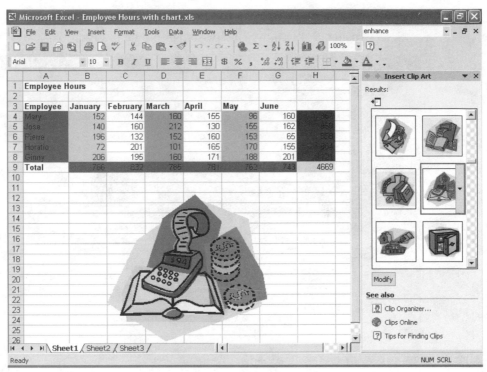

Figure 7.42: Clip Art

7.1.8 Saving and Printing

Describe how to save and print a worksheet.

While working on a worksheet, it is important to save the worksheet for later access. A worksheet may need to be printed as handouts for a meeting or be used as part of a presentation or research paper.

Saving Worksheet

Selecting **File → Save** saves the worksheet with the same name. To save a document to another location or with another name, select **File → Save As**.

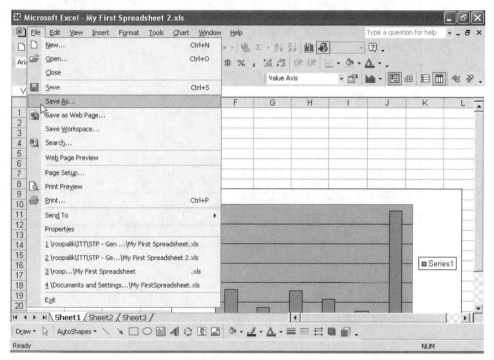

Figure 7.43: Saving a Worksheet

When the **Save As** option is selected, a name for the document and the location of the document needs to be entered, as shown in Figure 7.44.

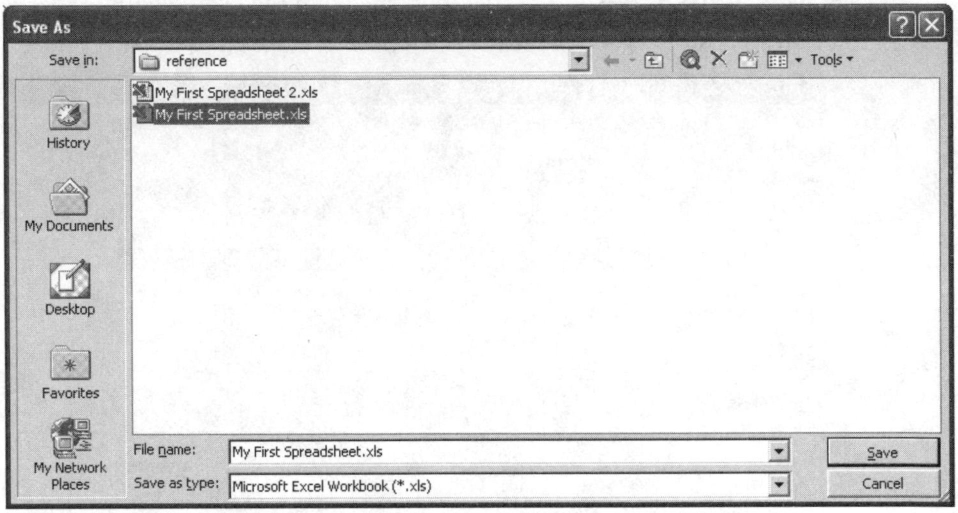

Figure 7.44: Save As Dialog Box

Excel files can be configured to save automatically as you work. From the **Tools** menu, choose **Options** and select the **Save** tab. Select the **Save AutoRecover info every:** checkbox. As shown in Figure 7.45, select in minutes how often to Auto Save and where to place the Auto Saved document.

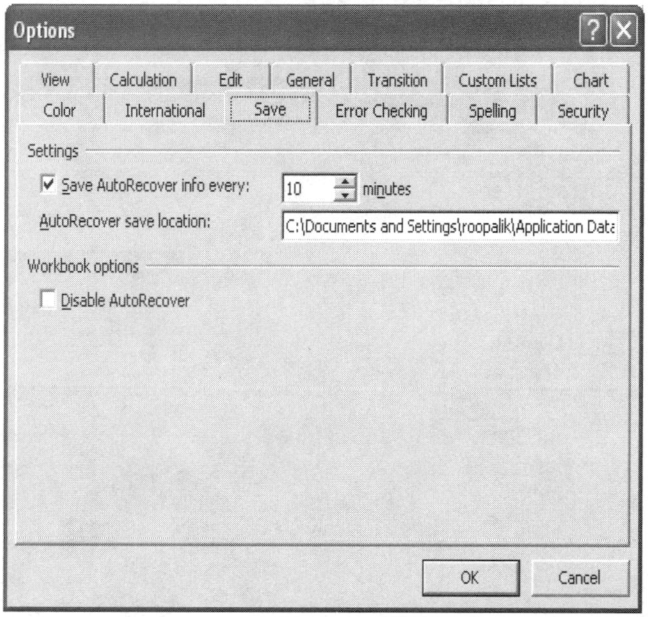

Figure 7.45: Setting AutoRecover Option in Excel

Printing Worksheet

It is advisable to preview your worksheet before printing as you can then check that the worksheet is within print margins. To preview your worksheet before printing, perform the following steps:

1. Select File → Print Preview.

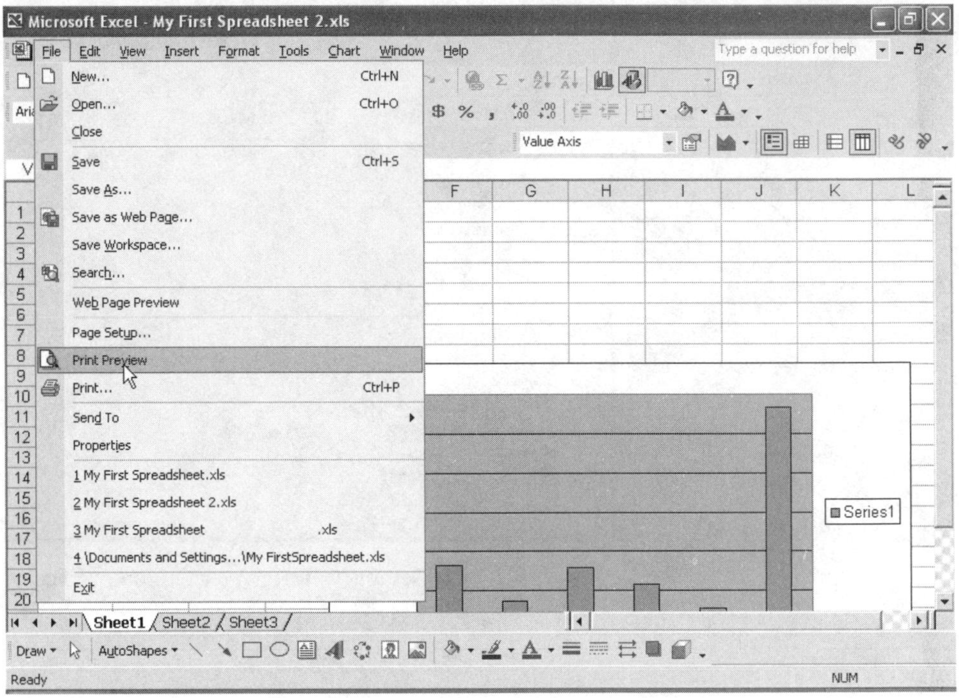

Figure 7.46: Selecting Print Preview of a Worksheet

You can preview how the worksheet would look like when printed. The print preview is displayed in Figure 7.47.

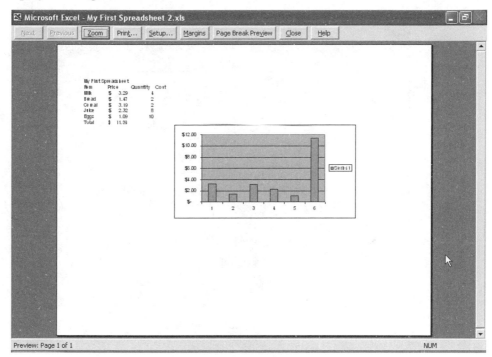

Figure 7.47: Print Preview

 It is advisable to set the Print area of your worksheet before you print. To set the print area, highlight the area of the worksheet you want to print. Then, select **File → Print area → Set Print Area**.

2. After previewing your worksheet, select **File → Print**. The Print dialog box is displayed. As shown in Figure 7.48, the options here are similar to those seen in Word.

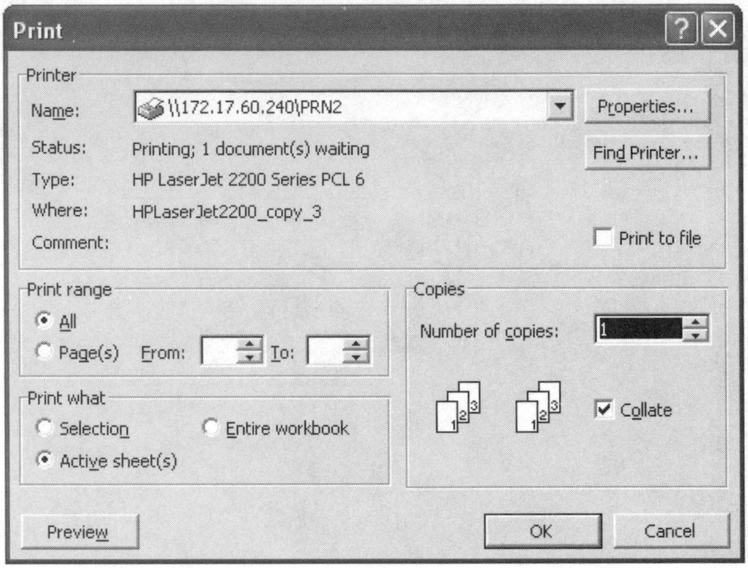

Figure 7.48: Print Dialog Box

The Print dialog box options include:

- **Printer selection**: Choose from a list of printers to send the document for printing.
- **Print range**: Choose to print all pages or selected pages.
- **Print what**: Choose selected data, active sheets, or entire workbook.
- **Copies**: Choose the number of copies to print.

3. Select the **Properties** tab to make additional print choices. The Properties dialog box is displayed in Figure 7.49.

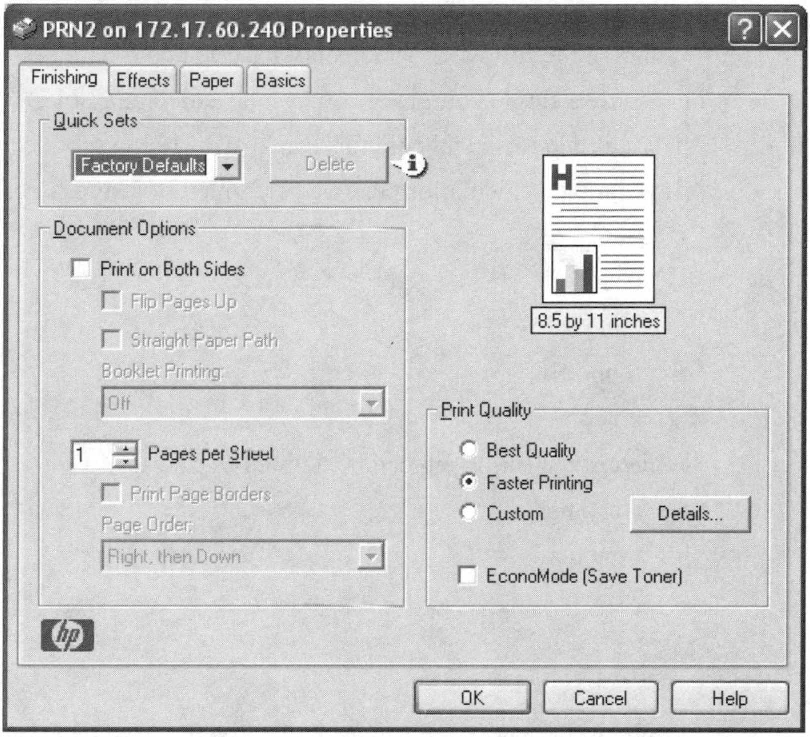

Figure 7.49: Print Properties

4. Choose your **Finishing**, **Layout**, and **Effects** and click **OK**.

Print properties in Excel are similar to those in Word. Use Excel Help for more information.

Selecting the printer icon from the toolbar will automatically direct the current active worksheet(s) to the last selected printer.

---

1. Which of the following statements are true about data in Excel?

   I.   Only a single column or row can be added at a time.

   II. Multiple rows and columns can be selected to produce a total.

   III. Complex calculations can be performed by using functions.

   a. I only

   b. II only

   c. I and II

   d. II and III

2. Which of the following can be defined as a series?

   a. Heading

   b. Function

   c. Row

   d. Cell

3. Which of the following is used at the beginning of cell contents to denote a formula?

   a. +

   b. =

   c. −

   d. /

7.2 Introducing Interactive Features of Spreadsheets

Multiple worksheets in a workbook allow you to store related information together. You can enter and edit data on several worksheets simultaneously. Linking worksheets and workbooks enables you to use data from one worksheet in another worksheet within the same or different workbook.

This section discusses some interactive features of spreadsheets including:

- Summary Worksheet—Linking data across worksheets and workbooks, creating summary worksheets to facilitate data usage and charting.
- Hyperlinking—Used to connect multiple worksheets.
- Web usage—Used to save a worksheet as a Web page.
- Help—Used to learn more about features or troubleshoot problems in a spreadsheet.

7.2.1 Summary Worksheet

Explain how to link data across worksheets and workbooks to create summary worksheets.

Creating summary worksheets is a useful technique in managing, analyzing, and presenting large volumes of data that are spread across multiple worksheets and workbooks. Data of different types and categories is generally segregated in multiple tables. On an as-needed basis, you will be required to correlate and analyze such diverse data.

The summary worksheet is designed for conveniently summarizing and consolidating data from several other worksheets and facilitating presentation of the consolidated data in the form of charts and graphs. Design of a summary worksheet will depend on the specific analysis needs.

A summary worksheet is created by linking data contained in several worksheets using the relative reference technique.

A relative reference points directly to a key cell or a block of cells in the worksheet that contains the original data. If you make any changes to the original data, the changes are automatically reflected in the summary worksheet.

To link cells from the original worksheet to a summary worksheet:

1. Create a new spreadsheet in Excel. Figure 7.50 shows a blank spreadsheet.

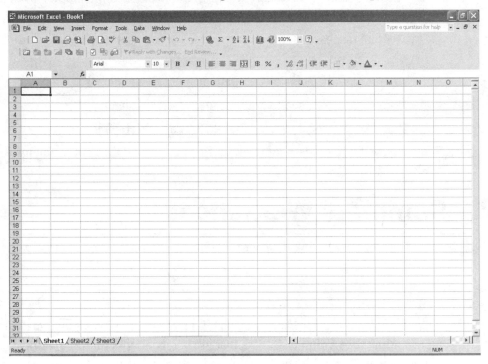

Figure 7.50: Blank Spreadsheet

2. Open an existing spreadsheet (named "Employee Hours.xls") by clicking on the **File** menu, selecting the file name from the listed files or using the **Open** option, as shown in Figure 7.51.

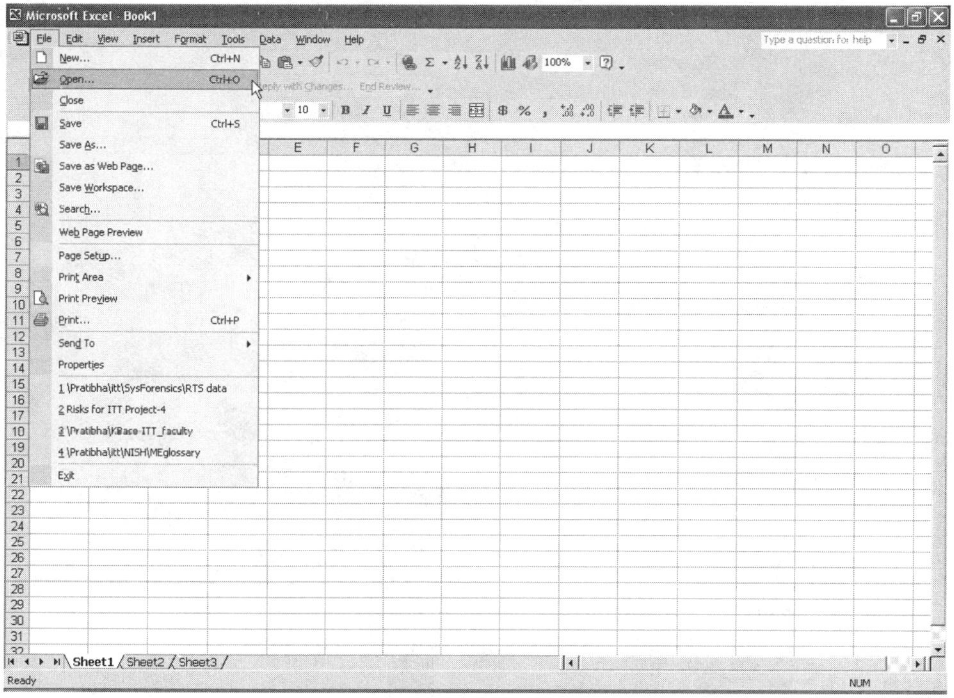

Figure 7.51: Open Existing Spreadsheet

At this point, two spreadsheets are open. The first spreadsheet is blank and the Employee Hours.xls spreadsheet contains data on the number of hours worked by each employee. Figure 7.52 shows the data in the Employee Hours.xls spreadsheet.

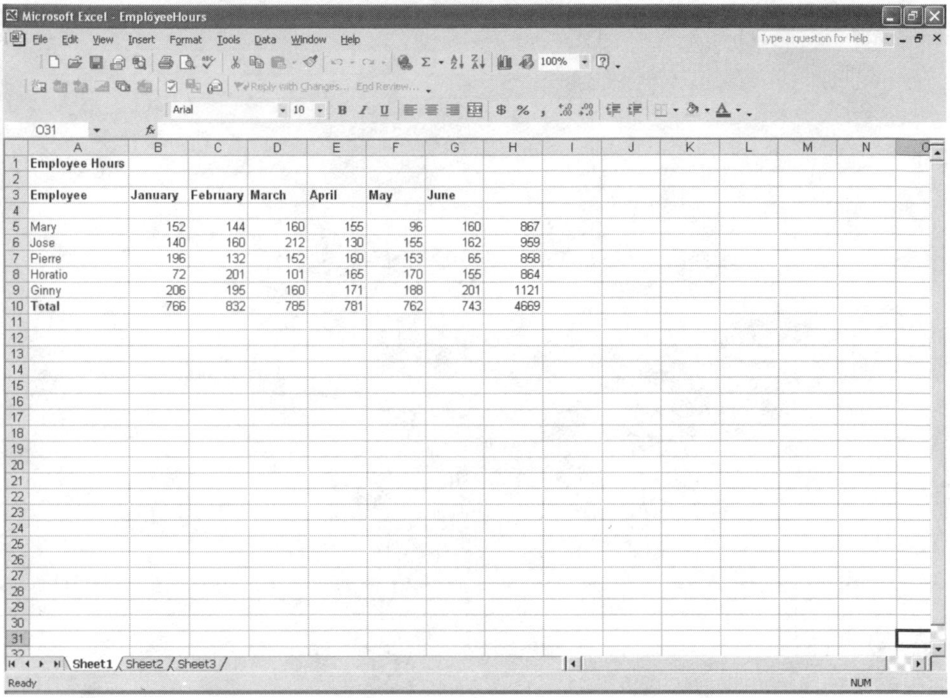

Figure 7.52: Data in Employee Hours.xls Spreadsheet

> To see the spreadsheets that are open, select the **Window** menu on the menu bar.

3. Select the data to be linked to the summary worksheet and then select the **Cut** option on the **Edit** menu. Figure 7.53 shows the Employee Hours.xls spreadsheet with selected data.

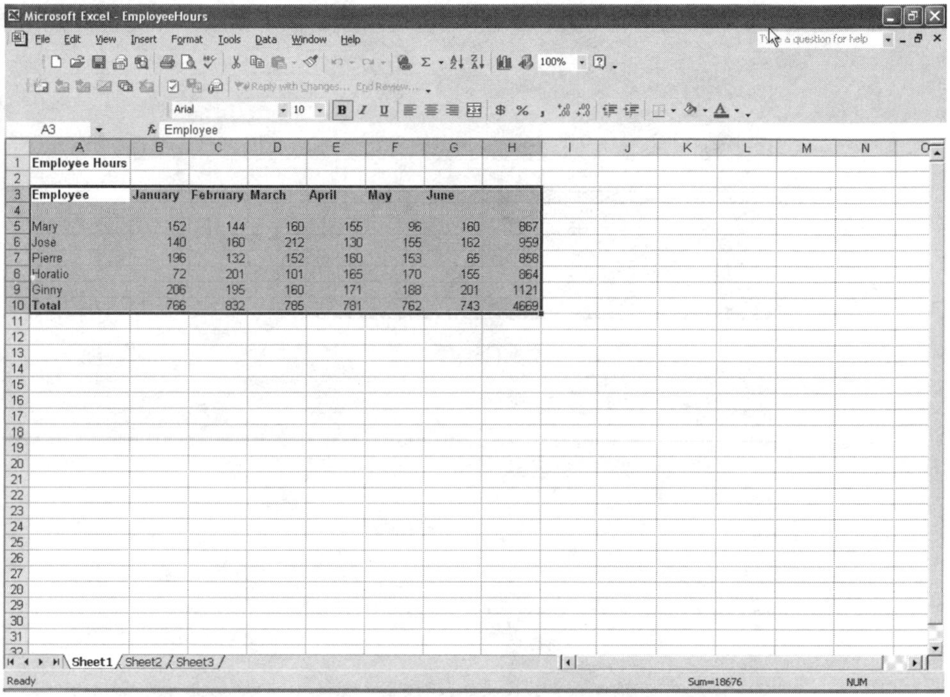

Figure 7.53: Selecting Data in Employee Hours.xls Spreadsheet

4. Open the blank spreadsheet and select the **Paste** option on the **Edit** menu. The Paste icon appears, as shown in Figure 7.54. Click the **Paste** icon and select **Link Cells** from the available paste options.

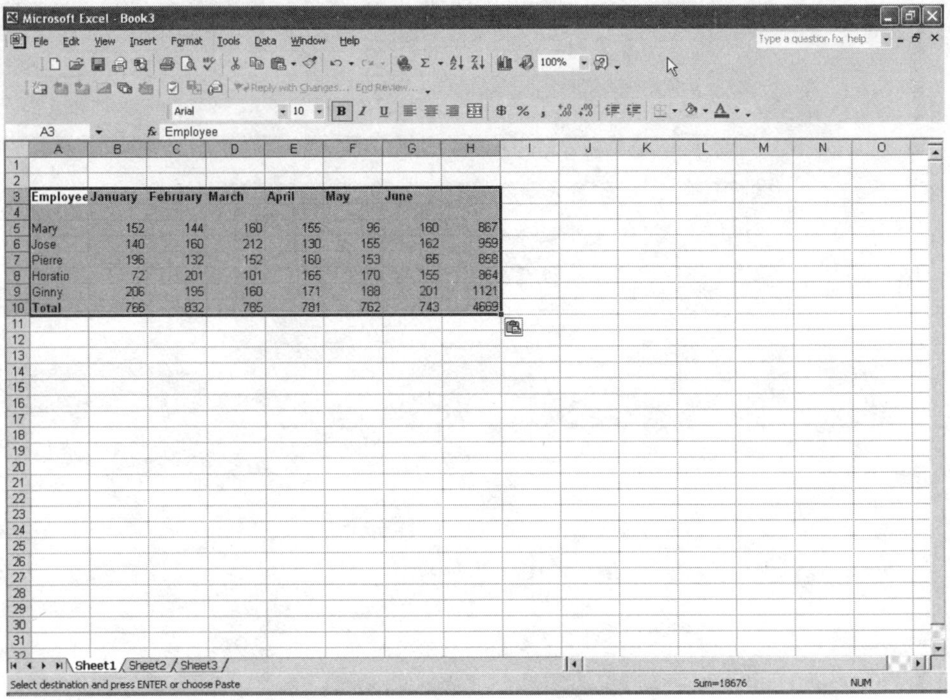

Figure 7.54: Spreadsheet with Paste Icon

5. Change the working hours for the employee named Ginny, in the original sprcadshcet (Employee Hours.xls) from 206 to 99, as shown in Figure 7.55.

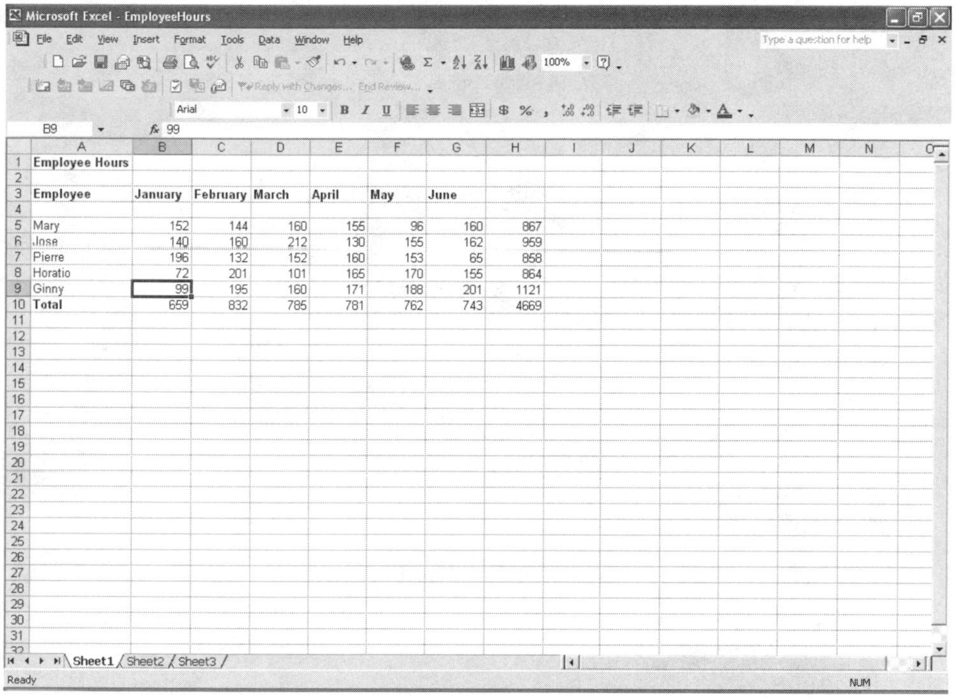

Figure 7.55: Changing Data in the Original Spreadsheet

The change made to the data in the original spreadsheet is reflected in the spreadsheet containing the linked data, as shown in Figure 7.56.

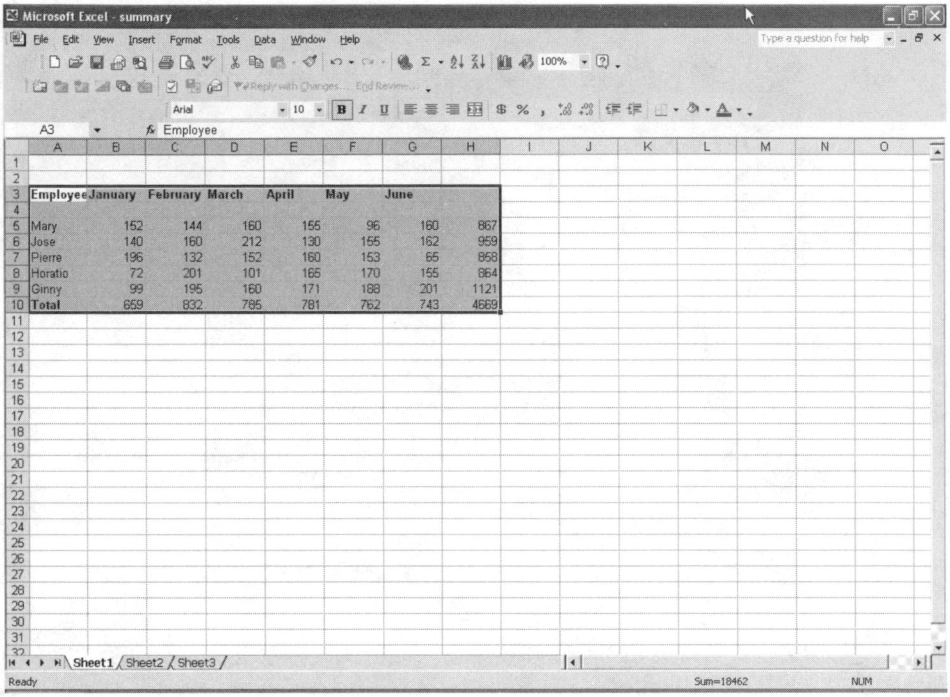

Figure 7.56: Worksheet Containing Linked Data

Multiple cells from the same document or other documents can be linked together through this process. Changing a value in any linked cell will be reflected in the entire linked data through this process.

Summary worksheets can be designed and built by linking the required data items from multiple data sources on other worksheets. The data can be consolidated using functions and formulae available in Excel. The functions and formulae can also be implemented using relative referencing across worksheets and workbooks. The summarized and consolidated data so captured in the summary worksheets can then be graphically presented using the graphs and charts functions available in Excel.

For implementing the above, refer to details and instructions available within the Excel Help feature. Additionally, you can find additional information at Microsoft's knowledge base Web site at:

http://support.microsoft.com/default.aspx?scid=FH;EN-US;KBHOWTO&sd=GN&ln=EN-US.

7.2.2 Hyperlinking

Describe how to insert a hyperlink in a worksheet.

Hyperlinking in an Excel spreadsheet is used to redirect a user from one spreadsheet to another by clicking on text. The text that represents the hyperlink is usually underlined and is colored differently from the normal text. Note that the color of the hyperlink text will be different depending on whether the hyperlink has been used so far in the current session. To add a hyperlink to an existing spreadsheet:

1.   Open the spreadsheet in Excel.

2. Select the **Hyperlink** option on the **Insert** menu, as shown in Figure 7.57.

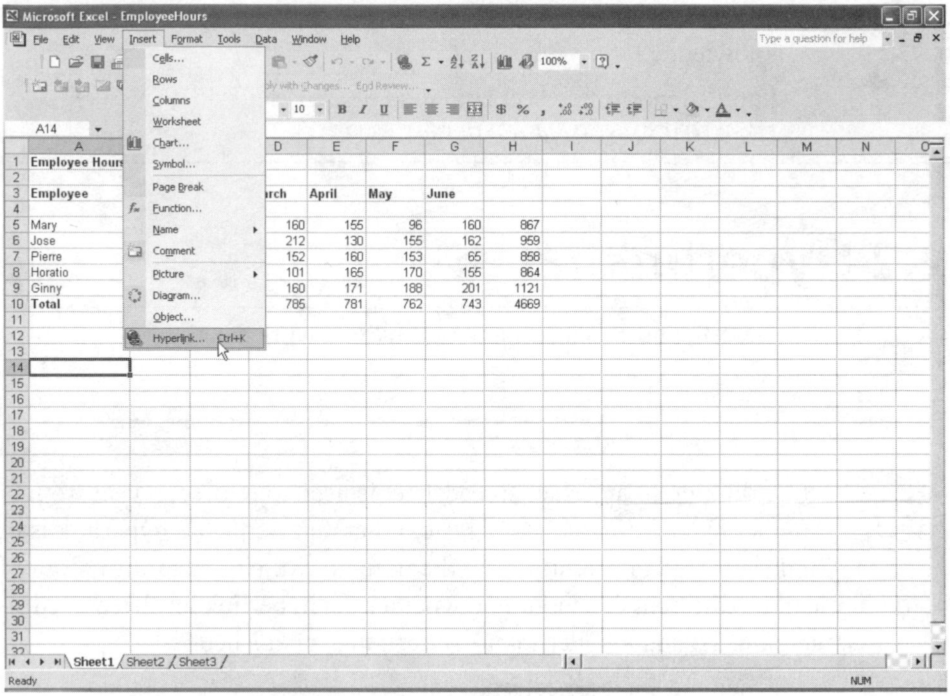

Figure 7.57: Adding a Hyperlink

3. Choose the location of the file or data cell(s) with which to link. Choose from one of the following options under **Link to** in the left pane:

- Existing File or Web Page
- Cell in This Document
- New Document
- E-mail Address

4. Select the actual file or data cell(s) using the following options under **Look in**.

- Current Folder
- Browsed Pages
- Recent Files

5. Enter the **Text to display** in the hyperlink. Click **OK** when complete.

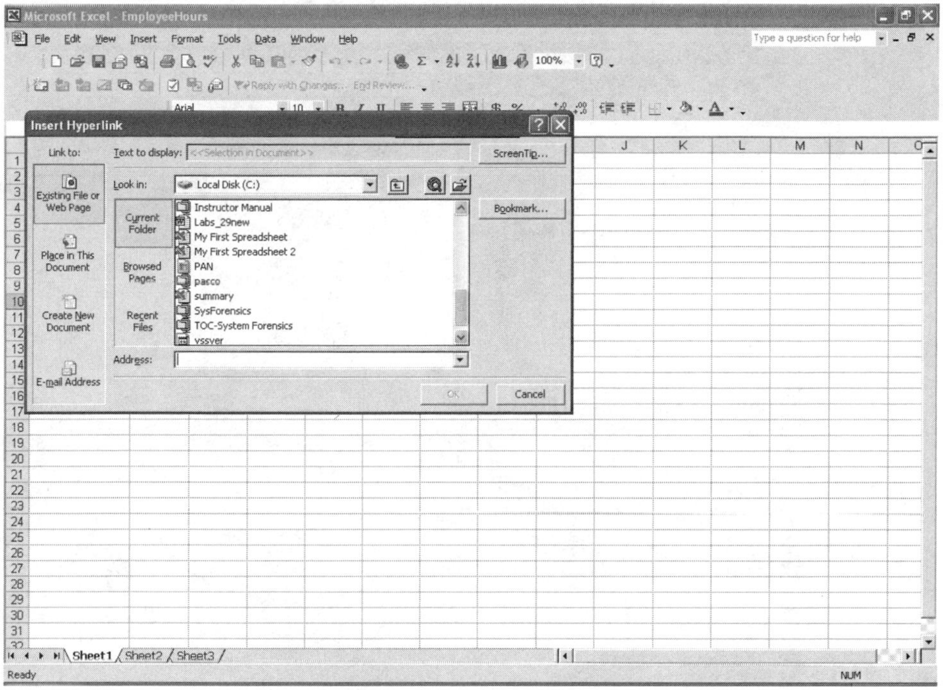

Figure 7.58: Hyperlink Configuration

Figure 7.59 shows the Employee Hours.xls spreadsheet after adding a hyperlink to the Payroll Calculator.xls spreadsheet.

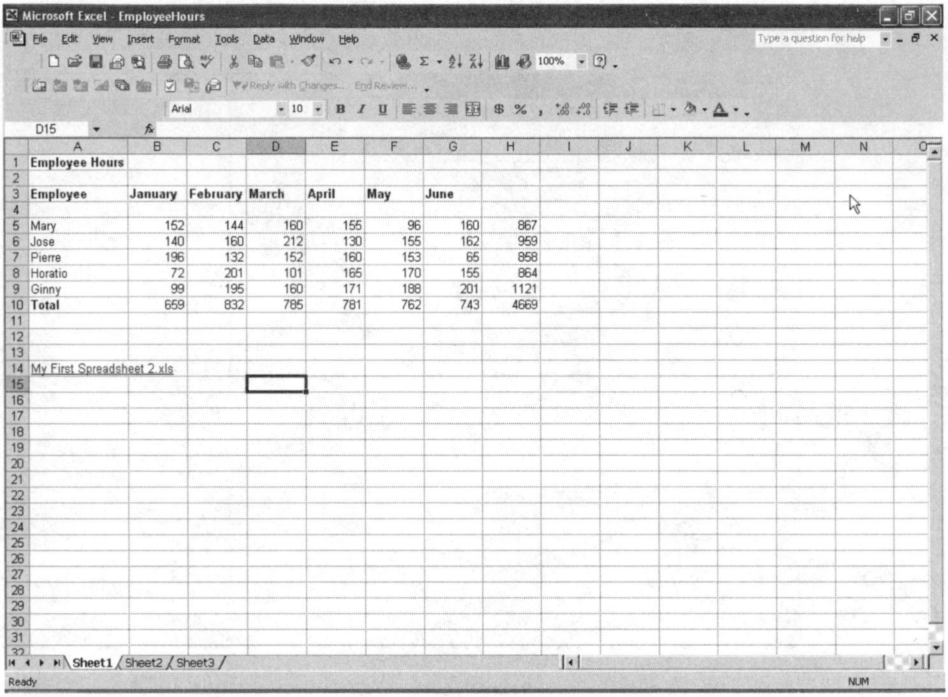

Figure 7.59: Hyperlink to the Payroll Calculator.xls Spreadsheet

6. Click the hyperlink to test whether it redirects you to the specified spreadsheet. Figure 7.60 shows the Payroll Calculator.xls spreadsheet.

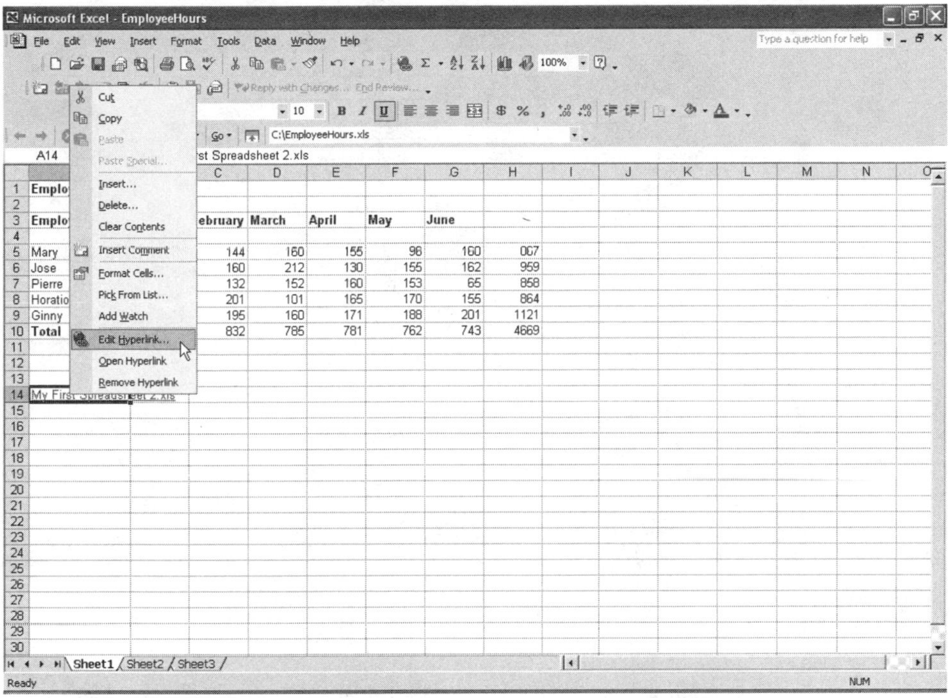

Figure 7.60: The Payroll Calculator.xls Spreadsheet

Use the back arrow button on the Web toolbar to return to the previous spreadsheet.

Hyperlink text, addresses, or locations can be edited, removed, or opened by right-clicking the hyperlink in the document and selecting the **Edit Hyperlink**, **Remove Hyperlink**, or the **Open Hyperlink** options on the shortcut menu.

Figure 7.61 shows a shortcut menu that is displayed upon right-clicking a hyperlink in a spreadsheet.

	A	B	C	D	E	F	G	H	I	J	K	L
1	Employee Hours											
2												
3	Employee	January	February	March	April	May	June					
4	Mary	152	144	160	155	96	160	867				
5	Jose	140	160	212	130	155	162	959				
6	Pierre	196	132	152	160	153	65	858				
7	Horatio	72	201	101	165	170	155	864				
8	Ginny	206	195	160	171	188	201	1121				
9	Tota		832	785	781	762	743	4669				

Shortcut menu items:
- Cut
- Copy
- Paste
- Paste Special...
- Insert...
- Delete...
- Clear Contents
- Insert Comment
- Format Cells...
- Pick From List...
- Add Watch
- Edit Hyperlink...
- Open Hyperlink
- Remove Hyperlink

Figure 7.61: Shortcut Menu Displayed Upon Right-Clicking a Hyperlink in a Spreadsheet

7.2.3 Web Usage

Explain how to save a worksheet as a Web page and use a spreadsheet on the Web.

To enable users to view an Excel spreadsheet from any location, you can make it available on a Web server. Data that is made available on a Web server is referred to as published data. You can publish data in Excel spreadsheets by using one of the following methods:

■ Place/publish an entire Excel workbook on the Web.

■ Place/publish a worksheet on the Web.

■ Place/publish a range of cells on the Web.

■ Place/publish charts on the Web.

An Excel spreadsheet can be easily transformed into a Web document. After a spreadsheet is saved with the appropriate file type recognized by the Web protocol, it can be made available on a Web site.

Publishing often requires contacting the Web administrator to place the Excel data on a Web server.

To save an Excel document as a Web document:

1. Open the Excel workbook that contains the data to be published.

2. Select the **Save as Web Page** option on the **File** menu, as shown in Figure 7.62. The **Save As** dialog box appears.

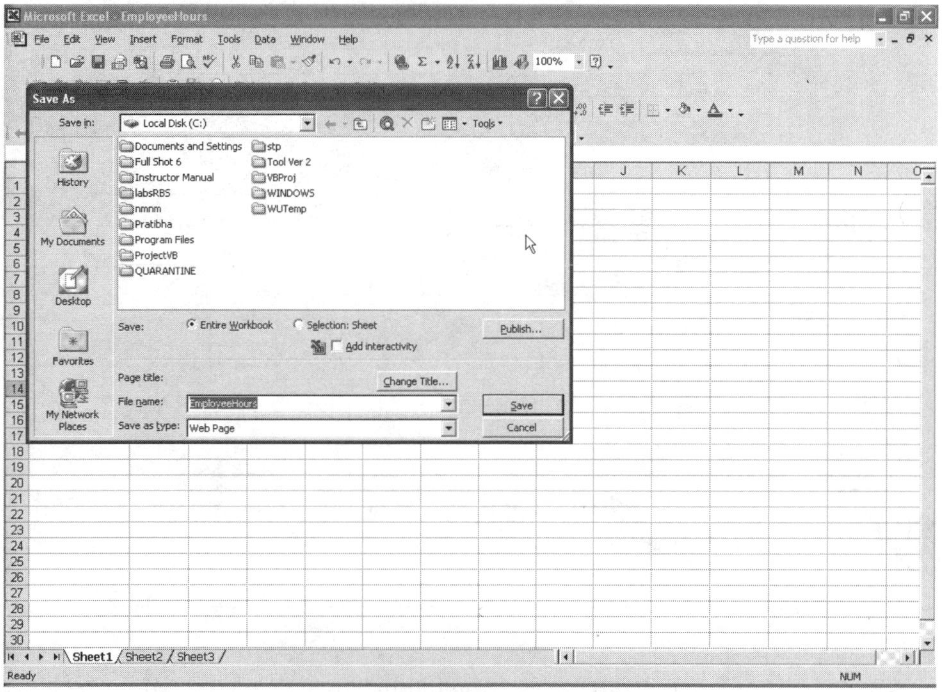

Figure 7.62: Selecting Save as Web Page Option

3. In the **Save In** drop-down list, select the folder in which the Web document is to be saved. You can save the entire workbook as a Web document. Alternatively, you can save selected data in a worksheet as a Web document. To save the entire workbook as a Web document, select the Entire Workbook option. In the **Save as type** drop-down list, select **Web Page (*.htm; *.html)**. Specify the name of the Web document in the **File name** text box, and then click the **Save** button. Figure 7.63 shows the **Save As** dialog box after entering the necessary details.

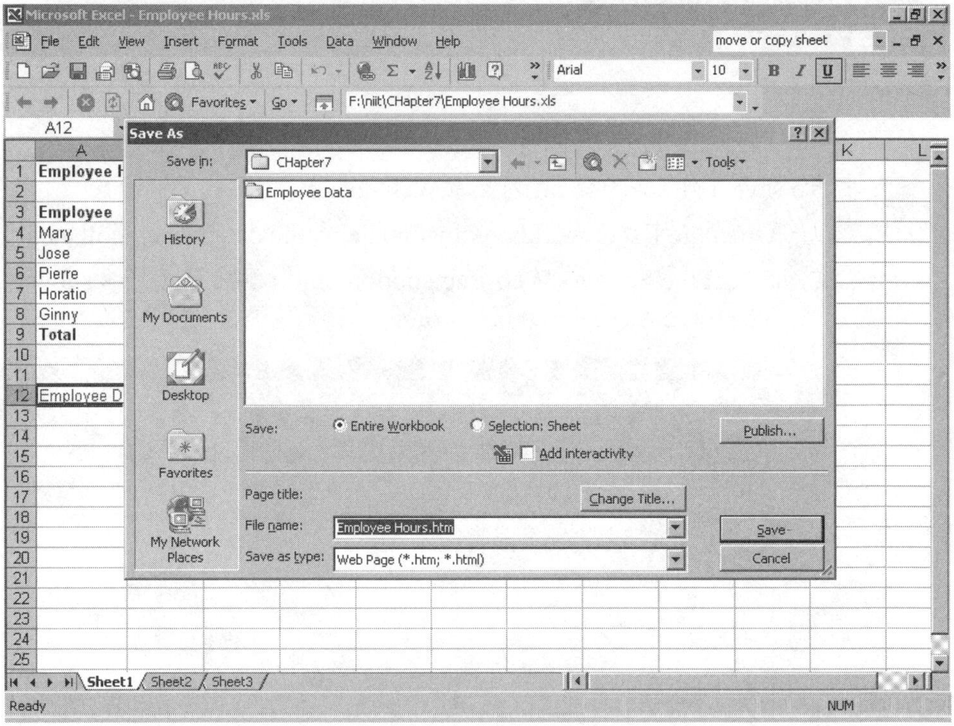

Figure 7.63: Saving as Web Page

 Select the **Add interactivity** check box in the Save As dialog box to edit the spreadsheet on the Web.

 For a detailed discussion on publishing data contained in Excel workbooks on the Web, refer to http://www.microsoft.com/mspress/books/sampchap/4751.asp.

7.2.4 Help

Use the Help feature to discover and apply additional features to troubleshoot your worksheet.

The Help feature in Excel is an important tool that can be used to obtain information on the various features provided in Excel. To obtain help on a specific topic, select one of the options on the Help menu. Figure 7.64 shows the Help menu.

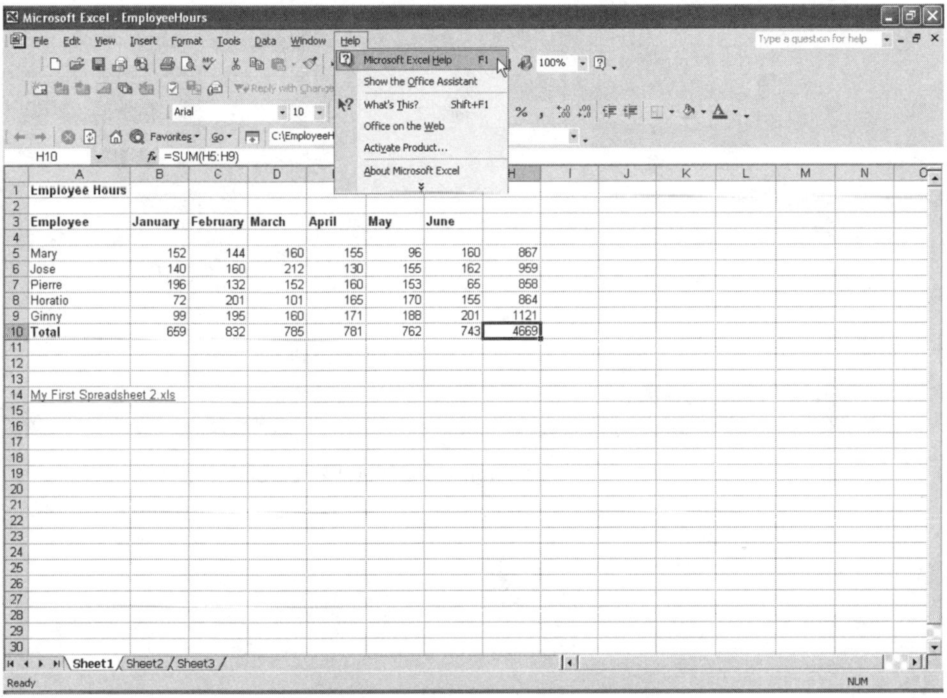

Figure 7.64: Open Help from the Toolbar

F1 is a shortcut to **Help**.

Enter a keyword or keywords about which you want to obtain help. Figure 7.65 shows the Help Assistant. The keyword **formula** has been typed in the text box.

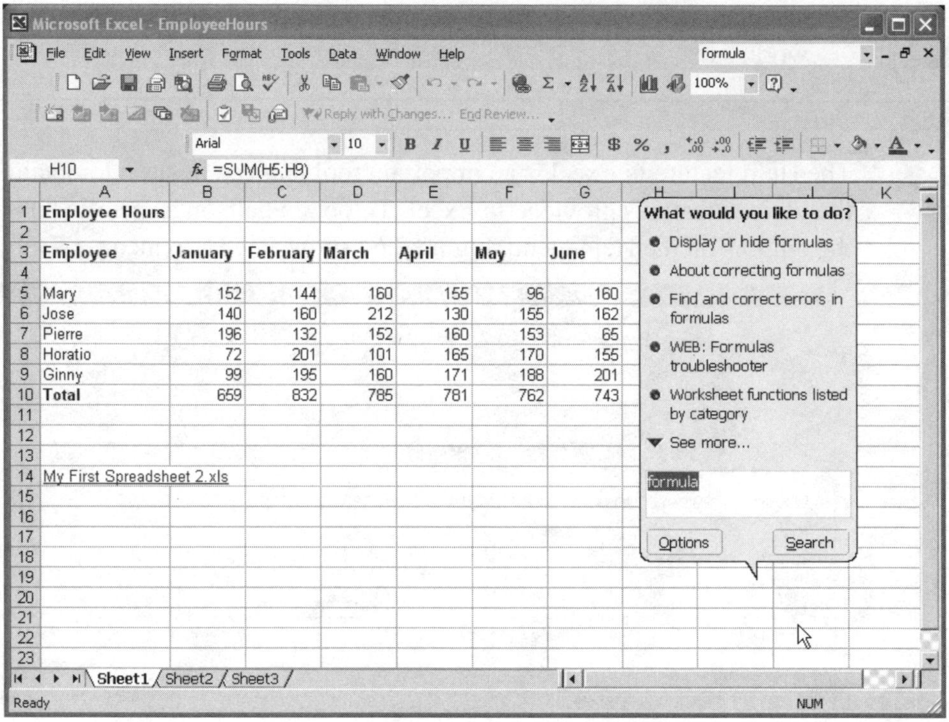

Figure 7.65: Help Search Results

1. Which of the following are valid hyperlink locations? (Choose all that apply.)
   a. Electronic Mail Address
   b. Web site
   c. Another Excel document
   d. A Word document

2. Which file extension would be used for a Web document?
   a. .xls
   b. .mct
   c. .htm
   d. .hmt

3. To make sure that users do not modify the Excel data published on the Web, what needs to be configured?
   a. Select the box for Add interactivity.
   b. Clear the box for Add interactivity.
   c. Do nothing. Excel worksheets only can be modified if they have a .xls extension.
   d. Only the creator of the spreadsheet can modify it.

7.3 Features of Databases

A database is a structured collection of information stored for a specific purpose. Information can be stored in file cabinets, Word documents, Excel spreadsheets, and so on. An automated database program like Microsoft Access makes it convenient to store, organize, and retrieve information. A database program makes it easy to define the organization of data storage, assist in adding new data, and modify the stored data through automated forms. It also enables you to query and report on the data in meaningful ways.

Some examples of databases are given below.

> **Example 7.1**
>
> A teacher can have a database of students, assignments, and grades.

> **Example 7.2**
>
> A retail sales company can have one database comprised of product information and a second database of customer information.

Information can be retrieved from a database using a defined query interface. Information can also be analyzed and organized in the form of reports. A teacher can generate a report on students and their grades. A sales manager can generate a report listing best-selling products by region.

Databases can be relational or non-relational. Databases that store all collected information in a location known as a **table** are *non-relational*. Relational databases provide the added advantage of storing information in multiple tables that are linked. Storing information in multiple tables minimizes repetition of information and improves efficiency and performance because important data is stored only once.

Microsoft Access is a relational database management system (RDBMS) that is used to collect, store, organize, manage, and manipulate various types of information in a

Windows environment. After the information is stored, you can retrieve it as required by using database objects, such as queries and reports.

In this section, you will learn about the Microsoft's Access database application. The topics covered include creating and querying a database, creating forms, generating reports, and using database help.

If you are unfamiliar with the basics of Access, it is strongly recommended that you use an online tutorial to increase your familiarity before proceeding. Access tutorials are available on the Web and can be found by using a search engine and typing in keywords "Access Tutorial." Microsoft provides its own Access Tutorial.

You may access a Microsoft Access online tutorial from the ITT Tech Virtual Library. Log on to the Virtual library at http://library.itt-tech.edu/. From the main menu, select the Learning Guides Link. Under the Online Tutorials, scroll down and select **Microsoft Office 2000 Tutorials**. Select Access from the list of Office Programs. Click the link **Begin the Access tutorial** at the top to begin taking the tutorial.

Additionally, a Microsoft tutorial for Access is available at http://www.microsoft.com/education/default.asp?ID=AnalyzeDataAccess2002.

7.3.1 Creating a Database

Explain the method of creating a database, such as Microsoft Access, with tables, fields, and primary keys.

In Access, the term database refers to a single file that contains a collection of information stored in various tables.

The most important step in creating a database is planning. Reviewing information that will be stored and determining how this information will be used is essential for creating a successful database design. The planning stage includes planning the database as a whole, including the tables and queries to be created and the reports to be generated. The cornerstone of a solid database design is a well-developed table structure based on how the tables will interact. The database design must be planned well to accommodate current and future business requirements and growth and change.

After planning the database, the next step is to create the tables for that database. You can create a database in three ways by:

- Using the design view
- Using the Table Wizard
- Entering data

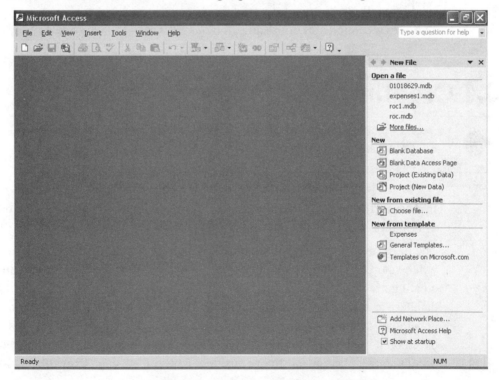

When possible, it is best to create all the tables at the time the database is created. This allows for more consistency among tables. If you create all the tables at one time, it is easier to identify missing fields and relationships that might have been overlooked. However, the reality is that the database is always growing and changing. Access allows you to modify and add tables to the database at any time.

Perform the following steps to create your database:

1. Select **Blank Database** in the right pane, as shown in Figure 7.66.

Figure 7.66: Access Database Startup Window

2. Enter a file name for the database document and a location to place the document by clicking **Create**.

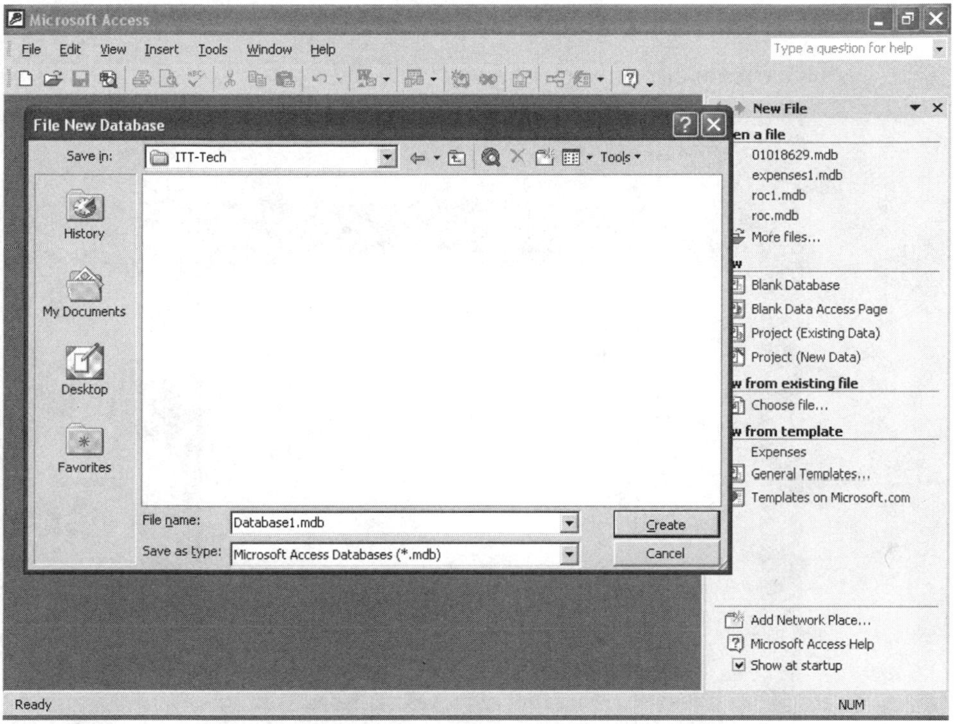

Figure 7.67: Creating an Access Database

Access provides three choices for database creation, as shown in Figure 7.68.

- ▓ Create table in Design view
- ▓ Create table by using Wizard
- ▓ Create table by entering data

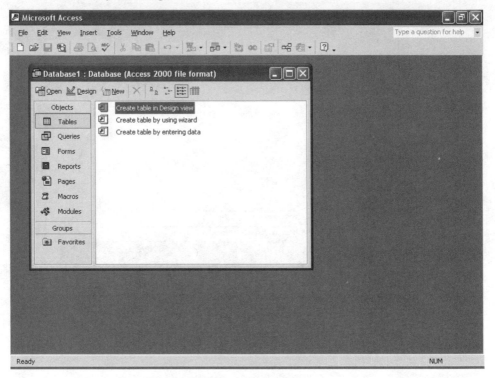

Figure 7.68: Options for Database Table Creation

 More information on the table creation options is available using the Access Help function or through Microsoft's official Web site.

In this example, the Table Wizard is used to create a student database. As shown in Figure 7.69, the Table Wizard offers the following choices:

- Table type
  - Business
  - Personal
- Sample Tables
- Sample fields in the table selected

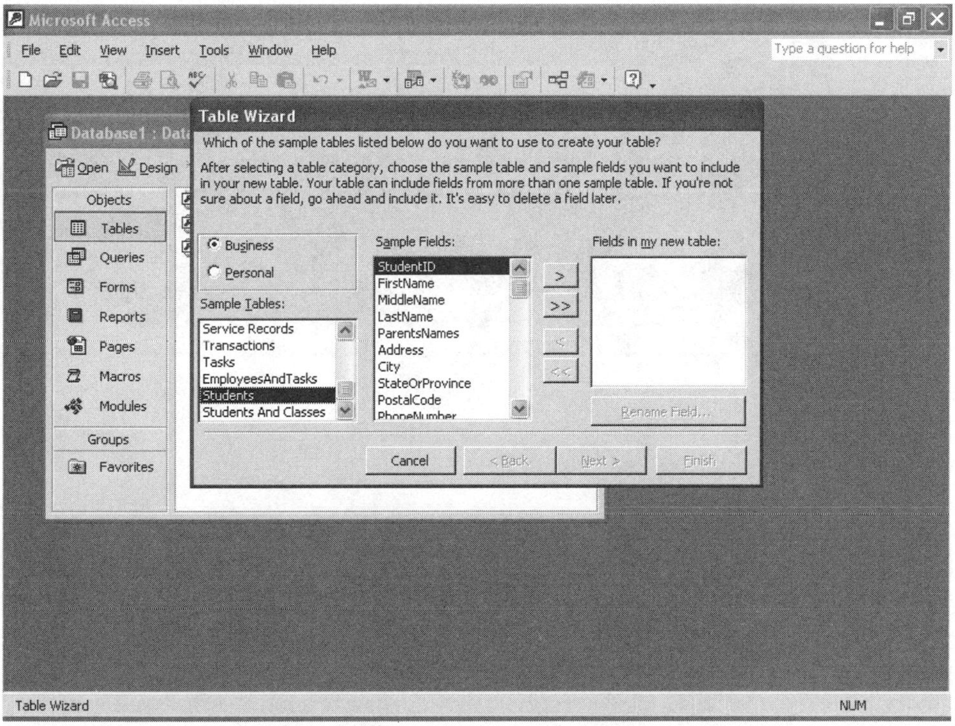

Figure 7.69: Creating Student Database Using Table Wizard

Add a single field by highlighting the selection and using the > symbol. To select all fields, use >>. To remove a selection, use the < symbol. To remove all selected fields, use <<.

---

3. Select the fields to enter in the table and click **Next**.

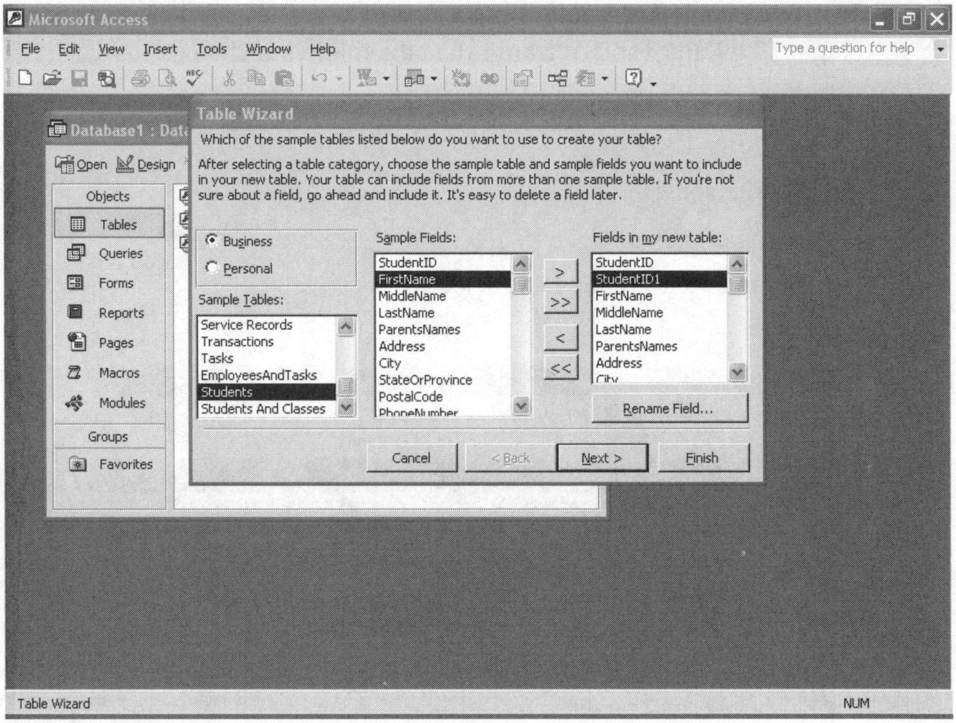

Figure 7.70: Table Wizard Fields Selection

4. Enter a name for the table and click **Next**.

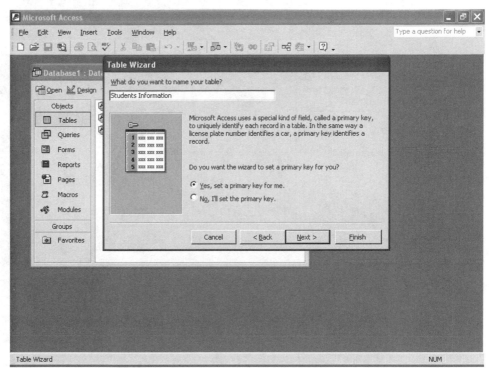

Figure 7.71: Table Naming

5. Select **Yes** to have the Table Wizard set the **primary key**. The primary key is used to identify each record in the table uniquely.

 The primary key is a field or combination of fields that uniquely identifies each record stored in a table. Primary key values cannot be duplicated. The primary key is often the first field or fields in a table.

6. Choose the option for what is to occur after the table creation wizard is complete.

   ▪ Modify the table design.

   ▪ Enter data directly into the table.

   ▪ Enter data into the table using a form the Wizard creates for me.

7. Table creation is completed once you select your desired option and click **Finish**.

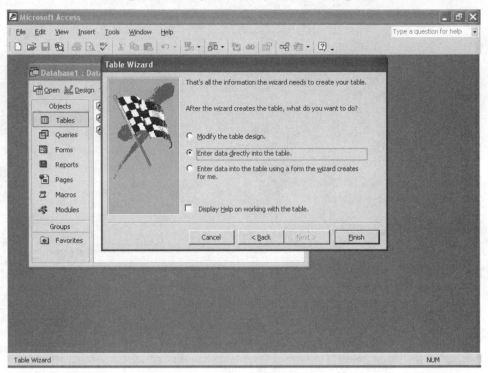

Figure 7.72: Table Creation Completed

The table is now ready to input data, as shown in Figure 7.73.

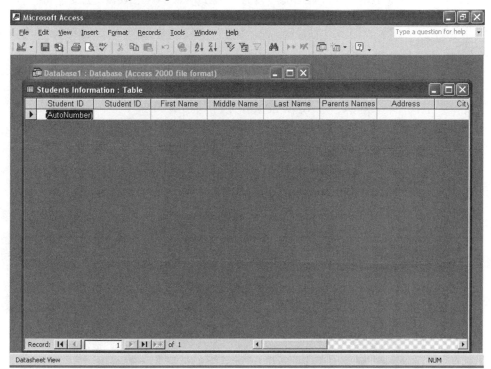

Figure 7.73: Table Input Screen

7.3.2 Querying a Database

Create and run queries to extract data from the database.

After you have created tables, you can create queries to retrieve the required data from the tables. Queries are created using tables and their corresponding relationships. Queries are built using the fields stored in the tables to produce a record set that answers a specific question or query. Queries can also be created using data retrieved by one or more existing queries or by using a combination of queries and tables.

The response to a query is referred to as a **dynaset**.

To create query, perform the following steps:

1. To open a database, choose from the list of databases under **Open a file** in the right pane.

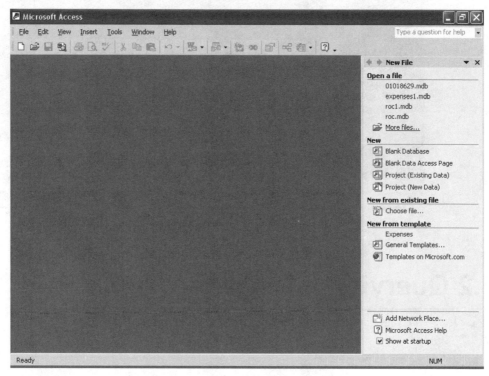

Figure 7.74: Access Database Startup Window

2. Choose **Queries** from the **Objects** column on the left and then choose query type.

    a. Create query in Design view

    b. Create query by using wizard

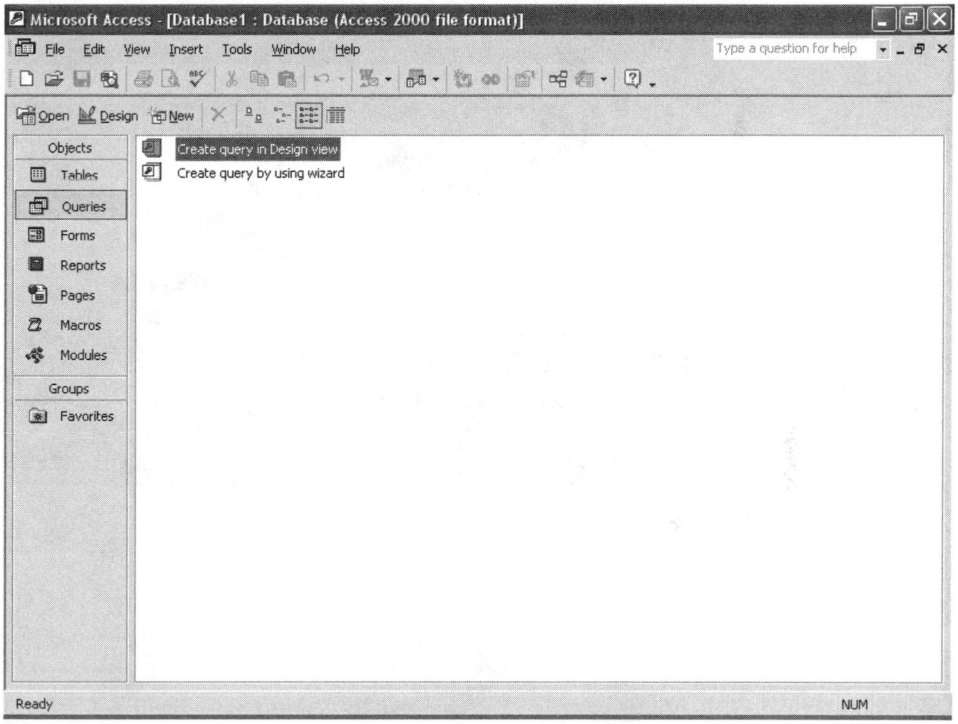

Figure 7.75: Create Database Query

In this example, the query Wizard will be used to retrieve data from the database.

3. Choose the field or fields to be displayed when the query is invoked.

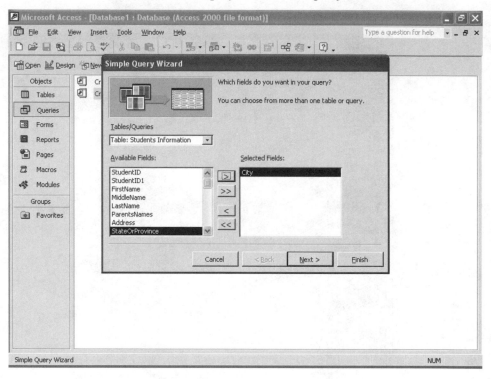

Figure 7.76: Select Query Field

4. Enter a name for the query. Select whether to open or modify the query. In this example, the open query option is selected.

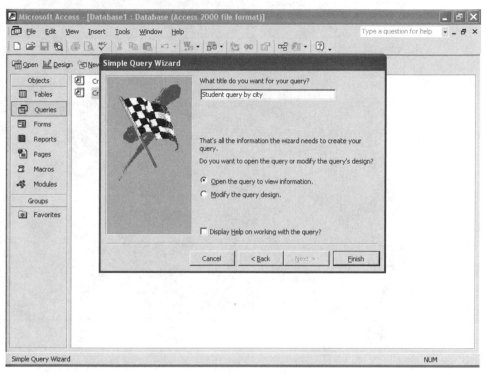

Figure 7.77: Query Name

A selection of all the cities in the database is displayed.

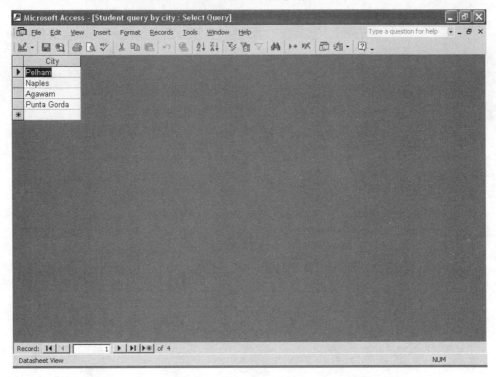

Figure 7.78: Query Field Results

7.3.3 Creating Database Forms

 Explain how to create and use forms for the database.

Tables display all the records in the table simultaneously in a spreadsheet-like structure, whereas forms display one record at a time in the format of your choice.

Forms use tables to retrieve data. Forms can be used to enter new records into the corresponding tables on which they are built. This makes data entry easier because data can be entered into more than one table at a time. Additionally, forms may contain labels and entry boxes and may also contain instructional information regarding the entries to be made, instead of rows of information.

Forms can use queries to review data that pertains to a specific set of criteria. However, it is not recommended that you enter or edit information using a form that has been created using a query. This is because information will not be stored in the table on which the query was based. Therefore, the added or edited information will be lost.

1. To open a database, choose from the list of databases under **Open a File** in the far right pane. Select **Forms** from the **Objects** column on the left.

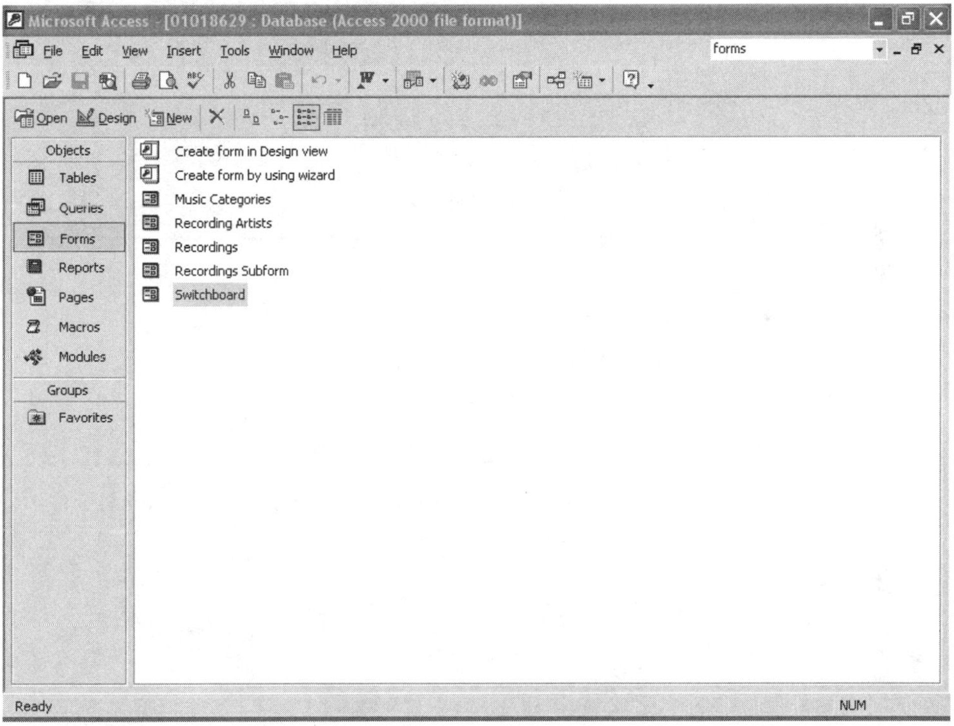

![Microsoft Access screenshot showing the Forms object selected in the database window with items: Create form in Design view, Create form by using wizard, Music Categories, Recording Artists, Recordings, Recordings Subform, Switchboard]

Figure 7.79: Form Creation

2. Select **Create form by using Wizard**. Select the fields in a table or query to be used in the form. Select the fields to be used in the form. Click **Next**.

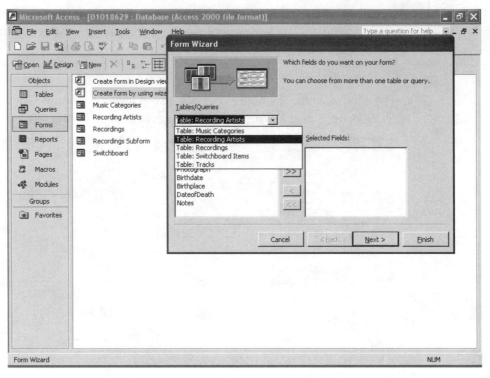

Figure 7.80: Form Field Selection

3. Select the fields in a table or query to be used in the form. Select the fields to be used in the form, as shown in Figure 7.81. Click **Next**.

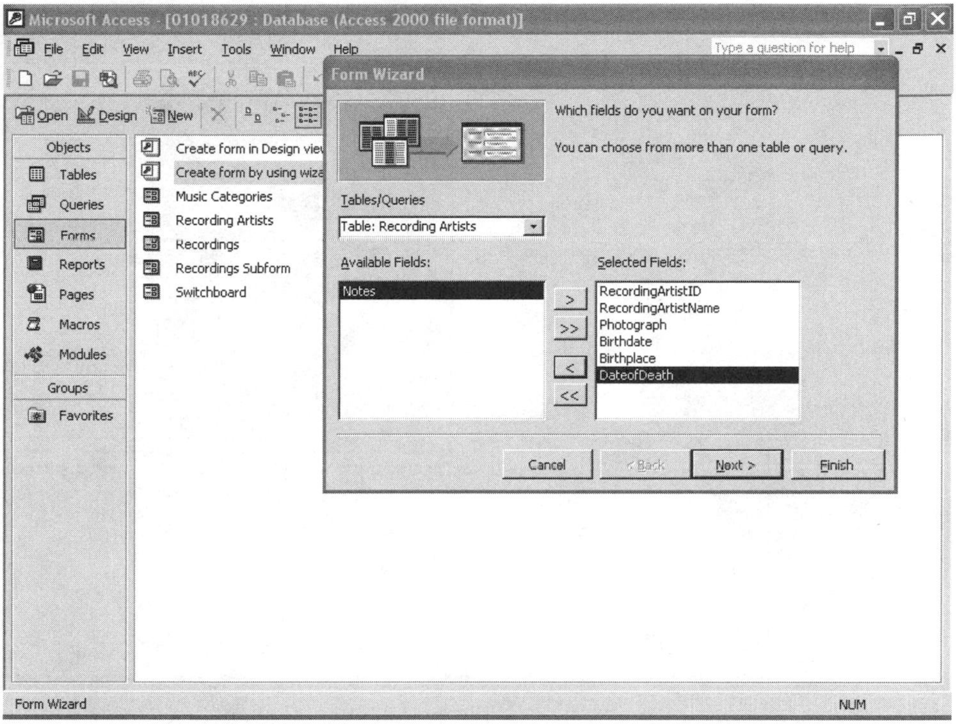

Figure 7.81: Form field selection

4. Select the form layout. Click **Next**.

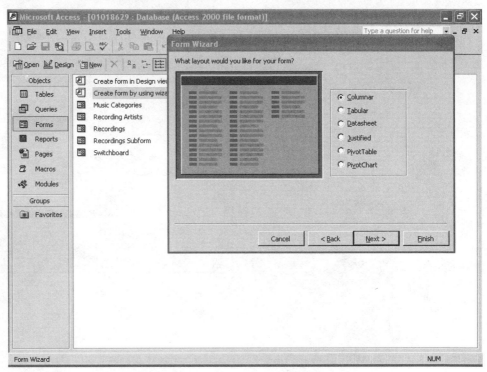

Figure 7.82: Form Layout Selection

5. Select the data style. Click **Next**.

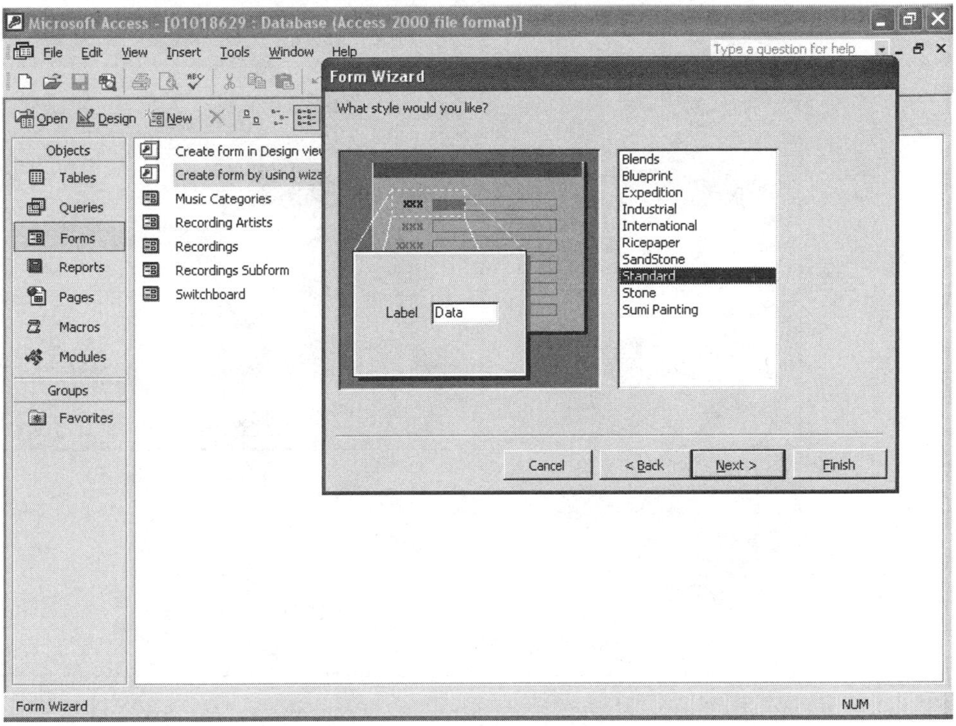

Figure 7.83: Form Data Style Selection

6. Select a name for the form. Select whether to make modifications to the form now or preview the form results. Click **Finish**.

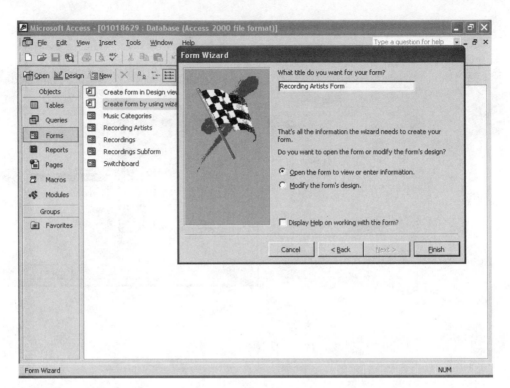

Figure 7.84: Form Wizard Completion

The form contains arrow icons at the bottom for moving between database records.

The completed form is displayed, as shown in Figure 7.85.

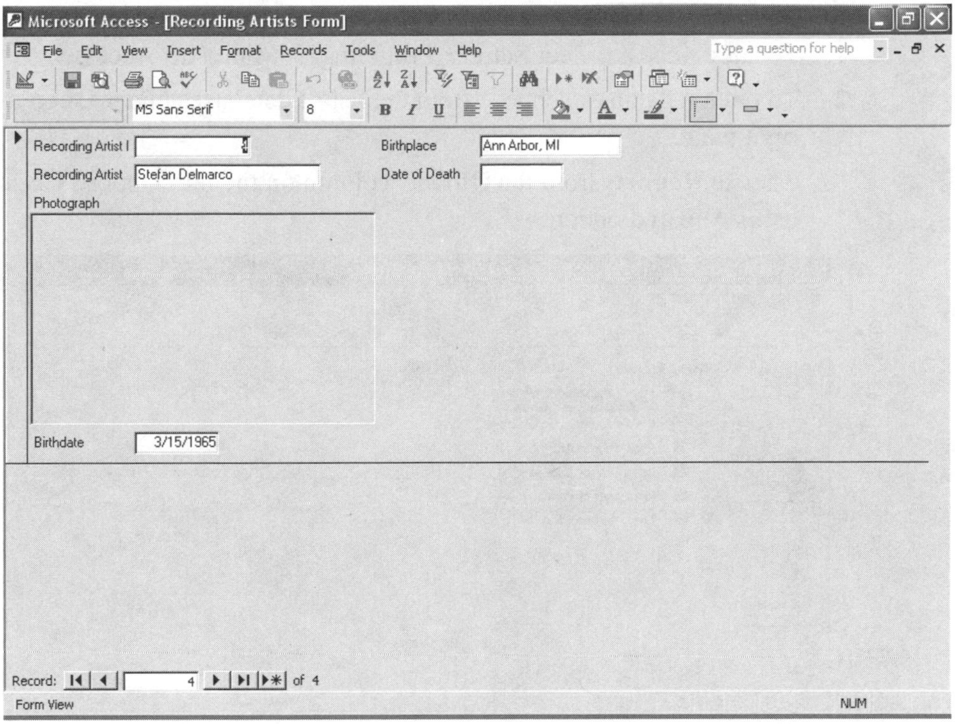

Figure 7.85: Completed Form

7.3.4 Generating Database Reports

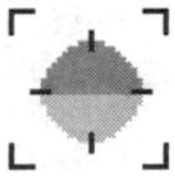

Explain how to generate and print reports from the database.

Reports are user-defined outputs created using one or more tables, queries, or both, and are generated to analyze the data stored in a database. They are often the end-result of a query. Reports are different from forms because they display multiple records at one time. This allows you to compare and contrast records based on specific criteria. Reports can also display headers and footers.

Various database objects work together to display required information as reports. They utilize data from each other, thereby creating a complete view of the data stored. The report can be customized to show the data in a particular order or display only selected fields of data.

1. To start Access, select Start → Programs → Microsoft Access.

2. To open a database, choose from the list of databases under **Open a file** in the far right pane.

3. Choose **Reports** from the **Objects** column on the left. Choose **Create a report by using Wizard** option.

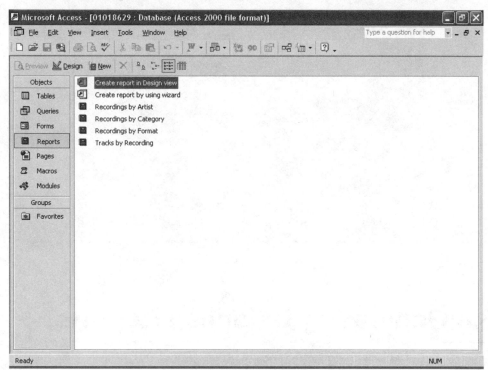

Figure 7.86: Creating a Report

4. Choose a field or fields from the database that will appear in the report. Click **Next**.

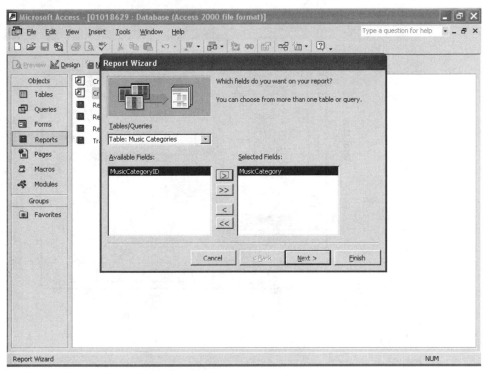

Figure 7.87: Report Field Selection

5. Choose the order in which the data records in the report are to be presented. Click **Next**.

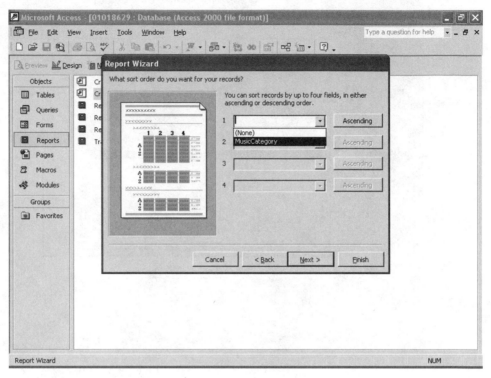

Figure 7.88: Field Sort Selection

6. Choose the layout format for your report. Click **Next**.

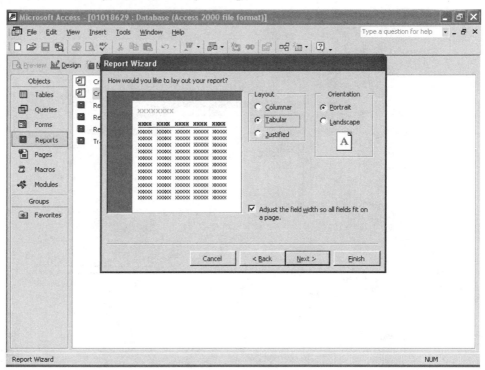

Figure 7.89: Report Layout

7. Choose the style for your report. Click **Next**.

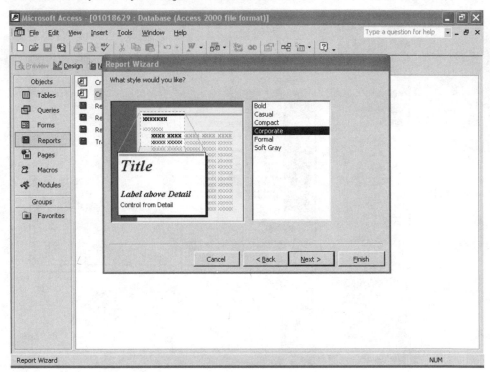

Figure 7.90: Report Style

8. Choose a title for the report.

9. Choose whether to preview the report or modify the report. Click **Finish**.

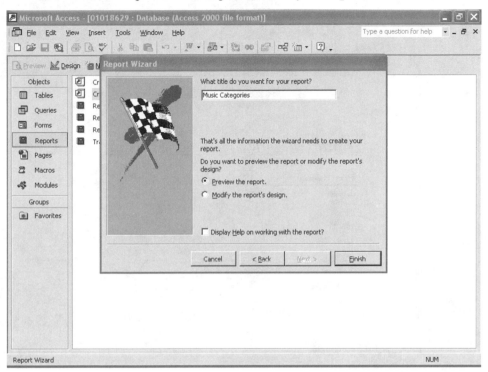

Figure 7.91: Report Title

10. The report listing music categories in the database is displayed.

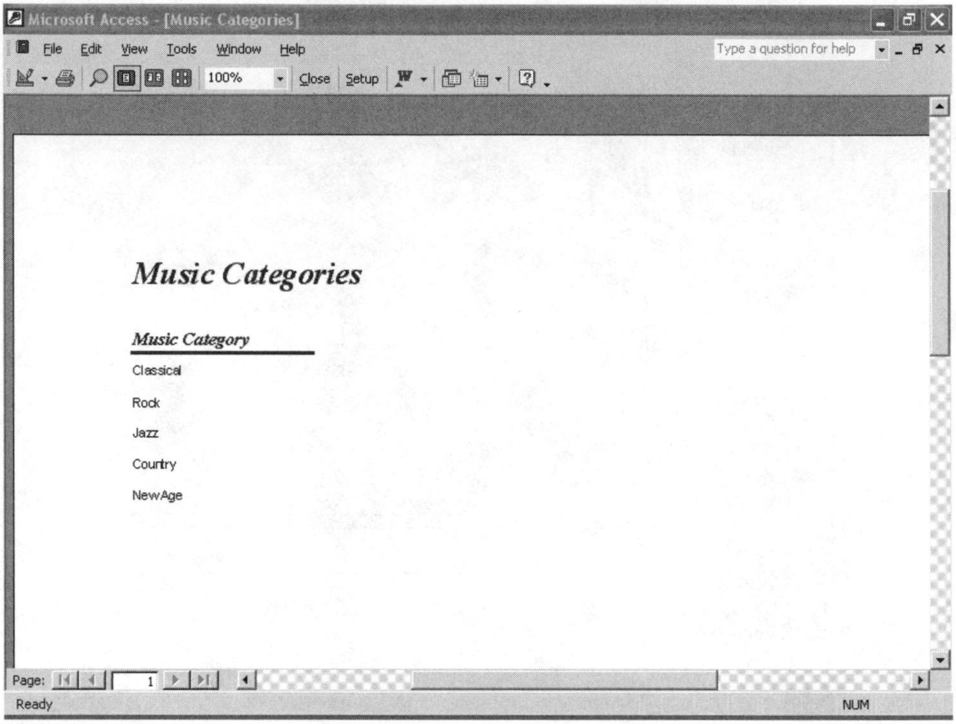

![Microsoft Access - [Music Categories] window showing the Music Categories report with the heading "Music Categories" and a column "Music Category" listing: Classical, Rock, Jazz, Country, New Age]

Figure 7.92: Report Results

The report contains arrow icons at the bottom for navigating between pages if the report results exceed a single page.

7.3.5 Using Database Help

 Describe how the Help feature is used to discover and apply additional features or troubleshoot your database.

Help in Access is a useful feature for learning how to maximize the potential of your database. Access Help can also be used as a troubleshooting tool.

Three options are available in the Access Help function. These are:

- Contents—Access help topics from predefined categories of common help inquires for Access.

- Answer Wizard—Post a question or use keywords to search through the Access Help database.

- Index—Search for topics in Help Index by making use of alphabetically-organized keywords.

To access the Help feature in Access, perform the following steps:

1. From the Menu Bar, select **Help → Microsoft Access Help**. Alternatively, you can press the **F1** key. The Access Help is displayed.

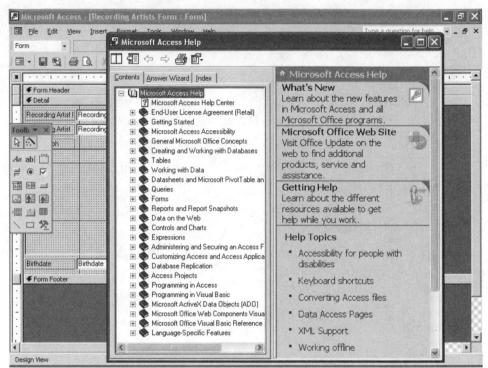

Figure 7.93: Access Help

2. The **Contents** tab provides help on everything from Access licensing to getting started with Access. This tab also offers to redirect users to the Microsoft Web site for information on what is new or learning how to get help.

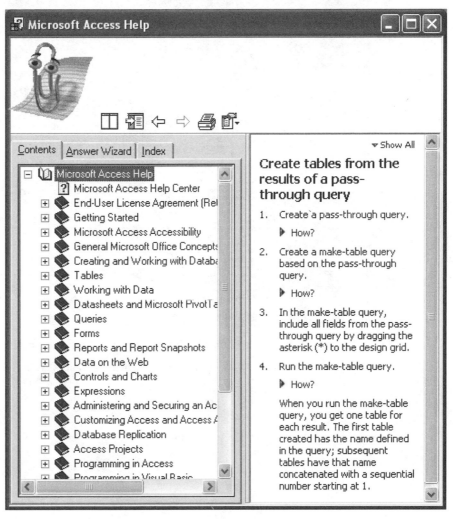

Figure 7.94: Contents Tab in Access Help

3. From the **Answer Wizard,** you can search for a Help topic by entering a question or a keyword.

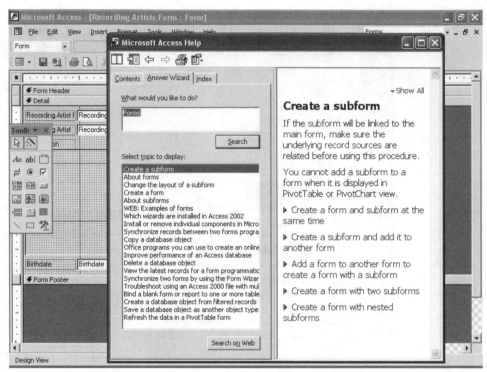

Figure 7.95: Answer Wizard Tab in Access Help

4. In the **Index** tab, you can type keywords of a Help topic separated by a semi-colon and then click **Search** for the results.

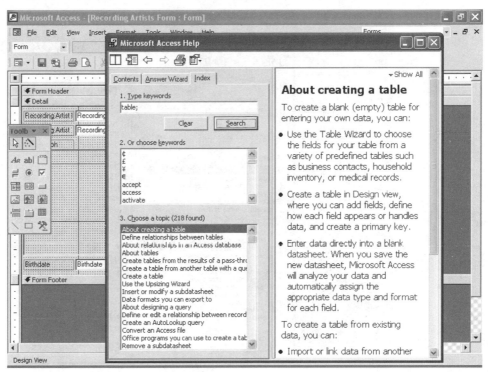

Figure 7.96: Index Tab in Access Help

5. For troubleshooting with Access Help, use keywords to describe the function. Alternatively, enter "troubleshoot" in the **Answer Wizard** tab field.

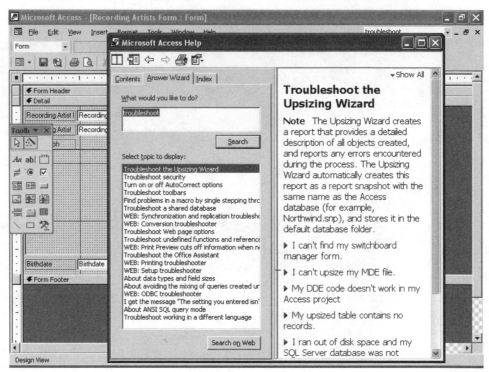

Figure 7.97: Using Help to Troubleshoot

You can use Access Help to explore and learn about any feature of the application. Alternatively, you can also explore online help available at the Microsoft site.

You likely have noticed that the Help features in all Microsoft Office applications are similar in their offerings and usability. As an independent learner, it is advisable to use Help frequently to move from a beginner to an advanced level in using these applications.

Practice Questions

1. Through which process is information retrieved from a database?
   a. Asking the creator of the database
   b. Typing data into the database
   c. Recalling data included in tables
   d. Querying the database

2. What is the screen called that is used to input data or retrieve data?
   a. Report
   b. Form
   c. Display
   d. Entry

3. Which of the following would be best located in a database?
   a. Birthday card list
   b. Presentation for your science research project
   c. The cover letter for your dream job
   d. Products, their price, and buyer information for your online auction

Summary

In this chapter, you learned:

- Data is entered into cells in a worksheet. The data entered in a worksheet can be a combination of a descriptor for a value and the value itself.

- Basic calculations can be performed in a spreadsheet using formulas and functions.

- Formulas are preceded by the symbol = to distinguish them from other data.

- Formulas inserted in worksheet cells can be copied to other cells.

- Formulas can contain cell references.

- Functions are built-in, ready-to-use calculation tools available in Excel. Functions perform a specific operation on selected data.

- Text as well as numerical data can be sorted in ascending or descending order in Excel. You can sort or arrange a list in a logical order, ascending or descending in alphabetic order, or in numeric order.

- Excel allows you to insert rows, columns, and cells to add new data in your worksheet. You can insert either a single row or multiple instances of rows, columns, or cells.

- Excel allows you to copy or move cells and thereby rearrange existing data in a worksheet. You can copy or move single cell or many cells.

- The appeal and effectiveness of worksheets can be increased by converting data into charts or graphs. Excel allows you to create many types of charts and graphs, including the following:
  - Bar/column graphs and clustered bar/column graphs
  - Pie charts
  - Line graphs
  - Area graphs
  - Scatter diagrams
  - Surface charts
  - Radar charts
  - Bubble charts

■ It is possible to modify any of the worksheet settings in Excel to enhance its appearance and make it easier to usc. Tcxt can be made bold and italicized. Additionally, color of the cell, text, or graph bars can be modified.

■ While working on a worksheet, it is important to save it for later access. A worksheet may need to be printed as handouts for a meeting or be used as part of a presentation or research paper.

■ Interactive features of spreadsheets include:

- What a summary worksheet is.

- How to add hyperlinks to a worksheet.

- The method to make a spreadsheet into a Web document.

- The importance of Excel Help and its use.

■ A database is a structured collection of information stored for a specific purpose. Microsoft Access stores, organizes, and retrieves information. It makes it easy to define the organization of data storage, assist in adding new data, and modify the stored data through automated forms. It also enables you to query and report on the data in meaningful ways.

Reference

- *ONLINE! Microsoft Education,*
  http://www.microsoft.com/Education/MSITAcademy/ITAPOnlineCampus.aspx

Soft Skills of Technical Professionals

8

Technical skills such as those learned in the previous chapters or those learned throughout your program of study are critical factors for success in your chosen field. Your technical skills define you as a technical professional. However, a successful career is not based solely on your technical expertise. You will need to demonstrate personal effectiveness and skills in relationships with coworkers in order to excel. These attributes, commonly referred to as *soft skills*, are often the key differentiators in determining who gets a job or a promotion.

This chapter presents concepts, tips, and techniques related to several important soft skills for technical professionals. This chapter prepares you to:

- Demonstrate effective time management practices.

- Describe techniques for mentoring, teamwork, and people management.

- Describe techniques for effective analysis, communication, and problem solving.

- Explain how setting goals, balancing work and personal life, creating a personal portfolio, and managing stress can enhance your career.

8.1 Time Management

You may have found yourself wishing many times that you had more time to do or complete something. Many people find themselves in situations where they wish that they could have managed their time better to accomplish goals. Time is a critical resource and to be successful you need to use it wisely.

This section describes the benefits of good time management and suggests strategies for improving your skills in this critical area.

8.1.1 Importance of Managing Your Time

 Explain how personal effectiveness can be enhanced through time management.

Success is a function of two important factors—ability and time. You can accomplish almost anything if you have the skill, ability, and an adequate amount of time. As you begin your program of study (and later your career), you are probably keenly focused on developing the technical skills that you need in your chosen field. You also need to learn to manage your time effectively, as depicted in Figure 8.1.

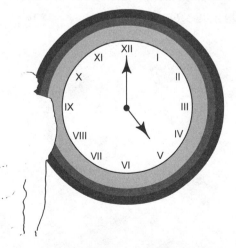

Figure 8.1: Time Management for Professional Success

The benefits of skillfully managing time are:

- You will be able to perform to the best of your ability: You may often find that you have the skill to perform a task, but not have enough time to complete it as well as you had planned. When you do not have enough time to do things the way you would like to, you may make mistakes or you may not have as much pride in your work as you want. By planning and managing your time well, you will have the opportunity to put forth your best effort on projects.

- You will experience less stress: Not having enough time to accomplish tasks can raise your stress level. By managing your time, you will feel more in control and approach situations with less worry.

- You will be more confident: Having the time to approach tasks in a calm, thoughtful manner with the opportunity to do your best work will lead to success. This, in turn, will build your confidence.

- You will be able to explore new opportunities: Effective time management implies that you are planning and prioritizing your tasks. You will be able to predict confidently how long tasks will take and strategically plan your schedule. As you perfect your skills, you will be able to branch out and explore new opportunities. This may involve learning new skills or looking at a new career option. Whatever the situation, you will need adequate time to explore and evaluate the opportunities.

These are a few ways in which your personal effectiveness can be enhanced by managing your time wisely. You will no doubt discover others throughout your career. As you start your education in your chosen career, it is important that you master the skill of managing your time. Your success will heavily depend on it.

8.1.2 Techniques for Effectively Managing Your Time

Describe the techniques for making effective use of your time.

The two key elements of managing your time are:

- Knowing your abilities.
- Creating and following a schedule.

Knowing your abilities implies that you are aware of your skills; you know what you can do. It also implies that you are aware of how much time you need to accomplish specific tasks. This aspect is variable, however, because as your skills change the time it takes to complete a given task also changes. As you gain proficiency in a given area, you may be able to complete tasks in less time.

The ability to create and follow a schedule is the cornerstone of time management. Your schedule is your plan for how you will spend your time. The extent to which your plan is feasible, as well as the extent to which you establish discipline and follow your schedule, will determine your effectiveness in managing your time.

A realistic plan or schedule consists of the following key elements:

- A list of the specific tasks or goals for a timeframe, usually a day or a week.
- Sufficient breaks for relaxation and fun.
- A buffer for unexpected occurrences.

Your aim in creating the schedule is to assess what you need to accomplish, create a workable plan, and meet your goals with minimal stress and maximum success. The process can help you to create an effective schedule or plan. A good process to follow is to:

1. Make a list of the tasks or goals you would like to accomplish in a given timeframe. You could make a list of goals for a week and then break the process down further to make schedules for each day of the week.

2. Prioritize the list, so that your most important goals have the highest priority. Refer to Table 8.1 for suggestions on prioritizing your goals.

3. Select the tasks from the prioritized list that you will accomplish in the timeframe.

4. Assess the amount of time it will take for you to complete each task.

5. Using a daily planner or a similar template, lay out your tasks for the timeframe. Include breaks for fun and relaxation and include a buffer for unexpected events.

6. Review your plan for the timeframe to ensure that it is feasible. Make sure you have sufficient flexibility and buffers to handle unexpected requests. The process for creating a schedule is shown in figure 8.2.

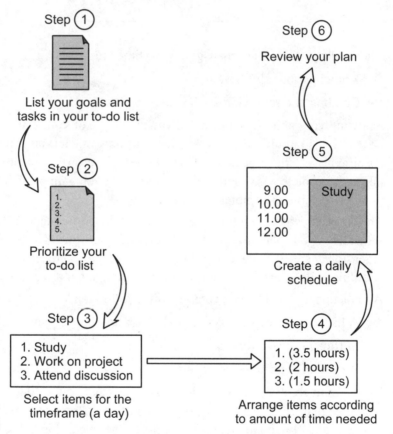

Figure 8.2: Process for Creating a Schedule

 Microsoft Outlook provides a Calendar feature. This is a useful tool for creating your schedule. Use the Help feature to learn how you can use it.

Prioritizing tasks is an important step in maximizing your success in time management. Do not fill your time with activities. Instead, make sure that you are prioritizing your most critical tasks to help you reach your most important goals.

Table 8.1 shows a method that you can use to prioritize tasks.

Step No.	Description	Rationale and tips
1	Create a list of goals or tasks that you would like to accomplish.	Break large tasks down into smaller subtasks. This will be your to-do list.
2	Create a list of criteria to rate your tasks.	The criteria should be areas that are important to you and critical to accomplishing the work. Examples can include difficulty, importance, due date, and required teamwork.
3	Set up a rating chart similar to the one shown in Figure 8.3 listing your goals/tasks on one side and criteria to rate the tasks across the top.	This format will make it easy for you to evaluate your ratings.
4	Rate each goal against the criteria. You could use a three-point scale, such as High (1), Medium (2), and Low (3). Include the actual due date of each task.	Be thoughtful in your evaluation of each goal against the criteria. Try to get an even distribution of ratings across your tasks. Otherwise it may be difficult to prioritize.
5	Sort your list of tasks by due date, placing items with the nearest due date at the top of the list.	Your ultimate goal is to get necessary tasks completed on time.
6	Decide which criterion is most important to you. In addition to maintaining the order established by the due date, sort the items based on their ranking within the chosen criteria. For example, if you have several items due on the same day, rank these items based on their individual criteria rating.	Think of this as a tiebreaker to help you get your high priority items to the top of the list.
7	If necessary, repeat the sub-ranking using the next most important criterion.	Remember to preserve the ranking.
8	Stop prioritizing when you have sorted items against all criteria or you feel comfortable with the list.	Go through iterations of prioritizing only as long as you feel it is productive. It is not necessary to prioritize against all the criteria if you feel there is no added benefit.

Table 8.1: Method for Prioritizing

Figure 8.3 shows a template of a form that you can use for prioritizing.

Task	Due date	Level of difficulty	Importance/criticality	Teamwork required

Figure 8.3: Rating Chart Template

Use Microsoft Excel to create your form for prioritizing tasks. Then sort the list on up to three criteria at a time, choosing the most important criteria as the first sort category, the next most important criteria as the second category, and so on. If you use this method, make sure that you use a rating scale, such as 1 for High, 2 for Medium, and 3 for Low, and sort items in ascending order so that items rated as High are placed at the top of the list.

After your list of tasks is prioritized, build your schedule using the method described in section 8.1.

Refer to Table 8.2 for suggestions on reevaluating your list in case you cannot create a feasible schedule.

Problem	Suggestions for revision
Your schedule does not allow you to complete all required tasks by their due date.	Reevaluate the amount of time you have allocated for each task. Try to complete tasks in less time. Shorten some breaks or eliminate some optional activities. It may be necessary to forego some personal time when you have important deadlines.
Your schedule for one day seems too busy with too many items.	Make sure that you complete important tasks before beginning new ones. Avoid scheduling too many tasks on one day.
You feel like you are changing tasks too frequently.	Regroup your schedule so that similar items are next to each other. For example, you may want to put study-related tasks next to each other so that you can block off a certain amount of time for studying rather than trying to study at different times during the day.

Table 8.2: Suggestions for Addressing Problems with Your Schedule

Remember, creating an effective schedule is a detailed process. You may need to refine your schedule several times before it is workable. Your abilities and timeframes for getting tasks done will also change as you gain proficiency, so be sure to reevaluate your scheduling practices from time to time.

8.1.3 Assessing Your Time Management Capability

 Assess your time management habits and create a personal plan to improve your effectiveness in managing time.

Having mastered the skill of creating a schedule and prioritizing your to-do lists, let us now focus on effectively managing your time and the need to evaluate the quality of your results. You need to assess whether you are doing your best work on projects—in essence, whether you are happy with the quality of the results, able to keep to your schedule with minimal changes, and at ease with your daily tasks. Another way to assess your time management capability is by evaluating your performance in certain critical areas.

Figure 8.4 shows one possible assessment that you can use to assess your effectiveness in managing your time.

A Time Management Assessment			
Answer the following questions by placing a checkmark in the column that describes your performance.			
	Rarely	Sometimes	Frequently
How often do you run out of time for your tasks?			
How often are critical tasks incomplete?			
How often do you need to change your schedule during a day?			
How often do you meet or exceed your expectations on the quality of your results?			
How often do you feel undue stress?			
Scoring			
	# Rarely	# Sometimes	# Frequently
Outstanding	3-5 checks	1-2 checks	0-1 checks
Average	1-3 checks	1-3 checks	1-3 checks
Poor	0-1 checks	2-5 checks	3-5 checks

Figure 8.4: Time Management Assessment Sheet

After assessing the effectiveness of your time management, decide on the next step. Assess whether you need improvement or whether you are performing above your expectations. Regardless of the results, take steps to enhance your effectiveness. Remember, managing your time is a process at which you are continuously improving. Even if you seem to be following your schedule precisely and with perfect results, you still have opportunities for enhancement.

Refer to Table 8.3 for suggestions on improving your time management effectiveness.

Time management performance	Suggestions for improvement
Poor: Not keeping to schedule and not achieving high-quality results.	Spend more time on critical tasks. Reevaluate your prioritization methods. Minimize interruptions. Plan fewer activities for the timeframe.
Average: You are keeping to your schedule with reasonable success and the quality of your results is acceptable, with room for improvement.	Keep working at refining your skills at prioritizing and allocating time for tasks. Look for ways to become more efficient in your daily schedule so as to make some time available for improvement.
Outstanding: You almost always keep to your schedule and often have free time available. The quality of your results is at or above your expectations.	You have the opportunity to take your skills to the next level. Look for opportunities to learn new skills or to explore career choices further. Dedicate some time to enriching your personal life.

Table 8.3: Improving Your Time Management Effectiveness

Keep the following strategies in mind as you look to enhance your time management skills:

- In addition to creating a schedule, keep a calendar of important milestones and appointments and a list of important tasks. Microsoft Outlook is a useful tool for managing your calendar and tasks.

- Look at your to-do list every day and evaluate your performance against it. Use your results to create your schedule for the next day.

- Be flexible. Make changes as necessary and be willing to give up personal time to achieve important goals.

- Always be realistic and do not overextend yourself.

- Remember to celebrate the accomplishment of key milestones, such as finishing a project or completing a course. This will help you to stay motivated.

- If you are having trouble in completing important tasks or you feel an undue amount of stress, ask for help. Talk to your instructor or an advisor to help form a strategy for success.

Practice Questions

1. What are two key elements to managing your time effectively?
   I. Knowing your ability
   II. Reducing your stress levels
   III. Creating and following a schedule
   IV. Exploring new opportunities
   a. I and II
   b. I and III
   c. I and IV
   d. II and III

2. Which of the following is an important step in creating an effective schedule?
   a. Prioritizing tasks
   b. Gathering feedback

    c.   Reducing stress

    d.   Brainstorming

3. If you find that your schedule does not allow you to complete all required activities by the due date, what could you do to help the situation?

    a.   Take a break to have fun

    b.   Plan similar tasks in adjacent time blocks

    c.   Eliminate optional activities and shorten breaks

    d.   Prioritize the tasks

4. When you find that, on a regular basis, you are able to keep to your schedule and complete tasks at or above acceptable levels of quality, what could you do as a next step?

    a.   Continue your excellent time management practices

    b.   Relax and have fun

    c.   Include more breaks in your schedule

    d.   Look for opportunities to learn new skills or further explore career choices

5. To prioritize your schedule, you have specified the following criteria for the tasks that you need to accomplish: due date, teamwork required, complexity, and special equipment needed. What is the first criterion you should use to prioritize your tasks?

    a.   Due date

    b.   Teamwork required

    c.   Complexity

    d.   Special equipment needed

8.2 People Management

One of the key learning points that will be important throughout your professional life is that people are the heart of an organization. There are processes and standards to which to adhere to and technology to support them, but at the center of every organization or initiative is the person or team of people who carry out the tasks and the leader guiding them. Success in organizations, therefore, depends on skill in handling interpersonal relationships and issues. Excellence in technology and process efficiency is critical, but without effective people, organizations cannot reach the highest levels of success.

This section describes the rationale for focusing on people as a key organizational asset and provides some techniques for effectively managing the development of people to achieve organizational goals. In addition, the team dynamics and suggestions for increasing the effectiveness of teamwork are discussed in this section.

8.2.1 People as Assets

Explain the importance of managing people as organizational assets.

Speed and flexibility are two key focus areas of businesses in the twenty-first century. High-quality products must get to the market quickly and organizations must be able to adapt to new technologies at a faster pace. Without these abilities, companies will find it difficult to gain a competitive advantage. To ensure that organizations have the ability to meet these and other challenges, a strong focus on people development is required.

People, as depicted in figure 8.5, are at the heart of every organization and successful companies begin by developing the skills of their employees.

Figure 8.5: People are Assets of Organizations

When you think about organizations for which you would like to work, you think about factors such as location, industry, and company size. In addition to these, a pleasant work environment, adequate tools to do a job, training for required skills, and an opportunity for growth are a few characteristics that are common to companies that are identified as ideal places to work. These characteristics focus on developing people within an organization.

The benefits of focusing on people as organizational assets are:

■ Longer work tenure: When opportunities to learn and grow exist within an organization, people tend to stay longer. This results in a workforce with greater knowledge about products and customers, leading to more satisfied customers, and ultimately a more successful business.

- Greater flexibility for the organization: A focus on developing people creates deep strength within an organization. People may gain exposure to many units in the company and may develop skill sets that are useful in several areas. This broad knowledge across the company helps to create flexibility, allowing the company to adapt quickly to changes in the marketplace.

- Higher employee satisfaction: Many employee surveys have shown that people are happier when a company puts a focus on training and development. When employees are happy, their performance improves and the company experiences increased success.

All these benefits result in stronger, more successful organizations. People development is a requirement for any organization that wants to succeed.

8.2.2 People Development

 Describe the techniques that can be used to develop organizational capabilities through personal development.

Realizing that success depends on developing people, an organization can ensure adequate people development through formal *development planning*. A formal development planning process involves:

- Setting clear requirements for what is expected of each employee
- Assessing employee performance against those expectations
- Identifying development areas that can enhance performance
- Creating a plan for personal development in those areas

The plan is typically reviewed on a regular basis. Both the employee and the manager should be held accountable for completing the development activities on the plan.

There are several benefits of formal development planning. These benefits are:

- A sense of accomplishment is gained by having formal, tangible plans for development. Employees can see what they have done to gain new skills and they also value the investment the organization has made in them.

- Managers have a basis for assessing the skills and capabilities of their groups. They can use this information to plan better for changes and upcoming projects.

- A constant focus is on developing skills and capabilities. By reviewing the plans on a regular basis, and making necessary modifications, an organization can ensure that employees maintain the skills necessary for current and future challenges.

Usually development plans outline training courses that employees can attend. However, not all development opportunities involve formal training courses. Often, experience gained on the job can be an effective way of learning specific skills or gaining exposure to important viewpoints and activities. A *mentoring program* can be an effective way to help people be successful in on-the-job learning.

In a mentoring program, people who are considered to be role models in specific areas are chosen as mentors. Mentors are assigned to work with people in the organization. The role of the mentor is to:

- Act as a coach and provide guidance

- Answer as well as propose questions to encourage learning

- Provide suggestions for further development

The mentor is not responsible for assessing performance against expectations set forth in the development planning process. That is the responsibility of the manager. Rather, the mentor is similar to a personal coach, providing guidance and direction to enhance a person's development.

A mentoring program can be either formal or informal. In a formal program, mentors are selected and assigned by the organization. In an informal program, individuals typically seek their own mentors.

Organizations can realize several benefits from a mentoring program, including:

- Strengthening organizational culture and values

- Enhancing interpersonal relationships throughout the organization

- Giving people exposure to different perspectives and functions across the company

- Making learning more effective by reinforcing it with actual experience

All of these benefits work toward building a stronger and more productive organization.

To ~~all~~ beat Dysfunction

8.2.3 Teamwork

- Explain the dynamics of teams.
- Describe techniques to enhance team performance.

Sports, school activities, volunteer activities, and work experiences all involve teams in one way or the other. Any time there is an opportunity for people to work together toward an end result, teamwork is involved. Teams may take the form of committees or groups and may have different organizations or structures. In work situations, it is common to have interdisciplinary teams in which people from different parts of the organization come together to work on a project. The different areas of expertise represented on multidisciplinary teams can lead to innovative results that meet the needs of the organization.

Almost everyone has had an opportunity to work with a team and almost everyone has had varied experiences with teams. Teams can be very effective, creating innovative solutions in a short period of time, with team members developing lasting respect for each other and enduring relationships. In essence, the collective skill and experience of a team can create a far better result than a single individual. This type of team experience is positive.

However, there are many team experiences that are not as successful. Unfortunately, it is common to hear about teams that were not able to achieve a desired result, took too long to complete a task, or ended with poor feelings among team members. Some dynamics of teams that cause these negative results include:

- Differences of opinion or understanding among team members that are not resolved
- Team members not contributing to the team
- Lack of organization or planning among team members

In the book, *The Five Dysfunctions of a Team*, Patrick Lencioni describes five negative characteristics or dysfunctions of teams that lead to ineffective results. These are:

- Absence of trust
- Fear of conflict
- Lack of communication
- Avoidance of accountability

■ Inattention to results

These characteristics do not occur in isolation, rather, they are interrelated, with one characteristic leading to another. If a team exhibits one of these characteristics, its likelihood of success is diminished, as the other characteristics will follow over time.

To overcome these negative dynamics, it is helpful to look at the opposite traits of these dynamics. Strong teams display the following characteristics among members:

■ They trust one another

■ They engage in free and open discussion around ideas and they are not afraid of conflict

■ They commit to decisions and plans of action

■ They hold themselves accountable for delivering against the plan

■ They focus on the achievement of collective results

There are several techniques that can be used to help build these characteristics among team members.

Table 8.4 describes the techniques that can be adopted at the organizational level.

Characteristic	Suggested techniques
Building trust	Create opportunities for team members to get to know each other. Knowing someone personally generates a level of trust.
Acceptance of conflict and free and open discussion of ideas	Encourage team members not to take criticism as personal attacks. Team leaders should allow conflict to be worked out. Do not push disagreements under the rug. Team leaders could take the role of the devil's advocate to help team members become comfortable with raising opposing viewpoints and discussing them.
Gaining commitment	Be decisive. Provide clear action plans and a rationale for decisions. Treat mistakes as opportunities for learning. Do not be afraid to make mistakes.
Building accountability	Provide clear structure for action plans with individual responsibilities clearly assigned.
Encouraging attention to results	Hold regular status meetings where team and individual progress are reviewed. Reward results.

Table 8.4: Techniques for Building Positive Team Characteristics

The techniques described in Table 8.4 refer to actions that can be taken by team leaders and organizations. Individual team members can participate in team activities and meetings with a positive attitude and open mind. In addition, team members should keep the five dysfunctional behaviors of teams in mind and attempt to steer clear of them. It is good practice for all team members to spend some time reflecting on their behavior with respect to overall team performance. Some questions for personal reflection may include:

- Do you trust other team members? What would it take for you to develop deeper trust?

- Are you holding back on expressing your thoughts in team discussions? Are you honest about your feelings and views?

- Are you committed to decisions made by the team? What would help you make that commitment?
- Are you following through on your commitments? Are you holding others to the same standard?
- Are you focused on the team's result or on your own personal performance?

Look for ways to align your attitudes and behaviors with the positive characteristics of effective teams. This will not only increase the success of your team, but will enhance your personal effectiveness as well.

Practice Questions

1. Companies find it beneficial to develop their people because it _____ .
   - I.   gives them greater flexibility to adapt to change.
   - II. makes the company a more desirable place to work.
   - III. can result in more satisfied customers and higher profits.
   - a.   II and III
   - b.   I and II
   - c.   I and III
   - d.   I, II, and III

2. What are the two techniques that can be used to develop people in an organization?
   - I.   Personal development planning
   - II. Prioritizing
   - III. Mentoring
   - IV. Problem solving
   - a.   I and II
   - b.   I and III
   - c.   I and IV
   - d.   III and IV

3. Which of the following is NOT a positive characteristic of an effective team?

   a. Members take disagreements offline to avoid distraction from the main plan of action.

   b. Members hold the team leader solely accountable for team results.

   c. The team creates effective schedules and clearly communicates its progress.

   d. Members engage in full and open discussion around ideas.

4. Which of the following activities could be part of a formal development planning process?

   I.   Setting clear requirements of what is expected of an employee.

   II. Assessing employee performance against expectations.

   III. Identifying development areas that could increase or enhance performance.

   IV. Creating a plan for personal development.

   a. II, III, and IV only

   b. I, II, and III only

   c. I, II, and IV only

   d. I, II, III, and IV

5. Which of the following is NOT the role of a mentor?

   a. Assessing performance against job expectations

   b. Answering questions

   c. Proposing questions

   d. Providing guidance

8.3 Analysis, Communication, and Problem Solving

In addition to managing time and people, there are several other essential professional skills that can help ensure success throughout your career and your life. *Analysis*, or the ability to separate a whole into parts, is an important skill for planning and developing solutions to problems. Effective analysis leads to creativity and innovation as you look for different ways to achieve results. This section discusses two important concepts related to analysis: critical thinking and creative thinking. Improving your skills in these areas will help you to analyze situations more effectively and develop innovative approaches or solutions to problems.

Communication is another important professional skill. Both written and oral forms of communication are essential for getting things done. Whether you are a manager delegating tasks to others or a subordinate reporting on results or problems, clear communication is essential to gaining mutual understanding and achieving optimal results. This section also presents techniques for effective communication and describes techniques for determining the effectiveness of the communication.

Finally, the ability to solve problems is a valuable skill in life. Whether you are faced with a critical business problem or a puzzling personal dilemma, your skill in assessing a situation, analyzing components, and developing scenarios to achieve the desired outcome will help you to solve any problem quickly.

8.3.1 Critical Thinking

 List the areas to explore in a critical analysis.

Have you ever thought about how you judge the quality of information? What do you think of commercials or infomercials on television? Do you trust the validity of information that you find on the Internet? Do you take newspaper stories at face value? Many people have reservations about these information sources, but that does not imply that all information from them is not trustworthy. Critical thinking can help you evaluate whether the information from any source is useful for your needs.

As shown in Figure 8.6, critical thinking involves looking at issues in a thorough manner.

Figure 8.6: Thinking Critically

Instead of taking things at face value, you look for deeper meaning and alternative conclusions. Critical thinking can help you make better decisions using the information available and produce higher quality reports and projects. Critical thinking can be used to support your viewpoints and to evaluate others' viewpoints. When using critical thinking to support your viewpoints, you need to examine thoroughly the rationale for your ideas and conclusions and prepare for any objection or questioning from others. You should attempt to address these potential questions and objections to your work to further support your ideas and to help you examine your ideas in a more complete way. Practicing critical thinking can help you clearly communicate your ideas.

Critical thinking can also help you evaluate others' viewpoints. Recall the techniques for validating and evaluating information from the Internet that were presented in Chapter Four, "Information from Electronic Sources." You can enhance your skills in this area by practicing critical thinking.

In the book, *Asking the Right Questions: A Guide to Critical Thinking*, authors M. Neil Browne and Stuart M. Keeley present eleven questions that can be used in critical thinking.

The following list presents questions that are adapted from that list, along with a brief explanation of their intent.

- What are the issues and conclusions presented?

This question examines the intent of the information. Before you can analyze information, you need to understand the issues being presented and the conclusions being drawn.

- What are the supporting reasons for the conclusion?

This question examines the explanations for the conclusion.

- What words, phrases, or statistics could have alternate meanings?

This question examines the content to determine if there is anything that needs further explanation, or is unclear or deceptive.

- What is the author's underlying bias?

The author may have some underlying values or beliefs that influence the conclusions being drawn. With this question you "read between the lines" to determine the author's personal beliefs about how things are, or should be, in the environment.

- Is there any information that is omitted from the author's argument?

With this question, you think about all possible information that could be relevant to the conclusion. It is possible that there exists information that would conflict with or disprove the conclusion?

- Are there any other conclusions that could be drawn?

With this question you look at the evidence, reasons, and arguments that were presented along with your own investigations to determine if there are any other plausible conclusions that could be reached.

These questions provide a thorough framework for critical analysis. It takes practice to be able to master the skill of critical thinking. You can begin by using these questions as a checklist for evaluating information. By practicing critical thinking to evaluate information, you will make better decisions about information, create better quality reports and projects, and ultimately improve the effectiveness of your communication.

8.3.2 Creative Thinking

 Describe how the techniques of brainstorming and developing analogies help foster creative thinking.

Creative thinking is a skill that can be applied in many situations. A common area in which creative thinking is useful is in generating possible solutions to a problem. Creative thinking can also be applied to generate a list of possibilities or opportunities, or in designing products. In general, creative thinking is used to spearhead innovation and improvements in developing products, refining processes, and solving problems. There are several techniques that can spark creative thinking. Two of these techniques, *brainstorming* and *developing analogies*, are discussed in this section.

Brainstorming is an activity that generates a list of possibilities. It is usually performed in a group. Individuals may also use brainstorming as a technique to generate ideas. There are several widely-accepted guidelines for brainstorming. These guidelines are:

- All ideas and suggestions within reasonable standards are accepted
- No ideas are criticized or evaluated
- Building up of ideas that have been suggested is encouraged

Several processes are possible within these rules or guidelines. One straightforward process is as follows:

1. The group appoints a scribe who is responsible for recording all the ideas. Alternatively, group members write their ideas on note cards, eliminating the need for a scribe. The group also appoints a leader if one does not already exist.

2. The group leader poses the brainstorming question to the group. Group members suggest their ideas in an unstructured, quick-paced manner. The scribe writes the ideas generated on a large sheet of paper so that the group can see them. Alternatively, group members write their ideas on note cards and post them on a wall or flip chart.

3. The group leader keeps the pace moving by encouraging all members to contribute ideas. If the process stalls, the group leader can contribute ideas or encourage members to build on some of the ideas that have already been submitted.

4. The process continues for 15-25 minutes or until the group has stopped generating new ideas. The group leader calls an end to the process.

5. The scribe or group leader collects the list and, after the session, transcribes the list to a useful format and distributes it to the group members.

Note that an individual can also follow this process, although the benefit of having multiple perspectives and viewpoints to generate a variety of ideas will not be realized.

You may notice that this technique for brainstorming requires participants to think of creative ideas, but provides only one suggestion—building up of ideas that have already been submitted—as a spark for creativity. One technique that can be used to spark further creativity, either with brainstorming or as a stand-alone activity, is developing analogies.

Analogies are comparisons between things that are typically thought to be dissimilar but have some underlying similarities. Analogies involve similarities in relationships. Thus, in an analogy, you analyze how one entity is similar to another and then apply that similarity to a relationship between two different items. An example of an analogy is:

A VCR is to a videotape as a browser is to HTML.

In this analogy, the relationship between a VCR and a videotape is compared to the relationship between a browser and HTML, as depicted in Figure 8.7. A VCR reads and displays data from a videotape, similar to how a browser reads and displays information in HTML code. You could use this analogy to spark creative thinking about new features for VCRs or browsers.

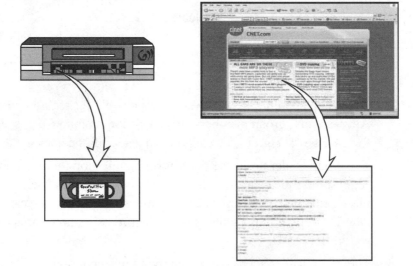

Figure 8.7: Analogies Help to Think Creatively

Another example of an analogy is:

A waiter is to a meal as a server is to data.

In this analogy, the action that a waiter takes with a meal, such as serving or presenting it to a patron, is compared to the action that a server performs in a network environment, which is to deliver data to an application that requests it. You can use this analogy to inspire creative ways of explaining the function of servers in a network.

Analogies help to foster creative thinking by helping you to see myriad possibilities. By making comparisons between items that are typically not similar, for example, meals and data, you can begin to think about ways to create new possibilities for products, solutions, or potential opportunities. You can also use analogies to explain difficult or abstract concepts in creative, understandable ways.

8.3.3 Effective Communication

 Describe the communication techniques that effectively convey ideas and gauge understanding.

Communication is generally described as an exchange of information. It involves two or more parties exchanging ideas through a medium, such as writing, speaking, signaling, or electronic means. For communication to take place, a message has to be sent and received. In other words, communication involves both the delivery and receipt of a message. This description of communication is fairly scientific and objective. It states the basic requirements that are necessary for communication to take place. However, when people refer to communication as a personal or professional skill, their expectations may differ.

Effective communication results in the mutual understanding of a message. It also establishes a rapport, as depicted in Figure 8.8. Therefore, effective communication is the process of sending a message that is understood by the intended receivers.

Figure 8.8: Effective Communication Establishes Rapport

Effective oral communication begins with speaking words, but involves much more. The tone of voice, body language, and facial expressions all influence the success of face-to-face communication by providing additional meaning to the words that are spoken. Body language and facial expression are often referred to as non-verbal communication. Non-verbal communication has an important influence on how messages are interpreted.

The medium of communication directly affects the success of an exchange. As discussed in chapter one, communication through telephone or e-mail presents additional challenges because some aspects of person-to-person communication that can convey additional meaning are absent. For example, tone of voice, body language, and facial expressions are not part of e-mail communication and the intended meaning of the communication can be misinterpreted. Your skill in effective communication is determined by how you handle the challenges of delivering a message so that receivers understand the intended meaning.

Table 8.5 presents some techniques that can be used to enhance your skills at non-verbal communication.

Technique	Description
Carry yourself with confidence	People will form a first impression of you based on how you approach them. Carrying yourself with confidence will make a good first impression.
Make eye contact	Looking away from someone gives the impression that you are interested in something other than the conversation at hand or that you are trying to hide something.
Don't fidget	Playing with trinkets, such as tapping a pencil or bending a paper clip during a conversation, conveys nervousness.
Be conscious of how you use your hands	Certain hand gestures, such as facing your palms upward or extending your hand, can convey positive messages. Other hand positions, such as placing your hands in your pocket, clenching your fist, or crossing your arms, convey negative messages.

Table 8.5: Techniques for Effective Non-Verbal Communication

Refer to Chapter 1, Table 1.2 for other suggestions on communication techniques.

In addition to delivering a message, you need to check that the intended meaning of the message was understood. Some techniques for determining this include:

- Asking questions to determine if the message that you sent was correctly understood
- Listening to what the recipients of your message are saying and addressing any questions
- Interpreting the body language of the listener

Mastering these skills, along with choosing words carefully, will help you to become a highly effective communicator. Effective communication will help you in many ways throughout your career, including helping you to persuade others to accept your point of view, to sell your ideas, and to make a positive impact in presentations.

8.3.4 Problem Solving

 Describe a structured approach to develop solutions to problems.

Problems are natural occurrences in business and in everyday life. Tough business situations, incorrect business decisions, and risk-taking all create a need to solve problems. A structured approach can help you to identify the problem to be solved, generate creative solutions, and select and implement the best solution.

In the book, *101 Creative Problem-Solving Techniques*, James Higgins describes a structured process called the Creative Problem-Solving process, or CPS process. Figure 8.9 provides an overview of the process.

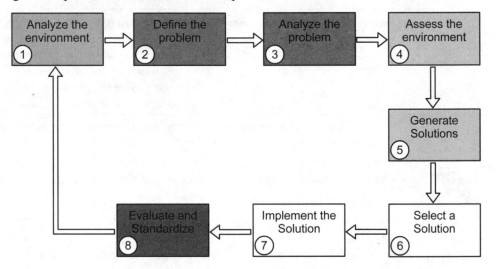

Figure 8.9: A Problem-Solving Process

The various steps are:

1. Analyze the Environment: In this step, you continuously scan your environment to be aware of the current state. Without the knowledge of what is currently occurring in the environment, you will not be in a position to identify problems or opportunities for change.

2. Define the Problem: In this step, the problem or opportunity is formally stated. Many problem-solving techniques suggest developing a formal statement of the problem to be solved or the opportunity to develop a creative solution.

---

3. Analyze the Problem: In this, you conduct a full analysis of the problem or opportunity and identify the possible causes of and potential solutions to the problem. The criteria for success or a description of how the intended solution or future state will operate are discussed in this stage. The goal of this analysis is to ensure that problems, rather than symptoms, are addressed and opportunities for problem-solving seized.

4. Assess the Environment: In this, you make inferences about certain aspects of the environment that affect potential solutions.

5. Generate Solutions: This is a creative process for generating potential solutions to the problem. It builds on solutions that may have been identified in Step 3.

6. Select a Solution: In this process, you select the optimal solution. There are several tools and processes that can help you to make good decisions among the alternatives generated. One is to generate a list of criteria that are important to the issue at hand and rate each alternative against the criteria. You then assess your ratings and select the most appropriate solution. This process is similar to the prioritization process discussed in Table 8.1. You could construct a rating sheet similar to the one in Example 8.1 to assist in your decision-making process.

7. Implement the Solution: This refers to implementing the selected solution.

8. Evaluate and Standardize: In this, you evaluate the solution against successful criteria and identify opportunities to improve the results. The control stage helps you guard against reverting to old practices and ensures a lasting implementation.

Many variations of this process exist, but all share similar stages of analyzing the current environment, identifying and describing the problem or opportunity, generating and selecting solutions, and implementing and controlling the solution. Using a process similar to this will help you develop effective problem-solving skills and implement solutions with positive results.

1. _____ involves not taking information at face value.
   a. Problem solving
   b. Communication
   c. Creative thinking
   d. Critical thinking

2. _____ involves using a structured method to develop and implement a solution.
   a. Brainstorming
   b. Problem solving
   c. Analysis
   d. Creative thinking

3. _____ is described as an exchange of information.
   a. Creative thinking
   b. Critical thinking
   c. Communication
   d. Analogy

4. _____ is a technique used to generate many ideas quickly.
   a. Developing analogies
   b. Problem solving
   c. Communication
   d. Brainstorming

5. The goal of using a structured problem-solving method is to be able to:

   a. develop a realistic schedule for implementing a solution.

   b. quickly implement high-quality solutions.

   c. develop creative solutions to problems.

   d. communicate progress on solving the problem.

8.4 Career Management

Your career choice has already started with the selection of your current program of study. You are gaining skills aimed at a particular type of career. As you will find in your work experience, your career will not be a simple, straight path. There will be many challenges along the way. The economy, new technologies, personal situations, promotions, job changes, and people you meet and interact with will all have effects on the direction your career takes. You will be able to control some circumstances, but not all. Your ability to cope with the changes, to set new goals, and to continue learning and developing skills will be critical as you manage your career through its inevitable twists and turns.

This section describes the rationale for continuous goal-setting and motivation throughout your career, tips for managing stress as you move through your career milestones, and a process for developing a professional portfolio to help you manage your career.

8.4.1 Goal Setting and Motivation

 Explain the importance of setting career goals and maintaining motivation..

Most people have their first career aspirations at the age of five or six. They may want to follow in their parents' footsteps or perhaps be a movie star or athlete. They typically have a role model that provides them motivation for an anticipated career. Of course, the choices made at such a young age rarely come to fruition but they do illustrate a basic process in career choice.

As shown in Figure 8.10, you first find something that interests or motivates you and then set goals to achieve it.

Figure 8.10: Motivation Helps to Set Goals

As you gain experience in a number of different areas, your motivation and goal-setting become more sophisticated. You learn to recognize the effort that is required to reach certain goals and that effort combined with potential rewards become key motivators. You become more selective in your aspirations and you set more realistic goals with a reasonable likelihood of success. You know more about what you want and you understand your abilities to get it. However, the same basic process still exists. You find something that motivates you and you set goals to achieve it.

You can see that focusing on developing your skill in setting goals is a critical factor in your lifelong success. Determining what you want or need creates your motivation, but, if you lack skill in setting reasonable goals to get it, you are less likely to succeed. How can you improve your skill in setting appropriate goals?

A common way to describe effective goals is through the often-used acronym, SMART. SMART goals are:

- Specific: They focus on a critical element or accomplishment

- Measurable: You can objectively determine if you have reached the goal.

- Achievable: You can expect to reach the goal, given reasonable resources and support.

- Realistic: It is not impossible to accomplish the goal.

- Time-bound: You set a timeframe for achievement.

By practicing the art of developing SMART goals, you can improve your skill in setting goals that will lead to success. You will be clear about exactly what you are aiming to do and you will set measurements and timeframes for your achievements. Developing SMART goals will not only give you clear direction, but also give you a framework for reevaluating and improving your goals in case you fall short of your objective.

At different points in your career, you may find that you lack motivation. You may lose interest in your current project or even in your career. If your motivation is lacking, then appropriate goal-setting and adequate performance are probably also falling short. Maintaining motivation is a key element to continued success in your career. Motivation is fueled by a desire or a need. If you want or need something, then you are usually driven to get it. Some suggestions for maintaining motivation are:

- Look for new challenges. Often, looking at a situation in a different way or trying to make an improvement in a lackluster environment can provide some motivation.

- Look for focal points, such as a motivational or inspirational quote, to help focus your efforts. You might also develop a personal mission statement. Quotes or mission statements can provide a source of purpose or inspiration to help motivate you toward a difficult or complex goal.

- Ask for feedback or suggestions on your situation. If you cannot think of ideas about what to do in a situation where you lack motivation, ask others for advice. Other people may be able to provide ideas that will give you a spark to ignite your motivation.

- If all else fails, consider a job or career change. If you cannot improve your motivation in your current situation, think about moving on to something new. Prolonged states of low motivation are not productive.

By maintaining your motivation and setting appropriate goals to achieve your objectives, you will find that you can reach your full potential in your career and in life.

8.4.2 Managing Stress

List potential causes of stress in professional life and describe techniques for managing stress.

Stress is a natural occurrence in everyday life. Although different people are affected by situations in different ways, almost everyone encounters stress at some point in his or her life. Occurrences in your professional life can be common causes of stress. Your ability to handle stress in professional situations is critical to success in your career.

Figure 8.11: Stress in Work Life

People typically think of stress in a negative way. The perils of stress, such as poor health and low personal effectiveness, are well publicized in almost any discussion of stress. But a certain amount of stress can be a motivator for some people. The key to managing stress is not necessarily to eliminate it, but rather to keep it at a manageable level so that your personal effectiveness is not affected by it. In professional situations, you want to manage stress so that you can maintain excellent performance and make the desired career choices.

Before you can effectively handle stress in your professional life, you should be able to identify potential causes of stress. The following list describes some common causes of stress in a professional environment:

- Lack of technical skill: Not having the skill or knowledge to perform a required task can create stress. You may be uncertain of how to accomplish the task or may get incorrect results because you do not know the proper way to do things.

- Lack of clarity about job responsibilities or expectations: Many people need direction about what they are required or expected to do on their job. Not knowing what is expected can be a cause of stress.

- Personality clash with co-workers or managers: Personality clashes can be evident or subtle. Clashes that result in arguments or other tangible conflicts can cause stress for people who prefer to avoid any type of conflict. Subtle personality clashes can also be detrimental. Often these types of clashes can be more difficult to pinpoint, raising the stress level even higher.

- Poor working environment: A noisy office, inadequate space, or unhealthy or unsafe working conditions are just some examples of a poor working environment that can cause stress.

- Unrealistic deadlines for projects: Not having enough time to do the required work is a classic cause of stress in professional life.

- Clash between personal and professional demands: At some point in career, almost every professional will find that the demands of personal life make it difficult to handle all the requirements of professional life. These conflicts of work-life balance can be a cause of stress. Examples of this include working parents needing to ensure that their children are cared for while they are at work or needing to relocate and change jobs or careers due to a spouse or partner getting a new job.

- Job loss: Some professionals may experience a job loss in their career. This may be due to a business closing, a layoff, or poor job performance. Whatever the cause, the loss of a job can be one of the most stress-inducing experiences in professional life.

There are several strategies you can use to help keep stress in your life at a manageable level. First, follow a healthy lifestyle. Eat nutritious foods, get enough sleep, and exercise regularly. Being healthy and fit will help you to handle stress appropriately. It will also help you to do your best work. Next, maintain good relationships with your co-workers and friends. In stressful situations, it is often helpful to be able to talk to and seek advice from someone you can trust. Maintaining a network of personal and professional contacts can provide you with a number of people to turn to when you need advice. Finally, take time to do things you enjoy. Having fun is one of the best ways to reduce stress.

Table 8.6 provides suggestions for handling some of the common causes of stress in the various professional situations.

Cause of stress	Suggestions
Lack of technical skill	Obtain training or documentation. Ask co-workers for help and talk to your manager if you have a serious skill deficiency. Be proactive about seeking help.
Lack of clarity about job responsibilities or expectations	Ask your manager for direction. Ensure that you and your manager have a mutual understanding of responsibilities and expectations. Clarify in writing, if required.
Personality clash with co-workers or manager	Try to work things out. Seek the help of a trusted co-worker or advisor to handle difficult situations.
Poor working environment	Make your working environment as comfortable as possible. Report serious situations to your manager or higher authority.
Unrealistic deadlines for projects	Propose a realistic schedule, backed up with factual data. Work with your manager to try to improve the situation. Use your experience on the project to ensure that the situation is not repeated in future projects.
Demands of personal life interfering with professional demands	Set priorities in your life and ensure that your professional and personal actions are aligned with these priorities. Set time for pursuing activities that make you happy.
Job loss	Maintain a positive focus, and take steps to secure new employment as quickly as possible. Using your professional network can help to lead you to job opportunities and relieve some of the stress associated with the loss of a job.

Table 8.6: Suggestions for Managing Stress in Professional Situations

8.4.3 Developing a Portfolio

 Describe the process and benefits of developing and maintaining a personal portfolio as a career management tool.

As you look for different job opportunities, potential employers will be assessing your skills, personality, and accomplishments. They will be looking for evidence of your abilities and creativity. One way to provide evidence is through a portfolio of your work.

A professional portfolio presents examples of your best work. You strategically select pieces for the portfolio to show the range of skills that you wish to highlight. Your portfolio should be aligned with the strengths and accomplishments you focus on in interviewing so that you present a strong, cohesive picture of yourself to potential employers.

A professional portfolio can help you in two important ways:

- It can help you get the job of your choice by serving as a unique marketing tool of your skills and accomplishments

- By maintaining the portfolio, you will remain focused on your key accomplishments and skill development throughout your career

Many people begin building the skills required for assembling a portfolio early in their life without even realizing it. Most school-age children participate in show-and-tell at school where they bring in an object that has some significance to them and describe it to their classmates. Assembling your professional portfolio requires many of the same basic competencies as show-and-tell: assembling objects that have significance, creating a story line around them, and describing the objects with passion and enthusiasm. By viewing your professional portfolio in this manner, you can create a collection that will set you apart from your peers and have fun while doing it.

A recommended process for creating a portfolio is described in Figure 8.12.

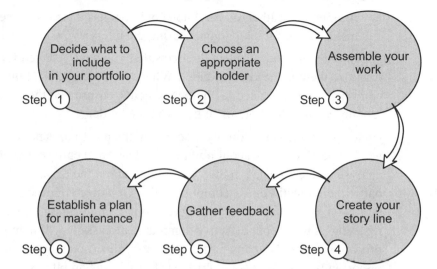

Figure 8.12: Creating a Professional Portfolio

A process for creating a portfolio would include:

1. Decide what to include in your portfolio: The analysis of what to include in your portfolio is critical. You should begin by making a list of your key strengths and accomplishments and then brainstorming the tangible items that highlight the areas on which you wish to focus. The items to consider for your portfolio may include:

   ▤ Your resume

   ▤ A transcript of grades

   ▤ Awards or recognition you received

   ▤ A sample of your work, such as writing, code, or a screen shot of an application or Web site that you designed

   ▤ Excerpts from project plans or reports you created

   ▤ Technical documentation you developed

2. Choose an appropriate folder for the contents of your portfolio: Selecting the appropriate folder is important. You want to create a well-organized, professional appearance for your portfolio and be comfortable handling it. Do not select a folder that is too small to hold your work or too large for you to carry during an interview. You want to be able to carry your portfolio discretely, yet refer to it effortlessly during your conversations. Some suggestions for a folder include:

   ▤ A three-ring binder of an appropriate width

- Sturdy folders with pockets
- A zippered, leather, or vinyl notebook that has a means for securing your work inside, a pad for taking notes during the interview, and a business card holder

3. Assemble your work: Collect the items that you have selected for your portfolio and organize them in the chosen folder. Whenever possible, print the items on a sharp color printer. If you need to photocopy items, ensure that the copies are clear and legible. Make sure all items fit neatly in the holder.

4. Create your story line: Simply assembling the portfolio is not enough. You also need to be able to talk about it with confidence and enthusiasm. Return to the analysis you completed in Step 1 and think about the reasons why you selected the particular strengths and accomplishments. Organize your thoughts into a story line that you can use to present your portfolio in an interesting, organized, and meaningful way. Your effective communication skills will help you here. Be prepared to talk about any part of your portfolio. You may not always have the opportunity to present your entire portfolio during an interview.

5. Gather feedback from others: After you have created your portfolio, present it to some of your co-workers, classmates, and friends to get feedback. Your goal is to have a portfolio that is well-organized and effectively highlights your strengths. Feedback in non-interview situations is critical to testing the impact of the portfolio on others. Gathering this feedback also gives you practice in effectively using the portfolio and helps you to become more familiar with it.

6. Establish a plan for maintaining your portfolio: The first step in maintaining your portfolio is to analyze the feedback you received and make improvements prior to your first interview. Spend time evaluating and fine-tuning your portfolio after every interview. Keep your portfolio up-to-date even if you are not actively seeking a new position. Assess your portfolio every six-to-twelve months to ensure that you do not forget about key accomplishments.

The process seems straightforward, but you may encounter several problems.

Table 8.7 lists some common stumbling blocks in developing a portfolio and suggests methods for overcoming them.

Problem area	Suggestions
You do not have enough material to highlight your focus areas adequately.	If you have less work experience, look for experiences outside of work, either from school or volunteer work.
Some work that you want to include is confidential information belonging to your employer.	Eliminate all confidential information from your portfolio. Under no circumstances should you include confidential items, such as customer information or proprietary code, in your portfolio. Describe the work you did in general terms. Seek advice from your employer if you are not sure about an item that you want to include in your portfolio.
You sometimes find yourself flipping through your portfolio in a somewhat disorganized fashion.	Use tabs to organize your portfolio. Create a table of contents for your portfolio and use page numbers to identify the contents. Practice using your portfolio in mock interviews.
Your portfolio looks worn after several uses.	Place your portfolio items in plastic sheet protectors and then organize them in a binder.
Your portfolio seems too long.	Eliminate similar items, keeping only the most illustrative or strongest examples of your work. Limit your portfolio to no more than 15 or 20 items.

Table 8.7: Common Problem Areas in Developing Portfolio

Remember that your portfolio is an important example of your professional skills. It shows tangible evidence of your accomplishments and also gives an indication of your presentation and organization skills. If done well, it can set you apart from your peers and help you to get the job of your choice.

Practice Questions

1. The Realistic characteristic of SMART goal-setting implies that:
    a. the goal can be accomplished.
    b. the goal is focused on a current project.
    c. you can determine when you have reached the goal.
    d. the goal has objective measurement criteria.

2. _____ is fueled by desire or need.
    a. Stress
    b. Career management
    c. Motivation
    d. Problem solving

3. _____ stress refers to keeping stress at a level such that it does not hurt your personal effectiveness.
    a. Allowing
    b. Managing
    c. Creating
    d. Avoiding

4. Which of the following is NOT a benefit of a professional portfolio?
    a. It helps you maintain a focus on your skills and accomplishments.
    b. It can help you get the job of your choice.
    c. It provides a unique marketing tool for your skills and accomplishments.
    d. It helps you reduce stress.

5. The Time-bound characteristic of SMART goal-setting refers to:

    a. sticking with a goal until you have reached it.

    b. creating a schedule to manage your time.

    c. setting a timeframe for achieving the goal.

    d. tracking how long it takes you to accomplish a goal.

Summary

This chapter presented several important *soft skills* for technical professionals. These skills will help you achieve success throughout your career. In this chapter, you learned that:

■ Effective time management can help you to do your best work, experience less stress, increase your confidence, and give you a chance to explore new opportunities. *Prioritizing* and *creating a schedule* are two important aspects of time management.

■ By focusing on developing employee skills, organizations can reduce their employee turnover, realize greater flexibility in adapting to changes, and enjoy higher employee satisfaction. All these benefits lead to a stronger, more successful organization.

■ *Formal development planning* and *mentoring* are two ways that organizations can ensure effective development of employees.

■ Teamwork is necessary whenever two or more people work toward a common end result. Effective teams exhibit the following characteristics among members:

- They trust one another
- They engage in free and open discussion around ideas
- They commit to decisions and plans of action
- They hold themselves accountable for delivering against the plan
- They focus on the achievement of collective results

■ *Critical thinking* and *creative thinking* are two analytical techniques that lead to creativity and innovation. Critical thinking involves looking at issues in a thorough, investigative manner. Creative thinking sparks innovation. *Brainstorming* and *developing analogies* are two techniques for creative thinking.

■ Effective communication involves delivering a message that is understood correctly by its recipients. Words, tone of voice, and non-verbal factors such as body language and facial expressions, all affect the interpretation of the message.

- Problem-solving skills can be enhanced by following a structured process. Structured problem-solving processes involve:
  - Analysis of the environment
  - Recognition and analysis of the problem
  - Generation and selection of a solution
  - Implementation of the solution and control to ensure continued success
- Setting goals and maintaining motivation are important factors in managing your career. Effective goals can be developed using the acronym SMART, which describes goals as:
  - Specific
  - Measurable
  - Achievable
  - Realistic
  - Time-bound
- Stress is a natural occurrence in everyday life as well as in professional environments. Managing stress involves keeping it at a level that does not negatively affect your personal effectiveness.
- A professional portfolio is a tangible representation of your strengths and accomplishments. Assembling and maintaining a portfolio can help you get the job of your choice and encourage you to maintain a focus on accomplishments and skill development throughout your career.

References

■ Browne, M. Neil and Stuart M. Keeley. *Asking the Right Questions: A Guide to Critical Thinking, 7th edition.* Upper Saddle River, NJ: Prentice Hall, 2004.

■ Griffin, Jack. *How to Say It at Work.* Paramus, NJ: Prentice Hall Press. 1998.

■ Higgins, James M. *101 Creative Problem Solving Techniques: The Handbook of New Ideas for Business.* Winter Park, FL: New Management Publishing Company. 1994.

■ Lencioni, Patrick. *The Five Dysfunctions of a Team: A Leadership Fable.* San Francisco, CA: Jossey-Bass. 2002.

Project Planning and Execution

9

Projects are common to both business and personal life. Planning a party, renovating the house, implementing a new system, or reorganizing a department, are all different kinds of projects. The process of defining, planning, doing, and evaluating the work is the hallmark of a well-run project. This chapter incorporates concepts, strategies, and techniques that facilitate the completion of projects efficiently.

At the end of this chapter, you will be able to:

- Explain the benefits of project management.
- Describe how to define the requirements and scope of a project.
- Develop a project plan.
- Identify and manage risk on a project.
- Manage project resources as changes occur on projects.
- Describe best practices to follow at the end of a project.

Need a car

5 ques

What kind of car interested in

make, model

New or used

Color

Options

what cylinder

Saftey features

gas mileage

leatherseating

6 cylinder engine

CD player   Adio options

Rear wheel Drive

9.1 Overview of Project Management

Think about the last project you worked on. It may have been work-related or it may have been a personal project, such as buying a car or remodeling a room in your house. How did you feel about your last project? Most people view projects with some level of anxiety. Some projects require more input of work than anticipated or cost more than planned. In some cases, the result of a project may not have yielded the desired results. Not all projects end badly, but almost everyone has experienced a less-than-optimal result on at least one project.

What can we do to change this? We certainly can't avoid projects. But we can take steps to manage them better and effectively control their outcomes. Project management is a skill that is highly desired in professional organizations.

Most projects require us to follow a process. This process includes:

- Defining what is needed
- Planning how it will be done
- Doing the actual work
- Evaluating the results

Structured processes for managing specific projects differ in the specific steps and tools they suggest, but the general steps mentioned above are common to most project work.

A structured process for executing projects helps to add control and achieve predictable results. This section provides an overview of project management and outlines the foundation of the skills and techniques that help the effective execution of projects.

9.1.1 Definition of a Project

 Recognize a project, as distinguished from a business process.

Before considering how to manage a project effectively, it is helpful to be able to identify a project and distinguish it from a business process. Project management is a critical business skill, but it differs from standard business or people management.

Organizations have both projects and business processes. While there are similarities between the two, there are key differences that have implications for how they should be managed. Table 9.1 outlines some of the key differences between projects and business processes.

Project characteristics	Business process characteristics
A one-time event	A repeated event
Moderate to long duration	Usually shorter duration
Temporary cross-functional work teams	Permanent work teams, usually in the same department
Team members change for different projects	Team members remain constant

Table 9.1: Comparison of Project Characteristics and Business Processes

Some challenges of project management as opposed to business processes are:

■ Problems may be difficult to anticipate, as specific projects are unique.

■ It can be challenging to keep the team members motivated, as projects take longer than established business processes to complete.

■ It may be difficult for project managers to coordinate between project teams and exercise authority over project team members due to the temporary and cross-functional composition of project teams.

While these situations may also arise with business processes, they are more common to projects and so a disciplined approach and expertise is required for project management.

9.1.2 Common Problems in Projects

 Describe common problems that occur in projects.

The characteristics of projects described in the previous section can lead to several problem areas in projects. As shown in Figure 9.1, these problems include:

■ Customers' expectations on quality and functionality are not met: Customers may find that certain functionality is missing, not implemented as expected, or other quality problems with the project deliverable.

- Deadlines are not met: Projects that extend beyond the stated deadline are unfortunately a common occurrence.

- Project team members feel overworked: Despite planning, project team members may need to work extra hours to meet deadlines. If the extra work is not balanced with a sense of reward and accomplishment, team members can feel overworked.

- Communication on the project status is insufficient: Team members and others involved with a project sometimes feel that they are not aware of project issues. This lack of communication is often a cause for other problems in the project.

Figure 9.1: Common Problems in Projects

Given the nature of projects, as described in Table 9.1, it is easy to see how these problems could occur. Effective project management can help to avoid these problems.

9.1.3 Goal of Project Management

State the goal of effective project management.

Managing projects effectively can produce desirable project results. Due to project mismanagement, some project experiences may be very grim—too much work, too little time, not enough recognition, and unfulfilled customer expectations. These are not the types of experiences professionals look forward to. However, not all projects are negative experiences. Well-executed projects end with customers being delighted by a high-quality deliverable arriving on or ahead of schedule and project team members feeling appreciated and rewarded for their work. Hopefully, you have been involved in projects that resulted in positive experiences.

What makes the difference between good and bad projects?

There are many factors that influence the outcome of a project. Effective project management seeks to control these factors so that projects run efficiently and produce high-quality results. The goal of project management is to ensure that:

- The scope of a project is clearly defined.
- Customer and team member expectations regarding scope, quality, and schedule are understood and accepted.
- Everyone affected by the project has the desired level of involvement and information about the project.
- Project-related issues are handled with minimal harm to the project.
- The final project deliverable is of acceptable quality and is delivered as per schedule.
- Results are evaluated. The relevant information from the evaluation exercise is documented and analyzed for the benefit of future projects.

9.1.4 Project Stakeholders

Describe common project stakeholders.

Stakeholders are people who have an interest in the results and activities of a project. Stakeholders can be involved with overall management of project resources, business results, and/or budgets. In short, if a project affects the decisions you make about your business processes, you can be considered a stakeholder in the project.

Table 9.2 describes common project stakeholders and their roles.

Project Stakeholder	Role
Project Sponsor	▪ Proposes the idea for the project. ▪ "Sells" the idea to senior management members, who are the decision-makers. ▪ Supports the project.
Project Leader	▪ Responsible for driving the results of the project. ▪ Coordinates and manages activities of the project team. ▪ Communicates status and issues.
Functional/Resource Managers	▪ Provides resources to complete the project. ▪ Responsible for implementing and sustaining the final outcome of the project.
Team Members	▪ Provides input to the project. ▪ Complete the work on the project.
Customers	▪ Define the requirements for the project. ▪ Provide feedback on project deliverables. ▪ Accept the final deliverable.

Table 9.2: Common Project Stakeholders

It is important to collaborate with project stakeholders as soon as a project is initiated, since their involvement is critical to the success of a project. Stakeholders provide essential input to all facets of a project. Identifying and involving the appropriate stakeholders are important steps towards the projects being successful.

9.1.5 A Generic Project Execution Process

 Describe a typical process for managing projects.

Once a project is proposed, a structured execution of the project process can begin. Figure 9.2 shows a basic project execution process.

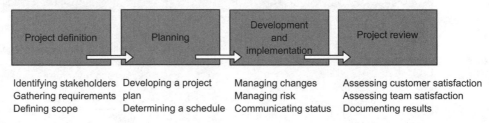

Figure 9.2: A Basic Project Execution Process

A basic project execution process includes the following stages:

1. The *project definition* stage is when the foundation for the project is established. The key players (stakeholders) are identified. They provide their input to decide the vision for the project. Requirements for the final deliverable are established and agreed upon. Finally, the scope of the project, issues the project will address, and items the project will not address, are defined and accepted by the stakeholders.

2. The *planning* stage provides the specifics about how the project will be executed. A project plan, which outlines relevant information about the project, is created and accepted by the stakeholders. A schedule that lays out when important tasks will be completed is distributed to the project team. This stage is critical to establishing a framework for project work that is acceptable to all stakeholders.

3. The development and implementation stage is where the actual work of the project is done. Effective project management is important at this stage. It involves controlling and handling changes in the project, managing issues that pose a risk to the project

outcome, communicating project status, and ensuring that desirable progress is made toward the final deliverable.

4. The project review stage is where results are evaluated and customer satisfaction is measured. The outcomes of this stage can provide valuable input to future projects.

The remainder of this chapter provides greater detail on activities throughout the duration of the development of the project.

Practice Questions

1. Which of the following are characteristics of a project?

   I.   It is repeatable.

   II. It has a unique, specific outcome.

   III. The team associated with it is temporary.

   a. I and II

   b. I and III

   c. II and III

   d. I, II, and III

2. Which of the following statement is true?

   Statement A: A common problem in projects is missed deadlines.

   Statement B: Potential problems in projects can be easy to predict if a structured project management process is followed.

   a. Statement A is true but Statement B is false.

   b. Statement A is false but Statement B is true.

   c. Both statements are true.

   d. Both statements are false.

3. Which of the following is NOT a goal of project management?

   a. To enable projects to be completed according to a schedule.

   b. To keep stakeholders informed about project status.

   c. To establish a team that will be dedicated to a specific activity and to build expertise with that activity over a period of time.

   d. To review results with an aim to improve future projects.

4. The _____ is typically responsible for promoting the project within the organization.

   a. Project Manager

   b. Project Sponsor

   c. Customer

   d. Functional Manager

5. At which stage of the project are stakeholders typically identified?

   a. Project Definition

   b. Planning

   c. Development and Implementation

   d. Project Review

9.2 Assessing Requirements and Defining Scope

When a project is proposed, there is often only a vague description of the desired outcome. "I'd like to buy a new car," "We need a web-based order processing system," or "We need a better way to manage our customer data" are some examples of directives that are given at the outset of a project. Before beginning work, the project team needs to understand more about the desired outcome. The team needs to understand the specifics about the customer and the situation before designing a solution.

9.2.1 Understanding the Customer

 Describe a process for determining the characteristics of the customer's environment.

Recall that the customer is the project stakeholder who accepts the final deliverable of the project. It follows that one of the first tasks of a project should be to define customer requirements. It is helpful first, to analyze the characteristics of the customer environment. This will help in the accurate interpretation of the project's requirements and create an acceptable deliverable.

The following questions can be useful in understanding customer characteristics:

- What is the problem or issue being addressed? Why is it a problem?
- What is the current situation? How do things work now?
- What is the ideal situation? How would things work in a perfect world?
- How many people will be using the solution implemented by the project?
- Are there any other characteristics of end-users that are important?

Your understanding of the customer's environment will influence the types of questions you ask to gain a clearer picture of the customer. After comprehending the customer environment and the problem being addressed, you will be ready to gather customer requirements.

9.2.2 Gathering Requirements

Describe a process for gathering customer requirements for a project.

Requirements are the specifications for a project. They specify the features and functions of the final deliverable. The requirements may also specify the timeframe in which the project must be completed.

Requirements are defined by talking to the appropriate stakeholders. For efficiency, groups of stakeholders can be called together in a meeting, instead of speaking with them individually. A brainstorming meeting or a focus group would be an appropriate method for gathering requirements. Example 9.1 shows a sample process for conducting a brainstorming meeting to gather requirements.

Example 9.1

1. The project leader or meeting facilitator poses a question about requirements. (For example, "What features would you like to see in the new customer tracking system?")

2. The group spends 15-20 minutes brainstorming features and requirements. Note cards can be used to record the ideas.

3. The ideas must be organized and evaluated. Similar ideas should be grouped together to simplify the evaluation process.

4. The project leader or meeting facilitator constructs an evaluation matrix. (see Figure 9.3) The group subsequently evaluates each requirement with respect to its impact on the customer's situation.

5. After the meeting, the project leader or meeting facilitator ranks the requirements in order of importance based on the input received in the meeting.

The group leader can use a content organizer tool to arrange the ideas logically during the brainstorming session. Organization of gathered ideas may be done in the form of a flowchart, a mind map, or a relationship diagram. You can search the Internet to learn how to use these tools.

An evaluation matrix may be created after all requirements have been collated. The evaluation matrix places the requirements in the order of their priority. Figure 9.3 shows a sample matrix for evaluating project requirements gathered during a brainstorming session.

Project requirements	Essential *(this requirement MUST be met)*	Helpful *(this requirement would be nice to have, but other alternatives may exist)*	Optional *(this requirement would have a low impact on the problem being addressed)*

Instructions:
List requirements in the left (grey) column
For each requirement, place a check in the column that best describes its overall impact to the project

Figure 9.3: Sample Matrix for Evaluating Project Requirements[MSOffice1]

It is important to ask the right questions to get a clear idea of customer requirements. It is critical to the planning, development, and ultimate acceptance of the final deliverable of the project. Unclear requirements can lead to a lot of problems, causing dissatisfaction to all stakeholders of the project. It may necessitate a lot of rework and lower the profit margin of the project.

Example 9.2 lists questions that would be useful for gathering requirements in a focus group.

Example 9.2

Some questions for gathering requirements in a focus group can be:

■ What are the problems in your environment? (Look for consistencies and highlight inconsistencies with information on problems that you have already gathered).

■ What would help you to overcome these problems?

■ If you were to design a *<proposed project final deliverable>*, what features would you include?

■ What is the best characteristic of your working environment right now? Why is it the best?

■ What is the worst characteristic of your working environment right now? Why is it the worst?

Additional questions could focus on specifics about current business processes or tools, especially if the participants in the focus group did not provide input on customer characteristics.

Gathering requirements is likely to take several meetings. Seeking input from a good cross-section of the stakeholders and user community and taking the time to evaluate the requirements with the audience will ensure a strong set of requirements with which to work.

9.2.3 Defining Scope

Explain how to define the scope of a project.

Once requirements are agreed upon, the scope of the project can be documented. The scope states the issues to be addressed by the project. It describes characteristics and features of the final deliverable and may also state problems that will be addressed. The scope defines the boundaries for the project.

For defining scope, it is important to describe both what is included and what is excluded from the project. Exclusions, or "out-of-scope" items, are important to mention to help control potential changes or additional requests once the project has started.

Some guidelines for defining the scope of a project include:

- Customer and environment characteristics in the description to help clarify why features have been included (or excluded) from the scope.

- Requirements and relevant input from all groups that participated in the gathering of requirements.

- A reality check of the final scope to ensure that it is of a manageable size and not overly ambitious. Projects that are too large are difficult to manage. On the other hand avoid being too conservative and defining too narrow a scope, as such projects may not address all important customer requirements.

A well-defined scope makes the task of project planning easier. In addition, it can also serve as a tool to keep the project on track through the development and implementation stages. Time spent up-front on defining and gaining approval on the scope is likely to pay dividends as the project progresses.

1. What understanding should you gain before gathering customer requirements?

    a. The project schedule

    b. Customer environment

    c. Technology required for the project

    d. The project scope

2. What methods can be used to gather customer requirements?

    I.   Brainstorming meeting

    II. Critical thinking

    III. Focus group

    a. I and II

    b. I and III

    c. II and III

    d. I, II, and III

3. Which of the following statement is true?

    Statement A: Gathering requirements usually takes several meetings.

    Statement B: Customer requirements help to define the project scope.

    a. Statement A is true but Statement B is false.

    b. Statement A is false but Statement B is true.

    c. Both statements are true.

    d. Both statements are false.

4. The project scope describes the ___ of the final deliverable of the project.
    a. timeframe
    b. stakeholders
    c. characteristics
    d. metrics

5. Which of the following is true?
    Statement A: The project scope should describe what is excluded from the project.
    Statement B: A well-defined project scope can help to control the project in the development stage.
    a. Statement A is true but Statement B is false.
    b. Statement A is false but Statement B is true.
    c. Both statements are true.
    d. Both statements are false.

9.3 Developing a Plan

The *project plan* can be developed once the scope of the project is defined and accepted by the stakeholders. The plan outlines what is to be done and how it will be accomplished. It provides the blueprint against which a project's progress will be measured. The project plan is instrumental for communication and setting expectations with project stakeholders and is a critical tool for managing the project to completion.

9.3.1 Components of a Plan

 Describe the typical components of a project plan.

The project plan describes all relevant aspects of a project. Plans can range from a few pages to over 20 to 30 pages in length. There is no set rule for how long a project plan should be or the specific headings to include. What is important is that the plan be clear and complete with regard to details that are relevant to the project. The plan will serve as a guide throughout the project and as a reference for future work after the project is completed.

Common components of a project plan include:

- A description of the problem or the customer's situation
- The names and roles of the project stakeholders
- A list of project team members and their roles
- The requirements for the project
- The tasks and milestones to be accomplished
- A project schedule

 Plans may include other information as well, depending on the nature of the project. For example, if a project requires the implementation of new technology, then a section on the description of the technology and relevant vendor information may be included. Budget information is also included in plans for larger projects.

Microsoft Project is a useful tool for creating a project plan.

The first four components of the project plan were incorporated in the Project Definition stage. The next two topics in this section describe the remaining components, which are the development of the tasks and milestones and the project schedule.

9.3.2 Defining Tasks

Explain the rationale for defining tasks within a project.

In order to plan the work for an entire project, the work needs to be separated into manageable components. These components of a project are called tasks. A well-defined set of tasks helps create a realistic plan and provides a tool to manage and communicate progress on the project.

It is advisable to break larger tasks into smaller subtasks. This makes them measurable and easier to track and accomplish.

Defining tasks is a skill. There are no hard and fast rules for defining tasks. Knowledge of work processes and the skills required to complete them is essential to developing a task list. For example, in a project to build a house, knowledge of the technical details about housing construction and building codes and requirements is essential to be able to develop a task list for the project. An appropriate task list cannot be created without this expertise.

The following list provides some tips and guidelines for defining tasks:

- Each task should be such that one or two people in a relatively short timeframe can complete it.

- Being aware of the skills and abilities of the project team members helps define tasks of a manageable size. If project team members are experienced, complex tasks likely will be appropriate. However, if team members are less experienced, tasks may have to be simpler.

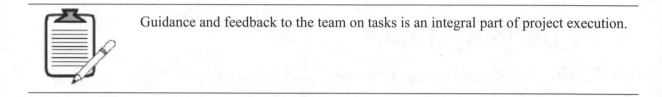

Guidance and feedback to the team on tasks is an integral part of project execution.

- Use your judgment in determining the number of tasks to specify. Too many tasks may make the project cumbersome and difficult to manage.

You may also group related tasks into a sub-project to simplify management.

Tasks should be planned in such a way that completion of one or more tasks results in the realization of a milestone. Achieving milestones is motivating for the project team. Milestones are delivery points of important aspects of the project. They are key points of accomplishment within a project. Tasks and milestones are the key components of the project schedule.

9.3.3 Developing a Schedule

 Describe a technique for developing a project schedule.

Developing a schedule is a critical component of project management. Once the planning is complete, the schedule is the guide for the remainder of the project. Ideally, a project schedule will meet the needs of the customer and provide sufficient time for project team members to develop a quality solution.

Always kccp buffer time in the schedule of tasks to accommodate unforeseen delays.

Unfortunately, it is often difficult to achieve an ideal schedule. Quite often the timeframes required by the customer do not provide the time the project team would like to have to develop the solution. In these cases, flexibility is important: adjustments and sacrifices must be made. Developing the schedule is a complex process and it may take several stages of planning to develop a workable schedule. Furthermore, despite even the best planning at this stage, it is likely that adjustments to the schedule will be made during the development stage of the project. Managing details of a schedule is one of the primary tasks of a project manager.

Figure 9.4 shows a sample process for developing a project schedule.

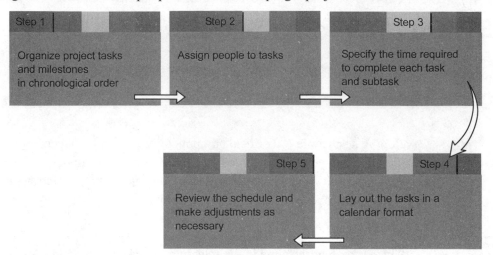

Figure 9.4: Process for Developing Project Schedule

A sample process for developing a project schedule would have the following steps:

1. Organize project tasks and milestones in chronological order: This is an initial and important step that requires thorough knowledge of the work processes necessary to develop the solution. Some tasks may be completed simultaneously, which will streamline the development effort.

2. Assign people to tasks: This is an important resource-planning step. People with the right expertise are required for each task. It is also important to plan resources appropriately around tasks that will be in progress simultaneously.

3. Specify the time required to complete each task and subtask: This requires knowledge of both the work processes and the skills and ability of the project team members. Flexibility is required in this step of the process to be able to meet customer timeframes and leave room for unexpected occurrences during development.

Figure 9.5 shows a template you could use to facilitate your work in Steps 1–3.

Task	Assigned resource(s)	Time required

Figure 9.5: Template for Planning Project Schedules

4. Lay out the tasks in a calendar format: You can use a standard calendar or a software tool such as Microsoft Project to complete this step. Be sure to take holidays and other special events into consideration.

5. Review the schedule and make adjustments as necessary: The schedule is rarely perfect after the first attempt.

Table 9.3 provides suggestions for addressing common problem areas in a project schedule.

Problem	Suggestions
Projected end date is later than customer requirements.	Check with the project team to determine if timeframes for completing tasks can be shortened. Shorten buffers for unexpected events. Explore whether additional resources can be added to the project.
There are no buffers in the schedule.	Look for resources outside the project team to provide a contingency plan.
Project team members are not comfortable with the timeframes in the schedule.	Document concerns and talk to the project sponsor about them. Seek an extension for the end date. Revisit the project scope and eliminate any unnecessary items. Be sure to get stakeholder approval on any changes to scope.

Table 9.3: Tips for Handling Common Scheduling Problems

Practice Questions

1. The ___ outlines what is to be done on a project and how it will be accomplished.
   a. project scope
   b. project schedule
   c. project sponsor
   d. project plan

2. Which of the following statement is true?
   Statement A: The project sponsor specifies a mandatory standard and required length for the project plan.
   Statement B: The project plan is usually developed before gathering customer requirements.

a. Statement A is true but Statement B is false.

b. Statement A is false but Statement B is true.

c. Both statements are true.

d. Both statements are false.

3. A _____ is a manageable component of a project able to be completed by one or two people.

a. sub-team

b. task

c. milestone

d. project plan

4. _____ are key points of accomplishment within a project.

a. Sub-teams

b. Milestones

c. Work processes

d. Requirements

5. In building a project schedule, what should you do before specifying the time required to complete each task?

a. Lay out the tasks in a calendar format.

b. Assign people to tasks.

c. Ensure there are buffers in the schedule.

d. Plan for holidays and special events.

9.4 Managing Risk

Once a project enters the development and implementation stage, focus shifts from planning to execution. The challenge at this stage is to keep development activity on target with respect to delivery date and quality. Many factors can affect a project and cause delays or problems. Effective project management can help to mitigate these factors and keep the project running smoothly.

9.4.1 Definition of Risk on Projects

 Describe the facets of risk in a project.

Risk can be described as any factor that could cause a project to miss a requirement. Risk elements can fall into three general areas:

- Technology
- Cost
- Schedule

Technology risk refers to the quality or availability of required technology for the project. In general, newer or emerging technologies carry a greater degree of risk than older, more established technologies. For example, a project that is based on a new or emerging technology might be at high risk, since the availability or quality of the technology may not yet be reliable or the expertise to work with the technology may not exist within the project team. Technology risk can also refer to infrastructure elements, such as network communications, special equipment, or access to data or information being available to a project.

Cost risk refers to the probability of overruns on the project budget. Whether a project is small-scale or large-scale, it may run a risk in this area. Several factors have to be considered in managing cost, including equipment, salary of project team members, and the preparation, marketing, and training costs for the final deliverable.

Schedule risk refers to the ability to adhere to the project schedule. The most important element of the schedule is usually the final delivery date, although other interim dates, such as training and marketing plans, can be important as well. Schedules can be affected by project team members becoming unavailable or by other external factors.

9.4.2 Assessing, Evaluating, and Mitigating Risk

 Describe how to identify and evaluate risk in a project and take steps to mitigate high risk factors.

Identifying and evaluating the risk factors that may exist in a project is an important aspect of managing risk. Familiarity with the work processes and skills required for the project is necessary for defining project tasks, creating the schedule, and assessing and evaluating project risk. It would be difficult to perform a detailed risk assessment without this knowledge.

The following processes can be used to assess and manage risk on a project:

1. List the possible elements of risk on the project: A brainstorming session with project team members helps to develop a list of risk factors. Follow the guidelines for brainstorming that were presented in Chapter Eight, Section 8.3.2, "Creative Thinking."

2. Evaluate the risk elements: The purpose of evaluating the risk elements is to estimate the probability of the occurrence of the risk and to assess the impact that occurrence might have on the project. In assessing the probability of occurrence, a scale of High (likely to occur), Medium (might occur), and Low (not likely to occur) can be used. In assessing the impact on the project, it should be considered whether the risk factor would cause a significant change in the schedule or quality of the final deliverable. A scale of High (significant impact), Medium (moderate impact), and Low (little to no impact) can be used to rate the factors.

Tally the information on a chart using a format similar to the template provided in Example 9.3[MSOffice2].

Example 9.3

Risk factors	Probability of occurence			Impact on project		
	HIGH	MEDIUM	LOW	HIGH	MEDIUM	LOW

3. Identify elements of high risk: After evaluating the risk elements for both probability of occurrence and impact on the project, data should be transferred to a risk assessment matrix. The risk assessment matrix, as shown in Figure 9.6, will help to identify risk factors that have a significant impact on the project. Each risk factor should be placed in the matrix according to its Impact and Probability ratings. Items in the upper right corner of the chart (high impact and high probability of occurrence) are high risk. Steps should be taken to mitigate the risk of these elements to the project.

Figure 9.6 shows a sample risk assessment matrix.

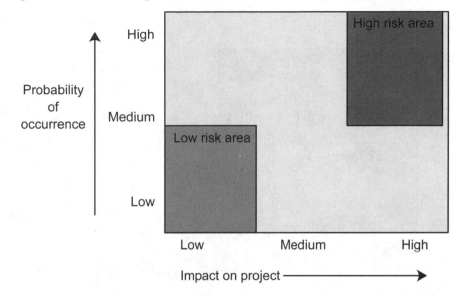

Figure 9.6: Sample Risk Assessment Matrix

Source: Adapted from Martin and Tate, *Getting Started in Project Management*, p. 122.

4. Generate measures to mitigate the high risk items: The goal should be to develop measures to lessen the impact or decrease the probability of occurrence of the high-risk items on the chart. Measures should be brainstormed with the project team and the best measures to help lessen the risk to the project should be selected.

 Be careful not to introduce measures that will impact other aspects of the project and create new risk.

---

5. Incorporate the selected measures into the project plan: Measures should be reviewed with the appropriate project stakeholders. Many of the measures may be kept as contingency plans to be implemented only if the associated risk factor occurs. A process for managing risk is critical to the success of a project. Every project has

risk factors and a failure to identify and manage them can have severe consequences for the schedule or quality of the deliverable.

Practice Questions

1. _____ can be described as any factor that could cause a project to miss meeting its objective completely.
   a. Mitigation
   b. Risk
   c. Impact
   d. Probability

2. You can use a _____ session to generate a list of risk elements for a project.
   a. risk assessment
   b. brainstorming
   c. contingency plans
   d. critical thinking

3. After identifying elements of high risk on a project, your goal is to:
   a. revise the project schedule.
   b. meet with the project sponsor.
   c. mitigate the high-risk items.
   d. begin development on the project.

9.5 Managing Resources

Project definition and planning are important stages of a project, and time spent up front in these stages certainly helps to eliminate surprises in the later stages of the project. But even the best planning is worthless without proper management during the development and implementation phases. The development phase is where the work of the project actually gets done. Effectively managing technical changes, handling issues with the project team, and communicating status to stakeholders are important activities in the development and implementation stage of a project.

9.5.1 Change Management

 Describe common types of changes that can occur during a project and explain how to handle them.

Change in a project is inevitable, despite thorough planning. Different technology may be required or project requirements may change due to external factors such as new regulations or management directives. Furthermore, critical issues related to the project may not surface until the development stage necessitating changes to the plan. A proper management of the changes is necessary to keep the project on track.

Some of the more common causes of change during the development phase of a project include:

- Additions to scope
- Changes in technology
- Modifications to design

Additions to scope, sometimes referred to as "scope creep," occur when customers continue to add requirements after the plan has been accepted. Customers may have forgotten to mention requirements, or, more commonly, they may think of additional beneficial features while viewing interim releases of the deliverable. It is important to manage these change requests carefully, as they could result in significant changes to the schedule.

Changes in technology can come about in several ways. Sometimes, the technology planned may not be available, either because it has phased out or perhaps earmarked for a different use. Technology is an important component of the infrastructure for the project and an integral part of the final deliverable. These changes need to be handled quickly and thoroughly in order to avoid significant delays or potential quality issues for the deliverable.

Modifications of design can occur as the project team works on the final deliverable. Team members may find alternatives to the proposed design they feel would make the project more efficient and enhance the quality of the final deliverable. Changes in business processes may also necessitate changes to the design, which also need to be handled quickly to avoid delays and confusion in the project.

The following list provides some suggestions for handling changes in a project.

- Always request that changes be accompanied by detailed justification. This will help the project team and stakeholders make quick and informed decisions about accepting or rejecting the request.

- Assess the impact on the schedule and the quality of the final deliverable before making any changes to the project. Make sure that a change is necessary and beneficial before implementing it.

- Obtain approval from the project sponsor and project stakeholders before implementing any change. Also, ensure that all project team members are aware of these changes.

9.5.2 Project Communications

 Describe best practices for communicating team activities.

Communication with the project team and stakeholders is essential throughout all phases of the project. It is common for project communication to fall short, leaving stakeholders, end-users, and sometimes even project team members unaware of changes or developments in a project. Poor communication can cause problems with the deliverable and leave project team members with negative feelings about the team.

As shown in Figure 9.7, several strategies can be used to help ensure sufficient communication about the project.

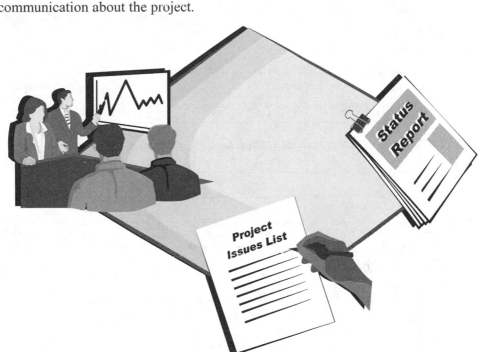

Figure 9.7: Effective Project Communication

The strategies include:

- Holding regular status meetings
- Maintaining a project issues list
- Sending interim status reports to project stakeholders

Status meetings not only provide a means for tracking the project, they also give team members a chance to collaborate and communicate on project issues. They help team members feel connected to the project. An agenda for these meetings is a must. The minutes from the meeting should be documented for the benefit of team members who are unable to attend.

Maintaining a project issues list is an important project management technique. The issues list provides a means for tracking problems with the project. Reviewing the issues list should be a part of regular team status meetings. A well-designed issues list can also serve as a useful communication tool for the project.

Figure 9.8 presents a template that can be used to maintain an issues list for a project.

X	Issue	Reported By	Date	Notes/Status
	X indicates that the issue has been resolved			

Figure 9.8: Template for Project Issues List

Sending interim status reports to stakeholders is a strategy to help keep stakeholders informed about project status. It may not be appropriate or possible for all stakeholders to attend project status meetings. The reports should be brief and focus on critical aspects of the project. Project leaders should use their judgment in determining how often to send status reports.

 Send the reports at critical milestones. Reports that are sent too frequently may tend to be ignored, while long delays between reports may give the impression that progress is not being made.

9.5.3 Recognition of Accomplishments

Explain the rationale for recognizing project accomplishments.

When people think of project management, they often consider only the technical and administrative aspects of managing the work to be done. Gathering requirements, setting the schedule, tracking issues, and completing the work on time and with acceptable quality are common focus areas in the field of project management. One additional area of focus is people management.

People management is often overlooked in project management, as project leaders may not be true managers in the organizational hierarchy. As many project teams are temporary in nature (recall the characteristics of projects discussed in section 9.1.1, "Definition of a Project"), people management is not necessarily considered for the project team; it is usually considered to be in the realm of the department or group manager responsible for the business results.

In order to keep the team motivated and focused on achieving the goals of the project, it is necessary to pay attention to the individual needs of the team members. Team members need feedback and recognition of their accomplishments to stay motivated. Without effective people management, the team is not likely to perform to the best of its ability.

Recognizing accomplishments is one way to keep the team motivated and focused on the project. Recognition throughout the project has the following benefits:

- Team members will feel that their accomplishments are worthwhile and appreciated.
- Recognition provides an additional way to highlight the progress being made on the project.
- Effective recognition maintains team morale and motivation, which is important as deadlines become stringent and as work increases.

Table 9.4 provides some strategies for recognition throughout a project.

Recognition strategy	Rationale
Provide an honorary award to be passed on to different team members at status meetings.	The award could be given to the person who handled the most unusual or difficult problem since the last meeting. This type of award helps to lighten the mood on difficult projects and can promote a sense of camaraderie among team members.
Recognize team members in status reports to stakeholders.	In addition to the administrative reporting on milestones, include the names of project team members who participated in the work. This provides visibility for team members and can encourage them to take pride in their work.
Celebrate important milestones.	Recognition should not occur only at the end of a project. Important milestones are also points to celebrate completion of significant work.

Table 9.4: Strategies for Project Recognition

Appropriately handling project changes, effective communication with team members and stakeholders, and thoughtful recognition of accomplishments for the duration of the project are all important strategies for effectively managing resources for a project. While projects can reach completion without a focus on these areas, project results will be better and team members and stakeholders will feel more positive about the project when these strategies are followed.

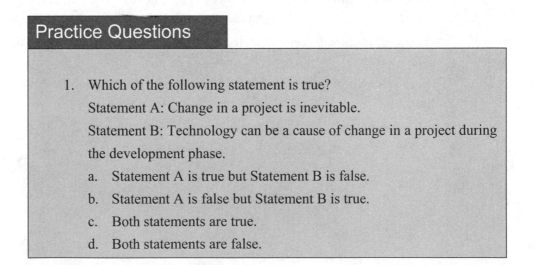

Practice Questions

1. Which of the following statement is true?

   Statement A: Change in a project is inevitable.

   Statement B: Technology can be a cause of change in a project during the development phase.

   a. Statement A is true but Statement B is false.

   b. Statement A is false but Statement B is true.

   c. Both statements are true.

   d. Both statements are false.

2. 'Scope creep' occurs when:

   a. customers make requests for new features after development has begun.

   b. projects fall behind schedule.

   c. projects progress slowly toward the final deliverable.

   d. contingency plans are enacted.

3. Which of the following statement is true?
   Statement A: Status meetings provide a means for tracking progress on a project.
   Statement B: Status meetings provide a chance for team members to collaborate on issues.

   a. Statement A is true but Statement B is false.

   b. Statement A is false but Statement B is true.

   c. Both statements are true.

   d. Both statements are false.

4. A(n) _____ provides a means for tracking problems on a project.

   a. issues list

   b. status report

   c. risk matrix

   d. change management process

5. Which of the following statement is true?
   Statement A: Recognition highlights progress being made on a project.
   Statement B: Project sponsors are responsible for recognizing progress made by the team.

   a. Statement A is true but Statement B is false.

   b. Statement A is false but Statement B is true.

   c. Both statements are true.

   d. Both statements are false.

9.6 Reviewing Results

Projects should not end with the delivery of the final product. Project issues should be documented for the benefit of future projects. It is also important to gather feedback from customers to determine if their expectations from the project were met. The team members should also assess their experiences in the project, so that any critical issues that caused problems can be addressed in future projects. Reviewing project results helps ensure that problems are addressed and success is replicable for future projects.

9.6.1 Customer Expectations

 Describe a technique for reviewing customer requirements and expectations at the end of a project.

In the initial phase of the project, customers participate in defining the requirements for the project. Customers may also have been involved in assessing interim project deliverables to help ensure that the required features for the product were implemented appropriately. It is also important to solicit feedback from customers after the final product has been delivered to determine their overall satisfaction with the project.

Customer feedback should also be obtained on:

- The overall quality of the final product
- The appropriateness of the product vis-à-vis the required specifications
- Overall satisfaction with the project

The quality of the final product is usually determined in acceptance testing or an evaluation of the features and functionality of the final deliverable as compared to the requirements outlined in the project plan. This is usually an objective measure of how the final product performs.

In addition to evaluating the quality of the product, it should also be assessed whether the product addresses the business problems that were outlined in the project definition stage. Following up on the questions that were used to gain a better understanding of the customer (refer to section 9.2.1, "Understanding the Customer") is one way to assess the appropriateness of the product for the customer environment.

Finally, it is good practice to assess the customer's overall satisfaction with the project. This is valuable information for improving future projects. A standard customer satisfaction survey can facilitate the execution of the primary goal of determining the customer's level of satisfaction with various aspects of the project. Areas to focus on in the survey include:

- Was the requirement gathering process thorough and efficient and did it include the right people?
- Was the project scope clearly defined?
- Was project communication easy to understand, complete, and at the right level of frequency?
- Did customers feel they had the right level of involvement in project activities?
- Did the project meet, exceed, or fall short of their expectations?

Customer needs are at the center of every project. The goal of a project is ultimately to meet the needs of the customer, so it follows that obtaining customer feedback at the end of the project is essential not only to evaluate the success of the current project but also to improve future projects.

9.6.2 Team Member Expectations

 Describe a technique for reviewing team member expectations at the end of a project.

In addition to assessing whether customer expectations were met on the project, it is also essential to get feedback from team members. Projects are not successful without full involvement and cooperation of team members. Evaluating their satisfaction with the way a project was run is important to be able to ensure that successful practices are continued and poor practices are rectified for future projects. Asking for feedback from team members also sends the message that team members are valued, which can help to maintain motivation and performance for future projects.

A team member satisfaction survey or focus group can be used to gather feedback from project team members. Areas of focus include:

- Was the communication adequate?
- Did the team members feel their contributions to the team and to the project were valued?
- Was the schedule realistic?
- Were changes to the project handled appropriately?
- What was the most positive experience on the project?
- What was the most negative experience on the project?
- What changes would improve future projects?

In gathering feedback, keep in mind that the project team is temporary and demands from the business organization or work team can often interfere with project work. It is often difficult to satisfy all project team members' concerns.

9.6.3 Final Project Activities

 Describe techniques for documenting project improvements and celebrating closure on a project.

It is not only important to document plans and expectations for the project at the beginning of the project, it is equally important to document results at the end of the project. The final project documentation provides a reference point for questions that may arise during future projects.

Table 9.5 provides a list of general project documents to be considered for final documentation.

Document	Rationale
Project Plan	The project plan contains the rationale for the original project design. If the original plan is significantly different from the final project results, the plan should be updated to reflect the project accurately. The plan should not be included if it does not describe the project accurately.
Customer Satisfaction Results and Feedback	Feedback from the customers on the results of the project can provide valuable information for handling future issues related to the project.
Final Project Statistics	Statistics on how long it took to complete the project, changes made during the project, and final costs associated with the project are all important to communicating the results of the project. They are valuable in helping to estimate future project work accurately as well.

Table 9.5: Suggested Final Project Documentation

As shown in Figure 9.9, it is also important to recognize the final accomplishment and celebrate the closure of the project.

Figure 9.9: Recognize Final Accomplishments and Celebrate Project End

Suggestions for celebration include:

■ Demonstrating the final product to the organization at large:

The end-users and project stakeholders are familiar with the project, but the rest of the organization may not be aware of the project. A demonstration of the final product can be a way to make others aware of the work that was done and also give project team members recognition for their accomplishments.

■ Organizing a team dinner or other event:

Providing a different venue for the celebration is a good way to show appreciation and reward team members for their work.

■ Providing certificates of achievement or other mementos of the project:

A visible reward that team members can display in their offices can give a sense of pride and accomplishment.

1. On what areas should you obtain customer feedback at the end of a project?

   I. Requirements for the next project.

   II. Overall quality of the final deliverable.

   III. Overall satisfaction with the project.

   a. I and II

   b. I and III

   c. II and III

   d. I, II, and III

2. What benefits are there in assessing team member satisfaction at the end of a project?

   I. It helps ensure that successful practices in managing the project are continued.

   II. It sends a message that team members are valued.

   III. It helps to focus future teams on project work rather than standard business work.

   a. I and II

   b. I and III

   c. II and III

   d. I, II, and III

3. What are the two activities that should be done at the end of a project?

    I.   Celebrate.

    II. Gather requirements for the next project.

    III. Evaluate stakeholder participation in the project.

    IV. Document project statistics.

    a. I and II

    b. II and III

    c. III and IV

    d. I and IV

Summary

In this chapter, you learned:

- The goal of project management is to control factors that influence the outcome of a project so that projects run efficiently and produce high-quality results.

- A project management process involves several general phases: Project Definition, Planning, Development and Implementation, and Project Review.

- During the Project Definition phase, stakeholders are identified, customer requirements are gathered, and the project scope is defined. Brainstorming meetings, evaluation sheets, and focus groups are commonly used to gather data during this stage of a project.

- The project scope defines the characteristics and features of the final deliverable. It should clearly define what the project will and will not address. The project scope can serve as a tool to keep the project on track during the development phase of the project.

- The project plan serves as the documentation for what is to be accomplished and how it will be done. It typically contains:
  - A description of the problem or the customer's situation
  - The names and roles of the project stakeholders
  - A list of project team members and their roles
  - The requirements for the project
  - The tasks and milestones to be completed
  - A project schedule

- Once a project moves from planning into development and implementation, the challenge is to keep development activity on target with respect to delivery date and quality. Factors that could cause projects to miss these requirements are referred to as risk.

- Risk elements can fall into three general categories: technology, cost, and schedule. Brainstorming and an evaluation matrix are tools that can help to identify and assess risk on a project.

- Despite thorough planning, change is almost certain to occur on a project. Causes for change include additions to scope, changes in technology, and modifications to design.

■ Appropriately handling project changes, effective communication with team members and stakeholders, and thoughtful recognition of accomplishments for the duration of the project are all important strategies for managing project resources effectively.

■ Final project activities should include:

- Documenting project issues for the benefit of future projects

- Gathering feedback from customers to determine if their expectations were met

- Gathering feedback from team members to assess their experience on the project

- Celebrating the end of the project

Reference

Martin, Paula and Karen Tate. *Getting Started in Project Management*. New York, NY: John Wiley & Sons, 2001.

The Impact of Technology

10

What is technology, and how does it affect our lives? This may seem like a strange question to ask in the twenty-first century, because technology is widely integrated into everyday life. The way you communicate, entertain, conduct business, receive medical care, and perform basic daily activities all depend heavily on technology. Technology is a basic expectation in today's society.

As a technical professional, you are focused on using technology to improve business results, society, and everyday life. By focusing on the impact of technology in recent history, and looking forward to future trends, you can form a strategy to use technology responsibly.

After completing this chapter, you will be able to:

- Identify several technological milestones over the last 20 years.

- Describe the effects of technology on the evolution of organizations.

- Describe social, economic, and psychological impacts of technology in recent history.

- Discuss strategies for individuals and organizations to enhance effectiveness through technology.

10.1 Advances in Technology

Technology is defined, in a general sense, as the application of scientific methods to enhance or provide necessities for society or business. Technology applies to advances in medicine, education, transportation, or even craftsmanship. Most people, however, think of technology as anything relating to electronic products or automation. This is sometimes also referred to as *high technology*. Advances in high technology over the last 20 years have led to noteworthy improvements in business and society. Not only have businesses and individuals had the opportunity to increase productivity dramatically due to the advances, but there have also been many societal and economic impacts. This section describes major advances in technology since the late 1970s, and highlights some of the most important advances that have occurred.

10.1.1 Technological Advances over Time

Identify the major technological milestones over the last 20 years.

For many younger people in today's society, it is difficult to imagine what life would be like without many of our modern inventions. Indeed, it is hard to imagine what life would be like without automobiles and mass transport systems, television and DVD players, computers and modern household appliances. These and many other inventions have resulted in great improvements in personal comfort and productivity. Similarly, technological advances have greatly enhanced organizational productivity.

Figure 10.1 lists some of the major technological advances between 1979 and 2000.

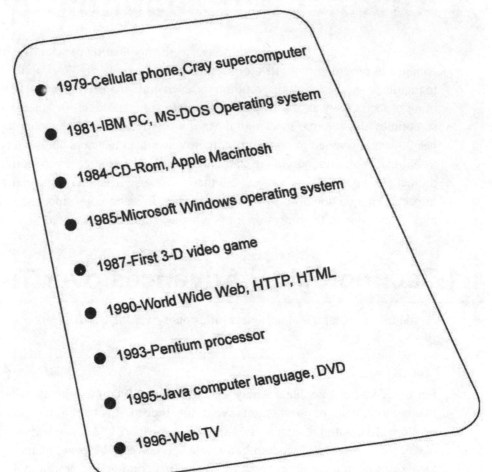

Figure 10.1: Selected Technology Milestones between 1979 and 2000[1]

In 1979, wireless communication over cellular phones became widespread. The concept of cellular phones was developed as early as the late 1940s, however, due to the limited frequencies available for communication, the technology was not considered practical for widespread use. In the late 1960s and 1970s, more frequencies were made available for cellular communications, leading to the commercial development of cellular phones. Today, cellular phones are commonplace and have had a dramatic influence on communications.

The Cray supercomputer was also developed in the late 1970s. The development of the Cray supercomputer was significant in that it involved the use of several processors that worked simultaneously to solve complex calculations. The speed with which Cray could perform calculations was unmatched by any computer at the time, making advanced scientific research possible. It served as a model for multiprocessing. Today, many forms of multiprocessor computers exist for business and research purposes.

In the early 1980s, the IBM Personal Computer (PC) and the MS-DOS operating system were invented. At that time, business leaders could not imagine the potential usefulness of a personal computer. Some considered the PC to be unworthy of commercial development. Few people envisioned the impact that the PC would have across business and society.

In 1984, the Apple Macintosh was released. This small PC had an intuitive graphical-user interface and became a popular alternative to the IBM PC with its cryptic MS-DOS operating system. With the Macintosh, PCs became easier to use and more appealing to the average person. Also introduced in 1984 was the CD-ROM. It was several years later that this storage medium had an impact. However, the mechanisms for a breakthrough in computer usage were beginning to be developed. Ease of use, effective data storage mechanisms, speed in processing, and the ability to share and communicate data eventually led to the point where personal computers soared in popularity.

A year after Apple Macintosh, Microsoft introduced its own operating system with a graphical-user interface—Microsoft Windows—in 1985. The era of point, click, and drag had begun.

In the late 1980s, the first 3-D video game was introduced. The first computer games had been invented in the late 1950s, and while interesting, these games primarily relied on hand-eye coordination and participant reaction time for enjoyment. 3-D video games provided much more visual enrichment and set the stage for complex strategy to be incorporated into games. The widespread popularity of video games provided further demand and motivation for PCs and related technology, and also influenced end-user expectations for future functionality and quality of interaction with PC software.

In 1990, the World Wide Web (WWW or Web), along with HTTP and HTML, were introduced. Initially, this method for sharing data with virtually any PC that was connected to the Web was somewhat overwhelming to the average person. However, as the speed at which data was transmitted improved and PC capabilities advanced, the Web became more popular.

The Pentium processor was introduced in the early 1990s and dramatically increased the processing speed of personal computers. This fueled the growth in the popularity of the Internet and also spurred the development of more sophisticated software and games for PCs.

In the mid 1990s, the Java computer language was developed. This made it possible to develop computer programs that would run on any machine. Previously, computer programs were confined to systems for which they were specifically designed and written. With Java, programs could be accessed over the Internet and run on almost any PC.

Web TV was introduced in 1996. This development used television as a means to view data over the Internet. Web TV was designed to make communication over the Internet accessible to everyone without the burden of learning to use and maintain a personal computer.

These technological milestones affected personal, societal, and organizational productivity. As technology products have improved steadily with regard to accessibility and usability, individuals, society, and businesses have been able to reach higher levels of performance and lives have been enriched.

10.1.2 Breakthrough Advances in Technology

Describe major technological breakthroughs and their impacts.

Technological advances have always resulted in improvements in the standard of living. These advances typically lead to improvements in existing capabilities. For example, technological advances have made laptops and mobile computing possible, and cellular phones and pagers have made communication more convenient. Occasionally, however, advances have created new powerful capabilities that did not previously exist on a widespread basis. One example of such a breakthrough advance is the development of the World Wide Web, or the Internet.

ARPAnet, a network designed in the late 1960s by the company Bolt Beranek and Newman was the predecessor of the Internet. ARPAnet was designed to facilitate the transfer and sharing of data between military installations. The network connected the research departments of four major universities with supercomputer installations. The supercomputers were not part of the network; rather the network was intended to facilitate the transfer and sharing of important research data. The original ARPAnet consisted of four DEC PDP-10 computers, which by today's standards would be considered relatively slow and lacking in features. In the early 1970s however, they were state-of-the-art computers. Innovations associated with ARPAnet include e-mail and FTP.

ARPAnet was eventually replaced by a faster network, called the National Science Foundation Network (NSFnet). NSFnet linked the original supercomputer sites that were part of ARPAnet and included other major university sites as well. NSFnet became the foundation for the Internet.[2]

In the early 1990s, the scientist Tim Berners-Lee developed the foundation for the Internet. Berners-Lee developed the specifications for HTTP, HTML, and URLs. HTTP was used to dictate how data was sent to Web browsers, HTML was used to create Web pages, and URLs were developed, which became Web addresses. These specifications, along with the first Web browser—Mosaic—developed a few years later, set the groundwork for widespread accessibility of the Internet.[3]

In the early years, no one could have predicted the enormous impact the Internet would have on society and business. Although many could foresee the wide potential for the Internet, the technology did not exist to enable that potential to be realized. Further technological advances, such as faster PCs and more powerful programming languages, helped the adoption of the Internet to skyrocket across society and business. In years to come, society will certainly look back at the development of the Internet as one of the most significant breakthrough technologies of the twentieth century.

Using the development of the Internet as a guide, it is possible to outline the characteristics of breakthrough advances in technology.

The general characteristics of breakthrough technologies include:

- Application of technology dramatically changes standard processes or norms, as shown in Figure 10.2. The Internet gave people a new forum for communication, commerce, and learning. E-mail, chats, and instant messaging have become new modes of communication. Buying products online rather than at a traditional store has become widely accepted. Research capabilities are greatly enhanced and expanded and opportunities to learn are plentiful and accessible with the advent of the Internet.

Figure 10.2: Technology Dramatically Changes Standard Processes

- Adoption of technology occurs quickly after the technology becomes accessible to the general population: The speed at which people and businesses adopted the Internet is virtually unsurpassed.

- Breakthrough technology spurs the development of other products and technologies that enhance it: The Internet and networking in general have spawned the development of several other products and technologies. Network or Internet security, faster PCs, writeable CDs, and enhanced multimedia capability have all been developed to take advantage of the capability of the Internet.

Other products, such as the development of automobiles and television and advances in medical techniques (for example, laser technology), have also served as breakthrough milestones during the twentieth century. As a technical professional, it is important to recognize the contribution made by significant technological milestones of the past as you develop and perfect the technologies of the future.

1. The introduction of _____ enabled applications to be run on almost any computer over the Internet.

    a. HTTP

    b. Microsoft Windows

    c. the Java computer language

    d. the Pentium processor

2. The _____ was the first computer with a graphical-user interface.

    a. IBM PC

    b. Apple Macintosh

    c. Pentium Processor

    d. WebTV

3. Which of the following is true?

    Statement A: Breakthrough technologies provide capabilities that were not previously possible.

    Statement B: The Internet is not considered a breakthrough technology because it requires other technologies to enhance its capabilities.

    a. Statement A is true but Statement B is false.

    b. Statement A is false but Statement B is true.

    c. Both statements are true.

    d. Both statements are false.

4. Which of the following is true?

   Statement A: The MS-DOS operating system featured a graphical-user interface.

   Statement B: The first 3-D video game required a Pentium processor.

   a. Statement A is true but Statement B is false.

   b. Statement A is false but Statement B is true.

   c. Both statements are true.

   d. Both statements are false.

10.2 Evolution of Organizations Through Technology

Advances in technology can certainly contribute to improved standards of living for individuals and the society as a whole. The effects of technology can also be seen in organizations. There is no doubt that advances in technology spur growth in existing businesses and foster the development of new ones. But changes in technology affect the structure of organizations in business as well. This section describes how organizations have evolved due to the changes in technology and presents some examples of how technology has been used to improve business results.

10.2.1 Organizational Changes over Time

 Describe significant organizational changes due to technology.

As businesses have grown to take advantage of the opportunities that advances in technology have provided, the organizational structures that run businesses have also changed and developed. Many of the changes in organizations are a result of opportunities and attitudes that have developed through advances in technology.

Organizations are generally characterized by a hierarchical structure. Managers and decision-makers are at the top of the hierarchy, while workers who carry out the tasks are at the bottom of the hierarchy. Within the hierarchy, departments that specialize in important business functions carry out processes and tasks that produce the outputs necessary for overall business operations. This structure was developed to mirror the efficiencies of an assembly line and served businesses well in the past. However, as technology and attitudes have changed, the characteristics of the traditional organizational hierarchy and business workspace have also changed in order to keep businesses competitive and attractive to potential employees.

As shown in Figure 10.3, some of the changes to organizations and business environments include:

■ Dispersed management and a remote workforce

■ Flatter organizations with a focus on teamwork and communication

■ Access to technological amenities

Figure 10.3: Changes in Working Styles

Dispersed management and a remote workforce are a direct result of the rapid growth in businesses. Improved communication and data sharing have made it possible for businesses to expand their reach, and, as a result, an organization can cover a wider area. In the past, managers had direct contact with and supervision over the work done by employees. Current organizations are increasingly faced with managers and workers who are in separate locations or even different countries. Organizations that previously relied on face-to-face meetings now must use technology to collaborate, evaluate work, and communicate information. Not only is the physical workspace affected, but attitudes and expectations about the organization must adapt to the changes as well.

While technology has enabled businesses to grow and expand their reach, it has also led to increased competition between companies. As a result, organizations have become more flexible and versatile to be able to respond quickly to changes and remain competitive. Thus, organizations have become less hierarchical and more focused on teamwork and communication. This has shifted the organizational model away from specialization among departments toward more collaboration and teamwork. Advances in technology facilitate this shift, and, again, attitudes and expectations about the organization must shift as well.

As shown in Figure 10.4, the physical business environment has also changed in response to advances in technology.

Figure 10.4: Changes in Physical Business Environments

These changes include:

- More open layout of offices and cubicles
- Access to collaboration tools, such as portable white boards that create electronic copies of whatever is written on them
- Desktop access to PCs, printers, and the Internet

All of these are necessities for organizations to be able to adapt and remain competitive. Not only does the physical workspace and access to technology aid in communication and teamwork, it also makes the environment more attractive to potential employees. With increased pressures to produce quick and efficient results, combined with the need to access data and communicate with remote members of the organization, employees need direct access to the tools and technology that will enable them to perform their jobs well. Organizations must provide an environment that supports the work to be done in order to remain competitive.

10.2.2 Organizational Characteristics Affected by Technology

 Describe characteristics of an organization that may be impacted by technological changes.

Technological advances have created competitive pressures that have forced changes in the physical look, attitudes, and expectations of business organizations. While the changes discussed in the previous section are primarily aimed at keeping a business competitive in response to advances in technology, there are also some subtle and dynamic organizational changes that may occur due to technology. Technical professionals should be aware of the organizational characteristics and requirements that can be affected by technology. This will enable them to set their expectations about the organization and adapt to changes that may occur. The ability to anticipate changes and quickly adapt will help increase your effectiveness and overall satisfaction throughout your career and lifetime.

Table 10.1 summarizes several organizational characteristics that may be impacted by changes in technology.

Characteristic	Description
Outsourcing as a workforce model	Advances in technology make it possible to share data more easily and to collaborate better across different organizations. This capability, coupled with business pressures to lower costs, can make outsourcing of some organizational components an attractive option for businesses. Outsourcing of functions, such as human resources or application programming to companies specializing in these areas, is becoming increasingly popular.
Extended support for customers	As advances in technology increase the global reach of companies, it becomes necessary to provide extended support to accommodate different time zones and customer demands for a product. In order to reach a broader audience for products, companies must provide additional support. This increased need for support can sometimes be accommodated through an outsourcing model, but other times it requires members of the organization to work in a different model. 24-hour, 7-day support is becoming more of a standard as businesses grow and compete to win customers.
Job security	Automation of certain job tasks is a direct result of advances in technology. Whether through automation or outsourcing of job functions, some workers will

Characteristic	Description
	face the possibility that their jobs will be eliminated from the organization. This can lead to high levels of stress.
Training	As new technology is introduced, organizations must be able to incorporate it effectively into their processes. In addition, workers must develop new skills to remain viable in the workforce. Training is an important function to help organizations and workers capitalize on technological advances.
Informational security	The Internet and networking in general have contributed to positive business results by enabling the efficient sharing of data. At the same time, they have added a significant threat to the confidentiality and integrity of data. Organizations must take care to protect access to confidential data and ensure that access to systems is strictly regulated and protected. The movement from physical access of data to electronic access has dramatically increased the need to focus on information security.
Ethical standards	The increased access to technology throughout an organization requires heightened attention to the use of the technology. Organizations must be aware of the limitations and restrictions of software licenses. In addition, care should be taken to ensure that computers and other technology are used for business purposes and not for personal or other intentions. Many organizations have policies regarding the use of technology only for business purposes, and, as technology becomes more accessible throughout the organization, the burden of enforcing the policy becomes greater.

Table 10.1: Organizational Requirements Affected by Technology

10.2.3 Uses of Simulations in Business

 Describe the use of simulations in forecasting, experimenting, and training.

Technology has changed the way in which businesses are organized and run and has set different expectations for workers. It has also provided significant opportunities for enhancing and improving processes and results. Technology has made it possible to develop *simulations* that aid in business forecasting, experimentation, and training. Simulations can help businesses make better decisions and provide employees with more comprehensive and efficient training.

Businesses use forecasting to predict the outcomes of certain actions or to set targets for planning purposes. Many businesses use spreadsheet applications to develop sophisticated budgeting models. By entering different values for the key aspects of the environment, such as changing the number of employees or varying the amount of expected pay increases, managers can see the predicted effects of potential actions they may take. Using simulations and models in this way aids managers in their planning and decision-making tasks.

Forecasting can also be used to predict certain levels of activity. Examples 10.1 and 10.2 present uses of forecasting.

Example 10.1

Traffic engineers may use simulations to predict the number of additional vehicles that roadways will need to accommodate if a housing project is built.

Example 10.2

City planners may use simulations to study the effects of proposed developments in a community. For instance, the effect a new office building may have on the traffic and the local economy. These simulations can be used to justify the proposed developments.

Another area in which simulations are extensively used is in experimentation and design. Computer-aided design (CAD) software provides powerful tools to help in designing and testing the feasibility of complex products. Other more complicated simulations, such as flight simulators, help to improve aircraft designs that would otherwise be difficult to develop.

Simulations also have helped create powerful training programs. They can teach decision-making skills and give employees an opportunity to practice skills in a controlled environment. Piloting an airplane and flying the space shuttle are two examples of situations where simulation plays an important training role. Without simulators, training in these areas would be quite difficult.

In addition to providing an opportunity to practice skills in a specific situation, simulations can also be used for general training purposes. Many software products now use integrated *wizards* as a training tool. Wizards act as modified simulations to help guide users as they perform unfamiliar tasks. Whether simple or complex, general or specific, stand-alone or integrated, simulations have had a significant impact on the way organizations make decisions and learn.

Practice Questions

1. Organizations usually have a _____ structure.
   a. hierarchical
   b. flat
   c. network
   d. technological

2. Which of the following is true?

   Statement A: Organizations have had to make technology and tools available to employees to remain competitive.

   Statement B: A dispersed workforce is the result of rapid growth in businesses.
   a. Statement A is true but Statement B is false.
   b. Statement A is false but Statement B is true.
   c. Both statements are true.
   d. Both statements are false.

3. Which of the following is true?

   Statement A: Technological changes have allowed organizations to focus more on teamwork and collaboration.

   Statement B: For organizations to adapt fully to changes in technology, attitudes and expectations must change.
   a. Statement A is true but Statement B is false.
   b. Statement A is false but Statement B is true.
   c. Both statements are true.
   d. Both statements are false.

4. _____ refers to the need for organizations to protect access to confidential data.
   a. Ethical standards
   b. Outsourcing
   c. Information security
   d. Training

5. Businesses can use simulations for experimentation, training, and _____.
   a. forecasting
   b. managing
   c. developing
   d. testing

10.3 Social, Economic, and Psychological Impacts of the Information Age

Breakthrough advances in technology, such as the Internet, have resulted in widespread changes. While individuals must learn new skills and organizations must adapt to remain competitive, there are also social, economic, and psychological impacts of this progress. The powerful capabilities of new technology touch every facet of society. Many of the impacts are positive and serve to raise the standard of living for societies. An awareness of the impacts of technological change will help professionals plan for the adoption of new technologies. This section discusses some of the effects of the Internet that fall outside the scope of organizational concerns.

10.3.1 Social Impacts of Technological Changes

 Describe the major societal impacts associated with breakthrough technology changes.

Breakthrough technology creates new possibilities for society and organizations.

As shown in Figure 10.5, the Internet has provided a catalyst for several cultural changes, including:

▪ Changes in language

▪ Development of new knowledge communities and relationships

▪ Greater access to information

Figure 10.5: Social Impacts of Technological Changes

As use of the Internet spread from universities and businesses into average households, the language describing the WWW developed and spread as well. The technical jargon associated with computers and networks became household terms out of necessity. If people wanted to take advantage of the capabilities being offered by the Internet, they had to become conversant in the language associated with it. From adults learning to download files, open a browser, and invest in dotcoms, to children reciting URLs, such as www.pbs.org and disney.com, the language of the Internet has become commonplace in society.

The relative ease with which individuals can access the Internet to view and provide information has led to the development of online communities and relationships. The Internet provides many opportunities for sharing information, including the development of personal Web sites, chat rooms, message boards, e-mail, and instant messaging. By using any or all of these capabilities, user communities and relationships can form around specific areas of interest. The ease with which communication and sharing can take place greatly facilitates the development of these virtual communities. However, individuals must use common sense and act responsibly when extending relationships beyond the electronic domain. In addition to enjoying the benefits of the virtual communities and relationships offered by the Internet, society must also adopt norms for responsible and ethical behavior within them.

The Internet has also brought increased access to information to the society as a whole. Governments, businesses, volunteer organizations, schools, and news and entertainment organizations all provide information over the Internet. Society benefits from this information because important messages and valuable content can be easily distributed to those who can benefit from it. Access to important services and interesting or entertaining material can prove beneficial to everyone. However, care must be taken to ensure that the information that is distributed is appropriate and accurate. Debate continues as to whether or not information on the Internet should be regulated and to what degree. Society and individuals will need to establish guidelines for responsible and ethical standards concerning information provided on the Internet.

10.3.2 Economic Impacts of Technological Changes

Describe the major economic impacts associated with breakthrough technology changes.

Throughout history, breakthrough technology has had positive economic impacts. The development of new technologies leads to new businesses and new products, which creates new economic opportunity for society. The introduction of the Internet and the information age is no different.

As shown in Figure 10.6, the Internet has created new opportunities for:

- E-commerce
- Money management
- Employment

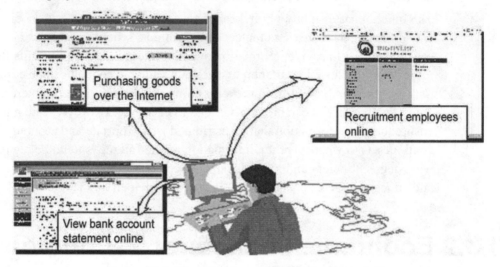

Figure 10.6: Economic Impacts of Technological Changes

The development of *e-commerce*, or the buying and selling of goods and services over the Internet, has been one of the most anticipated benefits of the Internet. Businesses rushed to make products and services available online, hoping to take advantage of the new distribution channel.

Consumers, however, were slow to adopt the change. Concerns over data security, uncertainties about receiving goods, and uneasiness about the inability to inspect goods before purchase have been common barriers for the average consumer to accept e-commerce. Some sites, such as amazon.com and eBay, have set standards for conducting consumer business over the Internet. Over time, as companies expand and develop their order-taking and return-handling capabilities, and as consumers gain more confidence with data security over the Internet, e-commerce will grow in popularity and provide a positive economic impact.

In addition to purchasing goods and services, consumers also have an opportunity to manage their money using the Internet. Many financial institutions provide online banking services, and companies offer electronic bill payment facilities. Investors can also trade stocks and manage portfolios over the Internet, providing quicker access and more control than they have with other access methods. Investors no longer have to call a broker to trade shares or purchase stocks. With more options and choices, consumers have the ability to make decisions and control their finances in ways best suited to their needs. Additional channels for money management have a positive impact on the economy.

Another economic impact of the Internet has been in the area of seeking employment. Job openings are now commonly posted on Internet posting boards, such as Monster.com. Search engines can find jobs suited to particular skill sets or geographic locations. Job seekers can also post their resumes for employers to access. Using the Internet for employment can help job seekers to locate available positions that meet their needs and can aid employers in finding employees that match their requirements.

While this makes locating potential matches between employers and potential employees more efficient, it can also result in an overflow of resumes and applicants for an available position. Thus, employers must develop adequate screening processes to find the best applicants and job seekers must develop effective online methods and alternate means of contact to gain visibility with potential employers. The process of finding employment has dramatically changed through use of the Internet.

10.3.3 Psychological Impacts of Technological Changes

 Describe common psychological impacts associated with breakthrough technology changes.

As discussed, breakthrough technology changes have led to dramatic changes for business, society, and the economy. All these changes ultimately require individuals to change and adapt as well.

As shown in Figure 10.7, there are several psychological impacts that individuals may face when adapting to the use of new technologies, including:

- Stress
- Confusion
- Empowerment

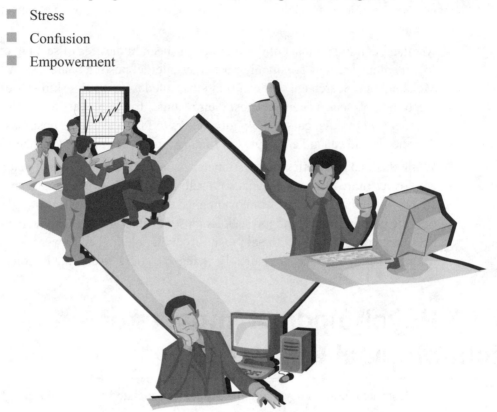

Figure 10.7: Psychological Impacts of Technological Changes

Stress is a common psychological reaction to change. The need to learn new skills and change familiar procedures can be unsettling for some people. A lack of confidence in learning the skills or a fear of the unknown can also contribute to stress. Many people may work through their stress in adapting to the change. However, for some people stress may be a barrier that prevents accepting the change.

Confusion is another common psychological impact of new technologies. As individuals learn about the new capabilities offered by the technology, they may be overwhelmed by the new opportunities that are possible. Confusion about how to apply the technology or determine its most beneficial features can hinder progress.

After the negative psychological effects of changes in technology are overcome, the opportunities offered by new technologies can give people a sense of empowerment. Empowerment can be described as a sense of ability, power, or control. It is natural that after a person has mastered the basic skills required to use the Internet, the opportunities offered on the Web can certainly provide a sense of empowerment. This sense of empowerment comes from the ability and control of individuals to seek information and perform transactions according to their needs and desires.

Practice Questions

1. Which of the following are the results of the impact of the Internet on society?

   I. Changes in language.

   II. Greater access to information.

   III. Development of new relationships.

   a. I and II

   b. I and III

   c. II and III

   d. I, II, and III

2. _____ refers to the buying and selling of goods and services over the Internet.

   a. eBay

   b. E-commerce

   c. Money management

   d. E-trade

3. Which of the following is true?

   Statement A: The use of the Internet has dramatically changed the process of finding employment.

   Statement B: Concerns over data security is a barrier to employers using the Internet to seek potential employees.

   a. Statement A is true, but Statement B is false.

   b. Statement A is false, but Statement B is true.

   c. Both statements are true.

   d. Both statements are false.

4. Which of the following is true?

   Statement A: Changes in technology can give individuals a sense of control and power.

   Statement B: Changes in technology can create stress and anxiety for individuals.

   a. Statement A is true, but Statement B is false.

   b. Statement A is false, but Statement B is true.

   c. Both statements are true.

   d. Both statements are false.

10.4 Strategies for Handling Technological Change

Given the rapid changes in technology over the last twenty years, changes in technology are inevitable. Despite the changes and improvements that have already occurred, there may be even more enhancements and new products invented. Some may find the changes exciting, while others some may find them daunting. Whatever the situation, a strategy for handling change is necessary to maintain and maximize positive results.

This section presents strategies for individuals and organizations to maintain technological competencies and effectiveness in the midst of technological change.

10.4.1 Personal Strategies for Handling Technological Change

Identify personal strategies for maintaining technical competencies.

Changes in technology can be unsettling. Not only can the new technology require you to learn new processes and procedures to complete familiar tasks, it may also require you to learn entirely new concepts to enable you to apply the technology. For example, learning to write a code using Java required programmers to learn both the syntax of the language and the concepts of object-oriented programming. Both elements are required to write efficient programs. These additional requirements for learning can make it challenging to maintain technical competency. However, developing a personal strategy for handling technological change can help.

Table 10.2 presents suggested strategies for maintaining technical competencies.

Strategy	Description
Use technology wherever possible	Look for ways to use technology outside of work requirements. Volunteer for opportunities that will give you exposure to new technologies or different applications of existing technologies.
Join an organization or subscribe to technical publications	There are numerous organizations and publications that focus on specialty areas in technology. Becoming a member of an organization or subscribing to a publication can give you information on current developments and trends.
Develop a plan for learning	Develop a plan and set goals to learn new concepts and skills. Technology is constantly changing and a plan for learning can help you focus on the skills you will need to develop in your career.
Assess your skills on a regular basis	To develop an effective plan for learning, you will need to assess your current skill levels and then determine where improvement is needed. Assessing your skills on a regular basis will help you to keep pace with the constant changes in technology.

Table 10.2: Strategies for Maintaining Technical Competencies

10.4.2 Organizational Strategies for Handling Technological Change

Describe the strategies that organizations can use to enhance their effectiveness through technological change.

To remain competitive, organizations should have a proactive strategy for adapting to changes in technology. An effective strategy will help the organization quickly incorporate new technology and increase business results.

As shown in Figure 10.8, the areas to consider in this strategy include:

- Training
- Organizational design
- Workforce management

Figure 10.8: Organizational Strategies for Handling Technological Change

Training is essential for organizations to adopt new technology. Training should provide instruction on concepts associated with the technology as well as hands-on practice in using the technology. Simulations may provide excellent opportunities for practice in these situations. Ideally, the training should blend general concepts with specific business applications related to the organization.

In addition to training for new technologies, organizations should also consider career development programs that allow employees to develop new skills on existing technologies. Encouraging employees to broaden their skills in existing technologies can result in greater flexibility for the organization. Unexpected events, such as skilled employees leaving the company, can be handled more easily. In addition, the incremented knowledge in the organization can spur innovations for improving existing processes and creating new opportunities.

Advances in technology inevitably lead to higher efficiencies in communication and processing. To take full advantage of these potential improvements, organizations will often need to reorganize to eliminate unnecessary functions or links. While reorganization is unsettling to employees, it can result in efficiencies that may ultimately energize employees and enhance business results. Developing a strong process to manage organizational changes and establishing a robust training program for the organization will help to make necessary reorganizations smooth and efficient.

Workforce management takes on new dimensions with advances in technology. A dispersed workforce, outsourcing, and the need for responsible decisions in the use of technology all require a new set of skills for traditional managers. Managers will need to become skilled in managing remote employees and in overseeing the use of technology to ensure that it is aligned with organization policies.

Practice Questions

1. Which of the following is true?

   Statement A: Changes in technology are inevitable.

   Statement B: A strategy for handling changes in technology is necessary to be able to maximize positive results.

   a. Statement A is true, Statement B is false.

   b. Statement A is false, Statement B is true.

   c. Both statements are true.

   d. Both statements are false.

2. Which of the following is true?

   Statement A: As long as you develop a plan for learning, it is not necessary to assess your skills on a regular basis.

   Statement B: Using technology wherever possible can help you gain exposure to new technologies.

   a. Statement A is true, Statement B is false.

   b. Statement A is false, Statement B is true.

   c. Both statements are true.

   d. Both statements are false.

3. To take full advantage of changes in technology, organizations often must _____.

   a. reorganize

   b. outsource certain functions

   c. manage remote employees

   d. develop ethical standards

4. Training on new technologies should include instruction on concepts and _____.

   a. ethics

   b. hands-on practice

   c. communication

   d. business results

Summary

In this chapter, you learned:

▪ Over the last twenty years there have been many significant technological milestones. Some of these milestones involved the development of personal computers and the Internet. These developments have led to many changes for society and businesses.

▪ Breakthrough advances in technology dramatically change standard processes and norms and are adopted quickly once they are available to the general public. These advances spur the development of other products and technologies. The Internet is a significant breakthrough technology in recent history.

▪ Changes in technology require organizations to change in order to remain competitive. Some changes to organizations due to technological advances include dispersed management and remote workforces, flatter organizations, and access for employees to technological amenities.

▪ Organizational requirements affected by technology include outsourcing as a workforce model, extended support for customers, job security, training, information security, and ethical standards.

▪ Technology has enabled the development of simulations that can aid businesses in forecasting, experimentation, and training.

▪ Social impacts associated with new technology such as the Internet include changes in language, development of new communities and relationships, and greater access to information.

▪ Economic impacts associated with the Internet include the development of e-commerce, enhanced money management, and new processes for seeking employment.

▪ Psychological impacts of technological changes include stress, confusion, and empowerment.

▪ Personal strategies for maintaining technical competencies include using technology, joining a technical association, developing a learning plan, and regularly assessing your skills.

▪ Organizations should develop a strategy that includes training, organizational design, and workforce management to maintain and enhance effectiveness through periods of technological change.

References

Bellis, Mary. *Modern Inventions: 20th Century Inventions 1976–1999*. 2003. <http://inventors.about.com/library/weekly/aa010500a.htm> (28 September 2003.)

Bellis, Mary. *Inventors of the Modern Computer: ARPAnet - The First Internet*. 2003. <http://inventors.about.com/library/weekly/aa091598.htm> (28 September 2003.)

Massachusetts Institute of Technology, MIT School of Engineering. *Tim Berners-Lee: The World Wide Web*. 1999. <http://Web.mit.edu/invent/iow/berners-lee.html> (28 September 2003.)

End Notes

Adapted from:

- [1] Bellis, *Modern Inventions: 20th Century Inventions 1976–1999.*
  <http://inventors.about.com/library/weekly/aa010500a.htm>

- [2] Bellis, *Inventors of the Modern Computer: ARPAnet - The First Internet.*
  <http://inventors.about.com/library/weekly/aa091598.htm>

- [3] Massachusetts Institute of Technology, MIT School of Engineering, *Tim Berners-Lee: The World Wide Web* http://Web.mit.edu/invent/iow/berners-lee.html

Bibliography

Bibliography

Armstrong, Thomas. *7 Kinds of Smart: Identifying and Developing Your Many Intelligences*. New York, NY: Penguin Group, 1993.

Berkman, Robert I. *Find It Fast*, Fifth Edition. New York, NY: Harper Resource. 2000

Browne, M. Neil and Stuart M. Keeley. *Asking the Right Questions: A Guide to Critical Thinking*, Fifth Edition. Upper Saddle River, NJ: Prentice Hall, 1998.

Davis, James R. and Adelaide B. Davis. *Managing Your Own Learning*. San Francisco, CA: Berrett-Koehler Publishers, Inc, 2000.

Gardner, Howard. *Intelligence Reframed: Multiple Intelligences for the 21st Century*. New York, NY: Basic Books, 1999.

Lencioni, Patrick. *The Five Dysfunctions of a Team: A Leadership Fable*. San Francisco, CA: Jossey-Bass, 2002.

Schneider, Gary and Jessica, Evans. *The Internet,* Third Edition. Boston, Ma: Course Technology—Thomson Learning, 2002.

Glossary

A

Achievement motivation: A person's desire to achieve results.

ActiveX: A dynamic Microsoft program that runs over the Internet.

Analogy: Comparisons between entities that are typically thought to be dissimilar but have some underlying similarities.

Animation: An animated cartoon that can be added to a document.

Auditory learners: People who prefer to learn by hearing information.

B

Blog: Personal online log, available over the Internet.

Boolean operators: Operators, such as AND, OR, and NOT, that help you refine searches by specifying combinations or exclusions of words.

Borders: Outer edges of a page or data that is inserted to add emphasis.

Brainstorming: A creative technique to generate ideas in which participants list ideas in a fast-paced fashion.

Broadband: A Wide Area Network (WAN) connection that connects two computers using a cable similar to the cable used for television connections.

Browser: Client application used to access Internet resources.

C

Cell: An area in a table or a worksheet in which data is entered, stored, and edited.

Client/server application: An application that runs between two computers. A client-based application interfaces with the server-based application for data transfer.

Clip art: A library of pictures that can be inserted in a document to enhance its appeal.

Critical thinking: A skill that involves looking at issues in a thorough investigative manner rather than taking them at face value.

D

Database: Large structured sets of persistent data, usually associated with software, to update, query, and retrieve the data. A database is a component of a database management system.

Dial-up: A connection between two computers that uses a standard telephone connection.

Domain Name: An alias name assigned to an IP address.

DSL (Digital Subscriber Line): A high-speed WAN connection that uses existing telephone lines.

E

E-commerce: The buying and selling of goods over the Internet.

E-mail: Electronic mail that involves transfer of messages from one person to one or more recipients.

Emotional maturity: An individual's ability to take action, control responses to situations, and take a broad perspective in terms of ideas and timeframes.

Empowerment: A sense of ability, power, or control.

Encryption: The process of masquerading data to secure it.

F

Footer: Content at the bottom of a page that is automatically displayed on all pages.

Formal development planning: A process in which managers and employees work together to create a plan to develop employee skills.

Formula: Mathematical statement of a fact, rule, principle, or other logical relation.

FTP (File Transfer Protocol): A client application used to transfer data from an FTP server.

Function: Mathematical formula that may be built into an application to perform calculations.

H

Hacker : A person who accesses data in an unauthorized manner and writes programs to damage data and operating systems.

Header: Content at the top of a page that is automatically displayed on all pages.

High technology: Technology relating to electronic parts or automation.

Home page: The first page of a Web site that loads by default and is returned to a client application when it performs a Web query.

HTTP (Hypertext Transfer Protocol): A client application used to access a Web page.

Hypertext link: A link to another page, document, or Web site.

I

Intelligence: The ability to gain knowledge and apply it in relevant situations.

IP (Internet Protocol): A protocol that serves as a unique numerical address assigned to all devices that connect on a network.

ISDN (Integrated Service Dial-up Network): Provides a connection between two computers using specialized telephone connections and devices.

ISP (Internet Service Provider): A company that provides a home user or small business a doorway to the Internet.

J

Java Applet: A small program from Sun Microsystems with dynamic content.

K

Kinesthetic learners: People who prefer to learn by using a hands-on approach.

Kiosk: Unmanned PC continuously showing a PowerPoint slide show.

L

LAN (Local Area Network): A network contained within a limited area.

Learning: The process of acquiring knowledge or skill.

Libel: Making false statements that are damaging to a person's character or reputation.

Listserv: Discussions that take place over the Internet through e-mail between subscribers of the listed topic.

Locus of control: Personal beliefs about how external events control the outcomes of your life.

M

Mentoring program: A program in which experts or role models work with less experienced employees to improve on-the-job learning and personal development.

N

Newsgroup: Discussions that takes place over the Internet through postings and responses.

Non-verbal communication: Aspects of communication, such as facial expressions and body language, that influence how the message is perceived.

O

Online reference: A category of information that encompasses traditional print-based reference material found on the Internet in an electronic format.

P

Plagiarism: Presenting someone else's words or ideas as your own.

Professional portfolio: A tangible representation of skills and accomplishments.

Project plan: A document that describes the relevant aspects of a project.

Project risk: Any factor that could cause a project to miss a requirement.

Project scope: A statement of what will be addressed by the project.

Q

Query: Request sent to a database to access the information stored in it.

S

Shading: A different color that is applied over the selected data to emphasize it.

SMART goals: Goals that are Specific, Measurable, Achievable, Realistic, and Time bound.

Spreadsheet: An accounting or bookkeeping program that displays data in rows and columns on a screen. Spreadsheets manipulate numerical data. The value in a cell can be calculated from a formula involving multiple cells. A value is automatically recalculated whenever another value on which it depends changes.

Stakeholders: People who have an interest in the results and activities of a project.

T

Table: A grid of rows and columns that can be used to place data in an organized format.

Teamwork: Two or more people working together toward a common goal or end result.

Technology: The application of scientific methods to enhance or provide necessities for society or businesses.

Template: Blueprint to be used on multiple instances of an application. Can be used for Word documents or PowerPoint slides.

V

Virtual directory: A location other than the home page on a Web server.

Virus: Program created to damage data.

Visual learners: People who prefer to learn by reading or sight.

W

Web server: A computer on the network that stores Web pages.

Wild cards: Special characters that represent one or more characters in a search string.

Word processing: Rapid and efficient processing (storage and printing) of linguistic data for composition and editing.

Worksheet: The interface in a spreadsheet where data is entered and manipulated.

WWW (World Wide Web): A network of Internet locations that contains resources.

Index

A

Achievement motivation, 1.6, 1.17, 3.3.18, 3.3.21, 3.3.24, 4.18, 4.21, 4.24, 5.18, 5.21, 5.24

Analogies, 8.28, 8.29

Animation, 6.1, 6.37, 6.48, 6.55, 6.56, 6.57, 6.62, 6.76, 6.79

ARPAnet, 10.6, 10.7, 10.33, 10.34

Auditory, 1.7, 1.17, 3.3.3, 3.3.4, 3.3.6, 4.3, 4.4, 4.6, 5.3, 5.4, 5.6

B

Blog, 2.9, 2.17, 2.18, 2.22, 2.23

Bodily-Kinesthetic, 3.3.10, 3.3.15, 3.3.16, 3.3.17, 4.10, 4.15, 4.16, 4.17, 5.10, 5.15, 5.16, 5.17

Bookmarks, 2.18, 2.65

Brainstorming, 8.13, 8.27, 8.34, 8.48, 9.16, 9.45

Breakthrough advances, 10.19, 10.32

Bullets, 6.19, 6.39, 6.47

C

Career Management, 8.1, 8.36

Cells, 7.10, 7.21, 7.27, 7.28, 7.29, 7.30, 7.42, 7.47, 7.62

Change Management, 9.31

Charts, 7.5, 7.31, 7.32, 7.38, 7.43

Communication, 1.8, 1.9, 1.10, 1.12, 1.30, 8.1, 8.24, 8.29, 8.30, 8.31, 8.34, 8.53, 9.5, 9.32, 9.33

Components, 1.27, 7.5, 9.18

Creative Thinking, 8.27, 8.24, 8.25, 8.50, 8.52

D

Database, 2.22, 2.31, 7.1, 7.77, 7.78, 7.79, 7.80, 7.81, 7.85, 7.86, 7.87, 7.90, 7.97, 7.105

E

E-commerce, 10.22, 10.25, 2.9

Economic impacts, 10.32

Emotional maturity, 1.6, 3.3.18, 3.3.20, 3.3.24, 4.18, 4.20, 4.24, 5.18, 5.20, 5.24

F

Favorites, 1.21, 2.6, 2.18

Footer, 6.47

Forms, 7.90, 7.91

Formulas, 7.11, 7.12, 7.112

H

Header, 6.18, 7.24

HTTP, 2.9, 2.12, 2.16, 2.17, 2.22, 2.23, 10.5, 10.7, 10.9

Hyperlink, 6.65, 6.66, 6.67, 6.68, 7.66, 7.67, 7.68, 7.69, 7.70, 2.12, 6.64, 6.76, 6.77, 6.79

Hypertext, 2.8, 2.9

I

Intelligences, 3.3.8, 3.3.12, 3.3.13, 3.3.14, 3.3.15, 3.3.16, 3.3.24, 3.3.33, 4.8, 4.12, 4.13, 4.14, 4.15, 4.16, 4.24, 4.33, 5.8, 5.12, 5.13, 5.14, 5.15, 5.16, 5.24, 5.33

Internet, 1.3, 1.4, 1.5, 1.17, 1.19, 1.21, 1.24, 1.25, 1.28, 1.29, 1.30, 1.33, 10.5, 10.6, 10.7, 10.8, 10.9, 10.13, 10.15, 10.19, 10.20, 10.21, 10.22, 10.23, 10.25, 10.26, 10.32, 10.33, 10.34, 10.35, 10.36, 2.1, 2.3, 2.4, 2.5, 2.6, 2.7, 2.9, 2.10, 2.11, 2.12, 2.13, 2.14, 2.15, 2.16, 2.18, 2.19, 2.22, 2.23, 2.26, 2.34, 2.35, 2.36, 2.42, 2.43, 2.65, 2.67, 3.3.23, 3.3.34, 3.3.35, 4.23, 4.34, 4.35, 5.23, 5.34, 5.35, 7.6, 8.24, 8.25, 9.12, 9.49

Interpersonal, 3.3.10, 3.3.11, 3.3.15, 3.3.16, 3.3.17, 4.10, 4.11, 4.15, 4.16, 4.17, 5.10, 5.11, 5.15, 5.16, 5.17, 3.3.10, 3.3.11, 3.3.15, 3.3.16, 3.3.17, 4.10, 4.11, 4.15, 4.16, 4.17, 5.10, 5.11, 5.15, 5.16, 5.17

ITT Course Management System, 1.1, 1.25, 1.26, 1.27, 1.29, 1.30

ITT Tech Virtual Library, 1.1, 1.13, 1.15, 1.19, 1.20, 1.21, 1.22, 1.23, 1.24, 1.27, 1.28, 1.29, 1.30, 1.33, 1.34, 1.35, 1.36, 1.42, 1.44, 1.45, 3.3.35, 4.35, 5.35, 6.3, 6.81, 7.6, 7.77, 9.49

K

Kinesthetic, 1.7, 1.17, 3.3.3, 3.3.4, 3.3.6, 4.3, 4.4, 4.6, 5.3, 5.4, 5.6

L

Learning Styles, 1.8, 3.3.1, 3.3.3, 3.3.14, 3.3.33, 4.1, 4.3, 4.14, 4.33, 5.1, 5.3, 5.14, 5.33

Linguistic, 3.10, 3.15, 3.16, 3.17, 4.10, 4.15, 4.16, 4.17, 5.10, 5.15, 5.16, 5.17,

Listservs, 2.15

Locus of control, 1.6, 1.30, 3.18, 3.19, 4.18, 4.19, 5.18, 5.19

Logical-Mathematical, 3.10, 3.15, 3.16, 3.17, 4.10, 4.15, 4.16, 4.17, 5.10, 5.15, 5.16, 5.17

M

Microsoft Access, 2.30, 2.31, 2.32, 7.1, 7.76, 7.77, 7.98, 7.106, 7.113

Microsoft Excel, 2.28, 2.29, 2.30, 7.1, 7.3, 7.6, 7.7, 7.8, 8.8,

Microsoft Outlook, 1.12, 2.1, 2.42, 2.43, 2.44, 2.45, 2.54, 2.56, 2.60, 2.65, 2.75, 2.76, 8.6, 8.13

Microsoft PowerPoint, 2.26, 2.27, 2.28, 6.1, 6.3, 6.33, 6.69, 6.70

Microsoft Word, 2.25, 2.26, 6.4, 6.69

Milestones, 10.4, 9.20, 9.24

Motivation, 8.36, 8.37, 8.38, 8.46

Musical, 3.10, 3.15, 3.16, 3.17, 4.10, 4.15, 4.16, 4.17, 5.10, 5.15, 5.16, 5.17

Myers-Briggs Type Indicator, 3.21, 3.22, 3.23, 3.24, 4.21, 4.22, 4.23, 4.24, 5.21, 5.22, 5.23, 5.24

N

O

P

Q

R

S

T

V

W